An Illustrated

Encyclopaedia of MYSTICISM

and the Mystery Religions

An Illustrated
Encyclopaedia of MYSTICISM
and the Mystery Religions

JOHN FERGUSON

THAMES AND HUDSON
LONDON

*For Dorothy,
who has often led us
into quietude*

*Filmset and printed in Great Britain by
BAS Printers Limited, Wallop, Hampshire*

Foreword

This is an example of a book which has mushroomed, as in some atomic explosion. I was originally invited to compile a *Dictionary of Mysticism and Mystery Religions in the Ancient World.* It became clear that it was not meaningful to include Plotinus and exclude Dionysius the Areopagite, to include Dionysius and to exclude Eckhart, to include Eckhart and exclude Fox. With that we had reached the Society of Friends, who are still with us. Again, it seemed scarcely meaningful to compile a volume on mysticism which took no cognizance of some aspects of mystical exploration of considerable topical interest, such as experiment with drugs and Zen Buddhism, and this last opened the door to oriental mysticism generally. So the result is much more comprehensive than was originally planned, though nothing could be wholly comprehensive, and I must accept full responsibility for omissions, as for errors. In particular I took a deliberate decision to steer clear of demonology, magic and witchcraft.

Inevitably I am not equally expert in all areas of the subject, and have drawn widely on secondary sources. If, as the epigram puts it, to copy from one book is plagiarism, to copy from more than one is research, I can at least claim that this is a work of research! Secondary sources are listed in the bibliography, but I have not listed primary sources there. Even so there must be many other works I might have consulted, and no doubt should have consulted. Primarily, however, I have tried to let the mystics speak for themselves. I have indicated the translators of verse. Unacknowledged translations are either my own version or a version whose attribution I have failed to trace; in the event of any oversights, I offer my apologies. In some of the Graeco-Roman articles I have used language already to be found in my *Religions of the Roman Empire.* Cross-references are indicated by capital letters. They are not comprehensive, and are shown only when one article illuminates or completes another. I do not defend the inconsistencies of my handling of names and terms from other languages; but I do not believe that perfect consistency is possible. I have tried to draw some threads together in one or two more comprehensive articles. For though mystical experience tends to express itself within the framework of the particular religion in which the mystic was brought up, there is an impressive coherence of testimony from all ages and all parts of the world. But in general I do not take sides in the debate in interpretation; simply record.

Among many debts of gratitude two must be singled out for particular expression. One to Geoffrey Parrinder, a fellow Old Coaster and friend of long standing, who has given me the benefit of his enormous expertise in the religions of the world, but who is not to be blamed for my obstinacies and follies. The other to Margaret Bartlett, secretary extraordinary, who has coped magnificently with a miscellaneous manuscript.

JOHN FERGUSON

A

Abhidharma

Buddhist term for advanced doctrine. The books expounding this have come down in Pali, and in a Chinese translation from Sanskrit. They originally seem to date from somewhere about the fourth century BC. They are directed to the adept, and consequently dry and forbidding in style. They represent means of approaching wisdom through the elimination of the self, and the analysis of personal experiences into a nexus of impersonal forces.

Abraham ben Ezra
(1092–1167)

Mediaeval Jewish mystic theologian. Born in Spain, he travelled widely in Africa, Italy and France. He was a scholar and poet who himself said that he composed songs 'with which he adorned the Hebrew scholars as with a necklace'. Al-Harizi said of his poems that they 'cause refreshing rain in time of need'. His religious philosophy was much influenced by NEO-PLATONISM.

Absolute

Philosophical term for that which exists in and by itself without necessary relation to anything else; the unconditioned; the Ultimate. The Absolute is vital to the philosophies of HEGEL and BRADLEY. Mystical exploration may be considered as the attempt to find communication or communion with the Absolute. The BRAHMAN of philosophical HINDUISM is the Absolute.

Abulafia, Abraham
(13th century)

Jewish mystic, born at Saragossa. Abulafia travelled in the Near East, where he seems to have encountered some form of YOGA, since he recommends similar control of breathing and bodily postures. Abulafia's aim was vision and illumination through mystical CONTEMPLATION. He used the letters of the alphabet to divert the soul from the outside world, and held that contemplation of the name of God would lead to mystical ECSTASY, human language being a medium to lead men to divine language. Abulafia spoke of a kind of spiritual *guru* or Master named Metatron, who seems to be a semi-divine angel. But sometimes God seems to be the Master, and Abulafia goes further than other Jewish mystics in his identification with God: 'The man who has felt the divine touch and perceived its nature is no longer separated from his Master, and behold, he is his Master, and this Master is he, for he is so intimately united to Him that he cannot by any means be separated from Him.'

Abu Said ibn Abi 'l-Khayr
(967–1049)

One of the great mystical Sufis of Islam. When young he learnt some thirty thousand verses of secular poetry by heart. He studied theology at Merv. He tried to win spiritual peace from learning, passed through a spiritual crisis in which he continually repeated the name of Allah, spent some years in solitary MEDITATION and ascetic practices, led a nomadic life and eventually settled down to develop a monastic community at Nishapur until his final years of retirement.

Abu Said adds little to the philosophy or intellectual understanding of mysticism. His mysticism is an account of practical experience: 'Take one step out of yourself to arrive at God.' Any man who begins to know himself – as not-being – knows God as true Being. God Himself communicates to the heart the consciousness of God (*sirr*). All comes from God; as long as we say to God 'Thou and I' we remain self-centred; our worship becomes a reality only when we can say, 'Thou! Thou!' Abu Said tends in his mysticism to be a pantheist: 'There is nothing other than God.'

He chose his own epitaph: 'This was love's servant.'

Abu Yazid
(?801–74)

Mystic of ISLAM, also called al-Bistami or Bayazid, of particular interest because his thought shows some signs of interaction with the Hindu VEDANTA. In one vision God said to him, 'Abu Yazid, my creation is yearning to see you.' He answered: 'Adorn me with your unity; clothe me with your selfhood, raise me to your oneness, so that when your creatures see me, they may say, "We have seen Thee and Thou art that". Yet I will not be there at all.' Another experience he describes in lively language: 'I sloughed off myself as a snake sloughs off its skin, and I looked into my essential being and saw that "I am He".' He had the experience of passing beyond time and space: 'This servant is with God in all places and no place is without him.' More, he found himself one with all things; he was All and, being All, was one with God, was indeed God.

This – to orthodox Islam blasphemous – identification of himself with God was the greatest impression which Abu Yazid made. But at other points he sees himself as detached from God, in the familiar image of lover and beloved: 'The man who is advanced is lashed with the whip of love, slain with the sword of passionate yearning, propped up against the gate of awe.' 'The perfection of the mystic is that he should burn in his love for his Lord.' 'It is impossible to know you and not to love you.' 'The lover's thirst is never satisfied, his tongue hangs out, and he says "More".' 'There is nothing wonderful in my love for you, for I am a poor slave, but there is something quite extraordinary in your love for me, for you are a mighty king.' This is the language of many mystics. But at one point Abu Yazid makes a remarkable discovery, that his very love stands in the way of his reaching the object of his love.

This profound realization led Abu Yazid into his extreme position. He now had to accept frustration or claim attainment. He claimed attainment. He renounced conventional religious practices, reading the QUR'AN, the worship in the mosque, the pilgrimage to Mecca; he did not need them. He renounced the practices of mysticism, ASCETICISM and MEDITATION; he did not need these either. They were for the unenlightened, for those incapable of mystical experience. He claimed to be above the Prophet; the banner which he carried was a banner of light.

It is hard not to see Abu Yazid as a man carried away by his own imagination. But among his aberrations there is much of lasting value and insight. One of the best stories of him (a similar story is told of SCHOPENHAUER) tells how someone knocked at his door. He called out, 'Whom do you seek?' 'Bayazid.' 'I too have been seeking for Bayazid for thirty years and have not yet found him.' Of one thing he was certain. Attainment was not achievement. All was of God, not himself: 'At the beginning I was mistaken in four respects. I concerned myself to remember God, to know Him, to love Him, to seek Him, and when I had come to the end, I saw that He had remembered me before I remembered Him, that His knowledge of me had preceded my knowledge of Him, His love towards me had existed before my love to Him, and He had sought me before I sought Him.' So he was able to say 'I have known God by means of God, and what is other than God by the light of God.'

Acarie, Barbe Jeanne
(1566–1618)

Generally referred to as Madame Acarie. Foundress in France of the Carmelites of the Reform; after her husband's death she took the veil under the name of Mary of the Annunciation. She was a great admirer of TERESA DE JESUS. Though herself an ecstatic and a visionary, she unfortunately has left no record of her experiences.

Acarie, Marguérite
(17th century)

Youngest daughter of Madame ACARIE, and herself, like her two sisters, a Carmelite nun, she combined a rare spirituality with a lively gaiety, down-to-earth practicality and simple directness. It has been said that she above all others translated the spirit of TERESA DE JESUS into French terms. She once rebuked a nun who was trying to look 'religious': 'There is no sin in being thought silly, but there may easily be sin in trying to look so correct! Do let yourself be natural!' Her basic philosophy is summed up in her saying: 'The interior life consists in very few words, and a very great tendency to God.'

Acosmism

Philosophical attitude which denies reality to the ordered universe, and attributes reality only to the ABSOLUTE. It is thus an extreme form of PANTHEISM. The term was coined by HEGEL to describe the system of SPINOZA.

Acquired contemplation

Stage of non-verbal mental prayer reached through the exercise of the normal faculties, as opposed to INFUSED CONTEMPLATION.

Adam Kadmon

In the mysticism of the KABBALAH the original spiritual form of man, formed of light, and endowed with all wisdom, living in unity with God in the Garden of Eden or the higher celestial earth.

Adamites

Second-century Christian sect who believed that by laying aside clothing they might recover Adam's personal innocence. Similar doctrines were revived at the Reformation especially among the BRETHREN OF THE FREE SPIRIT.

Advaita

Indian term meaning 'non-twoness', philosophically rendered by 'monism'. *Advaita* as taught by SANKARA means that True Being is of itself, the eternal BRAHMAN, One only, unchanging and unchanged, undivided and without parts. The 'manyness' of things exists through MAYA, appearance or illusion. Change rests simply on a word; it is a mere name.

Æ

Pen-name (from Æon) of G. W. Russell (1867–1935), Irish theosophist, mystic, painter and poet. Painting, his natural genius, became his hobby and relaxation. He is a minor poet, but his poems are in their own way unique, for they reflect a mystical awareness of the past in the present, the cosmic in the parochial, the eternal in the temporal and the divine in the human.

Aelred
(1109–67)

Cistercian monk of Rievaulx, and author of *The Mirror of Love (Speculum Caritatis)*, a work influenced and encouraged by BERNARD OF CLAIRVAUX. His family were hereditary married priests at Hexham. *The Mirror of Love* was written by Aelred as novice-master, and it reflects his educational programme. It is on a less exalted plane than Bernard's work. God has loved man, man is made to love God. The soiled image of God can be renewed by divine love; we seek our true Sabbath of rest. Aelred has a moving account of his own experience: 'You called me, Lord, you called, you shouted, you terrified me, you compelled my deaf ears to hear you, you struck me down, beat me, overpowered my hard heart, you sweetened and softened and dispelled my bitterness.'

Æon

Literally 'age' or 'world'; spiritual being of GNOSTIC mythology.

Affective prayer

A prayer which consists of acts of loving desire. Augustine BAKER calls it the 'affective prayer of the will': it involves 'forced acts', deliberate acts of will directing the soul to worship; affections, such as love, joy, hope and desire, which flow out spontaneously, but which must be watched and balanced by acts of humility or they may lead to mere sentimentalism; and aspirations 'purely flowing from an internal impulse of the Divine Spirit'. 'The soul's aim', says Augustine Baker, 'is to recollect herself by that general notion that faith gives her of God; but being not able to do this presently, she doth in her mind, and by the help of the imagination, represent unto herself some Divine Object, as some one or more perfections of God, or some mystery of Faith; and thereupon, without such discoursing as is used in meditation, she doth immediately, without more ado, produce acts or affections one after another towards God.'

Affirmative way

See VIA AFFIRMATIVA.

African prophetic churches

During the twentieth century, extending back into the late nineteenth, the whole of Africa has seen the emergence of independent indigenous Christian churches. Sometimes the motive has been political, sometimes schism has been occasioned by a personal dispute. Sometimes the move has come from the appearance of a strong, charismatic, prophetic leader. Such was William Wade Harris of Liberia, with his white gown and turban, the great evangelist of the Ivory Coast. Such was Garrick Braid of the Niger Delta with his great healing powers, or Joseph Babalola of Ilesha in Nigeria, a visionary of genius. Such was Simon Kimbangu of Zaïre, healer and pacifist, who spent thirty years in a Belgian gaol. Such was Alice Lenshina of Zambia, who believed that she herself had been resurrected from the dead, and given a new Bible by angels, who insisted on strict morality, and was apolitical. Such was Isaiah Shembe, visionary, healer, ascetic and exorcist, who established the new community of the Ama Nazareth outside Durban.

Many of these churches, and many smaller sects and groups, are marked by ecstatic worship, fostered by drumming and expressed through dancing, speaking in tongues and the like. Dreams and visions play an important part in such groups as the Cherubim and Seraphim; it was said of Alice Lenshina's Lumpa church that 'dream and taboo were the two front doors through which Christians went back to the African past'. Prayer is important, as in the Aladura churches of West Africa; and it involves congregational participation and is sometimes itself associated with a dissociation of the conscious senses.

Agrippa von Nettesheim, Heinrich Cornelius
(1486–1535)

Heinrich Cornelius was born in Cologne. He was a scholar and alchemist, theologian and magician, lawyer and secret service agent. He took the grandiloquent Latin name himself. In

Portrait of Agrippa. The frontispiece of his Occult Philosophy

his work *Occult Philosophy*, written when he was a young man but not published till 1531, he put forward a system in which everything is linked together in one single whole, which is God. Man, made in the image of God, is a microcosm, a small universe. The macrocosm, being like man, has a world soul. There are 'correspondences throughout the universe, mysteries which a select few can penetrate and control. Man has in himself All that is contained in the greater world. There are in him the four Elements in just proportion, and the quintessence of Æther, the chariot of the soul. There are in him the vegetative life of plants, the senses of animals, of celestial spirits, the Angelical reason and the Divine understanding.' Man receives and contains even God Himself. In *The Uncertainty and Vanity of Sciences and Arts* Agrippa outlines the knowledge of his day with encyclopaedic scholarship, but concludes that it is nothing compared with the divinely revealed Word of God.

Ahura Mazda

The Lord of Light, the Wise Lord, the One God of ZOROASTRIANISM.

Akhenaten
(d. 1358 BC)

Name taken by the Egyptian Pharaoh Amenhotep IV, who reigned 1375–1358 BC. He abandoned polytheism and fostered a monotheistic worship of a single divine power dwelling on light invisible behind the disk (*aton*) of the sun. He moved the seat of government to Tell-el-Amarna, where he built glorious temples. But he offended the priests and neglected foreign policy, and his revolution was soon undone.

Alacoque, Margaret Mary

See MARGARET MARY ALACOQUE.

Alain de la Roche
(1428–75)

Breton Dominican, who spread Confraternities of the Holy Rosary. He was not an ecstatic but claimed revelations, including historical revelations, which he used in his discourses, published after his death as *Sponsus novellus Beatissimae Virginis Mariae* (1498). He evidently believed passionately in their genuineness, but the general view of posterity is that 'he was undoubtedly a religious of sincere piety, but one who was led by a feverish imagination to strange hallucinations'.

al-ʿAlawi, Abu ʾl-ʿAbbas Ahmad ibn Mustafa
(1869–1934)

Mystical poet from Algeria, with a strongly intellectualist bias, as the following extract shows:

I am Essentially One, Single, Unencroachable
By the least object. Leave I any crevice,
Any space vacant that to another might go?
For the Inside am I of Essence in Itself
And the Outside of the Quality, Diffuse
  Concentration.
'Thither' is there none whither I am not turning.
Doth other than Me exist, empty of My
  Attribute?
My Essence is the Essence of Being, now,
Always. My Infinity is not limited by the least
Grain of mustard. Where can the Creature
Find room to intrude on the Truth's Infinite?
Where other than It, when All is Full?
Union and separation are thus in Principle the
  same,
And to behold creation is to behold the Truth,
If creation be interpreted as it truly is.

(*tr. Martin Lings*)

He set himself towards the goal of Supreme Sainthood, the Great Peace, inward intoxication and outward soberness. He experienced many visions, especially in sleep. He became an almost hypnotic teacher. His doctrine was the oneness of being, oneness in essence, qualities and actions. So in his verse the Creator says:

The veil of creation I have made
As a screen for the Truth, and in creation there be
Secrets which suddenly like springs gush forth.

The letters of the alphabet were for him symbols, and the exterior acts of ritual purification and prayer an essential part of interior religion.

Albertus Magnus
(1200–80)

Dominican theologian, somewhat overshadowed for posterity by his more systematic pupil THOMAS AQUINAS. Albertus was one of those revolutionaries who brought in the philosophy of ARISTOTLE to modify the current Platonism. His philosophy has been described as an attempt to combine scholasticism and mysticism. His own mysticism is best seen in the little monograph *De adhaerendo Deo*. If God is a Spirit, to be worshipped in spirit, the mind must be cleared of images, the doors of the senses must be shut. The mind freed from distractions is in some sense transformed into God; the man who penetrates into himself and in so doing transcends himself, ascends to God. It is through darkness of mind that we reach the uncreated light. To find union with God we must detach ourselves from the world, and then strip from our idea of God, first physical attributes, then intellectual qualities, and finally the very idea of being, for that keeps Him among created things.

Alcantaran method

See PETER OF ALCANTARA.

Alchemy

'Alchemy', wrote Pierre-Jean Fabre in 1636, 'is not merely an art or science to teach metallic translations, so much as a true and solid science that teaches how to know the centre of all things, which in the divine language is called the Spirit of Life.' The transmutative process is an integral part of the Great Work, which is a material and spiritual realization. Essential to alchemy is the understanding of 'correspondences' between the material and spiritual. The alchemist was seeking under suitable astrological conditions (another aspect of the theory of correspondences) to bring together Primary Matter and the Primary Agent (also called secret fire), first to produce a pure mercurial substance, then an incombustible sulphur and finally the Philosophers' Stone, which had the power of transmuting base metals into gold, but whose discovery was also a necessary part of the realization of man's full faculties, and a precondition of the discovery of the Panacea, the Elixir of Life which would transmute the human body into an incorporate body of light, so securing for the Adept omniscience, omnipotence and the joy of divine love. The process is picturesquely illustrated and all through is the sense that regeneration comes through putrefaction, life through death.

Christian alchemists do not hesitate to identify Christ, already called the Corner-Stone, with the Philosophers' Stone. So BOEHME, of all the great mystics the one most influenced by alchemical thought: 'In this stone there lies hidden all that God and Eternity, heaven, the stars and elements contain and are able to do.

The Green Lion disgorging the Sun, an alchemical illustration of the generation of wisdom (the sun) through the transformation of matter (the lion)

There never was from eternity anything better or more precious than this. It is offered by God and bestowed upon men. Everyone may have it . . . It is in a simple form, and has the power of the whole Deity in it.'

Man then is the true subject of the alchemist's art. The three principles, Sulphur of his earthly part, Salt of the intellect and above all Mercury, the Mercury of the Wise, 'Snowy Splendour', the spark of the soul, the mystical spirit, must be brought together in the Azoth or Philosopher's Egg set within the Athanor or cauldron, which is man himself, and by the fire of love. Then the transmutation of natural into spiritual man may begin. The first stage of the process is Blackness, the stage of purgation; the second is whiteness, the stage of illumination; the climax is redness, the colour of alchemical gold, and is also called the Marriage of Luna and Sol, the human and the divine, the finite and the infinite.

Alcohol

Alcohol (ethanol or ethyl alcohol) is the commonest of all drugs; it acts as a depressant on the brain. Its use can be traced back to the earliest stages of civilization. Alcoholic beverages are fermented from grain, potatoes, fruit juices, honey, pepper and other sources. The capacity of alcohol to dispel care and create illusion has given it in the past religious significance, as in the mysteries of DIONYSUS. The invention of distilled spirits, in which the drug is more concentrated and more potent, intensified this. Arnauld de Villeneuve (*c.* 1300) called brandy 'a water of immortality', and indeed some brandies, in France, are still generically called 'eaux de vie'.

The Hindu Soma, and Persian Haoma were ritual libations of fermented juice. The god Indra drank great quantities of Soma and said, 'I have drunk Soma, I have become immortal.'

Allegory

Allegory seeks for a meaning beyond the literal and obvious. Heraclitus (not the philosopher), a first-century AD Homeric scholar, says, 'That is called allegory which, as the name implies, says one thing but means something other than what it says'; he claims to derive his principles of interpretation from the practice of the mystery religions. It is thus a means of taking seriously passages in sacred scripture which are not immediately edifying to the reader, and as such was used by the Christian Platonists of Alexandria in relation to the Old Testament (they did not in general allegorize the New), the Stoics in relation to Homer (Heraclitus insists that Apollo's anger is a scientific description of plague, and Athene pulling Achilles by the hair is a picture of Achilles' psychological state), and the Kabbalists in relation to the Torah. It was at the same time a device of the mystics to read mystical meaning into these and other passages. The Alexandrians insisted on three dimensions of interpretation,

Jesus healing the blind men of Jericho. An illumination from a 17th-century Ethiopian Gospel book

literal (the body), moral (the soul) and intellectual (the spirit). For example Jesus heals two blind men at Jericho. The literal interpretation is simply the account of an event which actually took place. In the intellectual interpretation the beggars are Israel and Judah, and Jericho is the world. The moral interpretation speaks directly to the reader. His eyes must be opened by the Word of God; he must come out of his Jericho. Occasionally the literal sense is passed over but not often; sometimes, as in the command to the rich man to sell all and follow Jesus, the literal sense is all. More widely, allegory may assume an infinite network of meanings and correlations in which there is an infinite depth of meaning to every representation; allegorical meaning thus cannot be exhausted.

Alphabet

Much mystical and religious thought regards a name as having power and bearing a substantive relation to its object. The letters of the alphabet thus become in a sense the elements of the universe and fit objects for contemplation.

See also ABULAFIA, AL-'ALAWI, HURUFISM, KABBALAH, ROSICRUCIANS.

Alphonsus Maria de'Liguori
(1696–1787)

Neapolitan, who started on a brilliant legal career, but withdrew from the pursuit of worldly success and in 1726 took Holy Orders. He was a preacher of winsome directness, an immensely influential moral theologian who opposed alike moral laxity and fanatical rigorism, and the author of numerous mystical and ascetical treatises, notably *A Succinct Exercise of Perfection* (1743), *The True Spouse of Jesus Christ* (1760), *The Practice of Loving Jesus Christ* (1768). The essential points of his mysticism lie in detachment from created things, love towards God, prayer and meditation. Alphonsus contributed to the devotion paid to the Sacred Heart of Jesus. His devotional writings have been charged with overexuberance; it springs from the sincerity and enthusiasm of the man. He founded the Redemptorist order.

Alumbrados

The name, the Enlightened, was applied to a group of sixteenth-century Spanish ecstatics, who claimed that direct religious experience did away with the need of sacraments and of the prayers of the Church; that the only true prayer was an ecstatic union making no use of words or mental images; and that this mystical union once achieved was never lost. They were repressed by the Inquisition.

Amalric

Latinized form of AMAURY.

Amaury
(d. *c.*1206)

Influential teacher at Paris, whose views were condemned both before and after his death only to survive through his followers and disciples. He held that God is the one essence of all beings created and uncreated, and the universe an emanation from the Divine. God is not distant therefore; His being is in the lives of those who open themselves to Him. Those who live in the love of God are incapable of sin and are raised above external observances. This mystical experience may be achieved through silence and inward awareness. Once the soul has risen to God by means of LOVE, it sloughs off its own nature and receives the being of God. It is no longer a creature; it no longer sees and loves God as a being external to itself; it *is* God.

Amida

Abbreviation of AMITABHA, 'endless light', or *Amitayus*, 'endless life'. In BUDDHISM, Boundless Light, personified as a Buddha. Repetition of the words '*Namu Amida Butsu*', 'Lord of Boundless Light, I adore you', is believed by some Japanese Buddhists to guarantee LIBERATION.

Amiel, Henri Frédéric
(1821–81)

Swiss philosopher, professor at the University of Geneva, whose democratic sympathies isolated him from his fellows. He kept an introspective diary at considerable length, which was excerpted after his death under the title *Fragments of an Intimate Journal*. It is ironical that Amiel, who regarded his failure to write a *magnum opus* with depression, should have influenced so many people by this private record. To its making went vast reading, a keen enjoyment of friendship and natural scenery, disappointment in his worldly failure, the sense that everything in the universe is matter for thought.

Amiel's religious experience is mystical and personal. TRUTH comes at the point of interaction of NATURE and the soul, each operating under its own law, and the soul's inward law is the only revelation of God: 'There is but one thing needful – to possess God. All our senses, all our powers of mind and soul, are so many ways of approaching the Divine, so many modes of tasting and adoring God. Religion is not a method: it is a life – a higher and supernatural life, mystical in its roots and practical in its fruits; a communion with God, a calm and deep enthusiasm, a love which radiates, a force which acts, a happiness which overflows.' The secret is the renunciation of the will: 'To love, to dream, to feel, to learn, to understand – all these are possible to me if only I may be dispensed from willing – I have a sort of primitive horror of ambition, of struggle, of hatred, of all which dissipates the soul and makes it dependent on external things and aims. The joy of becoming once more conscious of myself, of listening to the passage of time and the flow of the universal life, is sometimes enough to make me forget every desire and to quench in me both the wish to produce and the power to execute.' But Amiel is ambiguous: some of his appeal lies in his very human weaknesses. He is aware of his 'too restless search for perfection'. He is aware too of what he calls *l'éblouissement de l'infini*: the Infinite is at once dazzling and dizzying. His highest certainty comes when he writes: 'All is well, my God envelops me.'

Amitabha

The Buddha of Infinite Light, in Buddhist popular mythology the Ruler of the West, a great object of personal devotion especially in China and Japan. *See also* PURE LAND.

Anabaptists

General name covering several groups which arose in Europe in the sixteenth century, united by the practice of believers' baptism. There was a strong mystical strain in the movement. Thus Balthasar Hubmaier (*c.* 1485–1528) wrote of his own experience, 'I believe and trust that the Holy Ghost has come in me and the power of the most high God has, as with Mary, overshadowed my soul, to conceive in me the new man; so that in the living, indestructible Word, and in the Spirit I might be born again, and see the kingdom of God.' So Hans Denck (*c.* 1495–1527) spoke of 'an inner voice, a Spark of Truth which I partly feel in me'. This voice gave him his certainty: 'The voice of my heart, of which I assuredly know that it renders the truth, says to me that God is righteous and merciful, and this voice speaks in every good heart distinctly, and intelligibly, and it speaks the more distinctly and clearly the better one is.' Those who listen experience mystic union: 'All who are inspired with the Spirit of love are one with Christ in God.' So with the Zwickau Prophets, amongst them Nicholas Storch (d. 1530) an ecstatic visionary, who believed that all godly men were under the direct inspiration of the HOLY SPIRIT, and Thomas Münzer (*c.* 1490–1525) who claimed the immediate command of the Spirit upon his life, and taught a doctrine of the INNER LIGHT, similar to that of the SOCIETY OF FRIENDS.

Ancrene Riwle, The

Thirteenth-century English volume of rules for anchoresses, of uncertain authorship. Not itself a treatise on mystical theology, it sets the background for mediaeval mystical experience. The writer says that there are only two rules: LOVE, and, to serve that, bodily discipline. The treatise falls into eight sections: Devotional exercises; the government of the senses in keeping the heart; Moral lessons and examples; Temptations and means of avoiding them; Confession; Penance and amendment; Christian love; Domestic and social duties. There is good straight common sense; injunctions not to be always gazing out of the window, chattering to visitors, gossiping among themselves; there is tenderness towards the nuns who overdid the physical ASCETICISM; there is insight, as in the advice that the severest temptations come later, not earlier. This attractive volume is the framework of the experiences of JULIAN OF NORWICH and others like her.

Androgyne

A single being coupling the male and female powers and energies, also called hermaphrodite (from two Greek deities). Many mystical religions see the Ultimate Power as bisexual ('God created man in his own image . . . male and female created he them.' Gen. I, 27); it is explicitly stated in the *Corpus Hermeticum*. In Chinese TAOISM, and in Indian TANTRISM the Ultimate is often portrayed as a pair of lovers, and all over the world bisexual gods of fertility are found. In many gnostic theosophies human perfection is imagined as an unbroken unity. Aristophanes in PLATO's *The Banquet* gives an entertaining picture of an originally spherical humanity, sexually divided, each half seeking for its mate. The Brihadaranyaka UPANISHAD (I, 4) has a similar idea. Christian GNOSTICISM is full of phrases suggesting that a reunited humanity would find omnipotence, eternal life, the Kingdom. Thus in *The Gospel according to Thomas* Jesus says, 'When you make the two become one, you will become the Son of Man, and if you say, "Mountain, remove yourself", it will remove itself.' In the second *Letter* of Clement the Kingdom will come, according to Jesus, 'when the two shall be one, the outside like the inside, the male with the female neither male nor female'. So in *The Gospel of Philip*: 'Christ came

The androgyne as an illustration to Aurora consurgens, *a 14th-century alchemical text*

to re-establish what was thus divided in the beginning and to reunite the two. Those who died because they were in separation he will restore to life by reuniting them.'

The figure of the androgyne, representing the conjunction of opposites, predictably plays an important role in ALCHEMY. Jakob BOEHME took over the idea from the alchemists. According to Boehme, Sophia, the Divine Wisdom, was part of Primal Man, but when he tried to dominate her she was separated from him, an episode which Boehme does not hesitate to compare with Christ's crucifixion. All love of man for woman is really a mystical yearning for the lost part of himself, the Divine WISDOM.

The myth of the androgyne gripped the imagination of the nineteenth century; it received magnificent expression in Balzac's *Séraphita.*

Angela of Foligno
(*c.* 1248–1309)

Thirteenth-century Umbrian mystic, born of a wealthy family and married. After her husband's death she became a Franciscan tertiary. 'During my whole life I have studied how I might obtain the fame of sanctity,' she remarks naïvely. She had simplicity and fervour, and a strongly romantic temperament. She describes the eighteen steps she took in penitence and self-discipline as her PURGATIVE WAY. She received many visions, especially of the Passion of Christ, which were recorded by her confessor, Brother Arnold. But once she had emerged from the period of wrestling with the world her visions do not at all conform with the idea of hysterical illness. On the contrary she says that 'a divine change' took place in her soul, and she appears as one of those whose ecstasies renew them for normal life.

Here is a characteristic passage from her *Book of Visions*: 'The eyes of my soul were opened, and I discerned the fullness of God, in which I understood the whole world, here and beyond the sea, the abyss, the ocean, everything. In all these things I could see nothing except the divine power, in a way that was utterly indescribable. My soul was brimming over with wonder and cried out in a loud voice "The whole world is full of God".' She describes how she apprehended God through Goodness, Beauty, Power, Wisdom, Love, Justice. In another passage she describes the vision of God through DARKNESS. Her scribe found difficulty in understanding this: 'Christ's faithful one told me that her mind has been uplifted but three times to this most high and ineffable mode of beholding God in great darkness, and in a vision so marvellous and complete. Certainly she had seen the Sovereign God countless times and always darkly; yet never in such a high manner and through such great dark.' In another passage Angela says, 'I beheld a Thing, as fixed and stable as it was indescribable, and more than this I cannot say, save what I have often said already, namely, that it was all good. And though my soul did not behold love, yet when it saw that ineffable Thing it was itself filled with unutterable joy, and it was taken out of the state it was in and placed in this great and ineffable state. . . . But if you want to know what it was that I beheld, I can tell you nothing, except that I beheld a Fullness and a Clearness, and felt them within me so abundantly that I cannot describe it, nor offer any image of it; for what I beheld was not bodily, but as though it were in heaven. Thus I beheld a beauty so great that I can say nothing of it except that I saw the Supreme Beauty, which contains in itself all goodness.' Here language is wrestling with experiences which it has no vocabulary to express.

Angelico, Fra
(*c.* 1387–1455)

Italian painter. Giovanni da Fiesole became a Dominican friar and prior of his convent; according to one story he was offered, but refused, an archbishopric. One of the most delicate and sensitive of all painters, he produced his masterpiece in the incomplete series of paintings of the life of Christ designed as an aid to meditation for the friars in their cells in the convent of S. Marco in Florence.

Angelus Silesius
(1624–77)

Poetic *nom de plume* of Johann Scheffler, a Lutheran converted to Catholicism because the Lutherans rejected the Christian's highest wisdom, the *Theologia Mystica*. He was himself influenced by an admirer of BOEHME named Abraham von Franckenberg; his own verses show the impact of the *Song of Songs* and of ECKHART. Angelus writes pithily and epigrammatically. He seeks to startle his reader. He will begin a verse 'God is a sheer Nothing' or 'God foresees nothing' or 'I disbelieve in Death' or 'I am myself eternity.' He is concise:

Go out – God goes in
Die to yourself – live to God
Be not – He is
Do nothing – His bidding's done.

It would be hard to find a finer compendium of mysticism. But in numerous verses of short compass he explores the whole gamut of mystical experience. Phrases, memorable phrases, ring from his page: 'I am not I nor Thou: Thou art the I in Me', 'All you would have lies already within you', 'The password is Love', 'The Knower must be one with the Known', 'A single Light and a single Splendour', 'I must be pregnant with God.' Angelus's mysticism is explicitly Christian:

In Christ is God God
In angels, angelic form
In men, Man
In all, All.

Or his most familiar couplet:

Though Christ a thousand times in Bethlehem
be born,
Unless he's born in you, then are you still
forlorn.

Sometimes he reaches profound depths of mystical insight:

Who in this mortal life would see
The Light that is beyond all light,
Beholds it best by faring forth
Into the darkness of the Night.

(tr. J. E. C. Flitch)

In addition to his poetry Scheffler was in his day a formidable controversialist.

Anker-Larsen, Johannes
(1874–1957)

Danish novelist whose books explore the mystical life and are at the same time rooted in the countryside of Denmark. His best-known work is *De Vises Stein (The Philosopher's Stone)*.

Ankh ☥

Egyptian symbol of life, shaped like a Christian cross except that the top piece is in the form of an oval loop. Also called *crux ansata*.

Ansar, Pir-I
(d. 1088)

Persian poet and mystic, otherwise known as ʿAbd Allah al-Ansari. He composed an important sketch of Sufi philosophy, but his lasting qualities lie in his devotional poetry, especially his *Munajat* or *Orisons*, in which rhyming prose is interspersed with verse quatrains.

O Powerful, Who of Godhead worthy art!
O Creator, who shewest the way to every
erring heart!
To my soul give Thou of Thy Own
Spotlessness,
And to my eyes of Thy Own Luminousness;
And unto us, of Thy Bounty and Goodness,
whatever may be best
Make Thou that Thy Bequest.

O Lord, in Mercy grant my soul to live,
And patience grant, that hurt I may not
grieve:
How shall I know what thing is best to
seek?
Thou only knowest: what Thou knowest,
give!

(tr. A. J. Arberry)

Anselm
(1033–1109)

A Christian from northern Italy who came north to Normandy, and later to Canterbury as Archbishop; he gave an intellectual leadership such as no other incumbent has matched. Something of a Platonist, he equated God with the Form of the Good. He also put forward a form of the ontological argument for God's existence: God is 'that than which nothing greater can be conceived', and if He lacked existence would not be such. His *Meditations* show his mystical devotion. The very impulse towards God comes from God: 'Let me seek Thee in longing, let me long for Thee in seeking: let me find Thee in loving and love Thee in finding.' The eye of the soul is darkened in itself and dazzled by God's splendour. 'Everywhere Thou art wholly present, and I do not see Thee. In Thee I move and in Thee I have my being, and cannot come to Thee, thou art within me and about me, and I do not feel Thee.'

Anthroposophy

Mystical system evolved by Rudolph STEINER; the name implies a THEOSOPHY which puts man at the centre instead of God. The object is that through concentration and MEDITATION the believer comes to an 'intuition' which enables his lower self to have a vision of his higher self. Anthroposophy brings together strands from many parts of the world, including India, Persia, Egypt and Palestine. It teaches a doctrine of REINCARNATION, and the escape from the material through and into the spiritual.

Antony of Padua
(1195–1231)

Born in Lisbon, he became an Augustinian and later a Franciscan. He was noted as a powerful preacher, and a man of great holiness of life. His visionary reception of the Christ-Child in his arms is commemorated in numerous statues and pictures. He is associated with many miracle stories.

Apex of the Spirit

In Christian mystical writers that part of the soul which is united with God in mystical experience.

Apocalyptic

The word, which means 'uncovering' (cp. 'revelation'), is applied especially to a class of literature in Judaism and CHRISTIANITY, which was especially prominent in the last two centuries BC and the first two AD. The apocalyptic writers stand in the line of descent from the PROPHETS, but the tone of their works is very different. Apocalyptic literature habitually has reference to the past, present and future. All three may be illustrated from the first great apocalyptic work, *The Book of Daniel.* It is projected back into the past as if relating to the reigns of Nebuchadnezzar, Belshazzar and Darius; it is called out by a present crisis, clearly by the attempt of Antiochus Epiphanes to hellenize Judaea; it offers a vision of the future, the climax of the age, the time of judgment, and the glorious KINGDOM OF GOD. Among other Jewish apocalyptic writings must be mentioned three associated with the name of Enoch, one in Ethiopic, one in Slavonic and one in Hebrew. In the Slavonic apocalypse Enoch is escorted by two angels through the seven heavens. In the first he sees the angels who guard snow, ice and dew; in the second are the fallen angels who sinned with mortal women; in the third he is shown the Paradise of the blessed and the torments of the wicked; in the fourth are the sun, moon and stars and their attendant angels; in the fifth are the Watchers, the primary rebels among the angels, led by Satan or Sataniel; in the sixth come the angels who govern the world of nature; in the seventh is God in His glory surrounded by the archangels. From there the book goes on to the revelations received by Enoch at the command of God, the plan of creation in seven millennia, of which the last is a Sabbath of rest. Another

The 'beast with seven heads and ten horns' making war on the saints. From a 14th-century text of the Apocalypse (Revelation) of St John

important document is the *Apocalypse of Ezra* (2 Esdras 3–14), which comprises seven visions granted to Ezra in Babylon. In the first he is told that the end of the age is drawing near, that it will be marked by desolation, horrors and portents and the rule of a kind of Antichrist. In the second the end is heralded by the opening of the book of judgment and by a trumpet blast. In the third Ezra is given the promise of the New Jerusalem, the four-hundred-year reign of the MESSIAH, universal death, a seven-year silence, followed by resurrection and judgment. In the fourth Ezra sees a sorrowing woman, Jerusalem, mourning her fall (the events of AD 70, the contemporary point of reference), and transfigured into the New Jerusalem. The fifth is a reinterpretation of Daniel's vision of an eagle, with a symbolic sketch of history and the coming of the Messiah to crush the oppressor and liberate the righteous. The sixth also takes off from Daniel, and shows one in the likeness of a man rising from a stormy sea, and coming with the clouds of Heaven as liberator of his people. Finally in the seventh vision Ezra is promised deliverance.

Among Christian apocalyptic writing we must note the passage in the Synoptic Gospels (e.g. Mk 13), known as 'The Little Apocalypse'. It shows Jesus proclaiming 'the last things'; the signs will be wars and destruction and persecution, the abomination of desolation desecrating the Temple, natural portents, presaging the arrival of the Son of Man with his angels to gather the faithful. But no one, men, angels, not even the Son, knows the time or hour. 'Watch therefore.' This apocalypse is of particular interest. All the Jewish apocalypses are pseudonymous. Either then this is a separate 'pamphlet' pseudonymously attached to Jesus, or Jesus broke with tradition in proclaiming his own apocalyptic vision. Further, this apocalypse is closer to prophetic traditions than some of the others. It is not only a vision of the Ultimate, but also a proclamation that spiritual blindness leads to disaster, that the way to glory lies through tribulation, and that there is constant need for vigilance.

The Apocalypse of John or The Book of Revelation is the best known and most impressive of all these apocalyptic writings. It too is not pseudonymous; there is no reason to doubt that its writer was named John though he was not the evangelist John. He was a visionary, who was caught up in the spirit on the Lord's Day, and offers visionary but very practical messages to the seven churches of Asia. Then he is transported to heaven, and sees the throne of God with lightning flashing from it, and twenty-four elders, and the seven torches of fire which are the seven Spirits of God, and four fantastic creatures singing 'Holy, holy, holy'. He sees the book of the divine mysteries, sealed with seven seals, and opened only by a sacrificial Lamb. (The infusion of the historical events connected with JESUS of Nazareth into the visionary symbolism is of great interest.) From the opening of the first four seals come four horsemen bringing conquest, war, famine and death. The fifth releases the cry of the martyrs, the sixth earthquakes and portents and the survival of a faithful Remnant, the seventh silence for half an hour. These are no doubt the signs that the end is near. But they are now succeeded by a second and then a third series of seven woes, and a spectacular vision of the fall of Babylon (which is clearly Rome; here we have the legendary historical setting, the present crisis, the future vision). So come the first resurrection, the reign of Christ and his saints, Satan's final fling and defeat, the general resurrection and final judgment, the new Heaven and new earth with no more sea (in Jewish tradition water is often the power antithetical to God), and the vision of the New Jerusalem. Much of this belongs to the common stock of apocalyptic writing, though there are some unusual elements and it is explicitly Christianized. But the visions are woven together and presented with consummate artistry. Not for nothing did Austin Farrer call his great study of it *A Rebirth of Images*.

Of the other Christian apocalyptic writings the most important is *The Apocalypse of Peter*, which was regarded as canonical by some. A fragment shows Christ granting a vision on a mountain to the twelve Apostles, showing them the glory of two departing brethren, the blessings of Heaven ('a great place outside this world, shining with light, the soil of it blooming with immortal blossoms, and full of perfumes and sweet-smelling flowers') and the horrors of Hell.

Apocalyptic is an important section of mystical and visionary literature. It was nearly all (the Slavonic Enoch is an exception) produced under stress and with a sense of urgency: 'the times are at hand'. It shows the interaction of good and evil and the ultimate triumph of good. As revelations of an immediate future, the visions were unfulfilled. As symbolic expressions of ultimate truths they retain their fascination and their challenge.

Apophatic theology

The name given to the theology based on the VIA NEGATIVA.

Apostolic state

Term applied by Madame GUYON to the highest state of mystical experience, equivalent to that called by others SPIRITUAL MARRIAGE.

Apprehension

The One, the Ultimate God, is not to be comprehended by the human mind, only apprehended. Such apprehension takes two forms. One entails the 'flight to God'; it is ecstatic, outgoing and uncontrollable. The other lies through inward CONTEMPLATION; it is more a matter of inward discipline, more controllable. Some writers speak of them as intensity and withdrawal. Probably the two forms are obverse and reverse of a single coin, and come together in what RUYSBROECK calls 'the peace of the summits'.

Arcana

Secrets or mysteries. SWEDENBORG entitled one of his works *Arcana Coelestia*.

Arctic hysteria

Phenomenon among the Tungus of Siberia, characterized by extravagant crying, wild singing, passive withdrawal alternating with passionate activity, desire for darkness. It is interpreted as POSSESSION by spirits and regarded as one indication of vocation to be a SHAMAN. If the condition recurs in response to stimuli such as drumming, the vocation is confirmed, because uncontrolled possession has now become controlled possession, or, to put it differently, instead of the spirits possessing the subject, the subject possesses the spirits.

Arintero, Juan Gonzalez
(1860–1928)

Spanish spiritual writer who combined the academic studies of science and theology, but at about the age of forty turned completely to mystical theology. His great work was the four-volume *Desenvolvimiento y vitalidad de la Iglesia*. Arintero denied the possibility of ACQUIRED CONTEMPLATION. He held that all Christians were called to perfection and to allow their devotional life to develop into mystical contemplation.

Aristotle
(384–322 BC)

PLATO's greatest pupil was in many ways the most unmystical of philosophers. But at two points his thinking is of major importance for MYSTICISM. One is the distinction between active and passive reason (though the latter term does not occur). In Aristotle's philosophy, the actual is brought out of the potential by the actual. So the process of thought requires actual, active reason to produce the change in passive reason: 'Without active reason there is no thought.' Active reason then is a divine force, working within the human – not the transcendent God of Aristotle's *Metaphysics*, but a divine power possessing all knowledge and imparting it to us.

In *Ethics* Aristotle fixed the true end of man as happiness, a self-contained activity exercising the highest part of our being, the intellect, in accordance with the highest virtue, theoretical wisdom. It is in fact CONTEMPLATION. Aristotle places at the highest point of his universe a God engaged in abstract thought, and man similarly finds his fulfilment in contemplation.

A Tatar shaman under the influence of Arctic hysteria. From an 18th-century travel book

Aristotle exercised an indirect influence on mysticism through a curious work called the THEOLOGY OF ARISTOTLE. This is in fact a late Neo-Platonic treatise, though it is possible that it incorporates material from Aristotle's lost early works, when his thinking was close to that of Plato.

Arnauld, Antoine
(1612–94)

French theologian, much influenced by his sister Angélique and her work at PORT ROYAL. He was regarded as unorthodox, because of his support of Cornelius Jansen and his doctrine of the all-embracing power of divine Grace. His total output amounted to over 300 volumes.

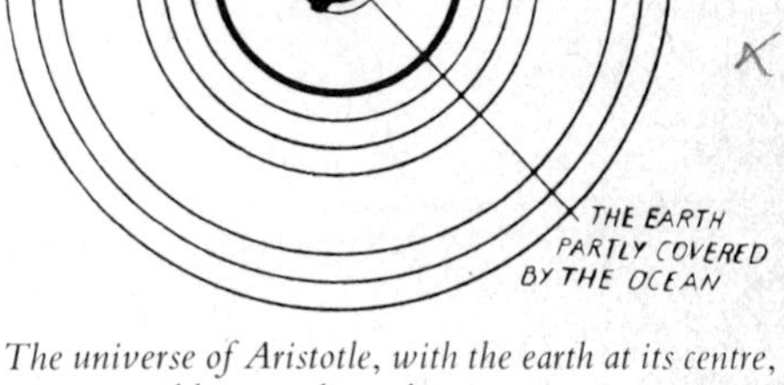

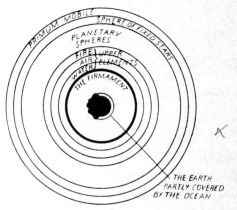

The universe of Aristotle, with the earth at its centre, as conceived by a mediaeval writer

Arnauld, Jacqueline Marie

See PORT ROYAL

Arnauld, Jeanne Catherine Agnès

See PORT ROYAL

Ascension

Mystical experience of rising, sometimes associated with flying, sometimes with the ascent to Heaven in a 'three-tiered universe'. Jewish mysticism acknowledges three forms of ascension: direct ascension into Heaven of a few chosen ones such as Enoch and Elijah; ascension and return, granted to Moses; and the ascension of the soul in Hasidic mystical experience. The ascension of Jesus closed his earthly appearances, and an ascension of Muhammad took place in sleep. Mystical powers of flight are attributed to the Asiatic SHAMANS, who in the early stages of their initiation are sometimes found entranced among the treetops. The Indian rope-trick is a popular example of ascension. The idea of a mystical ladder reaching to Heaven is common in many cultures as in the story of Jacob's dream. It is found in *The Egyptian Book of the Dead*; in the mysteries of Mithras; in Islamic mysticism, where there are seven steps to God; and in DANTE's vision, to name only a few. *See also* LEVITATION.

Asceticism

Ascesis is literally athletic training, and athleticism has, in STOICISM and CHRISTIANITY, been used as an image of the religious life. It comes to be applied to the renunciation of worldly pleasures and the mortification of the flesh.

A Hindu ascetic, whose untended hair and fingernails, and permanently upraised arms, express his detachment from the world. An 18th-century Indian painting

Asceticism has been associated with religion, and especially mystical religion, for a variety of reasons, some relatively good and some relatively bad. One is an essentially dualist view of the universe: matter is evil; only the spiritual and immaterial is good. So we may seek to escape from this weary wheel of birth and death by mortifying the flesh. Or, secondly, without regarding matter as evil, life here may be seen as a distraction from the life of the spirit. Or, thirdly, it may be a way of escaping the jealousy of the gods, as the Greek dictator Polycrates flung away his most precious possession (a ring – its return meant that the gods doomed him), or as BROWNING's Caliban says of his god:

> The best way to escape his ire
> Is, not to seem too happy.

Or, fourthly, it may be regarded as a way of acquiring merit before God by renouncing all claims in face of His almightiness. Or, fifthly, it may arise from a psychological abnormality, great or small – as Bernard Shaw observed, human beings assume they are at their most religious 'when they were the most uncomfortable'. Or, sixthly, it may be a physical means of inducing visionary states. Or, seventhly, it may spring from a desire to imitate the sufferings of a divine figure such as Christ; this was certainly a strong motive in the appalling self-tortures inflicted by Henry SUSO over a quarter of a century till a vision of God called a halt.

Some mystical writings warn against excess in ascetic practice. The *Gita*, for example: 'Yoga is not for him who eats too much nor yet for him who does not eat at all, nor for him who is all too prone to sleep, nor yet for him who always stays awake. Rather Yoga is for him who is moderate in food and recreation, controlled in his actions and gestures, moderate in sleeping as in waking' (6, 16–17).

Some authorities have seen mystic CONTEMPLATION and renunciation as being closely intertwined, and have argued that asceticism lies at the roots of mysticism.

Asclepius

Greek god of healing, called Æsculapius by the Romans (to whom he was brought in the form of a snake). Asclepius was the object of intense personal devotion from people who combined bad health and religiosity. One such, Aelius Aristides, in the second century AD, left a notable record of his religious commitment. This includes a mystical experience. While in the sanctuary he saw the cult-statue brilliantly lit up (such 'illumination' is not uncommon). The head blurred and swam till it became three, a power of Heaven, earth and the underworld, Zeus-Asclepius-Sarapis. Aristides cried 'One', a formula of unity from the Sarapis cult, and heard a voice: 'That is you.' This is mystical communion.

Asclepius, the Greek god of healing, and his companion servant-guide Telesphoros

In HERMETICISM Asclepius was one of the names of Hermes Thrice-Greatest, and three of the tractates are named after him.

Astrology

The concept of astrology depends on the great backcloth of the stars, seemingly operating as a single system, and the seven heavenly bodies visible to the naked eye which move independently in relation to the stars, the sun, the moon and the five planets Mercury, Venus, Mars, Jupiter, Saturn. The power of the sun and moon and the free movement of the planets ('wanderers') make it natural to endow them with life and divinity. The stars are sometimes treated as children of the sun and moon, or as translated heroes or ancestors. The patterns made by groups of stars suggested shapes, which in turn led to a development of myth.

In the temperate zones the course of the sun plainly affects vegetative growth on earth. The cycle of the moon and of menstruation in women correspond. It was therefore natural to see the heavenly bodies as powerful deities controlling life on earth. With the three-tiered picture of the universe prevalent until the last few centuries, earth was the abode of living humans, the dead were down below, the gods up above. Again, divine power was in the sky. How to fence it in, understand it, control it?

There were two main observational factors. First, the course of the sun or ecliptic (and indeed of the planets) was limited to a narrow band of the sky. This was divided in Mesopotamia into twelve, each section being dominated by a particular constellation or sign of the Zodiac. Second, it was observed that some stars would be visible just above the horizon shortly after sunset one day, and then not seen for a period of about a month reappearing shortly before sunrise. These heliacal settings and risings were carefully recorded. The observer divided his field of observation into twelve 'houses'.

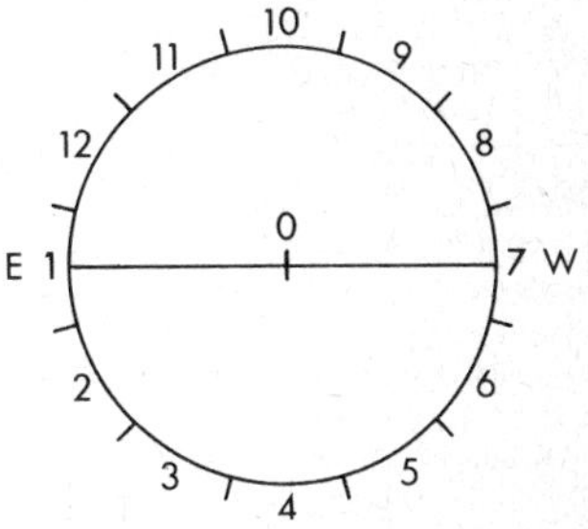

These were however more often represented in the form of a square.

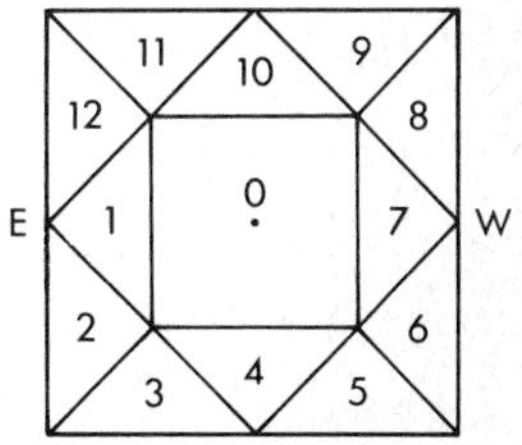

Positions were expressed in relation to signs (of the Zodiac) and houses. These triangles gave the astrological symbols for the points of the compass – though they were reversed in the process – so that △ = N, ▽ = S, ▷ = E, ◁ = W. They also gave the alchemists signs for the elements, Fire △ and Air 🜁 being over our heads and Earth 🜃 and water ▽ under our feet. The synthesis of fire and water gives ✡, which is a sign for alcohol ('burnt water'), but in Kabbalistic mysticism, because the combination of the Hebrew consonants for fire and water gives the word for Heaven, became a symbol for God.

There are three principal ways in which astrology has affected mystical religion. The first arises out of the belief that the planets, signs of the Zodiac and positions of the heavenly bodies at the moment of birth affect character and destiny. Our words *jovial, saturnine, mercurial, martial* reflect this belief. The calculation of horoscopes is used to reveal the destiny of the individual. The second is through the picture of the universe as a series of concentric spheres, with the Divine above and outside them. The

Venus as both goddess of love and sign of the Zodiac. From a 15th-century Italian astrological treatise

soul on its way to being born descends through the spheres, and as it passes away from the Divine becomes tainted by each of the spheres through which it passes. The spheres are dominated by the planets. Thus from Jupiter comes love of power, from Venus lust, from Mercury greed for gain, from Mars violence, from Saturn sloth. This is the picture offered by MITHRAISM, which promised the means of escape from these pollutions and their effect. The third is connected with a theory of correspondences, that all parts of the universe are interrelated, the heavenly bodies, and the sublunary world and the microcosm that is man, and that therefore we do well to relate all that we undertake to the total world-picture. This is a potent element in ALCHEMY in which the alchemical process will be invalid unless it is carried out with the appropriate conjunction of heavenly bodies.

Athanor

See ALCHEMY.

Atman

In Hindu mysticism the Self or Soul. In the *Mandukya Upanishad* the Self has four conditions: the waking life of outward consciousness; the dreaming life of inner consciousness; the sleeping life of silent consciousness; the awakened life of supreme consciousness, *Atman* in all its purity. Hindu monistic mysticism is linked with the proposition 'Brahman is all and Atman is Brahman'; it is the realization of identity between the Self and the Divine.

Atonement

In Christian theology Christ through his sacrifice (variously interpreted) brings man to a state of being at one with God. This is the at-onement. This is naturally important to mystical Christians, for whom the union (which is to say at-onement) of man and God is the goal, and who brought together this mystical goal with the theology of Christ's atoning work and the Pauline concept of being in Christ. This can be well exemplified by William LAW, for whom Christ is man's captain of salvation, the pioneer and pathfinder, who offers us an example and inspiration, and if we will respond by being 'in Christ', liberates us from sin and unites us with the Godhead. In some mystical writers atonement is directed to mankind as a whole, and is associated with UNIVERSALISM.

Attar, Farid al-Din
(d. 1229)

Persian Sufi poet who wrote an elaborate allegory called *The Parliament of the Birds* in which the birds set out on a quest for the lord of creation, the *Simurgh*. They have to pass through the valleys of Search, Love, Knowledge, Detachment, Unity, Wonder and Self-annihilation. Of all the thousands of birds only thirty win through. At the palace door they see thousands of resplendent suns and beautiful moons. A chamberlain comes out to test them; he calls them 'a feeble handful of dust'. The King has his being always and eternally and does not depend on their homage. But they are aflame with love, as the moth for the candle. They are admitted to the presence – and find that in seeing the *Simurgh* (which means Thirty Birds) they are seeing themselves. Without speaking he conveys to them this truth: 'The sun of my majesty is a mirror. He who sees himself therein sees his soul and his body, and sees them completely. Since you have come as thirty birds (*si-murgh*), you will see thirty birds in this mirror. If forty or fifty were to come it would be the same. Although you are now completely changed you see yourselves as you were before. . . . But I am more than thirty birds. I am the very essence of the true *Simurgh*. Annihilate yourselves gloriously and joyfully in me, and in me you shall find yourselves.' So the birds lose themselves in the *Simurgh* as the shadow in the sun. 'Seek the trunk of the tree, and do not worry whether the branches do or do not exist.'

Attis

See CYBELE.

Augustine
(354–430)

Augustine was born near Carthage, and became a Manichaean. Later he was influenced by NEO-PLATONISM, and this coloured his mysticism.

He was converted to Christianity in 386, and from 396 was Bishop of Hippo Regius, and an outstanding ecclesiastical statesman, scholar and scourge of heretics. He is a classic example of a mystic in the mainstream of the ecclesiastical development.

In his early work *On the Quantity of the Soul* (70–80) Augustine identifies seven stages in the soul's functioning. It is the principle of life, of sensation, of intelligence and of morality (which he identifies with purgation). Beyond these lie three more, the calming of the passions, the approach to contemplation and contemplation itself. The fourth stage, or purgation, is thus pivotal between natural life and mystical experience. God purges the soul, transforms it, leads it in and nurtures it. In its fullest sense CONTEMPLATION belongs to the next life, but glimpses or intuitions of the Divine are possible here.

This is paralleled by an analysis in *The Lord's Sermon on the Mount* (1, 3, 10) of the ascent of the soul through seven stages: (i) poverty of spirit, (ii) piety in openness to the scriptures, (iii) acknowledgment of our betrayal of God, (iv) earnest hunger and thirst after righteousness, (v) openness to God's mercy shown in care for others, (vi) through cleanness of heart and purity of mind preparation for the divine vision, (vii) full wisdom.

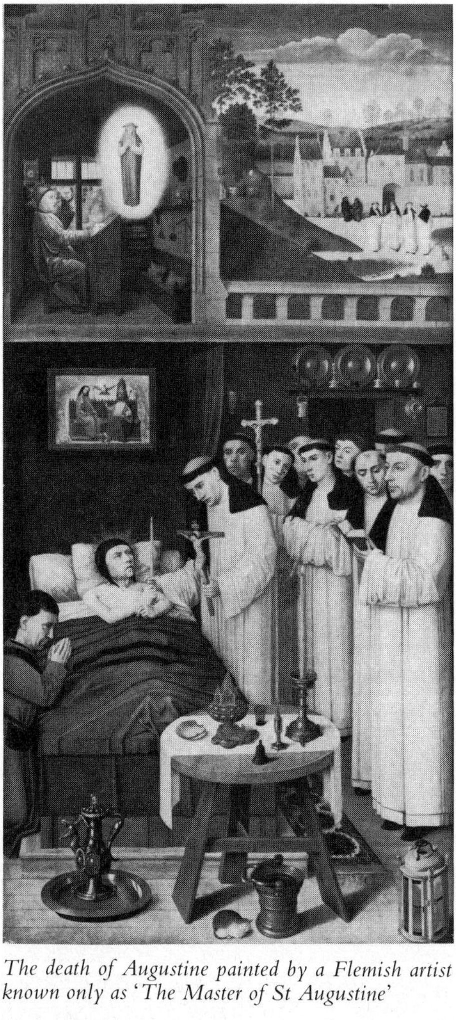

The death of Augustine painted by a Flemish artist known only as 'The Master of St Augustine'

That this is based on practice, not theory, is seen in Augustine's vision at Ostia (*Conf.* 9, 10, 23 – 9, 11, 27). He tells how he was with his mother Monica, speaking together of eternal life. They experienced first yearning for the Self-Same; in their search they scanned the material world, then passed to a more inward ascent, and for a moment touched with the full beat of the heart the life that never comes to be but always is. He concludes that if only all might be hushed, the tumult of the flesh, the sense-impressions of earth, sea and sky, the heavens, the soul itself, all imagery, all symbols, all things transient, then we might hear the very voice of the eternal, and if that experience were prolonged we would indeed enter into the joy of our Lord.

In his *Exposition of Psalm 41* Augustine gives a warm analysis of mystical experience. It starts from yearning. But before the soul can engage in contemplation, it must first destroy the serpents of iniquity, eliminate whatever is contrary to the truth and free itself from irrational passions. Now, in a state of faith but not of sight, the soul desires to see God. It searches through creation, it looks within; in neither is God to be found. It is carried above itself by the contemplation of the virtues of God's servants, into the mystic experience, the perception of something unchangeable, an experience which Augustine describes through the imagery of music.

Augustine did look inward for God; he found Him in the depths as well as the heights (*Conf.* 3, 6, 11). So that Augustine's mysticism springs from Neo-Platonist theory and his own practical experience. Maréchal says well of him: 'His serene luminous mysticism impregnates the Plotinian dialectic of which he is the tributary, and permits the emergence in unequivocal terms of a highly personalized experience characterized by an uncommon, supernatural passivity.' Cuthbert Butler calls him the Prince of Mystics, and finds in him the most penetrating intellectual vision into things divine, and a love of God that was a consuming passion. The source of Augustine's mysticism is in one sense simple. It is expressed in the affirmation at the outset of his *Confessions*, 'Thou hast made us for Thyself, and our hearts are restless till they find their rest in Thee.'

Aurobindo, Sri
(1872–1950)

Aurobindo was educated in England, and read widely in Greek and Latin, as well as in English,

French and German, and later Sanskrit. His mysticism stands in direct line of succession from the UPANISHADS, but it is expounded with an awareness of European metaphysical thought. His major work is *The Life Divine*, nearly half a million words in which he seeks to interpret metaphysically his own mystical experience.

Aurobindo's mysticism was notable for being directed to a transformation of this world, not an escape from it. S. K. Maitra, one of his best interpreters, has said: 'The fundamental idea upon which the whole structure of Sri Aurobindo's philosophy rests is that Matter as well as Spirit is to be looked on as real.' There is a ladder of being from the Absolute Divine Existence, down through Consciousness, Bliss, *gnosis*, mind, soul and life to matter; but all are part of the one reality.

Instead of freeing the spirit from the body Aurobindo spoke of bringing the spirit more perfectly into the body. 'It is the descent of the new consciousness which is the stamp and seal of my discipline.' This new consciousness would be achieved by a combination of YOGA disciplines and would lead to a new stage on the evolutionary staircase, the 'supramental'.

Aurobindo's own mystical experience may be seen in his account of the gates of the Transcendent, where 'stands that mere and perfect spirit described in the Upanishads, luminous, pure, sustaining the world but inactive in it, without sinews of energy, without flaw of duality, without scar of division, unique, identical, free from all appearance of relation and of multiplicity – the pure Self of the Advaitins, the inactive Brahman, the transcendent Silence. And the mind when it passes those gates suddenly, without intermediate transitions, receives a sense of the unreality of the world and the sole reality of the silence which is one of the most powerful and convincing experiences of which the human mind is capable.'

Automatic writing

Many creative writers have had a sense of being 'inspired'. PLATO in *Phaedrus* wrote of ' a kind of madness, which is possession by the Muses; this enters into a delicate and virgin soul, and there inspiring frenzy, awakes lyric and other poetry'.

> The lunatic, the lover and the poet
> Are of imagination all compact.

So de Musset speaks of poetic composition: 'It is not work, it is listening; it is as if some unknown person were speaking in your ear.' With the mystics this dissociation from the will of the writer seems to be carried further. CATHERINE OF SIENA dictated her *Dialogue* in a state of ecstasy. TERESA DE JESUS likened her writing to the speech of a parrot repeating without understanding the words of its master. BOEHME speaks of himself as impelled to write by a 'motion from on high': 'Art has not written here. There was no time to consider how to set it down deliberately according to literary understanding. All was ordered according to the direction of the Spirit. . . . The burning fire often forced forward with speed, and the hand and pen had to hasten directly after it; for it comes and goes like a sudden shower.' Madame GUYON would have a sudden urge to take up her pen; if she tried to resist, it was agony. Words and sentences, ideas and arguments tumbled from her so that one of her longer books was actually composed in a day and a half: 'In writing I saw that I was writing of things which I had never seen, and during the time of manifestation, I was given light to perceive that I had in me treasures of knowledge and understanding which I did not know that I possessed.' BLAKE is in some ways the best example of all. He declared that he wrote *Milton* and *Jerusalem* 'from immediate dictation . . . without premeditation and even against my will', and at his death declared that his works were the product of his 'celestial friends'.

Avoda

Jewish Hasidic term for the mystic's service of God in time and space, the practical fruits of mystical experience.

Azoth

See ALCHEMY.

B

Baal Shem, Israel
(*c.* 1700–60)

Jewish mystic, who founded the new HASIDISM of the eighteenth century. His name was Israel ben Eliezer, but he was widely known as the Baal Shem Tov, the Good Master of the Name (of God), or BEShT. He was born of a simple family, was early orphaned, was the butt of his fellows for his vague dreaminess, followed a variety of occupations in a seemingly desultory way, then at the age of thirty-six revealed powers of healing and prophetic insight. He was something of a pantheist. The whole world is a manifestation of the Divine Being. It is not an emanation, for nothing can be separated from God. Even evil exists in God; there is no absolute evil, only relative; it is a divine thing for a man to admire a woman's beauty, and evil only if he sees it in relation to himself instead of a manifestation of God. So every man must be considered good; no man has sunk so low that he cannot raise himself to God. Life-denying asceticism is not pleasing to God; on the contrary we should make joy our aim. Every act of worship should involve enthusiasm and ecstasy. Mysticism is not the KABBALAH; it is the sense of true oneness, which is as incomprehensible to the normal state of mankind 'as dancing to a dove'. But the man who has it, the *tsaddiq*, the righteous man, becomes a bridge between the Creator and the creation, and a source of Divine mercy. The Baal Shem was close to the people, and deeply loved. Many anecdotes, miracle stories and legends accrued to his name.

Bacchant

See DIONYSUS

Baker, Augustine
(1575–1641)

Christian spiritual writer, restored to faith, after a period of disillusion, by what he regarded as a miraculous escape from death. In 1605 he joined the Benedictine order. He would spend five to six hours a day in interior prayer, concentrating on intellectual vision. Like many mystics he experienced a long period of spiritual drought, but in 1620 his spiritual powers returned. In 1624 he was sent to the new convent at Cambrai to aid in forming the spiritual character of the religious. Here he produced the majority of his writings on ASCETICISM, prayer and spiritual union, which were collected after his death in the two volumes *Sancta Sophia*. In 1633 he moved to Douai. Ordered back to London, he was constantly on the move to escape persecution. Worn down by strain and by the effect of his own austerities, he died of the plague.

Augustine Baker taught the mystical union of God and 'the summit of the mind, the fund and centre of the spirit, the essence of the soul'. *Sancta Sophia*, though diffuse and unsystematic, is widely regarded as containing one of the most thorough and profound accounts of interior prayer. It lays strong emphasis on AFFECTIVE PRAYER.

Bankei
(1622–93)

Japanese ZEN Master, a man of the people, and a preacher of great popular appeal, who spoke directly to the people rather than from learned tomes. His preaching centred on 'the unborn Buddha-heart'. A peasant was told that if he did his work with his whole heart he would be practising the unborn heart. If he did his work in anger the work would become toilsome; if his work was free from passion, it sprang from the Buddha-heart. His general precept was 'Only sit up with the Buddha-heart, be only with the Buddha-heart, sleep and arise only with the Buddha-heart, and live only with the Buddha-heart'.

Banquet

Image used by mystical writers to express their mystical experience. God is the host; the soul is the guest. The experience is pleasurable, life-giving and satisfying. So MACARIUS: 'Sometimes, like guests at a royal feast, they are satiated with indescribable enjoyment.'

Baqa

Sufi concept of eternal life, 'the continued existence in eternity of that which has never ceased to be in Truth, through the shaking off of what was not, by obliterating it'. Its precondition is thus FANA, the dissolution of everything except God.

Baraka

Grace in Moslem mysticism: the root has many connotations, but basically that of blessing, and the mysterious power of holy men.

Basil the Great
(*c.* 329–79)

Christian leader, who became Archbishop of Caesarea. His cardinal importance in Christian history lay in diverting monasticism from solitary retirement to a communal life linked with the practical service of others, while retaining a basis in the mystical contemplation of the Divine Beauty. Prayer, purity, fasting, self-discipline are the essential means to union with God, a union which lifts us out of space and time; hence those who have reached this goal have foreknowledge of the future, understanding of the mysteries, and lasting joy; they abide in God, they are made like God, they are made God. Once this is granted it is not lost: 'The indwelling of God is this – to have God ever in mind, established within us. So we become temples of God whenever our recollection of Him is not interrupted by earthly thoughts, nor the mind disturbed by unexpected passions, but escaping all these, the lover of God withdraws to Him.'

Basilides
(2nd century AD)

Alexandrian GNOSTIC, contemporary with VALENTINUS, he claimed to inherit a mystical secret going back to the Apostle Peter. Basilides was by far the profoundest of the Gnostics intellectually, and was trying to bring together a Semitic religion of salvation, Indian concepts of MAYA and NIRVANA and some of the acutest speculations of Greek linguistic philosophy. Basilides was an exponent of the VIA NEGATIVA; he claimed that it was misleading to make any statement about the supreme God; all we can say is that the non-existent God made a non-existent cosmos out of the non-existent. Basilides, a child of his time, could hardly avoid letting his thought emerge in a revealed myth, telling how the ungenerated Father generated Mind, from whom came Logos, then Understanding, then Wisdom and Power, then powers, principalities and angels, and from them a whole succession of 365 heavens; how in the seed of the universe was a triple sonship, of which the third stood in need of purification and restoration; and how illumination descended upon Jesus and enabled him to save the third Sonship. The myth ends in cosmic annihilation when those who remain below will neither be saved nor know of their need for salvation.

Baudelaire, Charles
(1821–67)

French poet, and the primary creative force behind modern French poetry. *The Flowers of Evil*, regarded as obscene in their day, were designed to instil a sense of his own involvement in the 'Hypocritical reader – my fellow – and my brother!' Baudelaire's great importance lies in his sense that the exploration of the world outside and of the inner world are one and the same thing. In his sonnet 'Correspondences' he writes of the interrelatedness of all things, the universal symbolism, the interaction of all the senses with one another and with the spirit. So

Charles Baudelaire in 1863. A photograph by Etienne Carjat

the artist's task is to express and clarify the consciousness which acts within the material world, but at the same time transcends time and space. Baudelaire was fascinated by the occult, and by the effect of drugs, and wrote a work called 'The Poem of Hashish'.

Bauls

A movement in Bengal, independent of Hinduism and Islam, mainly among the lower castes. The word means 'madcap'. The aim is freedom, sometimes expressed through the Sufi concept of FANA, dying-to-self.

That is why, brother, I became a madcap Baul.
No master I obey, nor injunctions, canons, or custom.
Man-made distinctions have no hold on me now.
I rejoice in the gladness of the love that wells out of my own being,
In love there is no separation, but a meeting of hearts for ever.
So I rejoice in song and I dance with each and all
That is why, brother, I became a madcap Baul.

The Bauls reject formal external religious observances: 'At every step I have my Mecca and Kasi: every moment is sacred.' One interesting aspect of the Bauls is their attitude to the *guru* or teacher. Sometimes they describe him as 'emptiness'. This is in fact a mystic attitude, and they sometimes claim that their only *guru* is God.

Would you make obeisance to your *guru*, O my heart?

He is there at every step, on all sides of the path,
For numberless are your *gurus*.
To how many of them would you make your
  obeisance?
The welcome offered to you is your *guru*, the
  agony inflicted on you is your *guru*,
Every wrench at the heart strings that makes
  the tears to flow is your *guru*.

Important aspects of Baul doctrine are the balance of material and spiritual needs (including the harmony of earthly and divine love), and the unity of past, present and future: life is a bridge to connect both banks of the river.

Beatific vision

The vision of the Divine Being in glory. In Christianity Pope Benedict XII in 1336 formally declared that the Divine Essence would be seen by intuition and face to face. In general Christians have held that this is the ultimate destiny of the redeemed at the last day, but some theologians, including THOMAS AQUINAS, have held that it was granted to individuals (such as Moses or PAUL) for brief periods during their earthly life. Mystics have claimed this, or something approaching it. In *The Little Flowers of St Francis* it is described as 'a rapture and uplifting of the mind intoxicated in the contemplation of the unspeakable savour of the Divine sweetness, and a happy, peaceful and sweet delight of the soul, that is rapt and uplifted in great marvel – and a burning sense within of that celestial glory unspeakable'. Here is SUSO: 'The highest stage of union is an indescribable experience, in which all idea of images and forms and differences has vanished. All consciousness of self and of all things has gone and the soul is plunged into the abyss of the Godhead and the spirit has become one with God.'

The concept of the Beatific Vision is also found in Islamic mysticism, for example as the culmination and climax of AL-MUHASIBI's work, or in this passage from al-Arabi (d. 1240): 'In the Beatific Vision God manifests Himself to the elect in a general epiphany which, nevertheless, assumes various forms corresponding to the mental conceptions of God formed by the faithful on earth. There is, then, one single epiphany, which is multiple only by reason of the difference of forms by which it is received. The Vision impregnates the elect with Divine light, each experiencing the Vision according to the knowledge of the Divine dogma or dogmas gained by him on earth.' Here it is in poetic form from IBN AL-FARID:

With my Belovèd I alone have been,
When secrets tenderer than evening airs
Passed and the Vision blest
Was granted to my prayers.
That crowned me, else obscure, with endless
  fame,
The white and red between
His Beauty and His Majesty
I stood in silent ecstasy
Revealing that which o'er my spirit went and
  came.
Lo, in His face commingled
Is every charm and grace;
The whole of Beauty singled
Into a perfect face
Beholding Him would cry,
'There is no God but He and He is the most
  High.'
(tr. R. A. Nicholson)

Something very similar is found in the Neo-Platonic mysticism of Plotinus (1, 7): 'Beholding this Being – resting, rapt, in the vision and possession of so lofty a loveliness, growing to Its likeness – what beauty can the soul yet lack? For this, the Beauty supreme, the absolute and the primal, fashions Its lovers to Beauty and makes them also worthy of love'; or before him, in his master Plato who writes of the vision of 'a Beauty eternal, not growing or decaying, waxing or waning . . . Beauty absolute, separate, simple and everlasting . . . Beauty genuine, pure, unmixed'. Al-Ashari said that believers will see God 'with the eyes' at the Resurrection.

The Beatific Vision has been equated with the Hindu concept of *Sat Cit Ananda* (Being-Awareness-Bliss).

In the BHAGAVAD GITA (11) it is a tremendous vision of the Divine Being.

Becoming

The realm of change, intermediate between BEING and Not-Being, normally in mystical religion something to be escaped from.

In PARMENIDES, Becoming is illusory. So too PLATO contrasts the world – which is always becoming and never has any being, which is perceived by the senses, and belongs to 'opinion', not knowledge, which is subject to change, and passes away as it comes to be – with the world of true reality, which always is and has no Becoming, which exists immutable, eternal, deathless, and is perceived by reason through true knowledge.

Béghards

See BÉGUINES.

Béguines

About the end of the twelfth century groups of women began all over Europe to form themselves into communities, dedicated to religious purposes, but gathered freely and without being tied by religious vows. They were given various nicknames, *humiliatae* or *bizzocchae* in Italy, *Coquennunnen* in Germany, *papelardae* in France and *Béguines* in the Low Countries, where they were most successful in combining normal life with the dedication of a religious community. The Church looked suspiciously on them, and sniffed out heresies among them; the Fourth

Lateran Council in 1215 forbade the formation of new religious orders except as an expansion of those already approved. But in 1216 Innocent III specifically authorized the *béguinages* of the Low Countries. The women lived in communes, in dormitories or single rooms, paid their way by doing manual work, lived in poverty and chastity, looked after the sick and needy. The springs of this action were in their devotional life, in sacramental processions and frequent communion services and in private meditation on the birth, humanity and suffering of Jesus and mystical union with him. Their male counterpart were the *Béghards*.

Being

'Being is God,' says ECKHART, 'God and being are the same – or God has being from another and thus himself is not God', 'Everything that is has the fact of its being through being and from being. Therefore if Being is something different from God, a thing has its being from something other than God. Besides, there is nothing prior to being, because that which confers being creates and is a creator. To create is to give being out of nothing.'

The concept of Being is central to most mystics. Mystical religion is a search for Being, pure Being, absolute Being, the absolute value from which all values are derived. There is a good saying by the Sufi Shabistari:

> Being is absolutely good.
> If it contains any evil, it is not Being.

But there is a sense also in which mystics look beyond Being. Thus Eckhart says: 'Great masters teach indeed that God is unconditioned Being. . . . But that is not so: He stands as high above Being as an angel above a gnat. It is as wrong to call God Being as to call the sun pale or black.' So too SANKARA: 'When I say "God is Being", that is not true. He is something quite transcendent. He is a Not-Being above Being.' So too PLATO calls the Form of the Good 'beyond Being'. This is to emphasize that the Ultimate is not to be limited by any of the normal categories of human experience.

Benet of Canfield
(1562–1610)

William Fitch was born in Essex of a Protestant family and went to London to study law. On 23 July 1585, however, his dissatisfaction with worldliness came to a head, and he resolved on a new life. A day or two later there came to him a sudden revelation of the truth of the Catholic faith, and on 1 August he was received into the Catholic Church. His spiritual autobiography records the religious emotions of the three stages – moral conversion, religious conversion and the subsequent entry into the Capuchin order. He took Benet as his religious name. He was imprisoned for his faith and died in exile. He wrote while in prison a detailed allegory, *Le Chevalier Chrestien*, but his lasting reputation rests on *The Rule of Perfection*: 'Divided into three Partes. The First treating of the Exterior Will of God, contayning the Active Life. The Second of the Interior Will contayning the Contemplative Life. The Third of the Essentiall Will concerning the Life Supereminent.' The rule of perfection is quite simply the surrender of the human will to the will of God, and Benet sees the supreme example of this in the Passion of Christ. The book was immensely popular because it spoke to all alike, worldly and unworldly, sinner and saint.

Benjamin Minor

Treatise on CONTEMPLATION by RICHARD OF ST VICTOR.

Berdyaev, Nicolas
(1874–1948)

Russian philosopher, expelled from university for radicalism, converted from an unorthodox Marxism to Christianity after the 1905 revolution, exiled by the Bolsheviks in 1922. He was still active as a radical socialist, and one of his colleagues described the experience of meetings under Berdyaev's leadership: 'It was as if the walls of the hall dissolved, and revealed endless vistas; this comparatively small meeting became the threshold of the Universal Church. Speeches were made which sounded like prayers and prophecies. In this fiery atmosphere it seemed that all things were possible; a miracle was about to happen; the barriers dividing men would collapse, and the reunion and integration of all would come about.'

Berdyaev's thought centres on the unity of God and man in Christ. From this he brings God and man into a wider universal relation. God's revelation to man is in the depth of our being, and this implies our creative participation. 'One cannot arrive at God, to him there are ultimately no "ways"; one can only go out from God; he is not merely at the end; he is at the beginning.' So he defines mysticism as 'knowledge which has its source in vital and immediate contact with the ultimate reality' and regards it as 'the foundation and source of all creative movement'.

Bergson, Henri
(1859–1941)

French philosopher, who rejected the static God of Aristotelian theology for a dynamic God, who is Himself growing and learning and developing, who endures with us and conquers the ravages of time, who is seen emergent in the evolutionary process as the *élan vital*, the vital drive which gives to evolution purpose and direction. According to Bergson there are two sources of morality and religion. One lies in social processes which act as a conservative and repressive influence and lead to the closed society. The other source is the direct intuitive grasp of spiritual reality. Bergson claims that despite differences the great mystics do cohere in what they say about their experience, and that ordinary men, without aspiring to their heights, can all share in that experience sufficiently to grasp its truth. The fruit of this second approach is the open society. Bergson has an important theory about art, that it is the artist's business to convey a direct vision of true reality, pulling from our eyes the veils which hide the Truth from us. Bergson is one of the great philosophers about mysticism, as distinct from mystical philosophers.

Bernard of Clairvaux
(1090–1153)

Born near Dijon, he entered the monastery of Cîteaux in 1112 and founded his own monastery at Clairvaux three years later. From there he wielded immense influence, helping to establish Innocent II, opposing Abelard, fostering the Crusades.

Bernard's mysticism is a mysticism of LOVE. There are four degrees of love: the love of self for self; the love of God for what He gives; the love of God for what He is; the love of self only for God's sake. The soul is the bride and God the husband. But the initiative is God's. He rapes the soul, obliterates its proud individuality and merges it with His own spirit. This is the ecstasy of pure love. Mystic union, the highest degree of love, is 'a perfect participation in the love which God has for Himself in the unity of the Spirit' and 'to become thus is to be deified'. The outcome is action; Bernard uses the image of a reservoir filled to overflowing with love which spills over into the lives of others. Bernard does not have as his ideal the contemplative life as such, but the contemplative life which has its fruits in action: 'The act of contemplation is like sleep in the arms of God, but the soul returns fired with a most vehement love of God, inflamed with zeal for righteousness, and filled with extreme fervour in all spiritual desires and duties' (*Cant.* 4, 9, 4).

The Virgin Mary appearing to St Bernard of Clairvaux, by Filippo Lippi

Berserk

Norse warrior filled by Wotan with mystic frenzy in battle, releasing him from fear of death.

Bérulle, Pierre de
(1575–1629)

Founder of the French Oratory in 1611, he established the Order of the Discalced Carmelites in France. Bérulle was taught the principles of contemplative prayer by BENET OF CANFIELD, and was himself a close associate of VINCENT DE PAUL, Charles de CONDREN and FRANÇOIS DE SALES. He was a great trainer of souls, and was able to combine a public life of high distinction with personal devotion and pastoral care. His mysticism is God-centred and not man-centred; it starts from adoration; indeed he claimed that complete surrender to God was all that is required of men. Vincent called him 'one of the holiest men I have known . . . of a *solid* sanctity which you will hardly find elsewhere'.

Bhagavad Gita

The Song of the Lord, the best-loved of all the Hindu scriptures. It is of uncertain date, perhaps about 300 BC. It was included in the massive epic of war, the *Mahabharata*, but in the *Gita* the war is symbolic, and the main participants Arjuna and KRISHNA are the soul of man and the divine charioteer of the soul. It belongs to the period identified by S. N. Dasgupta as Classical Devotional Mysticism.

In the *Gita* the approach to mystical experience is through faith in a personal God. The real climax of the *Gita* is the theophany in Chapter 11, when Krishna appears to Arjuna in his supreme and divine form and Arjuna sees countless visions of wonder. The path of the Transcendent is hard for mortals to attain by knowledge but easy by devotion (12, 7), and there are different approaches to the same end:

'the faith of every man is according to his nature' (17, 3). The *Gita* is the justification of personal encounter as an approach to the Divine.

The *Gita* allows the value of the traditional approaches of YOGA through good works (*karma-yoga*, though these may become a force dragging the soul down unless combined with non-attachment) and contemplation (*jñana-yoga*), but offers personal devotion (*bhakti-yoga*) as a higher way. It is in fact a book about the love of God.

The 'most secret doctrine' of the *Gita* is that after release man's soul, finding its true essence outside time, will experience immortality as BRAHMAN, will know God, will share in His life. But there is a doctrine more secret and more precious still. This is the love of God for man: 'Because I greatly desire you, I will tell you your salvation. Keep me in your thoughts, worship me, sacrifice to me, honour me. Then you will come to me. This is a firm promise; for you are very dear to me' (18, 64–5).

Bhakti

Hindu term for personal devotion and love of God.

There are five degrees or 'flavours': quiet contemplation, active service, friendship, filial attachment, passionate love. Important *bhakti* practices are *shravana*, listening to the praise of God and reading the scriptures; *kirtana*, singing the praise of God, (a central part of CHAITANYA's practice); and *smavana*, repetition of the name of God, before which sins 'fly like wolves frightened by a lion', and which leads to the loss of self in RAPTURE.

Bilocation

The power of being present in more than one place at once, a gift attributed to some ecstatics, e.g. ALPHONSUS LIGUORI, PHILIP NERI.

Birgitta of Sweden

(1303–73)

Daughter of a wealthy family, she was married at thirteen to Ulf Gudmarsson and had eight children, as well as becoming chief lady-in-waiting to the Queen of Sweden. After her husband's death in 1343 she devoted herself to the religious life, founding the Ordo Sanctissimi Salvatoris (popularly known as Brigittines: Syon in Middlesex, England, was one of their best-known foundations). She moved to Rome, where she advised the powerful and served the poor.

Blake, William

(1757–1827)

English poet, painter and visionary.

Blake had visions even in childhood. At the age of four he saw God looking in through the window. Five years later in Peckham Rye he saw 'a tree filled with angels, bright angelic wings bespangling every bough like stars', and a little later angels walking in a harvest scene. Such visions remained with him all his life; he might witness a fairy's funeral, or see heaven in a wild flower, or find himself in the Good Shepherd's arms.

Blake's life follows typical mystical patterns; the innocence of childhood, the experience of adolescence, the new birth of his young manhood, the dark night of Felpham, the attainment of his old age.

Basic to the understanding of his mysticism is his doctrine of fourfold vision. Single vision is spiritual blindness; it is the uninformed work of the eye; it is the mechanical, material, Newtonian outlook. Twofold vision is through the eye, not of the eye. It is the perception of a spiritual reality behind the material. A thistle reveals a frowning old man, a grain of sand reveals Infinity, the rising sun becomes 'an innumerable company of the Heavenly host crying "Holy, Holy, Holy is the Lord God Almighty".' Threefold vision is associated with Beulah, Palestine blessed by God, Blake's name for the subconscious as the source of creative art. Fourfold vision he calls 'my supreme delight'; it is the mystical ecstasy where God and man, and the whole world become one. But although selfhood must be annihilated, Blake believed in the sacredness, eternity and indestructibility of the individual.

Blake did not practise or advocate the way of negation. He believed in opening the senses, not closing them.

Blake is insistent on the Ultimate being revealed through every thing:

To see a World in a Grain of Sand
And a Heaven in a Wild Flower,
Hold infinity in the palm of your hand
And Eternity in an hour.

He describes how he challenged the prophet Isaiah with daring to assert that God spoke to him. Isaiah answered: 'I saw no God nor heard any in a finite organical perception, but my senses discovered the infinite in everything.' A series of aphorisms includes the propositions 'Man's desires are limited by his perceptions; none can desire what he has not perceived. . . . Therefore God becomes as we are that we may be as he is.' Although Blake was critical of SWEDENBORG's ethics, he learned much from him, especially in the vision that 'God is very man.' So Blake himself writes:

Each grain of Sand,
Every Stone on the Land,
Each rock & each hill,
Each fountain & rill,
Each herb & each tree,
Mountain, hill, earth & sea,
Cloud, Meteor & Star,
Are Men seen Afar.

Blake created a vast symbolic system of his own. He speaks of the four Zoas ('Four Mighty

'*Urizen struggling with the waters of materialism*' *from William Blake's* The Book of Urizen *(1794)*

Ones are in every Man'), each associated with a compass-point: Tharmas (the physical body, the senses, corresponding to the Father), Luvah (the emotions, especially Love, corresponding to the Son), Urthona (the creative imagination, corresponding to the Holy Spirit, manifested in time as Los, creative art), and Urizen (reason, corresponding to Satan, the fallen part of the Divine Substance). From the interaction of these four Blake builds a vast canvas of the drama of creation which is also the drama of the individual. Within the individual he speaks correspondingly of Shadow, Emanation, Humanity and Spectre. In Blake's cosmic drama we must annihilate Selfhood. One of his most vivid symbols is that of the Sunflower, man's spiritual aspiration, 'weary of time'.

Bodhidharma
(*c.* 470–543)

An Indian Buddhist monk who went to China about AD 520, where he was known as Ta Mo, and established ZEN Buddhism. Many legends are told about him. There is a verse summary of his message:

> A special gospel outside Scripture,
> not involving words or letters,
> pointing straight at men's souls,
> discerning the true self and the
> way to Buddhahood.

His method was described as 'gazing at a wall'. This was one of his own metaphors, though later it was taken literally, and he was alleged to have spent nine years gazing at a monastery wall. Rather he meant that there seems an impenetrable barrier between ourselves and the Ultimate. There is no gradual penetration, only a sudden disappearance of the barrier.

Bodhisattva

'Wisdom-Being', as aspirant to Buddhahood, as the Buddha declared himself a *Bodhisattva* before his enlightenment. The *Bodhisattva* is characterized by nine aims: (i) to free himself from false views of existence, (ii) to free himself from convention, (iii) to grasp the unreality of the 'external' world, (iv) to see SAMSARA and NIRVANA as aspects of one single reality, (v) to cultivate practical compassion, (vi) to perform righteous acts without effort, (vii) to cultivate mystical contemplation, (viii) to have perfect wisdom, (ix) to manifest the Buddha-body. Nagarjuna says, 'The change from an ordinary being to a Bodhisattva takes place when his mind has reached the stage when it can no longer turn back on enlightenment. Also he has by then gained five advantages; he is no longer reborn in the states of woe, but always among gods and men; he is never again born in poor or low-class families; he is always a man and never a woman; he is always well-built and free from physical

The Buddha with Bodhisattvas and disciples on the Vulture Peak. An embroidery from the Caves of the Thousand Buddhas, Tun-huang, China

defects; he can remember his past lives, and does not again forget them.'

According to the MAHAYANA a *Bodhisattva* becomes a divine saviour who postpones *nirvana* to help others to salvation. Each *Bodhisattva* takes the vow:

> However innumerable beings are, I vow to save them;
> However inexhaustible the passions are, I vow to extinguish them;
> However immeasurable the things of the faith are, I vow to master them;
> However incomparable the Buddha-truth is, I vow to attain it.

Above these are the Great *Bodhisattvas*, celestial beings, who also save by their grace.

Boehme, Jakob
(1575–1624)

A farmer's son, who became a first shepherd and then a shoemaker. He claimed to be a visionary: 'I saw the Being of all Beings, the Ground and the Abyss; also, the birth of the Holy Trinity; the origin and first state of the world and of all creatures. I saw in myself the three worlds – the Divine or angelic world; the dark world, the original of Nature; and the external world, as a substance spoken forth out of the two spiritual worlds. . . . In my inward man I saw it well, as in a great deep; for I saw right through as into a chaos where everything lay wrapped, but I could not unfold it. Yet from time to time it opened itself within me like a growing plant. For twelve years I carried it about within me, before I could bring it forth in any external form; till afterwards it fell upon me, like a bursting shower that kills where it lands, as it will. Whatever I could bring into outwardness I wrote down. The work is none of mine; I am but the Lord's instrument, with which He does what He wills.'

From about 1612, and particularly from 1618, he was writing down his THEOSOPHY in works of tantalizing obscurity. God then is the Being of all Beings, the Ground, the Abyss, and as the Being of all Beings is neither good nor evil but the source of both. The Ultimate knows itself in the Son and expresses itself in the Spirit; this is Boehme's reconciliation of his mystical experience with Christian theology. The Godhead has two wills, love and wrath, one good and one evil. From the tension between these arise the seven Spirits of Nature: the will to resist, the tendency to expand, the struggle between the two, the passage from inorganic to organic existence, vegetable life, animal life, man. We are thus involved in the conflict between good and evil, though in the end good will triumph over evil, love over wrath. Man finds his victory in Christ: 'I am inwardly dead, and he is my life; I live in him, and not in my selfhood.' In unity with Christ the soul will conquer on earth and replace the fallen angels in the heavenly city.

Jakob Boehme

Boehme's system sometimes seems pantheistic, but he was insistent that it was not: 'I do not say that Nature is God. He Himself is all, and communicates His power to all His works.'

Boehme has had a powerful influence subsequently, influencing people as various as Isaac Newton, William LAW, William BLAKE. His antitheses affected the dialectical thinking of HEGEL, and so, by an ironical quirk, Karl Marx.

Bogomili

Mediaeval neo-Manichaean sect found in Constantinople and the Balkans. They perhaps derived from the EUCHITES, and came into prominence in the twelfth century: the name either means 'Beloved of God' or is derived from the prayer 'God have mercy!' The sect was dualist, holding a twofold creative principle, one good, one evil. God the incorporeal Father had two sons, Satanael and Jesus or Michael. Satanael formed man of earth, but his life came from the Father. Jesus took the semblance of a body, to combat and conquer Satanael. The soul is thus to be redeemed from the body, and the Bogomili condemned meat-eating, marriage and many of the visible manifestations of religious worship.

Bonaventura
(1221–74)

Giovanni di Fidanza was a Franciscan intellectual, who wrote the official life of FRANCIS and in *The Journey of the Mind to God* and *The Triple Way* offers a philosophical exposition of Francis's mystical experiences; Gilson called him 'a Saint

Francis of Assisi gone philosopher and lecturing at the University of Paris'.

Man can be orientated in three principal directions: through the bodily senses to the material world; through spirit to himself; through mind to realities which transcend the self, that is to pure TRUTH, Christ and God. There are seven stages in the ascent of the soul: the apprehension of the external world as God's work; the apprehension of God's presence in the external world; the apprehension of the self as made in God's image; the apprehension of the renovated self as the very mirror of God; the apprehension of the light emanating from God; the apprehension of Jesus Christ, the Mediator, the Highest Principle of all; and then beyond all these the experience of union and mystic rest. There are three paths to perfection. Purification, or withdrawal from evil, leads to peace through the expulsion of sin. Illumination, or perfection in good, is concerned with the imitation of Christ and the reception of Truth. Union is the marriage of the soul with the best and highest. The first two use meditation, prayer and contemplation; the third is the path of LOVE.

Book of the Dead, The

See EGYPTIAN and TIBETAN.

Book of the Holy Hierotheos, The

Christian mystical treatise, probably of about 500, perhaps written by a Jerusalem monk named Stephen Bar-Sudayli. The book, which is heavily influenced by NEO-PLATONISM, deals with the ascent of the soul to the First Cause, the Self-Existent Universal Essence, who is the natural aspiration of the mind; and its union with him. The ascent starts from purification, and the crucifixion of the former self, and humble self-surrender and sanctification. It is directed by LOVE, but Love belongs only to the first stages of the ascent, for Love implies a distinction between Lover and Beloved, and can lead us only to unification, not to the ultimate union or commingling. Of the mystery of that final commingling the book does not speak; it is beyond speech. But 'when the Minds have reached the fullness of divine growth and holy perfection, then they acquire the designation of the Godhead – rather, to speak mystically, they become the Essence of God'.

Book of the Nine Rocks, The

Mediaeval mystical treatise, associated with the FRIENDS OF GOD, giving an account of a series of visions received by the author about 1351. A series of visions expose the corruptions of the present Church, and proclaim the calling of a few, without whom Christianity would come to an end. In the second part of the book the writer sees a gigantic net covering the earth, from which it is possible to escape only up a mountain with nine great rocky steps. The first is confession; the second the resolution to give up one's own will and submit to a Friend of God; the third is self-mortification for salvation; the fourth is self-mortification for God's glory; the fifth is the beginning of the sacrifice of self-will; the sixth the complete dependence on God, though desire is not yet extinguished; the seventh is the abandonment of desire for revelation but a still selfish joy in revelation; the eighth the abandonment of all for God and the readiness to receive; the ninth and highest the experience of beholding the Divine Origin.

In one of the most remarkable passages of the book the writer asserts that an honourable Jew or 'Mohammedan' is closer to God than many so-called Christians: 'When God finds a good Jew or Mohammedan of pure life, he feels a thrill of love and infinite compassion for him . . . and will find some way of saving him unknown to us . . . baptizing him in the holy desire of his will.'

Book of Privy Counsel, The

Work by the author of THE CLOUD OF UNKNOWING: in order to explain some of the more difficult passages of the earlier work, more concise and carefully planned; and single-minded in its insistence that mystical prayer is the highest form of spiritual life, a house in which the Lord is both doorkeeper and door, and that we should offer ourselves to God as pure Being.

Bossuet, Jacques-Bénigne
(1627–1704)

French scholar and preacher, Bishop of Condom and later Meaux, disciple of VINCENT DE PAUL and himself a noted spiritual adviser to individuals and communities (for whom he wrote *Méditations sur l'Evangile* and *Elévations sur les mystères*). Bossuet was an opponent of FÉNELON and QUIETISM, while himself showing a solid grasp of the principles of MEDITATION and the contemplative life. It seems that it was he who coined the phrase 'prayer of simplicity'.

Bourignon, Antoinette
(1616–80)

Flemish mystic and visionary, who lived in Liège and Hamburg, and tried unsuccessfully to found a new ascetic order. Later she came to identify herself with the woman clothed with the sun of *Revelation* 12. She influenced Pierre POIRET, and through him whole tracts of later mysticism. A sect of Bourignonians survived in Scotland into the eighteenth century.

Bradley, Francis Herbert
(1846–1924)

English philosopher, author of *Appearance and Reality*. Bradley held that science, ethics and religious thought are riddled with contradictions; that the notions of personality and selfhood are similarly contradictory; and that the only true reality is to be found in the ABSOLUTE.

Brahman

In Hindu mysticism, the Spirit of the universe, transcendent and immanent. Hindu monistic mysticism can be summed up as the realization of the identity between the Self in man, ATMAN; and the Divine, BRAHMAN: 'Brahman is all, and Atman is Brahman.' For RAMANUJA and others there is union without identity.

Brancusi, Constantin
(1876–1957)

Rumanian sculptor who settled in Paris. He achieved his effects by a combination of high craftsmanship and formal simplification. Brancusi's art is an art of mystic symbolism: two of his major symbols, both taken from Rumanian folklore, are the soulbird and the column of the sky: both are associated with the shamanistic and mystical vision of ascent. Brancusi succeeded in endowing his works with a numinous quality: they became starting-points for contemplative experience.

Breath-control

An important aspect of the practice of meditation, stressed particularly in YOGA. The object is negative. Regular breathing does not assist meditation, but irregular breathing does distract. One well-known breathing exercise (not to be

Endless Column *(1937), by Constantin Brancusi*

Brahmins depicted as 'Knowers of Brahman' in a 17th-century Indian painting

overdone by the beginner) is to let the inhalation, held breath and exhalation be in the proportion 1:4:2. A familiar aid is to repeat the word *puraka* (inhalation) once while inhaling, *kumbhaka* (held breath) four times while holding the breath and *rechaka* (exhalation) twice while exhaling. Another is to close the right nostril with the right thumb, inhale, hold the air inside for as long as comfortably possible and then exhale through the right nostril; follow this by inhaling through the right nostril and exhaling through the left. This is recommended twenty times four times a day. Advocates claim that even if it does not lead to enhanced meditation it will certainly lead to sounder health.

Bremond, Henri
(1865–1933)

A Jesuit from 1887 to 1904, he was author of the attractively written and sympathetic *Histoire Littéraire du sentiment religieux en France*, a major study of French spirituality, copiously illustrated from the original sources.

Brethren of the Common Life

Free religious community founded by Geert de GROOTE in the fourteenth century. There were no external vows; the members were held together by their spiritual commitment. They combined a religion of personal experience with practical social service, especially in education. One of their communities has been described as 'the silent, motionless centre of a whirling and incomprehensible world'. Love, humility, simplicity, service – this was the way of life. The body was made efficient for the purposes of the soul, which were the free exercise of love to man and God, and the imitation of Christ. Among those they influenced were THOMAS À KEMPIS and NICHOLAS OF CUSA.

Brethren of the Free Spirit

Originally known as the Sect of the New Spirit, a loose association of Christians, which began in Strasbourg *c.* 1200 and spread to Switzerland. They were mystical and pantheistic in tendency. Every man is of the same substance of God, and can, if he has the will, rise to union with God. In that state of union he finds freedom. External observances become irrelevant, and the Holy Spirit endows him with sinless holiness, since sin is the will to offend God, and his will has become God's will. Although some of the followers transformed liberty into licence, the movement was in essence a reassertion of the spiritual and the need for an inward experience of God.

Bride

The image of SPIRITUAL MARRIAGE in which the soul is the bride of the Divine or ABSOLUTE (in Christian mysticism sometimes the bride of Jesus) is frequent in mystics of all religions. In Christian mysticism the expression of the experience is influenced by THE SONG OF SONGS. Sometimes the experience seems more immediate and overwhelming; then, the image is of ravishing. But the mystical disciplines recognize the necessity of preparation before union, and the stages of betrothal, marriage and consummation are not inappropriate. *See also* SEX, SPIRITUAL MARRIAGE.

Brigid

See BIRGITTA

Brown, Thomas Edward
(1830–97)

Manx poet, for many years a schoolteacher, who has the misfortune to be remembered for the ugliest phrase of one of his less happy poems ('A garden is a lovesome thing, God wot!'). He was in fact a mystical poet of some merit. He was a solitary, living close to the throne of Heaven, and able to see Catherine Kinrade forgiving Bishop Wilson after death, and to hear Samuel Sebastian Wesley thundering a fugue upon the organ of God, and to watch the prayers arriving and being sorted. He was a nature-mystic who could see how 'The true God rushes in the salmon'. He was something of a pantheist. Certainly he found his God in communing with nature. But he also understood interior mysticism. He longed to come to God 'with one swift arrow-dart'. He knows the obstacles:

If thou couldst empty all thyself of Self,
Like to a shell dishabited,
Then might He find thee on the ocean shelf
And say: 'This is not dead,'
And fill thee with Himself instead.

But thou art all replete with very thou
And hast such shrewd activity,
That when He comes He says: 'This is enough
Unto itself – 'twere better let it be,
It is so small and full, there is no room for Me.'

But he knows also the fulfilment, as in 'Praesto':

Expecting Him, my door was open wide:
Then I looked round
If any lack of service might be found,
And saw Him at my side:
How entered, by what secret stair,
I know not, knowing only He was there.

Browne, Sir Thomas
(1605–82)

Physician and writer. His work *Religio Medici*, written when he was only thirty, seemed dangerously sceptical in its day; it is ironical that it has come to be treated as a textbook of piety. Browne is a curious mixture of the erudite mind reflecting on the ideas of others, and a kind of self-absorption. There is in his work no trace of personal mystical experience. But his wide-ranging mind plays over some mystical, and Platonic or Neo-Platonic, ideas. He insists for example that the visible world is but a picture of the invisible, or that 'there is a common spirit that plays within us yet makes no part of us; and that is the spirit of God, the fire and scintillation of that noble and mighty essence which is the life and radical heat of spirits (I, 32). He plays too with the ideas of the alchemists: 'The smattering I have of the philosopher's stone – which is nothing else but the perfectest exaltation of gold – hath taught me a great deal of divinity, and instructed my belief how that immortal spirit and incorruptible substance of my soul may lie obscure and sleep awhile within this house of flesh. Those strange and mystical transmigrations that I have observed in silkworms turned my philosophy into divinity.' These are not part of a consistent philosophy of life, but a reflection of ideas current in educated circles in the early seventeenth century.

Browning, Robert
(1812–89)

English poet, one of the most original and forceful of Victorian writers, whose central themes were art, love and religion. His early poems show a general undogmatic religion, which later under his wife's influence became explicitly Christian. He has sometimes been praised or blamed for an easy optimism.

God's in His heaven,
All's right with the world.

Yet those very words are the expression of a mystic faith, sung as they are by a ragged, destitute mill-girl in the middle of a story charged with sordid realism. They may be optimistic, but not cheaply or easily so. Browning is no Wordsworthian nature-mystic; his strength is his understanding of the human soul. In *Pauline* he describes the soul's aspiration to God:

What is it that I hunger for but God?
My God, my God! let me for once look on
Thee
As though nought else existed: we alone.
And as creation crumbles, my soul's spark
Expands till I can say, Even from myself
I need Thee, and I feel Thee and I love Thee.

In *Abt Vogler*, a study of a musician, he gives Platonic expression to the Ultimate: 'On the earth the broken arcs; in the heaven a perfect round.' In *A Death in the Desert* he offers within a Christian framework a profound discussion of the mystical relation between God and man.

Bruno
(*c*.1032–1101)

Founder of the CARTHUSIAN order, born in Cologne, he moved to Rheims, where he became Chancellor of the diocese. In 1084 he went with eight companions into the mountains near Grenoble and founded La Grande Chartreuse. From there he was called out by his former pupil, Urban II, to a life of active ecclesiastical politics, but was allowed to retire to Calabria, where he founded the monastery of La Torre. Bruno held together in an extreme way the poles of public activity and the contemplative life.

Bruno, Giordano
(1548–1600)

Italian natural philosopher, he was at one time a Dominican friar, but came under charges of unorthodoxy. He held strongly pantheistic views. Copernicus had opened his eyes to the immensity of the universe. He saw the stars as sons of God, 'a living mirror of the infinite Deity'. God is everywhere present in the whole of the world, filling it with his infinity and with his immeasurable greatness. The distinction between sacred and secular, divine and earthly disappears. Reality is an eternal spirit, one and indivisible. From this spirit, which is One, all being flows. God is in every grain of sand; man, the macrocosm within the macrocosm, is a mirror within a mirror. For these views Bruno was burned at the stake.

Buddhism

Of all the world religions perhaps the one which lays the deepest stress on enlightenment. At its origin lies the story of how the prince GAUTAMA in the sixth century BC left his life of privilege to be a wanderer in the world of suffering. He looked for liberation through asceticism but did not find it there. He then turned to the way of meditation, and in a spiritual experience as he sat under the bo-tree he became the Buddha or the Enlightened. 'The Perfected One is the holy highest Buddha.' From this he proclaimed the Four Noble Truths: (i) there is Suffering everywhere in the world; (ii) the cause of Suffering is desire; (iii) the remedy for Suffering is the extinction of desire; (iv) the path that leads to this extinction is the Eightfold Noble Path. He also identified the Eightfold Path to Salvation, of Right Understanding and Right Thought, which provide the initial faith and the ultimate WISDOM; Right speech, Right Bodily Action and Right Livelihood, which provide the ethical content of the Way, and Right Moral Effort, Right Mindfulness and Right Concentration, which provide the element of MEDITATION.

The goal of the mystic way is NIRVANA or the annihilation of desire. Negatively conceived (the root *nir* is negative), it is none the less a state of bliss. Buddhist mysticism however differs from much other mysticism in repudiating any doctrine of the self. There is no belief in an individual self, in personal identity, in an underlying 'I'; only in what we would today call a stream of

Amitabha, Infinite Light, rising above the mountain of the material world. A Japanese painting on silk, 13th century

consciousness. And there is no belief in a universal Self, Supreme Being, First Cause or God. Buddhism is that rare phenomenon a religion without an ultimate God. Images of the Buddha with different symbolic poses are used as an aid to devotion, but he is not worshipped as a god, though called 'the god above the gods'. 'I go to the Buddha for refuge' is the first part of a threefold formula which continues 'I go to the doctrine for refuge; I go to the monastic order for refuge'.

Buddhism is represented by two schools: the northern, found in Tibet, China and Japan, with scriptures in Sanskrit, Tibetan and Chinese, teaches the doctrine of the MAHAYANA ('greater vehicle'); and the southern (or Theravadins), found in Sri Lanka, Burma and south-east Asia, with scriptures in Pali, teaches the doctrine of the *Hinayana* ('lesser vehicle'). Both are mystical in approach, since the essence of Buddhism is mysticism. ZEN is a branch of the *Mahayana*. One notable *Mahayana* story tells how the saints set out in a great ferry boat (i.e. *Mahayana*), which is to carry them across the river of SAMSARA (i.e. the phenomenal world) to *nirvana*. As they cross, the shore they are leaving fades. The great vehicle arrives and they disembark. And now all distinctions have become void. The farther shore has faded out, so has the shore on which they have landed. The ferry boat itself has dissolved; it is not that it has disappeared, but that it never had any existence. The passengers have dissolved. *Nirvana* itself is nothing.

In the traditions of *Mahayana* Buddhism the Buddha performs numbers of miracles. When we look beneath the surface of those miracles we see that each is designed to express some mystical truth. Spiritual facts cannot be intellectually apprehended.

The spread of Buddhism in India was fostered by the Emperor Asoka in the third century BC. Through missionary concern it spread first to Ceylon, then to Burma and Thailand, and right across the continent of Asia to China and Japan. One of the best-known centres of Buddhism is Tibet, but some of the more familiar features of Tibetan popular religion are pre-Buddhist. Buddhism is primarily practised by communities of monks or nuns, but it also has considerable lay support. There are three fundamental monastic rules, no possessions except nine ritual objects, non-violence and celibacy, as well as detailed injunctions. The four sublime states are benevolence, compassion or love, joy in sympathy, and peace of mind. Compassion, care for others, is vital. The would-be *Bodhisattva* must renounce self. The highest monastic life is meditation. In Tibetan Buddhism and in much contemporary Asiatic Buddhism there is great stress on the five Buddhas of meditation, the blue Akshobhya, the Unshakable, in the east; the red Amitabha, Infinite Light, in the west; the green Amogha-Siddhi, Infallible Success, in the north; the golden Ratna-Sambhava, Jewel-born, in the south; the white Vairocana, the Immaculate, at the zenith. Beyond them all is the primordial Adibuddha, whose essence is seen in Vajra-Sattra, the Universal Soul or Intelligence.

> O Jinas, deliver us from the world of illusion.
> I offer you salutations, oblations,
> confession of our sins against the Religion.
> I proclaim our repentance.
> May what virtue we have gathered be of
> benefit to us.
> Om Mani Padme Hum.

One of the finest expressions of Buddhist mysticism comes from HUI-NENG: 'Within our mind there is a Buddha, and that Buddha within is the real Buddha. If Buddha is not to be sought within our minds, where shall we find the real Buddha? Do not doubt that a Buddha is within your mind, apart from which nothing can exist.'

Bulgakov, Sergei
(1870–1944)

Russian Christian mystical theologian, who spent the last part of his life in exile in Paris. Like SOLOVIEV, Bulgakov found in WISDOM the bridge between the world and God; and it was his major work to give a comprehensive reinterpretation of all the main traditional teaching in the light of this principle.

C

Cabasilas, Nicholas
(*c.* 1350)

Follower of Gregory PALAMAS, mystic and writer. His mystical experience lies within the bounds of a strict Christian ecclesiastical orthodoxy. It is an experience of union with Christ the Saviour, who 'is closer to us than our own soul'; and it is founded upon the SACRAMENTS.

Cabbala

See KABBALAH.

Cabeiri

See SAMOTHRACE.

Camaldolese order

Monastic order of hermits founded by ROMUALD at Camaldoli in the Apennines on principles of high austerity and solitary contemplation, which were somewhat relaxed and modified in later foundations. The painter LORENZO MONACO was a member of the order.

Cambridge Platonists

A group of Christian scholars in seventeenth-century Cambridge, dominated by the saintly Benjamin Whichcote (1609–83) and including the scholarly Ralph Cudworth (1617–88), John Smith (1618–52) an attractive writer who died young, and the eccentric Henry More (1614–87). They were important, first for their reconciliation of Platonism with Christianity; second, for their rejection of the negative way of Dionysius the Areopagite, and their sturdy rationalism; third, for their insistence on the indwelling of God in the mind (their favourite text was 'The spirit of man is the candle of the Lord'); fourth, for their doctrine of 'plastic nature', the teaching that nature herself plays a part in the creative process, and that this accounts for the imperfections in the material world. John Smith has a magnificent exposition of NATURE-MYSTICISM.

Carthusian order

Contemplative order founded by BRUNO at La Grande Chartreuse in 1084. There was at first no rule, but withdrawal from the world, MORTIFICATION, long periods of silence, solitary work and mental prayer were the practice from the beginning; it might be said that the Carthusians reintroduced some of the traditional eremitical practices into the monastic life. The name Chartreuse has entered the English language in the form Charterhouse.

Cassian, John
(*c.* 360–434)

A widely travelled monk, allegedly born in Scythia (i.e. Russia), and who visited Bethlehem, Egypt, Constantinople, Rome and Marseilles, where he founded two monasteries. He was a semi-Pelagian who believed that in salvation the human desire to be saved and divine grace must cohere. Cassian's two books, called *Conferences* and *Institutes*, systematize eastern mysticism for the West, and develop AUGUSTINE's thoughts on CONTEMPLATION. Cassian distinguishes two ways of life, active and contemplative, and two forms of knowledge, factual and spiritual. Contemplation is the aim of the religious life; in its fullness it can be found only after death, but it can be anticipated here by the work of the HOLY SPIRIT in a righteous soul.

First the obstacles of temptation and vice must be overcome. For this are needed practical virtue, ASCETICISM and renunciation of the self, and prayer. Prayer at its highest culminates in silent ECSTASY, the 'prayer of fire'. Spiritual knowledge and prayer are inseparable; contemplation in its fullest sense is 'perpetual prayer'.

Cataphatic theology

The name given to the theology based on the VIA AFFIRMATIVA.

Catherine dei Ricci
(1522–90)

Alessandra Lucrezia Romolo entered a Dominican convent in 1535, and remained there till her death. For a period of some twelve years she had a weekly RAPTURE lasting from noon on Thursday to 4 pm on Friday. During this period she not merely contemplated the Passion of Jesus, but re-enacted its events, stretched her hands to be tied, standing to receive the scourge, bowing her head for the crown of thorns. She experienced STIGMATIZATION.

Catherine of Genoa
(1447–1510)

Caterinetta Fieschi was of noble birth, married at sixteen, and for ten years lived a life of pleasure and luxury. When she was twenty-seven she experienced CONVERSION: 'Her heart was pierced by a sudden and immense love of God, and in a transport of pure and all-purifying love, she was drawn away from all the miseries of the world.' She from that point lived a life of profound practical devotion, on the one side with the EUCHARIST almost daily (very rare at this period for a member of the laity) and an intense sense of the presence of God; on the other in work among the sick.

She speaks of God under a variety of images. He is Goodness, Beauty, Truth, Love. He is Sun, Light, Fire, Air, Ocean. He is the Essence, the very Being of all things, visible and invisible. He is the 'one true divine root-centre' of her soul.

The impulse to union comes from LOVE. 'The love of God is our true self-love, since these selves of ours were created by and for Love itself.' 'Pure love loves God without any why or wherefore. The soul offers and remits itself entirely to Him, so that it can no more operate except in the manner willed by tender Love Himself; and from that point it does not produce works except such as are pure, full and sincere, works which please God-Love.' And love seeks the God who is Love; so Catherine cries 'Love, I want You, the whole of You.'

The condition of union is PURIFICATION. On earth this means ASCETICISM. But Catherine is unusual in seeing the process of purification as continuing after death. The soul actually is eager for Purgatory owing to the 'impetuosity of that love which exists between God and the soul, and tends to conform the soul to God'. God, being FIRE, burns away the imperfections in the soul till it finds its BEING in God.

In the experience of union Catherine (who was a STIGMATIC) goes beyond the language normally used by Christians: 'My Being is God, not by simple participation, but by a true transformation of my Being – God is my Being, my Me, my Strength, my Beatitude, my Good, my Delight.'

Catherine is the subject of a palmary study by Baron von HÜGEL.

Catherine of Siena
(1347–80)

The daughter of a dyer, Catherine had visions in her childhood, and despite home difficulties grew up practising the MORTIFICATION of the flesh. At fourteen she became a Dominican nun and devoted herself to CONTEMPLATION and good works. In 1370 she experienced a mystical death and resurrection under the command of God to save souls and minister to those in need. She tells of 'the sweetness of serving God, not for her own joy; and of serving her neighbour, not for her own will or profit, but from pure love'. She saw love as the supreme reality of the universe, and says of Christ in a magnificent sentence, that 'nails would not have held the God-man fast to the cross had not love held him there'. She had a deep devotion to Jesus, which found expression first in a mystical espousal to him, and later in the experience of STIGMATIZATION, the sensation of her own body being pierced with the five wounds of Christ. This came to her in a vision of Christ crucified coming in a blaze of light, and five blood-red rays streaming from his wounds to her hands, feet and side, changing to the splendour of pure LIGHT as they came: 'So great is the pain that I endure sensibly in all those five places, but especially within my heart, that unless the Lord works a new miracle, it does not seem possible to me that the life of my body can endure such agony.' She set herself to reform the Church. She was in the counsels of the Pope, whom she addressed as 'sweetest Babbo mine', and urged him in his vacillations to quench self-love. Her object was that 'Holy Church should return to her first condition, poor, humble and meek, as she was in that holy time when men took note of nothing but the honour of God and the salvation of souls, caring for spiritual things not for temporal'. So she pressed on the Church leaders the need for a life of direct devotion: 'I desire to see you seek God in truth, without anything between.' She could testify from her own experience that the soul 'bears ever within it the place where God lives by grace – the house of our soul wherein holy desire, prays constantly'. She knew 'that sea of peace where you shall never have any fear of being separated from God'.

Caussade, Jean Pierre de
(1675–1751)

French spiritual writer, who joined the Jesuit order in Toulouse at the age of eighteen. He travelled, preached and was a notable spiritual director; in old age he bore with courage increasing blindness. In 1741 he published anonymously his *Spiritual Instructions*, twenty-seven dialogues designed to justify contemplative practices by appeal to the authority of BOSSUET. This met with some criticism, not so much for its contents as for misleading omissions. Still, it contains much good sense and much profound wisdom: 'There is nothing more sublime than contemplation as we find it in books; nothing more beautiful or grander than passive prayer in theory. But in practice there is nothing more humiliating, more crucifying.' Perhaps more important is the volume put together from notes of his discourses and published a century after his death as *L'Abandon à la providence divine*. *Abandon* is the key to Caussade's mysticism: it implies a total acceptance of God's will. So all may attain sanctity for it is offered to all. One of his great phrases is 'the sacrament of the present moment'. Caussade's thinking has been moulded by FRANÇOIS DE SALES and JUAN DE LA CRUZ, but he is himself; BREMOND called him 'the incomparable Caussade'.

Chaitanya
(*c.* 1485–1533)

Viswambar, better known by his nickname Gauranga, or his initiation name Chaitanya, was born in Bengal. At the age of sixteen he began to devote himself to learning, and grew into a scholar of exceptional gifts. But in 1509 he became a devotee of KRISHNA, and experienced a series of ecstasies, sometimes spending long periods in silent meditation, sometimes being subject to uncontrollable tears, and sometimes engaging in wild dancing and shouts of praise. He used and recommended the name of Krishna as a MANTRA: 'Chant the name while sitting, standing, walking, eating, in bed and everywhere. The name is omnipotent.' From then on his life was one of preaching, healing and helping the needy. A true devotee, he maintained, seeks nothing from God, but is simply satisfied with loving him. Such love can spring only from one who leads a virtuous life; one who is kind, truthful, impartial, non-injurious, magnanimous, tender, pure, selfless, at peace with himself. LOVE of God transcends all religious duties. There are five stages in such love: attachment; service; friendship; sonship; spiritual marriage. In the highest, the lover and the beloved melt together as one, and become a single manifestation of love. Chaitanya remains one of the outstanding representatives of VAISHNAVISM and practitioners of BHAKTI.

Ch'an

Chinese school of Buddhism; the origin of the Japanese ZEN. The word comes from Sanskrit *dhyana*, which means 'meditation'. The school dates from the early eighth century.

Chantal

See JEANNE FRANÇOISE DE CHANTAL

Chao-chou
(778–897)

Chinese ZEN Master, disciple of NAN-CH'ÜAN, and master of the paradox. Asked about Enlightenment he answered 'Go and wash your bowl.' Asked about the destiny of the soul he answered 'The wind is blowing again this morning.' Asked what to give a beggar he answered 'He lacks nothing.'

Chapman, John
(1865–1933)

Henry Palmer Chapman (who took the spiritual name John), was an English Christian scholar who converted to Roman Catholicism in 1890, and subsequently became Abbot of Downside. His *Spiritual Letters* are among the more attractive and profound spiritual works of the twentieth century. They contain much practical sense: his two favourite precepts on prayers were 'Pray as you can, and don't try to pray as you can't!' and 'The less you pray, the worse it goes.' Souls must expect to go through the DARK NIGHT OF THE SOUL, part of which comes from our active self-mortification, part from our passive experience of God taking from us all that shuts Him out. What is needed all through is hope, which consists of courage and perseverance. His judgment of mysticism is of considerable interest:

The marbled decoration on this Ming dynasty dish symbolizes the Chi, or Vital energy of the Cosmos

'Mysticism is not merely a preternatural perception of the Divine, but may also be a means of knowing something about the Divine, just so far as God wills to use the faculty for his gracious purposes. Consequently, though neither the mystical act nor the mystical faculty are supernatural, God can make them a vehicle of supernatural communication, in fact a "means of grace". And so it is that saintly mystics find that it is in this way that God gives Himself to them, granting revelations to prophets, inflaming contemplatives with his charity, transforming the perfect by union.'

Chasidim

See HASIDISM.

Ch'i

In TAOISM the Moving Spirit or Vital Energy of the Cosmos, breathed in by means of special breathing exercises, and expressed in art by marbling.

Christianity

JESUS of Nazareth was born and bred within Judaism, and his primary work was done among the people of that faith and culture. But there is evidence that he was proclaiming a universal gospel and that he himself began to reach out to non-Jews. This was carried on by his followers, especially PAUL, and was intensified by the rejection of the Jewish leaders, so that what started as a reformist movement within Judaism became an independent world-wide missionary religion.

As Christianity spread within the Graeco-Roman world it appeared to the Greeks and Romans as another of the MYSTERY RELIGIONS which offered a revelation of the truth to its initiates. And there were indeed many parallels, so that Christian writers (like Paul) are not afraid to use the language of the Mysteries; and at the same time the resemblances of the mystery religions to Christianity are attributed to devilish parodies. The more obvious features common to the mystery cults and Christianity were: admission on individual profession of faith, an initiatory rite (in this instance, baptism), special gatherings of the faithful in private, a common sacramental meal, special devotion to a saviour-God, a special wisdom revealed to the faithful (cf. Lk. 8, 10), the promise of a new life beyond the grave linked in one tradition with the grain which dies to live and in another with the language of the Mysteries (Jn 12, 24; 1 Cor. 15, 51).

Something of this, although there are contradictory elements, is reflected in the primary sources, the four Gospels. There is a sense of a secret not fully revealed. For example in the healing miracles Jesus continually instructs the demons (Mk 1, 34: 3, 12), the people healed (Mk 1, 44–5; 8, 26) and those around (Mk 5, 43; 7, 36) not to say what they had experienced. Further, the disciples who receive a special revelation of the nature of Jesus's relation to God (Mk 8, 30; 9, 9) are given the same charge. Even with Jesus's teaching the parable is regarded as an account of a mystery which is revealed only to those with understanding (Mk 4, 10–12). And there is a constant sense that the disciples are a special group who are expected to have this understanding, but who constantly fail (Mk 4, 40–41; 6, 52; 8, 16–21; 9, 10; 9, 32). These examples are all from the earliest Gospel, According to Mark; small wonder that Martin Dibelius termed it 'a book of secret happiness'.

But Christianity as a mystery religion was different in some ways. In the first place the saviour-figure was unequivocally historical. 'Suffered under Pontius Pilate' is a central affirmation of the traditional Christian creed. This could not be said of DIONYSUS or Mithras, or ISIS AND OSIRIS, or CYBELE and ATTIS, or Demeter and Kore, or the CABEIRI. Secondly, what was revealed was not a *gnosis*, a piece of knowledge, but a way of life summed up in the word *agape* or LOVE: it is precisely this point which Paul insists on to the Christians in Corinth (1 Cor. 13, 2). Thirdly, the fellowship of the initiate was not exclusive. Many of the mystery religions were single-sex; the fellowship between men and women in the Christian churches was something rare enough to be the occasion of salacious gossip. Further, in most of the mystery religions initiation was expensive. The sacrifice of a bull was far beyond the resources of the majority of the inhabitants of the Roman Empire. Baptism in water cost nothing, and there were no monthly or weekly 'dues'; there was a fellowship of sharing. This is why the great scholar A. D. Nock said, 'It was left to Christianity to democratize mystery'.

As Christianity spread, and particularly after it became officially recognized, it lost, except externally, the characteristics of a mystery religion. But throughout its story individuals and groups have sought or received a more intense personal mystical experience of God. Christian mysticism developed especially in the Middle Ages and in the sixteenth and seventeenth centuries. Examples of outstanding Christian mystics are BERNARD OF CLAIRVAUX, FRANCIS OF ASSISI, RUYSBROECK, TERESA DE JESUS; for a sect with a strongly mystical approach see SOCIETY OF FRIENDS, and for some modern approaches see PENTECOSTALISM. Christian mysticism has two special qualities. First, it tends to focus on the person of Jesus rather than on God in His ultimate Being, or to find the way to God in His ultimate Being through the person of Jesus. Secondly, for this very reason Christian mysticism tends to be strongly passionistic. There is a strong element of concentration on and identification with Jesus in his suffering, even to the extent of STIGMATIZATION. The mystic seeks to experience in the spirit the life, death and resurrection which Christ went through in the body.

Chuang Tzu

Chuang Tzu (*c.* 369–286 BC) was a historical figure, but the treatise which goes under his name, one of the three classics of TAOISM, is a compendium of writings from many hands and many periods. Through a variety of literary means it conveys the idea of a knowledge which is the special prerogative of the Taoist mystic. To argue about it is idle, for those who do not possess it cannot comprehend it; the well-frog knows nothing of the sea, the summer-insect knows nothing of ice, the cicada knows nothing of the soaring flocks of migrating birds. The mystic finds his knowledge by losing himself in a trance, then riding on the wind, carried by cloud-chariots to the Infinite, where discord melts in harmony, opposites blend and 'Heaven and Earth came into being with me together, and with me all things are one'. The One is the Tao, which can do everything by doing nothing. It is BEING, and it is Not-Being. It is in the ant, in grass, in tiles, in excrement, everywhere. Its marks are Completeness, All-Embracingness, the Whole. It 'has reality and evidence, but no action and form. It may be transmitted but cannot be received. It may be attained to but cannot be seen. It exists by and through itself. It existed prior to Heaven and Earth, and indeed for all eternity. It causes the gods to be divine, and the world to be produced. It is above the zenith but it is not high. It is below the nadir, but it is not low. It is prior to Heaven and Earth, but it is not ancient. It is older than the most ancient, but it is not old.' It is for humans to conform, not to intervene. Man is born in Tao, as fishes in water. The true sage ignores God and man alike and takes things as they come. Perfection of vision is seeing oneself; perfection of life is yielding to the natural condition of things. Some passages of

Chuang Tzu anticipate ZEN Buddhism, as the philosophic cook who works with his mind, not his eye. And death itself, like life, is an aspect of existence: 'Life and death are one, right and wrong are the same.' One of the chapters is entitled 'The Equality of Things and Opinions'. So the mystic who attains pure experience also attains absolute freedom.

Cisneros, Garcia de
(*c.* 1456–1510)

Cousin of the great Cardinal Ximenez, he entered the Benedictine order at the age of twenty. He became sub-prior at Valladolid, and then life-abbot at Montserrat. An austere man in austere surroundings, his *Ejercitatorio de la vida espiritual* (*Exercises for the Spiritual Life*) is an important and valuable guide to the approach to contemplation, which is a bridge between mediaeval monasticism and the mystical writings of the Counter-Reformation. His *Directorio de las horas canonicas* set the pattern for the communal devotional life at Montserrat for two hundred years.

Clarisses

See POOR CLARES.

Clement of Alexandria
(*c.* 150–215)

Christian theologian and philosopher. Clement is important here for three reasons. First, he is one of those who draw together Christianity and Platonism, and offer the Christian Church an intellectual framework for the interpretation of mystical experience. Second, central to Clement's thought is the LOGOS; in Greek thought the Reason at the heart of the universe; in Jewish thought God's self-expression; in either case the revelation of God's eternal nature, in Christian thought identified with and manifested in Jesus. Third, Clement was living in a period when GNOSTICISM was strong. He combatted the views of the Gnostics. But he himself held *gnosis*, the knowledge of God, to be the chief element in Christian perfection. Like PAUL, Clement uses the language of the mystery religions in speaking of Christianity. Further, he holds that in receiving the gift of immortality the believer is receiving some part in the being of God. In one passage (*Tutor* 3, 1) he says: 'It is then the greatest of all lessons to know oneself. For if one knows himself he will know God, and knowing God, he will be made like God.' Such knowledge requires the disciplining of the lower nature, and the acceptance of the way of love: 'The more a man loves, the more deeply does he penetrate into God.' In *Miscellanies* (7, 10, 57) he has a fine account of the ultimate goal of the mystic: 'And so Knowledge easily translates the soul to the divine and holy which is akin to it, and by its own light conveys a man through the stages of mystery until it restores him at last to the supernal place of rest, teaching the man who is pure of heart to gaze on God, face to face, with perfect science and understanding. For in this consists the perfection of the soul of the true Gnostic, that, rising above all purification and service, it should be with God.'

Cloud of Unknowing, The

An anonymous fourteenth-century mystical treatise in English owing some debt to DIONYSIUS, whom the author perhaps also translated. It is directed to readers who by virtuous living are seeking the way to contemplative living. The first three chapters set out the central themes of the book. God in His love is calling us to him; we must respond with humble love; but it will be hard work because we are continually reaching out through a cloud of unknowing; but the gift of contemplative union is God's.

Throughout there is a stress on the grace of God. There is much incidental wisdom illuminated by vivid picture-language. When you cannot cope with distractions, cower before them; your father will rescue you. Use God's word as a mirror to show you the smudges on your conscience. If your house is on fire you cry 'Fire!' and should not be afraid to pray in the same manner. Play hide-and-seek with God, taking care that you don't hide yourself away so thoroughly that He can't spot you at all.

The symbol of cloud or DARKNESS is central. It is an image both of separation and of union; it seems to separate while it in fact unites. Indeed, as we flounder in the cloud of unknowing we must persist by separating our self from material cares in putting a cloud of forgetting between ourselves and other creatures. So too the cloud of unknowing can help us to perfect humility, and through humility to love, to aspiration, to love-longing. Yet at the same time 'ther was never yit pure creature in this liif, ne never yit schal be, so highe ravischid in contemplacion & love of the Godheed, that ther ne is evermore a highe & a wonderful cloude of unknowying bitwix him & his God'. But we are granted glimpses: 'Than wil he sumtyme, paraventure, seend oute a beme of goostly light peersying this cloude of unknowing that is bitwix thee & hym, & schewe thee sum of his privete,' (i.e. mystery) 'the whiche man may not, ne kan not, speke.' It is, the author continually insists, tough going but infinitely rewarding, and the climax of his book is an exalted account of what it means to be united with God (67–70). The last words of the book assert that God sees not what we are or have been, but what we would be.

Collegiants

Seventeenth-century group of Dutch Remonstrants who practised silent waiting upon God and held a doctrine of the INNER LIGHT. SPINOZA was for some time associated with one of their meetings.

Communion with God

Communion with God is a mystery. In many societies it is a privilege confined to the priest or king. Sometimes it is the prerogative of the initiates of a particular cult or secret society as among the GNOSTICS or in some MYSTERY-RELIGIONS.

Communion with God is not identical with MYSTIC UNION, though it may take that form. But it is found also in prayer and sacrifice, in a sacramental meal, of which the Christian EUCHARIST is a particularly good example, in worship generally. The five 'flavours' of BHAKTI are all ways of communion – CONTEMPLATION of the deity, active service and obedience, personal friendship, filial tenderness, passionate LOVE.

Sin is a breach on man's side in communion with God. The wrath of God, no doubt originally a projection of human response on to God, is in a more sophisticated age the expression of the incompatibility of sin with the divine purity. But the wrath of God is often seen not as a breach in communion but as the means of restoration: 'He chastens those whom he loves.'

Among mystics the view is widely held that communion is the gift of God. So in the UPANISHADS, 'Only the one the self chooses can understand him'; in the Hermetic writings, 'One cannot teach it; only God can awaken it in the heart'; in Plotinus, 'The beggar keeps waiting as near as he can to the door of the rich man; perhaps the rich man will open and give him an alms, perhaps once, perhaps twice; that is good fortune, not a work of his own.'

Condren, Charles de
(1588–1641)

French mystic, disciple of Pierre de BÉRULLE, whom he succeeded as Superior-General of the Oratory. He taught orally and through personal correspondence, and was a notable director of souls. His personal mysticism, and the spiritual experience towards which he guided others, was God-centred and found its expression in devotion to the mysteries of the Incarnate Christ and the Sacrifice of the Mass as an immediate temporal realization of a timeless event.

Constant, Alphonse Louis

See LÉVI

Contemplation

Term usually used by western Latin writers, where the eastern Greek writers prefer mysticism. There is on the face of it a slight difference of emphasis. Contemplation is man-originated and active, mysticism God-originated and passive. Contemplation is, however, distinct from MEDITATION; it has been defined as 'a simple regard, accompanied by love', or 'a loving sight' or 'a peering into heaven with the ghostly eye'. Evelyn Underhill has identified three forms of contemplation, associated with the Natural World of Becoming, the Metaphysical World of Being, and the Divine Reality within which these opposites are found as one. The first is the discovery of God in His creatures, whether Alp or insect. In the second the disciplined and recollected attention is 'directed towards a plane of existence with which your bodily senses have no attachments'; it is directed away from every image, every notion, every thing towards the Night of Sense. In one aspect this stage may be called speculation: the soul sees reality as in a mirror (*speculum*). In the third and highest, dying to your own will, in the Night of the Spirit, the mystics say that Absolute Love comes. These three may be associated with the three orders of reality which RUYSBROECK claims to have experienced, the natural world, the essential world and the superessential world; or with the three principles which Jakob BOEHME found in the Divine Essence, the image of the Eternal in the outer world, the manifestation of the Divine in the Eternal Light-world, and 'the deepest Deity, without and beyond Nature'; or with the three heavens of JACOPONE DA TODI. They correspond to the three phases in the contemplative consciousness identified by RICHARD OF ST VICTOR, enlargement of mind, elevation of mind and ecstasy of mind.

Delacroix has an excellent account of contemplation: 'When contemplation appears (a) It produces a general condition of indifference, liberty, and peace, an elevation above the world, a sense of beatitude. The subject ceases to perceive himself in the multiplicity and division of his general consciousness. He is raised above himself. A deeper and a purer soul substitutes itself for the normal Self. (b) In this state, in which consciousness of I-hood and consciousness of the world disappear, the mystic is conscious of being in immediate relation with God Himself; of participating in Divinity. Contemplation installs a method of being and of knowing. Moreover these two things tend at bottom to become one. The mystic has more and more the impression of being that which he knows, and of knowing that which he is.'

Contraction

Mystical experience corresponding to fear in the neophyte, but presently powerful rather than related to the future. It is the sense of desolation, abandonment, damnation, darkness, which is one aspect of mystic experience. The way out of it recommended to the religious mystic is concentration upon God. *See also* EXPANSION.

Conversion

A change from hostility or indifference towards a religion into the acceptance and practice of it; a change of allegiance from one religion to another; a change from a belief which, however sincere at the time, later seems nominal and shallow, to a deeper commitment.

As an example of conversion among mystics we may take FRANCIS OF ASSISI, in whom worldly pleasure and compassion for a long time struggled for mastery until he was praying in the chapel of S. Damiano and 'having been smitten by unworldly visitations, found himself another man than he who had gone in'. Heinrich SUSO's conversion was, according to his own account, gradual. He turned to God, and was constantly reaching out to Him, but only after a period of grim austerity did God deliver this 'Servitor of the Eternal Wisdom' (as he calls himself) by a complete conversion, which liberated his mystical and visionary powers. Rulman MERSWIN was already devout at the time of his 'conversion'. He was walking alone when an image of Christ crucified suddenly came before him with extraordinary vividness. He lifted his eyes to Heaven and solemnly swore that he would utterly surrender his own will, person and goods to the service of God. CATHERINE OF GENOA was dissatisfied with worldly luxury even while enjoying it, and with conventional religion, until kneeling before her confessor she was suddenly gripped by an overpowering sense of the love of God and of her own unworthiness, and cried out inside her, 'O Love! No more sins! No more sins!' Madame GUYON, like Catherine, had a gay youth and an unhappy marriage. She suffered from a surfeit of religiosity which gave her no satisfaction, till a Franciscan friar said to her, 'Madam, you are seeking without that which you have within. Accustom yourself to seek God in your own heart and you will find him.' These words suddenly gave her a shock of pain, and yet of joy, and directed her to the practice of CONTEMPLATION.

It will be noticed that these examples all have four points in common. First, the conversion to mysticism is from religious belief, not from atheism. Second, there is a preliminary period when the desire for a deeper religious life is strong but does not find fulfilment. Third, there is a definite moment of transformation; it is itself a mystical experience; and it is within the religious belief already held. Fourth, this leads to a release of mystical powers.

Cordovero, Moses
(1522–70)

The greatest systematic interpreter of Jewish mysticism. His basic thought can be summed up in the paradox 'God is all reality, but not all reality is God.' In more detail: 'The Holy One – blessed be He! – shines in the ten *sefiroth* of the world of creation, and in the ten heavenly spheres. In investigating this subject the reader will find: that we all proceed from Him; that our life is interwoven with His; that He is the existence of all beings; that the inferior beings, such as vegetables and animals, which serve us as nourishment, are not outside of Him; in short, he will discover that all is one revolving wheel, which ascends and descends – all is one, and nothing is separated from Him.' The Creator is thus knowledge, the knower and the object known. There is nothing which He does not find in His own substances. Creatures find their perfection in unity with Him, but fall away from that perfection in proportion as they are separated from Him.

Corpus Hermeticum

See HERMETICISM.

Cosmic consciousness

Phrase used by some philosophers to describe mystical experience without committing themselves to any particular religious interpretation.

Crashaw, Richard
(*c.* 1612–49)

English mystical poet, nurtured on The SONG OF SONGS and TERESA DE JESUS, to whom he wrote a notable 'Hymn'. From his combination of intellectual conceits with emotional fervour, and the tension within him between the sensual and Puritanical, comes verse of passionate power.

Criobolium

Baptism in ram's blood, leading to spiritual rebirth, associated with the mysteries of CYBELE and Attis, a lesser version of the TAUROBOLIUM. There is some indication that the bull was associated with Cybele, the ram with Attis.

Crux Ansata

See ANKH.

Cudworth, Ralph
(1617–88)

See CAMBRIDGE PLATONISTS.

Cybele

The Great Mother was worshipped in western Asia under a number of guises. In all of them she is the elemental feminine, creative and nutritive, a power of wild nature, and of the fertility of the earth. At Sumer she was Inanna, in Assyria Ishtar, among the Nabataeans Atargatis. At Ephesus she was Artemis, in Cyprus Aphrodite, in Cappadocia Ma. We encounter her as the Mountain-Mother or as Our Lady of the Animals. In the Graeco-Roman world, which she entered as the chief deity of a mystery religion, she was most often called Cybele.

Behind the cult stands a myth. Attis was a handsome lad and Cybele fell in love with him. But he was unfaithful and she drove him mad so

A 4th-century Roman silver dish showing an enthroned Cybele and Attis attended by the Sun, Moon and Stars

that he castrated himself under a pine-tree and bled to death. But this was not the end. There is a cycle of death and rebirth. The Festival of Mourning is succeeded by the Festival of Joy. The old year dies, but the new year rises again.

The priests were eunuchs, and self-castration in ecstasy was part of the initiation to the priestly service: the Roman Catullus wrote a breathtaking poem on the subject. Curiously, scholars are not agreed on the function of the castration; some hold that the priests were giving their fertility to the goddess, others that by removing the channel for the emission of the seed (which was believed to emanate from the head) they were preserving the life in the body dedicated to the Mother. In their later ritual they would reenact this. The music of horns, flutes, tambourines and cymbals would work them up (like DERVISHES) to an ecstatic frenzy of whirling dance, and they would lacerate their arms with knives so that their blood flowed again. It is clear that the religion has to do with fertility; and this is reinforced by the public festivals in spring, which took the form of an extended mystery play re-enacting the myth, and included the bathing of the cult-image, symbolizing the soaking of the earth in rain.

Alongside the public festivals were Mysteries in which individuals might be initiated through the baptism in ram's or bull's blood, CRIOBOLIUM or TAUROBOLIUM. As at ELEUSIS, the harvesting of grain, which is then sown again, becomes a symbol of life beyond death. Attis was called 'the reaped yellow ear of grain'. Initiation was a rebirth to eternal life, and the initiate received milk as a new child. In a sacramental meal, taken from the very musical instruments which enhanced the attractiveness of the cult (and, in the West, its unfamiliarity), the initiate took the divine life into himself. His affirmation of faith included the words:

> I have eaten from the tambourine,
> I have drunk out of the cymbal,
> I have become a mystic votary of Attis.

Another version of the formula shows the initiate identified with Attis as consort of the goddess:

> I have eaten out of the tambourine,
> I have drunk out of the cymbal,
> I have carried the holy dish,
> I have entered the bridal chamber.

'Be of good cheer, initiates of the god who was saved; you will have salvation from your tribulations.'

D

Dance

Dance plays a significant part in many religions. In mystical religion it may be part of the preparation for ecstatic experience: so with the Maenads of DIONYSUS, the DERVISHES, or VOODOO or some contemporary AFRICAN PROPHETIC CHURCHES. As such, it may be an attempt to be one with the rhythms of the universe, or with the movement of creation, God being usually conceived as the still centre of the turning world. So PLOTINUS compares us with a Greek chorus dancing round the One, out of time when we do not concentrate on the centre. In a Christian context Ambrose, Bishop of Milan, speaks of the believer as dancing the spiritual dance in the ecstasy of faith. One of the most interesting survivals in this connection is in the apocryphal *Acts of John* (94–102) where there is a round dance of the Twelve Apostles with Jesus at the centre. In BOTTICELLI's *Nativity* the angels are shown in a round dance above the stable; Fra ANGELICO's *Last Judgment* depicts the souls of the blessed and the angels joining in a round dance with a mystic flower at the centre.

The souls of the blessed dancing at the Last Judgment. Detail from Fra Angelico's Last Judgment

Dante Alighieri
(1265–1321)

Italian Christian poet. In his young days he fell in love with 'Beatrice' Portinari, and idealized her from afar, for in truth he scarcely knew her. His love for her and his love for God remain inextricably intertwined all through his life. He became involved in the internal politics of Florence, and was exiled when his faction was defeated; finally, after years of wandering, he settled in Ravenna, where he wrote in the vernacular his great cosmic vision *The Divine Comedy*. This work is a poetic trilogy, *Hell*, *Purgatory* and *Paradise*. Through the first two sections the poet is escorted by Vergil, who stands for natural reason. He is taken into Paradise by Beatrice, reason enlightened by divine revelation, who leads him through the hierarchy of the nine heavens. From there BERNARD OF CLAIRVAUX, the great contemplative mystic, guides him towards the BEATIFIC VISION. And now his sight is strengthened, and is able to pierce through the beams of Divine LIGHT to their very source. And here he discerns the whole universe in God.

Dante Alighieri, painted by William Blake in about 1800

In that abyss I saw how love held bound
Into one volume all the leaves whose flight
Is scattered through the universe
around. . . .

(33, 85 tr. D. L. Sayers and B. Reynolds)

Gradually he sees the Creator through the creation, three circles of three colours, yet occupying one space, one reflected from the next, and the third of flame emanating from both (here the Christian theology of the Trinity has determined the details of the mystical vision), and through these a human form. Dante describes the way his understanding wrestled to bring together the vision of the circles and the human form, and it was revealed to him in a flash of revelation. Then:

High phantasy lost power and here broke off,
Yet, as a wheel moves smoothly, free from jars,
My will and my desire were turned by love,
The love that moves the sun and the other stars.

Darkness

Usually in mysticism the presence of God is expressed under the image of LIGHT. Darkness is the absence of light; life may even be seen as a battleground between Darkness and Light. But there is another side to this, the VIA NEGATIVA is one of the mystic's roads to God. When you have stripped away everything, what is left is Void, Emptiness, Nothingness, Desert, Darkness. And that darkness is the light. So The TIBETAN BOOK OF THE DEAD speaks of 'the clear light of the Void' and DIONYSIUS of 'the dazzling obscurity which outshines all brilliance with the intensity of its darkness'. RUYSBROECK too says that the contemplative must lose himself in a darkness in which he can never find himself in a creaturely way, and of the manifestation of God in the abyss of darkness, though RUYSBROECK goes on to speak of God as the light shining in the darkness rather than as the darkness itself. So too the poet VAUGHAN describes in God 'a deep but dazzling darkness'.

Dark Night of the Soul

Phrase taken from JUAN DE LA CRUZ and more generally applied to the common though not quite universal experience of mystics that after a period of illumination there is a swing of the pendulum back to emptiness, impotence, desolation. The Dark Night is divided between the Night of the Senses, the purgation of the lower part of the soul, the bodily senses, imagination and emotions, and the Night of the Spirit, the purgation of the higher part of the soul, the intellect and will. The enhanced awareness of divine Perfection leads to a deeper sense of human imperfection. The state of depression is in fact a natural reaction to the high tension of the earlier experience, especially in a sensitive mind unusually prone to oscillation between extreme psychological states. The depression may be acute. Juan de la Cruz writes, 'That which the anguished soul feels most deeply is the conviction that God has abandoned it, of which it has no doubt; that He has cast it away into darkness as an abominable thing.' 'He acts', says ECKHART, 'as if there were a wall erected between Him and us.' 'It is', says ANGELA OF FOLIGNO, 'a privation worse than hell.' But the mystics also see it as an agonizing but needful time of testing. It alone will produce the FANA, the dying-to-self, which is the precondition of BAQA, eternal life.

David of Augsburg
(*c.* 1200–72)

Franciscan evangelist and mystic, and the first mystical writer to use the German vernacular; though he also wrote in Latin. In *The Seven Stages of Prayer* he gives an account of prayer as a means to mystical experience. Prayer begins by being directed by an effort of will, and using spoken words. Gradually it becomes effortless; words are still formulated but spoken inwardly. In a higher stage words are dispensed with. The worshipper submits to the will of God instead of being preoccupied with his own will. The sixth stage is called 'mystic sleep'; the highest is the BEATIFIC VISION where 'the mirror is completely taken away through which we see God here, and we are completely like God and see Him face to face, just as He is'. David knows and illustrates the different aspects of mystical experience: jubilation, spiritual intoxication, joy, dissolution; he is familiar with the experience which JUAN DE LA CRUZ later calls 'the dark night of the soul'. He identifies three forms of vision – corporeal, imaginative and intellectual; and offers a salutary warning against self-deception, and visions which spring from sexual starvation. The ultimate aim of mystical experience is the union of the soul and its faculties of memory, understanding and will, with God.

David of Dinant
(d. *c.* 1210)

Pantheistic philosopher, condemned by the Church, because he held that God, intelligence and matter are identical in essence, and unite in a single substance; that everything in NATURE is one, and that individual qualities which distinguish beings are only appearances due to an illusion of sense.

Dead Sea Scrolls, The

See ESSENES.

Deification

Some Indian and Far Eastern religions have tended to break down the division between God and man; the religions which emanated from the Near East, Judaism, Christianity and Islam, have tended to insist on it. Mysticism thus fits more easily into the patterns of India and the Far East, for they see mystical experience as restoring an essential unity between man and God. In the western religions this thought may be considered paradoxical and shocking. The language is nevertheless found. Among the Greek Christian Fathers, such as Athanasius, we continually come on such phrases as 'He became man that we might be made God.' Here it is possibly only a paradoxical way of saying 'He became mortal that we might become immortal.' On the whole Christian mystics speak of the marriage between God and the soul. But some do make a point of deification, and this is scripturally based on JOHN (17, 21 'May they all be one; as you, Father, are in me, and I in you, so may they be in us') and PAUL, and especially 2 *Peter* (1, 4 'you may . . . come to share in the divine nature'). In Gregory of Nyssa it is associated with the communion service. Theologians of the Orthodox Church however insist that in union man becomes one with God's ENERGIES not with his Essence.

The philosophy of deification is well seen in the story of AL-HALLAJ, who made the notorious assertion 'Ana 'l-Haqq' ('I am God' or 'I am the Creative Truth'). He was seemingly asserting that man is in his essence divine. God created Adam in the image of His own eternal love; he revealed in his own humanity the secret of His radiant divinity. But the divinity of God cannot unite with the humanity of God except through an incarnation. So Hallaj:

> Your Spirit mixes with mine, as wine is
> mixed with water.
> What touches You, touches me. In all things
> You are Me.

Or:

> I am my Beloved, my Beloved is me,
> We are two spirits in one body.
> If you see me, you see Him.
> If you see Him, you see us both.

There have been attempts to defend Hallaj from the charge of blasphemy by suggesting that in his ecstasy he did not distinguish between the divine attributes and the Divine Essence, or that it was the voice of God speaking through Hallaj, not Hallaj himself. In general Hallaj's doctrine seems to have been one of *hulul*, a belief in an 'infusion' of the Divine Spirit, and later believers in this were called HULULIS.

Denys of Ryckel
(1402–71)

Popularly known as Denys the Carthusian, he was associated with the Charterhouse at Roermond. His mystical experiences were such as to win him the title *doctor ecstaticus*, a title which also paid tribute to his learning. His works extend to forty quarto volumes; most important for mystics being *De contemplatione* and *De fonte lucis*. He seems to have coined the term 'acquired contemplation'.

Dervishes

The word dervish means a poor man, a religious beggar and an ecstatic. There are many sects of

Mevlevi Dervishes in their ecstatic dance

dervishes; the best known is the Mevlevi, or Whirling Dervishes, founded by RUMI in the thirteenth century, whose whirling motion is a symbol of the rotation of the universe in the presence of God, and at the same time a means of attaining the ECSTASY which leads to a full awareness of the divine presence.

> O hearts! O worlds! Let love your master
> be . . .
> The leader of our round of love goes out
> Beyond the sun and dawn . . .

The Mevlevi are still to be seen practising their ritual in Turkey, Syria and Egypt. Another well-known dervish order is the Naqshbandi, named after its founder, but with a punning meaning of Painters or Designers, also nicknamed the Silent Order. Another is the Chishti, who make great use of music in their exercises and made a considerable impact in India.

Devekuth

The intense LOVE of God, a concept based on Deut. 11, 22, the ecstatic culmination of Jewish mysticism. Dov Ber of Mezhirich declared that 'the principal elements of Divine worship are *devekuth* and awe'. So Nahmanides: 'A man should always remember God and his love, never ceasing to think of him, so that even when he is talking to his fellow-men, his heart is with God.'

Devotio moderna

The movement for 'up-to-date' devotion originated in the Low Countries in the fourteenth century, influenced by Jan van RUYSBROECK but essentially created by Geert de GROOTE. Here the presence of God was found in daily life, in home and school and in the local worshipping community. It stressed personal religious experience and encouraged meditation on the life and Passion of Christ. It found its great expression in The IMITATION OF CHRIST.

Dhamma

Buddhist term for doctrine or teaching, from Sanskrit *dharma*. The Buddhists have a threefold formula of which the central clause is 'I go to the *Dhamma* for refuge.' The *Dhamma* consists fundamentally in the Four Noble Truths about suffering and the escape from suffering.

Dhikr

In Moslem mysticism incessant repetition of the name and attributes of God or of a simple MANTRA as a means of recollection of and concentration on God. 'The first stage of *dhikr* is to forget self, and the last stage is the effacement of the worshipper in the act of worship.'

Dhu 'l-Nun

(d. 861)

Egyptian Sufi, alchemist and mystic, who linked Islamic monotheism with the traditional wisdom of Egypt. Like RABI'A he wrote mystical poetry using the language of physical passion.

> I die, and yet not dies in me
> The ardour of my love for Thee,
> Nor hath Thy Love, my only goal,
> Assuaged the fever of my soul.
>
> To Thee alone my spirit cries;
> In Thee my whole ambition lies,
> And still Thy wealth is far above
> The poverty of my small love.

Central to Dhu 'l-Nun's thought is the *gnosis*, the mystical knowledge revealed only to the few. Dhu 'l-Nun was something of a pantheist, like many mystics; he found testimony to the Unity of God in the noises of animals, the murmur of the trees, the splashing sound of water, the song of birds, the whistling of the wind, the growling of thunder. To him God was All-Prevailing, All-Knowing, All-Wise, All-Just, All-True. His love of nature was such that it was said that the birds flocked above his coffin to give it shade. Another legend tells of an inscription appearing mysteriously over his grave: 'This is the beloved of God, who died from his love for God, killed by God.'

Dickinson, Emily

(1830–86)

American poet, who lived with a patriarchial father in a circumscribed world in New England. She was not the recluse some have made her out to be; but her real world was the world of the imagination, stirred particularly by two men ('My life closed twice before its close'), Ben Newton, a young, poor free-thinker, and Rev. Charles Wadsworth, a married man who (if it was he) 'tried to teach me immortality'. She scribbled verses of vivid imagery on the back of envelopes and other scraps of paper, verses slight and loose in form, but with a passionate sense of outward and inward experience, so that the home and garden and village became a vehicle through which the Absolute appeared, summer days became a sacrament, the breathing of air divine intoxication, a sunbeam a sacred liturgy, grass an emblem of the contemplative life. She is arguably America's leading mystical poet:

> It was a quiet way –
> He asked if I was his –
> I made no answer of the Tongue
> But answer of the Eyes –
> And then He bore me on
> Before this mortal noise
> With swiftness as of Chariots
> And distance as of Wheels.
> The World did drop away
> As Acres from the feet
> Of one that leaneth from Balloon
> Upon an Ether street.
> The Gulf behind was not,
> The Continents were new –
> Eternity it was before
> Eternity was due.
> No Seasons were to us –
> It was not Night nor Morn –
> But Sunrise stopped upon the place
> And fastened it in Dawn.

Ding-an-sich

'The thing in itself.' The unknowable metaphysical ground of being, in the philosophy of Immanuel KANT.

Dionysius the Areopagite

(*c.* 500)

A Christian writer who took the pseudonym of PAUL's Athenian convert. We know nothing of him except from his own writings, *The Celestial Hierarchy*, *The Ecclesiastical Hierarchy*, *The Divine Names* and *Mystical Theology*, in which he draws on his own mystical experience, and interprets it in the light of a philosophy which blends Christianity and NEO-PLATONISM.

Dionysius follows through the principle of the VIA NEGATIVA, that no predicates attach to God, and no words may properly be used to describe him. He speaks of God as the Divine Darkness, or says that God has made DARKNESS His secret place. He is the Darkness beyond LIGHT, the super-essential Darkness. A magnificent passage in *Mystical Theology* (c. 5) expounds the *via negativa*: 'Once more, ascending yet higher, we maintain that It is not soul, or mind, or endowed with the faculty of imagination, conjecture, reason, or understanding; nor is It any act of reason or understanding; nor can It be described by the reason or perceived by the understanding, since It is not number, or order, or greatness, or littleness, or equality, or inequality, and since It is not immovable nor in motion, nor at rest, and has no power, and is not power or light, and does not live, and is not life; nor is It personal essence, or eternity, or time, nor can It be grasped by the understanding, since It is not knowledge or truth; nor is It kingship or wisdom; nor is It one, nor is It unity, nor is It Godhead or Goodness; nor is It a Spirit, as we understand the term, since It is not Sonship or Fatherhood; nor is It any other thing such as we or any other being can have knowledge of; nor does It belong to the category of non-existence or to that of existence; nor do existent beings know It as It actually is, nor does It know them as they actually are; nor can the reason attain to It to name It or know It; nor is It darkness, nor is It light; nor error; nor truth; nor can any affirmation or negation apply to It; for while applying affirmations or negations to those orders of being that come next to It, we are not applying to It either affirmation or negation, inasmuch as It transcends all affirmation by being the perfect and unique Cause of all things, and transcends all negation by the pre-eminence of its simple and absolute nature.'

But Dionysius as a Christian finds it impossible to escape entirely from an account of God in terms of LOVE, righteousness, wisdom. In *The Divine Names* he tries to reconcile his Christian Biblicism with his mystical understanding. His answer is that God is in Himself unknowable, and every affirmation about Him is false in absolute terms. But we may loosely attribute qualities to God because He is the cause and origin of those qualities in the empirical world. It is misleading to speak of the existence of God, but the existence of the world has its origin in Him. It is misleading to speak of the goodness of God, but He is the source of goodness in others. There are difficulties here which Dionysius has not resolved, for he is still speaking of God as cause or source, but it is an ingenious attempt.

Dionysius, as a Neo-Platonist, is much concerned with the 'divine progression' from the Godhead to the world, the chain which links the ordinary mortal to the divine. There are three orders of angelic beings. In the highest are the 'great Intelligences', who stand at the vestibule of the Godhead. They possess 'the unsullied fixity of Godlike identity', and act as prisms conveying the Divine Light in such intensity as those below can stand; for 'it is impossible that the beams of the Divine Source can shine upon us unless they are shrouded in the manifold texture of sacred veils'; the beauty of intelligible pearls is not to be cast to swine! These great Intelligences are Seraphim, Cherubim and Thrones. In the second order are Dominions, Virtues, Powers; and in the third Principalities, Archangels and Angels. The transmission of Divine Light down is carried on from the Heavenly Hierarchy to the Ecclesiastical Hierarchy, another ninefold order of symbols and ministers headed by Christ. So in one sense God is all.

But all is not God. Equally important to the divine progression is the celestial ladder which leads the soul back to God. Dionysius has a compelling account of prayer. It is 'as if a luminous chain were suspended from the celestial heights, and we, by ever clutching this, first with one hand and then with the other, seem to draw it down, but in reality we are ourselves carried upwards to the high splendours of the luminous rays. Or as if, after we have embarked on a ship and are holding on to the cable reaching to some rock, we do not draw the rock to us but draw, in fact, ourselves and the ship to the rock.' The end of this is unity with the Divine. 'To be made divine is to be made like God, as far as may be, and to be made one with Him.' (The concept of being like God comes from Plato, *Theaetetus* 176B.)

The writings of Dionysius exercised an extraordinary influence on subsequent generations.

Dionysus

Dionysus was a god of nature, seemingly known in Greece in the Mycenaean age, but half-forgotten till he stormed in again from Thrace and won a place at Delphi and on Olympus. He is associated with vegetation and particularly the vine, so that he is the god of intoxication and the spiritual intoxication that is ENTHUSIASM, ECSTASY and inspiration. He is the god of animal life too, and takes the form of bull, snake and lion, and, more gently, of fawn and kid. He is closely associated with the pattern of nature which we still call spring and fall; his great festivals were in the spring. The antiquarian Macrobius saw in his myth the cycle of the seasons, birth, growth, decay and rebirth; we have other evidence of belief that he was asleep or shackled in winter and awakened or released in spring.

Dionysus supported by a bacchant. Detail from an early 4th-century BC *Greek cup*

The followers of Dionysus were ecstatic women, called Bacchants (from the god's name Bacchus) or Maenads (from the Greek word for 'madness'). They wore wreaths of ivy, oak or fir, and skins of animals, and carried the *thyrsus*, a staff wreathed in vine-leaves or ivy and tipped with a pine-cone. In their ecstasy they would range through the mountains in dizzying dances, and tear some animal apart with their bare hands and eat it raw. There is no doubt that this was a communion in the god's own body and blood; indeed at one centre the god was worshipped under the cult-title Raw. The inspiration of the god was believed to confer miraculous power, and, as often, a belief in miracles leads to the performance of miracles. We hear of them caught in a snowstorm so that their clothes were frozen stiff, but rescued unharmed, or falling asleep from sheer exhaustion in an enemy village during wartime, and being protected for their holiness.

During the Hellenistic and Roman periods, we hear of members of Dionysiac fellowships (*thiasoi*). One group caused a scandal at Rome in 186 BC: numbers were large; we hear of initiations, ecstatic prophesying, and scandalous behaviour. Another group was to be found at Pompeii in the first century AD in the VILLA OF THE MYSTERIES. The so-called ORPHICS constituted a kind of splinter sect. Lists of functionaries in inscriptions show that men and women, and indeed children, were involved. The titles are fascinating; they include such officials as Chief of the Mysteries, Chief Herdsman, Guardian of the Cave, Bearer of the Phallus, Head of the Hearth, Bearer of Milk, 'Papa', Torch-Bearer and the like. Children were important; there was something of a cult of the infant Dionysus, and we know of very young children (one who died at three years and two months) who were initiates.

The most characteristic symbol of the Dionysiac mysteries was the *liknon*, one of the god's titles being Dionysus Liknites. The *liknon* was an oblong basket open at one end, filled with fruit, and containing a phallus veiled in a cloth. It speaks of life, potency, fertility and ultimately of the promise of life through death.

What the promise of Dionysus meant can be seen in a magnificent series of sarcophagi, belonging to a family called Calpurnius Piso, and dating from the second century AD; parallel examples are known. Whether we see the childhood of Dionysus, Dionysus in triumph, or Ariadne abandoned by Theseus and taken as bride of the god, they all speak of the way in which our humanity can put on divinity, our mortality immortality. In general the Dionysiac mysteries were deeply concerned about the dead, who were promised, if initiated, an after-life of Bacchic revelry – the evening before without the morning after.

Divine Comedy, The

See DANTE.

Dogen

(1200–53)

The greatest of all Japanese ZEN masters, honoured as a BODHISATTVA. He became a monk at the age of thirteen, travelled in China, and in 1236 established his great monastery in Japan at Koshohoringji, which drew in many disciples of both sexes. Dogen was an adept at religious meditation through ZAZEN; he sought and taught the purification of the ego, the elimination of all selfish desires, and utter self-surrender. He also stressed personal devotion to the Buddha. Philosophically he was a pantheist; the ABSOLUTE and the sensible world are one. His most important book is the *Shebogenzo*.

Dostoyevsky, Fedor Mikhailovich

(1821–81)

Russian novelist, who suffered under a brutal father in his youth; became an epileptic; was sentenced to death for revolutionary activities, and when the sentence was commuted spent eight years in Siberia; had a brief marriage to a neurotic consumptive, a stormy love affair, and a happier second marriage; had to flee Russia to escape his creditors; and returned to spend his last ten years in the enjoyment of fame.

Dostoyevsky was fascinated by abnormal mental states, believing that they represent the essence of humanity. He was profoundly religious and yet at the same time critical and sceptical. He portrayed characters reflecting his own divided self, notably Ivan in *The Brothers Karamazov*, his masterpiece, a novel which calls for spiritual renewal. Zossima, in the same novel, is a profound study of spirituality and compassion, based on the mystic TIKHON. Dostoyevsky, to the end of his life, was exercised by the mysteries of good and evil, human personality, immortality and God.

Doukhobors

Russian Christian sect. Their origin is uncertain, but they appeared near Kharkov about 1740. The name, which means 'Spirit-fighters', was given them by the Orthodox, who claimed that they were fighting against the Spirit; they accepted it because they were armed with the Spirit. They believe in one God who is love, and that every man may be one with God, revealed as memory (Father), reason (Son) and will (Holy Spirit). They believe in reincarnation and the immortality of the soul. They are today found mainly in Canada.

Drugs and mysticism

See HASHISH, HUXLEY, LSD, MESCALIN, OPIUM, PEYOTISM.

Duvergier de Hauranne, Jean

See PORT ROYAL

E

Eckhart, Johann
(*c.* 1260–1328)

Eckhart, later nicknamed *Meister*, 'The Master', was born at Hochheim in Thuringia. He became a novice of the Dominican order, and was sent to Cologne to study theology; there he became deeply imbued with the scholasticism of ALBERTUS MAGNUS and THOMAS AQUINAS. Some mystics are all experience and no thought; not Eckhart. He returned to the priory at Erfurt and was elected prior. From there he went to the University of Paris, obtaining his doctorate in 1302. He attained high office in the Dominican order, first as Provincial Minister of Saxony, then as Vicar General of Bohemia. After a further period in Paris we find him in Strasbourg as a preacher with an enormous following. There follows an obscure period during which he seems to have been Vicar General of Saxony, from where he returned to the University of Cologne. But his last years were troubled. He was tried for heresy, died before the final verdict and was condemned posthumously. He himself declared that he was capable of error but not of heresy, 'because error depends on understanding, heresy depends on will'.

Eckhart is at once logician and mystic. His thought derives from the scholasticism of Albertus and Thomas on the one hand, and from the mystical NEO-PLATONISM of PLOTINUS, AUGUSTINE and DIONYSIUS THE AREOPAGITE on the other.

His great themes are God and the soul. He starts from the affirmation that God is; more, He is BEING, pure being, absolute reality. The first thing to say about God is 'He is', 'He exists'. Eckhart loves the Old Testament passage where God appears as 'I am that I am'. He distinguishes between God and the Godhead: 'God acts. The Godhead does not.' In the depths of mystical experience we pass beyond the God whose work is seen in this world to the Godhead. He speaks of the Wordless Godhead, the Naked Godhead, the Nameless Nothing, the Still Wilderness, the Immovable Rest. Eckhart's account of God is paradoxical, because it brings together the two sides of his philosophy. Thus he follows Dionysius in recognizing the limitations of our normal language in speaking of God. One of his heretical propositions was that 'God is neither good, nor better, nor best. If anyone were to say that God is good, it would be as incorrect as saying that white is black.' His defence was: 'Certainly God, who is above every name by which we might name Him, is as high above them as white is above black.' One of his hearers in a curious verse says that the Master 'speaks to us about Nothingness. If a man does not understand that, the Light Divine has never shone in him.' Yet he does not follow the VIA NEGATIVA, but follows Aquinas in his use of analogy in speaking of God. Similarly he was charged with obliterating the distinction between God and man. His scholasticism pointed him to divine transcendence, his mysticism to divine immanence; and he therefore taught paradoxically the actual dissimilarity between God and the soul, and yet the essential similarity.

The most distinctive part of Eckhart's teaching about the soul is that at the apex of the mind is the *seelenfünklein*, or spark of the soul, the *scintilla animi* of earlier theology. This is the part or aspect of the soul by means of which union with God takes place. It is the seat of conscience as well as of the religious consciousness, and it is indestructible: even in Hell it still persists. More, he seems to speak of the identity of God and the spark of the soul in the moment of mystical experience: 'The eye by which I see God is the same as the eye by which God sees me. My eye and God's eye are one and the same – one in seeing, one in knowing, and one in loving.' Equally distinctive is his teaching about the birth of Christ in the soul. Eckhart is more interested in this than in the historic life of Jesus of Nazareth. For him what matters is that in us Christ is born, dies and rises again. God is eternal, and therefore the cosmic generation of the Son from the Father is taking place eternally, and it is this which constitutes the experience of mystical union. The event is eternal, but we experience it in terms of 'before' and 'after'. 'God has spoken once: twice have I heard this' (Ps. 62, 12).

Eckhart is not greatly interested in the material world. The creation is utterly dependent on the creator. He was charged with holding that the world had existed from all eternity, but explicitly denied that the world is eternal in the same sense as God is eternal. He was also charged with denying the reality of the material world. In one sense this was a true bill: 'All things are a mere nothing. I do not say that they are slight or that they are anything, but that they are a mere nothing.' 'Nothing hinders the soul's knowledge of God as much as time and space, for time and space are fragments, whereas God is one! And therefore, if the soul is to know God, it must know him above time and outside space; for God is neither this nor that, as are these manifold things. God is One!' Still, he lived a life of practical good works within the world.

It is a tribute to the essential unity of mystical experience and to the profundity of Eckhart that during this century there have been two major studies: one, Rudolf OTTO's *Mysticism East and West*, comparing his thought with that of SANKARA; and one, Suzuki's *Mysticism: Christian and Buddhist*, drawing out its likeness to the teaching of the ZEN Masters. Yet Eckhart's thought remains distinctively Christian.

Ecstasy

A state of temporary mental alienation, associated with a feeling of timelessness, from a Greek word meaning 'displacement' or 'standing apart'. The experience, though it may be prolonged, is transitory and infrequent (except perhaps to some saints); and it is abnormal to such an extent that it seems to add another dimension to experience. The word has been trivialized, but the popular song 'O then, O gee, I'm in ecstasy When I dance with my girl' is perhaps a genuine expression of a sensation of timelessness. Ecstasy is sometimes used of religious trances. The experience of ecstasy is often described in terms of sudden light (though sometimes the distinction between light and dark seems to disappear), of a sensation of elevation or levitation, of a rising spring or flowing stream, of a heightened inner consciousness, of an increased intensity, of stillness and peace. There is a sense of release, of freedom from self and sin and sorrow and desire, of knowledge of a totally new kind, of identification with the universe or with all living things or with God, of timelessness or eternity, of glory, of joy and happiness and utter satisfaction.

Teresa de Jesus in ecstasy. Marble sculpture by Gian Lorenzo Bernini

Sometimes the experience is spoken of as indescribable or ineffable.

In TERESA DE JESUS's analysis of MYSTIC UNION ecstasy is the third and next-to-highest stage.

Teresa herself was forty-three when she had her first experience of ecstasy. Others are recorded much earlier, CATHERINE OF SIENA's even at the age of four.

Ecstasies are normally of quite short duration, and Teresa suggests that the effective period is not more than half an hour. There are however records of ecstasies lasting several days. The most remarkable example is Maria von Möerl (1812–68) from Kaltern in the Tyrol, who experienced continuous ecstasy during the last thirty-five years of her life, except when her confessor called her out from it; during these periods she went about her household and family tasks in a normal practical way.

Sadhu SUNDAR SINGH has an important contrast between the yogic states he experienced before his conversion to Christianity and the ecstatic states after his conversion. In the yogic states the emotions he was feeling before the trance were intensified, and if he was sad before the trance he would weep during the trance; in his subsequent ecstasies there was always 'the same feeling of calm satisfaction and being at home'.

In its physical aspect ecstasy is a form of trance, accompanied by depressed breathing and circulation, and sometimes by total anaesthesia. Such a psycho-physical condition is a commonplace of hysterical illness, and the mystics are aware of this and can distinguish in themselves the hysterical condition from what they regard as the true mystical ecstasy; this is particularly true of CATHERINE OF GENOA in later life. TERESA DE JESUS too is careful to distinguish what she calls 'raptures of feminine weakness' from the true intellectual vision. The mystics insist that the test of a true mystical ecstasy is not in its physical manifestation but in its inward grace. In its psychological aspect ecstasy is a form of 'complete mono-ideism', the full concentration of the attention on one single thing. It is thus an extreme form of CONTEMPLATION, the difference being that though the will may play a part in producing the state of ecstasy it is incapable of suspending it. In its mystical aspect ecstasy is a vivid apprehension of the transcendent.

Egyptian Book of the Dead, The

Collection of ancient Egyptian religious writings dating in its present form from the sixteenth century BC, but incorporating earlier material and found in more elaborate versions with fanciful illustrations at a later period. Copies of varying length (according to the wealth of the deceased) were buried in the grave: the object was simply to secure for the dead man eternal life. Sections tell of physical danger to the body from insects, and of spiritual danger in the other world. Chapter 125 deals with the Judgment

A papyrus fragment from the Egyptian Book of the Dead

(including the protestations of innocence). The whole displays a lively belief in resurrection and immortality.

Eisai

(1141–1215)

Founder of Japanese ZEN, who visited China in 1168 and 1187, and received the seal of enlightenment in the Lin-chi or Rinzai sect, building the first temple of that sect in Japan at Hakata. At first he met with hostility but won the support of the authorities with his patriotic treatise *The Spread of Zen for the Protection of the Country*. Eisai also fostered the cultivation of tea and wrote a book on the subject.

Eleazar of Worms

(d. *c.* 1230)

The most voluminous of all the mediaeval German Hasidic writers. His work was an attempt to present a comprehensive account of mystical theory and practice. This makes it impossible to summarize his thought in a small space. There are strong Platonic elements, the 'archetypes', which are the Platonic forms, and a doctrine of knowledge as recollection. Eleazar has a vivid picture of human life: man is a rope whose two ends are pulled by God and Satan; in the end, but only in the end, God demonstrates His superior strength. Hence the need for systematic exposition; Eleazar for example has a comprehensive account of a penitential system.

Eleusis

The myth behind the most famous mystery religion of the Graeco-Roman world told how Demeter, whose name means Earth-Mother or Grain-Mother, had a daughter named Kore (the Maid) or Persephone (a pre-Greek name of unknown meaning). Kore was picking flowers when the earth opened and the god of the Underworld, Pluto (whose name stands for both death and plenty), carried her off. Demeter was disconsolate and wandered looking for her lost child. She came in disguise to Eleusis, a settlement some fourteen miles from Athens, and became nurse to the young prince. After a while she revealed herself, and told them to build her a temple-house. In this she brooded for a year. During that year no crops grew, nature shrivelled up, a plague fell upon animals and death upon men. Zeus, the father-god, was forced to act and procure the Maid's release. But while in the underworld she ate some pomegranate-seeds which tied her to that land for a third of the year.

Plainly the myth has to do with the cycle of the year and the burial of corn-seed in the earth. The exact symbolism is controversial. The burial of seed in the ground and its emergence to new life suggests that the period of death is the winter. But in Greece the really parched bare months are those of the summer; and others have supposed that the point is the storage of the seed-corn in underground jars during the summer, and its emergence for the autumn sowing.

At Eleusis there developed a cult of Demeter and Kore, which certainly dates back to the second millennium BC; traces of a small temple-house of that date have been found which would fit the myth well. When Eleusis came under the power of Athens, there was expansion of the buildings, and by the time of the dictator Pisistratus in the sixth century BC it was becoming a pan-hellenic cult. The great Hall of the Mysteries, with its forty-two columns, belongs to the following century, and in Roman times the buildings on the site were greatly expanded and enriched.

The cult was entrusted hereditarily to two families, who provided the chief officials – the Hierophant, or chief priest, and his assistant; the priestess of Demeter and other priestesses; the Torchbearer; the Herald; and the Altar-priest. The cult was a mystery: there was admission for initiates only, and it was a grave offence, involving the death penalty, to betray the secrets.

There were two annual festivals. The Lesser Mysteries were held in spring in Athens, and offered some sort of preliminary initiation and PURIFICATION, involving fasting, sacrifice, ritual baptism and lustration, and the singing of hymns.

The Greater Mysteries were associated with the autumn sowing in September–October. Every four years they were held with special splendour. There was a fifty-five-day truce. On the day before the festival proper the cult-objects were taken from the Eleusis sanctuary in ceremonial procession to a shrine in Athens. On the first day of the festival the Herald called for celebrants: 'everyone who has clean hands and intelligible speech' (i.e. Greek), 'he who is pure from all pollution and whose soul is conscious of no evil, and who has lived well and justly'. On the second day the Herald cried 'To the sea, initiates!' The sea cleanses all human evils. With them they had each a sacrificial pig, which was similarly purified and then sacrificed. The third day was the day of public sacrifice for the communicants. The fourth was reserved for the purification of late arrivals. The fifth saw the great procession back to Eleusis with all the initiates and their sponsors. A deity called Iacchus (later confused with Bacchus) presided over their festive cries. At one point watchers on a bridge hurled obscenities at the procession – an ancient apotropaic ritual. The arrival was marked with extreme joy. The sixth day was spent in resting and FASTING and preparation. That night the mysteries were celebrated. The seventh day was another period of rest. The eighth was spent in libations and rites for the dead. The ninth was the day of dispersal: there was no formal procession back of Athens, and those going elsewhere were free to depart.

What were the Mysteries? The fact is that the secret has been well kept. We do not know for certain. We can discount the more obscene imaginings of Christian critics on the offensive. No doubt there was a dramatic re-enactment of the myth, in a spectacular and quite frightening manner. We know that it included music and ballet, and that a gong sounded at the name of Kore. It is possible that there was an enactment of the sacred marriage. At one point there seems to have been a kind of antiphonal cry of 'Rain', 'Conceive' (rhyming words in Greek). This could bring the language of nature to a mythical marriage, it could be going behind the myth to the fertility of the earth. The reuniting of Maid and Mother was celebrated with a revelry of torches. A papyrus fragment shows Heracles claiming 'I have beheld the fire . . . I have seen the Maid.'

But the supreme moment was not something acted but something seen, presented in a brilliant light, impossible without the use of reflectors. The sacred objects no doubt included ancient cult-statues; they may well have included replicas of the male and female sex-organs. But it seems that the climactic revelation was a reaped ear of corn, perhaps of brilliant gold.

There is evidence of a communion feast in cereal and barley-wine. According to one writer the participant spoke the formula 'I have fasted. I have drunk the barley-wine. I have taken things from the sacred chest, tasted them and replaced them first in the basket then in the chest.' The cereal seems to have been taken in the form of buns or cakes. There is also evidence of the use of pomegranates; these may be among the objects taken and replaced without consumption.

There seems in this to be some kind of identification with the Corn-Maid. The Roman Emperor Gallienus commemorated his initiation by putting on his coins *Galliena Augusta*; the form is feminine and suggests that he is one with the goddess. This is an identification with the goddess who dies and rises again. We may think similarly of the words of Jesus: 'Unless a grain of wheat falls into the ground and dies it remains alone, but if it dies, it bears much fruit.' So there is promise that through identification with the goddess there is a richer life beyond the grave and not just the shadowy meaninglessness of the

An Athenian boy receiving ears of corn from Demeter while Persephone crowns him with a garland in the Eleusis ritual: 5th-century votive relief

Homeric Hades. And the condition is moral and religious purity. Hence Cicero after his initiation: 'We have learned to live and die with a better hope.' Hence the Homeric Hymn to Demeter:

Blessed among men on earth is he who has
seen these things.
But he who is uninitiate and without share
in the holy rites
has no like fate when in death he lies
beneath the spreading dark.

Hence the triumphant words inscribed by an initiate on his tomb: 'Glorious indeed is that mystery vouchsafed by the blessed gods, for death is no ill to mortals, but rather a good.'

Elisabeth of Hungary
(1207–31)

Princess of Hungary, married to Ludwig IV of Thuringia. On Ludwig's death in 1227 she cried, 'The world with all its joys is now dead to me.' She had already shown herself a woman of great and practical charity. It happened that at this time the Franciscan cause had recently been established in Germany. Elisabeth now espoused it heartily. Her position prevented her at first from accepting absolute poverty, but soon she devoted herself completely to works of healing and a life of great austerity under the direction of the stern Conrad of Marburg.

Emanation

Phrase used especially by PLOTINUS and the NEOPLATONISTS to describe the generation of the world from the Ultimate. Thus the sun radiates light while itself remaining unchanged and undiminished; so too heat is an emanation from fire, cold from snow, perfume from a flower, the river from the spring.

Emmerich, Anna Katherina
(1774–1824)

Christian visionary, a nun of the Augustinian order at Dülmen, stigmatic, some of whose reflections are preserved in her meditations on the Passion, published posthumously as *Das bittere Leiden unseres Herrn und Heilandes Jesus Christ* by Clemens Brentano. Her visions include accounts of places, some of which were erroneous, some confirmed; through one of them the 'House of Mary' at Ephesus was discovered. She was carefully observed, and her stigmatization was authenticated.

Empedocles
(*c.* 493–433 BC)

Ancient Greek mystical philosopher, an orator and doctor of some distinction, a theorist who advanced the cause of physical science by proposing a complex rather than a simple basis to the universe, so paving the way for an atomic theory. Empedocles had a cyclical theory of the universe, the elements being brought together by LOVE and separated again by Strife. A varied world such as we know belongs to an intermediate stage, and Empedocles was enough of a pessimist to say that we are under the power of strife. Empedocles also wrote a poem called *Purifications* which describes the fall of man from unity and peace to disorder and strife, and the necessary steps for restoration. He believes in the transmigration of souls and claims himself to have been a boy, a girl, a bush, a bird and a dumb sea-fish. But he had escaped from the weary cycle of reincarnation.

Friends who live in the great town of golden
Acragas
up by the citadel, men who care about
righteous actions,
havens of respect for strangers, with no
touch of wickedness,
I greet you. I go about among you an
immortal God,
no longer mortal, duly honoured among you
all. . . .

Encratites

Name meaning 'the continent people', applied to groups of early Christians and GNOSTICS who sought salvation in ASCETICISM, vegetarianism, teetotalism and abstinence from sex.

Energies

Eastern Orthodox Christianity made a distinction between the essence or BEING of God, which is unknowable, inapprehensible, ineffable, and His energies or activities, through which we may be said to know Him and find union with Him.

En-sof

Jewish term for the Infinite, important in The ZOHAR and KABBALISTIC mysticism.

Enthusiasm

Literally 'the quality of having the god within', applied in the seventeenth and eighteenth centuries to those who saw religion primarily in terms of openness to the Divine Presence rather than intellectual creed, formal observance or good works, and who tended to confine salvation to those who received this revelation. The term was popularized in a sermon preached by Bishop Hickes in 1680, *The Spirit of Enthusiasm exorcised*, and was still topical when Isaac Taylor in 1823 wrote his monumentally dull *The Natural History of Enthusiasm.*

Ephraem of Syria
(*c.* 306–73)

Christian theologian, poet and mystic. To Ephraem God is the One Reality, unsearchable, indiscernible, incomprehensible, Hidden Infinite Being, the Divine Essence, Beauty and LIGHT. But though He is transcendent, all things have their being in Him, 'In His Majesty dwell powers, natures and angels,' and the human soul has its being in Him. So He is at once near and far off: 'Though He is in us, He is not in us; and though the Creation is in Him, it is as though it were not in Him.' God manifests Himself to us, speaks to us, through the LOGOS.

> Glory to the Silence that spoke by his Voice,
> Glory to the One on high, who was seen by his Dayspring,
> Glory to the Spiritual, to the Hidden One, to that Living One,
> Glory to that Hidden One, who even with the mind cannot be perceived by those who search after Him; but by his grace was experienced by men.

Man was made in the image of God, who mixed His salt in our minds and His leaven in our souls, to be a tabernacle for His unseen nature. For this we must prepare ourselves through penitence, self-discipline, PURIFICATION, vigil, prayer and especially the PRAYER OF QUIET. The soul whose eyes are opened may be allowed to look on the secret Light, the Beauty of God, and being flooded with the Divine Radiance, passes into heaven and by love is blended and mingled with the God who is LOVE.

Epiphany

Visible appearance of a divine being. The Epiphany of Jesus was his Manifestation to the Gentiles, the Wise Men.

Erigena, John Scotus
(*c.* 810–77)

Irishman (Erigena means 'born in Erin') who shines like a meteor in the Dark Ages. Somehow, in his thirties, he came to the court of Charles the Bald, who gave him high responsibility. He engaged in theological controversy on predestination and on transubstantiation. His prime importance in the story of mysticism is that his Latin translations of DIONYSIUS THE AREOPAGITE and MAXIMUS CONFESSOR made these works available to western Europe in the Middle Ages. His own world view, based on these, is found in five books *On the Division of Nature*, Platonic in form and NEO-PLATONIC in thought. Erigena sees the universe as a divine procession. There are four divisions of NATURE. That which creates and is not created is God in His own Being, the One, ABSOLUTE, the ground of our being, inapprehensible and ineffable. But this unknown God reveals Himself. The second division of nature is that which is created and creates. This is the immaterial world of the Platonic Forms, the thoughts of God and patterns of the visible universe. Erigena differs from PLATO in that he sees the Forms as dynamic and themselves creative. The third division, that which is created and does not create, is the visible universe, which exists only in appearance. The fourth division, that which is not created and does not create, is God as the ultimate destiny or consummation of all things. So that there is a kind of cycle. All things flow from God and back to God. He is the Alpha and the Omega, the source and the goal. 'This is the end of all things visible and invisible, when all visible things pass into the intellectual, and the intellectual into God, by a marvellous and unspeakable union' (4, 20). 'Everything that is shall return into God as air into light. For God shall be all things in all things, when there shall be nothing but God alone' (5, 8).

In contemplation the soul becomes one with God; it becomes that which it beholds; it is that which it sees; indeed it discovers its true nature. So 'there are as many theophanies of God as there are faithful souls' (4, 7). 'Whoever rises to pure understanding becomes that which he understands. We, while we discuss together, in turn become one another. For, if I understand what you understand, I become your understanding, and in a certain inexplicable way I am made into you. And also when you entirely understand what I clearly understand you become my understanding, and from two understandings there arises one' (4, 9). So with God and the soul. And it is a two-way process. The soul finds God, and God also finds the soul. The soul finds itself in God, and God finds Himself in the soul. Erigena writes at the end of his great work: 'Let everyone use the light he has until that light comes which will make darkness out of the light of those who philosophize unworthily, and which will turn the darkness of those who welcome It into light' (5, 80).

Eschatology

Doctrine of the 'last' things, an important element in Jewish and Christian APOCALYPTIC, the mystical vision of the end of the world, and the coming of the perfect KINGDOM OF GOD. C. H. Dodd has drawn attention in the teaching of Jesus to an element of 'realized eschatology'. In some sense the last things have already come: 'If I by the finger of God cast out devils, then is the Kingdom of God come among you.' In Jesus, according to this view, the final victory over sin and death is already won.

Essenes

Jewish sect found in Palestine between the second century BC and the second century AD. They were an esoteric group with a novitiate lasting three years. The first of these was spent outside the community, but with the three symbols of the sect, a pure white robe, a girdle, and a dibber for burying excrement out of God's sight (the Essenes seem to have identified Yahweh with the sun). Two years of moral probation followed. Only then was the initiate admitted to the common life after stringent vows of secrecy. They were all male and all adult, admission being on profession of faith; they renounced sex and money. They had rigid standards of ceremonial purity. Their life was communistic, pietistic and ascetic. One of their mysteries certainly had to do with the immortality of the soul, which they believed to be caught in the body as in a prison. They believed in a place of punishment for the wicked after death, and peaceful homes for the righteous. The Dead Sea Scrolls, found in caves near Qumran between 1947 and 1956, probably belong to an Essene community; they include *The War of the Sons of Light against the Sons of Darkness* (as it has been called), which is apocalyptic in language and thought, and *The Manual of Discipline* giving the rules of the community.

Estella, Diego de
(1524–78)

Diego de Ballestero changed his name on becoming a Franciscan. He was a famous preacher. His work *De la Vanidad del Mundo* went through four editions in Spanish and was translated into Latin, French and Italian before 1600. God is for him the still centre of the turning world, and the soul, drawn to God by love, will not find stillness till it reaches the centre.

Eternity

An aspect of the Ultimate. Eternity is not to be understood as the indefinite extension of time, but as qualitatively different from the time we experience. PLATO once called time 'the moving image of eternity'. Time is regarded by the mystics as an obstacle to our knowledge of God. Thus ECKHART says, 'Time is what keeps the light from reaching us', and RUMI, 'Past and future veil God from our sight.' Eternity is best apprehended as a kind of perpetual present. Boethius in *The Consolation of Philosophy* says that God has always an eternal and present state, and uses this as a means of reconciling divine omniscience and human free will: 'His knowledge, surpassing time's notions, remains in the simplicity of His presence, and, comprehending the infinite of what is past and to come, considers all things as though they were in the act of being accomplished.' This is the state the mystic enters. 'The Sufi', says Rumi, 'is the son of time present,' and it is the united witness of the mystics that in mystical experience there is no sense of the passage of time.

Ethics, Mysticism and

In general there is no particular ethic associated with mysticism, and the mystics tend to expound the ethic of the religious system with which they themselves are familiar, with the exception that because the mystics usually have a particularly deep religious concern they are likely to take that ethical teaching to a level of profound commitment.

To this however four points must be added.

First, in the earlier stages of the mystic's journey, while he is on the PURGATIVE WAY, there is a strong tendency to ASCETICISM, simplicity, abstinence from sex and indeed the more violent mortifications of the flesh. Secondly, during this and the next stages of CONTEMPLATION many mystics turn away altogether from even good works and any concern with righteous living. The motive behind this is complex. It is partly that concentration even on good works is not concentration on God; partly that the effort for righteousness is a distraction from the contemplative life (Martha and Mary!); partly that there is a kind of Pauline sense that you cannot achieve goodness by effort and that it always eludes you if you pursue it but that you can receive it; partly that the mystics realize the danger of self-righteousness over virtuous living; partly that they see good works not as the road to God but as the fruit of union with God. Thirdly, there is singular unanimity among mystics all over the world of the need for unself-centred love. Fourthly, the highest stage of mysticism leads the mystic back into the world to share the fruits of his experience with others. So did the Buddha remain in compassion for forty and more years after his enlightenment. So did PLATO's philosopher return to the cave. So did Jesus and his disciples come down from the Mount of Transfiguration to the valley where healing was needed. So did TERESA DE JESUS record: 'The most surprising thing to me is that the sorrow and distress which such souls felt because they could not die and enjoy our Lord's presence are now exchanged for as fervent a desire of serving Him, of causing him to be praised, and of helping others to the utmost of their power.'

Eucharist

Literally 'Thanksgiving'. The central act of Christian worship, also called the Holy Communion, the Lord's Supper or the Mass. At his last meal with his disciples Jesus broke bread for them, saying 'This is my body', and poured out wine for them saying 'This is my blood', and told them to continue in those acts in remembrance of him. In receiving the consecrated bread and wine the believer believes that he is receiving Christ. Christian mystics have thus seen the eucharist as central to their experience of union with the Highest.

Euchites

See MESSALIANS.

Eudes, John
(1601–80)

French mystic, founder in 1643 of the Congregation of Jesus and Mary at Caen. He was, along-

An early Christian celebration of the Eucharist in a wall painting in the Catacomb of Calixtus, Rome

side MARGARET MARY ALACOQUE, responsible for introducing devotion to the Sacred Heart of Jesus, and encouraged devotion similarly to the Admirable Heart of the Mother of God.

Expansion

Mystical experience corresponding to hope in the neophyte, but presently powerful rather than related to the future. The state of expansion embraces the whole of creation; it is a state of awesome joy. But the mystics recognize it as dangerous, because centring on the self rather than on God, and recommend quiet self-discipline and concentration on God to those in this state. *See also* CONTRACTION.

Extra-sensory perception (ESP)

Experiments in the twentieth century by Myers and Soal in England and Rhine in America have gone far to proving scientifically the existence of different forms of extra-sensory perception. Experiments have been directed to four ends. First is telepathy, communication between psyche and psyche at a distance without external means. Only the most obdurate reject the evidence for this. The other three are more controversial. Second is prediction; this emerged accidentally, but some subjects seem to have shown a capacity for prediction beyond the range of chance-variation, and there are some impressive records of dream prediction (popularly expounded in J. W. Dunne's *An Experiment with Time*). Third is the identification of unseen material objects (e.g. cards placed face downwards). Fourth, and most controversial, is the control of the behaviour of material objects by thought-force. All these experiments suggest that the resources of the human psyche may not be developed to their full potential.

F

Family of Love

Christian sect, founded in Holland by Heinrich Niklaes (*c.* 1502–80), and influential for about a century in Holland and Britain. Niklaes was a brooding, imaginative, solitary boy, brought up in a religious hothouse and with a naïve precocity. At the age of eight he had his first vision, of a mountain of light enfolding him, so that he felt penetrated by the Spirit of God, and a subsequent revelation of the saints of God, which he took as a call to himself. When he grew up he prayed for nine years for God to 'reveal His perfect truth on the earth'. Then suddenly 'God appeared to him, enwrapt him, became one being with him, and communicated to him the hidden things of his Divine nature and of the spiritual nature of man. The Holy Spirit of Love was poured out upon him, and he felt himself chosen to be the revealer of the Word.' So he organized the Family of Love. Outward observances are nothing; he rejected them: 'You will find in experience that God with His Christ and Holy Spirit and with the heavenly fellowship of all the holy ones will inhabit in you and live and walk in you, for He has chosen no other house or temple for His habitation but you.' This experience will come from prayer, and waiting in silence and stillness. True LIGHT comes from receiving the true BEING of the Eternal Life, from the incorporation of the inward man into that Life, and so from living in LOVE. The Family of Love is God's more perfect way, a community of holy ones, a community standing apart from violence, war and wrangling of all kinds, the only true seed and witness of Jesus Christ in the world.

The Family were charged with antinomianism; but that is clearly unjust, and Niklaes is specific on the matter. A juster charge might be that of spiritual pride. But it was a remarkable attempt to form a community of practical mystics.

Fana

SUFI concept of dying-to-self, well illustrated by a prayer of ABU YAZID: 'Adorn me in Thy Unity, and clothe me in Thy Self, Lord, and raise me up to Thy Oneness, so that when Thy creation see me they will say, We have seen Thee; and Thou wilt be That, and I shall not be there at all.' ANSARI calls it 'the dissolution of everything except God'. It is the precondition of BAQA, eternal life. 'True *fana* is the vision of the relation of the worshipper to God most glorious, and true *baqa* is the vision of the relation of God to all worship.'

Fasting

Fasting is a common practice at different stages in most of the world's religions. It is often seen as a purification, a preparatory rite for initiation, communion or festival. The ancient Egyptians fasted before entering a temple. The Mexicans fasted for a day before sharing in the sacramental meal of Huitzilopochtli. Among the Lapps the officiant fasted before offering sacrifice. There was a three days' fast before the Peruvian festival of Raymi. In the Eleusinian Mysteries the initiate had to fast before sharing in the sacred draught. In the ritual of the Great Mother at Rome there was a day of fasting in mourning for Attis before the day of joy. Apuleius records three fasts of ten days each as necessary for initiation into the mysteries of ISIS.

Fasting is often regarded as a necessary preparation for visionary experiences. It is part of the puberty rites of the American Indian, enabling the young man on the threshold of adult life to discern his guardian spirit. It is part of the training and initiation of seers and divines all over the world. Part of their practice too: the Greek medical scholar Galen declares that dreams produced by fasting are clearer than others, the Zulus say succinctly, 'The overstuffed body cannot see secret things'. So among the Greeks oracular priestesses, and those who consulted them, alike fasted.

Old Testament revelations came to Moses or Elijah or Daniel after a period of fasting; so too the visions of Jesus in the wilderness. The Christian writer John Chrysostom asserts that fasting makes the soul brighter and provides it with wings to mount and soar.

Fasting is sometimes seen in penitential or ascetic terms; it is a deprivation of the body. THE QUR'AN stresses penitential fasting, as does the Old Testament. The SUFIS devote themselves to fasting as an ascetic practice, and it is common as part of the self-discipline of mystics of all religions.

The most remarkable authenticated case of prolonged fasting is a twentieth-century ecstatic named Theresa Neumann. According to the records she spent many years with no food or drink, except a daily morsel of the Communion Host. In 1927 a medical commission appointed by the Bishop of Regensburg kept her under strict observation for a fortnight. Certainly during this period she took no food or drink, but her weight, though fluctuating within the period, was the same at the end as at the beginning. Theresa Neumann had extreme ecstatic experiences each Friday, but otherwise was living a perfectly normal life.

Faustus, Dr

Georg Faust was a real man who died about 1540. He studied at Cracow, travelled widely in Europe, had a reputation for eccentric scholarship and miraculous power, was a homosexual and was described by Philip Melanchthon as a 'sewer filled with devils'. Within fifty years he had become a legendary figure (blurred with an earlier Johann Faust), skilled in medicine, who forsook theology, sold his soul to the Devil, enjoyed a remarkable career for twenty-four years and then went to eternal damnation. Christopher Marlowe found in this theme the expression of Renaissance yearnings, Goethe turned it into a profound meditation on life, and particularly the need to strive. Faust has often been seen as representative of man.

Fa-yen
(885–958)

Chinese ZEN Master, founder of the Fa-yen sect, one of the FIVE HOUSES. He was a man of immense learning both in Chinese traditional philosophy and in the classics of Buddhism, and a teacher of deep psychological insight.

Fénelon, François de Salignac de la Mothe
(1651–1715)

One of the greatest of all French thinkers, writers and educationists, he met Madame GUYON in 1688 and defended her against BOSSUET's attacks. He became Archbishop of Cambrai in 1695; and two years later brought out *Explanation of the Maxims of the Saints*, forty-five articles designed to distinguish true mysticism from false.

Fénelon uses two cardinal principles of analysis: disinterested love and passive contemplation.

There are five kinds of love for God: the servile love of God's gifts rather than Himself; the covetous love directed to God for the sake of happiness; the love which springs from hope (as distinct from desire); 'interested' love in which the pure love of God is still mixed with self-regard; disinterested love. He takes the three familiar ways of the mystics. In the purgative way, love is mixed with the fear of Hell; in the illuminative way, with the hope of Heaven; only in the highest state is pure and unadulterated love found. But the lower loves are not to be repudiated as sinful; they are stages on the way, and the highest stages which many reach in this life.

'Pure contemplation is negative, being occupied with no sensible image, no distinct and nameable idea; it stops only at the purely intellectual and abstract idea of being.' Yet at the same time Fénelon maintains with seeming inconsistency that pure contemplation includes all the attributes of God as distinct objects. The contradiction perhaps arises from his concern for Christian orthodoxy. 'Pure contemplation is never unintermittent in this life.'

Scattered through Fénelon's writing are many gems. For example, 'We pray as much as we desire, and we desire as much as we love', or 'A man's self is his own greatest cross'.

Fénelon sums up his distinction between true and false mysticism under seven heads.

1 The idea that man can live in a permanent state of complete union with God is 'a poisoned source of idleness and internal lethargy'.
2 The practice of each particular virtue is a necessary part of the religious life.
3 Perpetual contemplation is impossible.
4 Passive prayer, without the co-operation of the free will, is impossible.
5 There can be no quietude except that which is the fruit of the Holy Spirit, who works in such a way that His distinct acts may seem to the unenlightened to be a continuous state of union with God.
6 If hope is always with us, we are not in a permanent state of pure love.
7 Pure love in its perfection is seldom found and always intermittent.

Fénelon thus does justice to the genuine character of mystical experience without allowing it to lead to the neglect of other aspects of life.

Ferrar, Nicholas
(1592–1637)

English contemplative, an outstanding scholar who travelled abroad widely in his early twenties, then embarked on a career in politics and business, which he gave up in 1625 for the religious life. At LITTLE GIDDING in Huntingdonshire he established a community dedicated to common worship, prayer and vigils, ASCETICISM and self-discipline, and practical work in healing, education and bookbinding.

Fichte, Johann Gottlieb
(1762–1814)

German idealist philosopher and follower of Immanuel KANT. Fichte's teaching has been termed 'ethical pantheism'. According to him God is the Absolute Ego, the 'living operative moral order'. The Absolute Ego develops in three phases. In the first it posits itself; in the second it posits a non-ego over against itself; in the third it posits itself as limited by the non-ego. True religion, according to Fichte, consists in 'joyously doing right'.

In *The Guide to the Blessed Life* (1806) Fichte wrote a major introduction to the philosophy of mysticism. The title is important; this is an existential work. Fichte offers a speculative ontology: 'Being is absolutely single, not manifold; there are not several Beings, but one Being only. The obvious truth of this statement must be clear to anyone who can really think. Only Being is; on no account *is* anything which is not Being or which lies beyond Being.' Consciousness is the only possible mode of existence of BEING. Divine existence is pure thinking, and to be apprehended only by thought. 'Just as Being is One only and not several, as it is unchangeable and unchanging whole and all at once, and internally absolutely homogeneous, so also its "being there" means consciousness, since this exists only through Being, and its "being there" means that consciousness also is an absolutely eternal, unchangeable and unchanging homogeneous One.' Yet there arises, in contrast to this eternal unity of consciousness, an apparent multiplicity in thought, both of thinking subjects, and of the objects of thought. Fichte explains this by the analogy of the prism which breaks up the purity of light, which can however be concentrated again in a single unity. 'The whole diversity is here revealed as existing only for us and as a result of our limitation, but in no way as existing in itself or immediately in the divine Being.' He goes on, 'Since knowledge or we ourselves are this divine existence itself, so there can be in us, in so far as we are this existence no change or turning, no plurality and no multiplicity, no parting, differentiation or cleavage. . . . In consideration, however, of what we are in ourselves, we are by no means that Absolute Being. Only in so far as we are knowledge, are we at deepest the Divine Being.' All the religions must 'go so far that one is inwardly convinced of one's own Not-being, and one's Being solely in God and through God'. So 'the impulse to become united with and dissolved into the immortal is the deepest root of all mortal existence'. 'Blessedness is to rest and remain in the One. Misery is to be dispersed into multiplicity and differentiation. Therefore the condition of becoming blessed is the withdrawal of our love from the Many back to the One.'

Ficino, Marsilio
(1453–99)

Son to Cosimo de Medici's court physician; chosen by Cosimo while quite young to translate PLATO, instruct Cosimo in Plato's philosophy and be instrumental in re-establishing Plato's Academy in Renaissance Florence. Ficino came to Plato through a background of science, theosophy, Neo-Platonism and Christianity. He translated Plato, PLOTINUS and DIONYSIUS into Latin with massive commentaries, and systematized his own thought in *Plato's Theology concerned with the Immortality of the Soul*. Ficino identified religion and philosophy, because he identified God and TRUTH. He offered a picture of the universe, derived from Plotinus but original to himself. It has God or the One at the top, and body or matter at the bottom, with man or the rational soul at the centre in a position of mediation. Ficino's system is dynamic; he believed that the whole universe interacted and

Marsilio Ficino (far left) in Ghirlandaio's fresco in the church of Santa Maria Novella, Florence

that the human soul, which was immortal, reached down (through the sphere of 'qualities') to the body and up (through the sphere of the world-soul) to God. The aspiration of the soul to God is Love reaching up to the perfect Form of Beauty. True love between individuals is never in isolation. It is always a triangle with God as the apex. Ficino's leading disciple was PICO DELLA MIRANDOLA.

Filiger, Charles
(1863–1928)

French painter, associated with Gauguin in his young days. He exhibited at the SALON DE LA ROSE + CROIX, and of all French symbolists is the most mystical and idealist. He died in poverty and obscurity.

Fire

It is a common experience of mystics that they feel that they are being consumed by fire. Stanislaus Kostka had to apply cloths dipped in cold water to his breast in order to temper the violence of the love he felt. On one occasion on a bitterly cold day he cried, 'I am burning, I am burning!' MARIA MAGDALENA DE' PAZZI could not wear woollens in winter 'because of the fire of love burning inside her'. On one occasion the fire within her seemed to be consuming her from outside, and she had to dash to a well and soak her whole body. The mystical experiences of PHILIP NERI caused him in extreme winter to throw off the bedclothes, open the windows and fan himself. CATHERINE OF GENOA in her last illness had continual sensations of burning, as if she were on the pyre. According to her biographer a bowl of cold water was brought to her; she plunged her hands in it for relief and the water was perceptibly heated. For some hours after her death her body retained abnormal warmth.

The imagery of fire is commonly used to describe mystical experience. For fire is a symbol of immense energy. So MECHTILDE saw deity as a stream of fire flooding over the world. Fire burns away impurity, and makes the things set in it incandescent like itself. So RICHARD OF ST VICTOR compares the soul plunged into divine love with iron in the furnace transmuted into a different quality of being, and RUYSBROECK had a vision of union as 'every soul like a live coal burned up by God in the heart of His Infinite Love'.

Five Houses

Schools or traditions of South Chinese ZEN. The oldest, the Wei-yang sect, was short-lived. Its special feature was the use of circular figures to represent the enlightened mind. The Yün-men sect specialized in single-word answers to questions about enlightenment. The Fa-yen sect arose from another Master, whose technique was rather to repeat a word or phrase. The other two Houses are more important. The Ts'ao-tung sect (in Japanese Soto) was famous for the doctrine of the Five Ranks: the Absolute within the relative; the relative within the Absolute; the Absolute alone, the relative alone; the Absolute and relative in conjunction. The doctrine expresses the essential unity of Absolute and relative, of the Void and the world of appearances. Finally there is the Lin-chi (Japanese Rinzai) sect in which shouting and beating are used as a means to Truth and enlightenment.

Foucauld, Charles Eugène de
(1858–1916)

Christian mystic. As a young man he lived a casual life, then was seized with a passion for exploration and ventured through Morocco. From physical exploration he passed to spiritual exploration, became for a time a Trappist, and lived in monasteries in Palestine. He returned to France, became a priest and settled to a life of meditation and neighbourly love in an oasis in the Sahara, where he was eventually assassinated.

Fox, George
(1624–91)

Founder of the SOCIETY OF FRIENDS. In 1643 he heard the voice of God: 'Thou seest how young people go together in vanity, and old people into the earth; thou must forsake all, young and old, and be as a stranger to all', and like GAUTAMA, he left home in search of enlightenment. Three years later, in dependence on the INNER LIGHT, he found it. From that point he set himself to preach in obedience to a command 'to turn people to that inward light, spirit and grace by which all might know their salvation and their way to God'. He faced persecution, riots and imprisonment with courageous faith and a refusal to meet evil with evil. His magnetism attracted followers whom he gathered in lasting fellowship. He lived simply, being known by his broad-brimmed hat (which he refused to doff except in prayer) and his leathern breeches. Fox's strength was that he had discovered the power of Jesus Christ 'experimentally', as he put it, 'without the help of any man, book or writing'. All his life he remained sensitive to the voice of God within him, to the inward Light. In his *Journal* he speaks of 'openings' (revelations) he has received. Sometimes they are visual, of an ocean of light flowing over an ocean of darkness, or of the mountains burning up; sometimes they are spiritual truths (as that to be bred at Oxbridge was not sufficient to fit a man to be a minister of Christ!). Contemporaries testify to his depth of spirit, to his power in prayer, to the love with which he countered evil. His teaching is fundamentally simple: that there is something of the Divine Spirit, the inward light, in every human being; that everyone can make direct contact with God without paid priest or set ritual; and that Christianity is a way of life, entering into everyday concerns. In a letter he writes of the inner world where 'live that doth not change, the unchangeable Life, the unchangeable Mind, the unchangeable Spirit and Wisdom, and the unchangeable worship and church of which Christ is the unchangeable head'.

Francesca Romana
(1384–1440)

Francesca Bussa di Lion was born in Rome, and, despite her desire to become a religious, married at the age of 13. In 1425 she founded the Oblates of Mary, and eleven years later, on her husband's death, became their superior. She had visions of her guardian angel in later life, which perhaps accounts for her becoming the patron saint of motorists.

Francis of Assisi
(1182–1226)

Rich, gay, open-handed, Francis Bernadone succumbed when twenty-two to a serious illness. For a period he lived in darkness; he could not recapture his former joy. He sought it in a new sensitivity to his fellow-men, which led him to kiss the wounds of a leper, or to identify himself with a line of beggars. Then one day while at prayer his eyes became riveted on the eyes of Jesus in the crucifix. He saw the figure move, speak, demand his life. Now he made a decisive choice of his Father in Heaven above Pietro Bernadone. Hearing the passage in which Jesus commissions his disciples to go out without material resources to preach and heal, he felt it as a personal commission. He took Poverty as his bride, he went out preaching 'in words like fire, penetrating the heart', and he practised the love which he preached. In self-abnegation he recovered his joyfulness. Followers began to join him. In 1210 the Pope authorized the formation of an order to live the apostolic life subject to the authority of the Church. This was followed by an order for women, and a third order of those who would commit themselves to the life of joyful and loving service without leaving home.

Francis was one of the great spiritual geniuses, and among all Christians seems closest to his Master. He had the gift of healing; he had an immense power of ascetic self-discipline combined with a boundless joy. He had a genuine humility. Because of his joyfulness and his humility his rebuke was terrible. He had a deep spiritual insight into the needs of others and an almost hypnotic power over them. He called his followers to love and to gladness; he called them to act as 'mirrors of perfection'. All this sprang from his own spiritual life. That life was supported by two great mystical experiences. The first was when the figure of Christ in the Church of S. Damiano cried to him, 'Francis, go and repair my church which, as you see, is falling down.' The second was towards the end of his life, in 1224. Brother Leo found Francis in ecstasy. As he watched he seemed to see a flaming torch descend from the sky and touch Francis as he knelt. He called his companions, and they watched and waited. Francis was praying for two gifts, to feel the passion of Christ in his body, and to feel in his heart the love that bore that passion. Suddenly a great glow illuminated the scene; it was visible from a long way; villagers thought dawn had broken and set out for work. In that brilliant light Francis had a radiant vision of Christ crucified. The vision lasted for over an hour. When the light faded Francis found on his hands, feet and side marks like the wounds of Christ. Two things must be said of this experience: firstly, that Francis was no hysterical exhibitionist, and tried to keep secret what had happened; second, that there is overwhelming contemporary evidence of the existence of the wounds on his body. See STIGMATIZATION.

Francis had a profound sense of the revelation of God in all creation; all are children of God, all brothers and sisters. Many stories reflect this, the preaching to the birds, or the taming of the ferocious wolf of Gubbio. This mystical joy comes out in the hymn called 'The Canticle of the Sun', written out of pain and weakness which would have led most men to despair:

St Francis of Assisi in ecstasy, as painted by Giovanni Bellini

Most High, Omnipotent, Good Lord,
Praise, glory and honour be given to Thee with one accord!

To Thee alone, Most High, does praise belong,
Yet none is worthy to make of Thee his song.

Be praised, my Lord, with all Thy works whatever they be,
Our noble Brother Sun especially,
Whose brightness makes the light by which we see,
And he is fair and radiant, splendid and free,
A likeness and a type, Most High, of Thee.

Be praised, my Lord, for Sister Moon and every Star
That Thou hast formed to shine so clear from heaven afar.

Be praised, my Lord, for Brother Wind and Air,
Breezes and clouds, and weather foul or fair –
To every one that breathes Thou givest a share.

Be praised, my Lord, for Sister Water, sure
None is so useful, lowly, chaste and pure.

Be praised, my Lord, for Brother Fire, whose light
Thou madest to illuminate the night,
And he is fair and jolly, strong and bright.

Be praised, my Lord, for Sister Earth our Mother,
Who nourishes and gives us food and fodder,
And the green grass and flowers of every colour.

During a violent civil dispute he told the friars to add:

Be praised, my Lord, for those who for Thy love forgive,
Contented unavenged in quiet to live.
Blest those who in the way of peace are found –
By Thee, O Lord Most High, they shall be crowned!

Right at the end he concluded his song:

Be praised, my Lord, for our Sister Bodily Death,
From whom none can escape that has drawn breath.
'Woe to those dying in mortal sin!' He saith.
Blest those who find that in Thy holy Will
The second Death to them will bring no ill.

Praise ye and bless my Lord, and do Him service due,
With humblest thanks for all that He has done for you.

(tr. F. C. Burkitt; slightly altered)

Franck, Sebastian
(1499–1542)

One of the earliest Protestant mystics, a voluminous writer who passed from the Catholic priesthood to the Lutheran pastorate, and eventually to a kind of liberal Christian humanism. To Franck, God is the first Cause and inmost Essence of all things. He is above all speech and all thought. We experience Him as personal, but that is on account of our experience, not of Him. He expresses Himself through the world but remains transcendent. In the end we can approach Him only through the VIA NEGATIVA.

François de Sales
(1567–1622)

François came from Savoy, and studied in Paris and Padua. He had the secular world at his feet, but felt an overwhelming call to the priesthood. He became Bishop of Geneva and was a spiritual spearhead in the Catholic counter-attack on Calvinism. François was noted for his simplicity and directness; his preaching was from the heart to the heart, and his writing has the same directness. His spiritual advice given to individuals was collected and given more general form in two notable volumes, *Introduction to the Devout Life* and *Treatise on the Love of God*. One outstanding feature is his rejection of élitism: 'It is an error – no, a heresy – to wish to banish the devout life from the army, from the workshop, from the courts of princes, from the households of married folk.' François writes for the ordinary Christian: 'Wherever we are, we may and ought to aspire to the perfect life.' So he offers what was later called the Salesian method of meditation, to lead the soul 'from her first desire for the devout life until she be brought to a full resolution to embrace it'.

The Salesian method begins from preparation, the practice of the presence of God, everywhere and in everything, the realization of the special sense in which He is in the heart, the use of the imagination to see Him at our side, and prayer for grace. Then follows the consideration or MEDITATION proper, introduced, if appropriate, by the use of the imagination on the subject; we must be ready either to concentrate intensively on a single theme, or allow our thought to pass to related themes. Third come resolutions; a true meditation will excite our love for God and man, our repentance, faith and zeal, and these affections must be 'expanded and extended' and given concrete expression. Fourth come thanksgiving, self-offering and prayer for strength. Finally there is a piece of advice which illustrates well

François de Sales

why François has proved such an attractive adviser: 'One should gather a little nosegay of devotion' – pick out one or two salient points in our meditation – 'in order to remember them throughout the day, and to inhale their perfume spiritually.'

François has much else to offer by way of practical wisdom. He is as firm as Seneca on the possibility of retreating within one's own mind from the clamour of the world and the pressures of business. He recommends the regular repetition, at different times of the day, of these words: 'I am no longer my own: whether I live or die, I belong to my Saviour; I have no longer any dominion over me or mine; my *self* is Jesus; my *mine* is to be his. O World, you are always yourself, and I have always been myself, but henceforth I will be myself no longer.' The kernel of François's devotional life is there. François was spiritual director to JEANNE FRANÇOISE DE CHANTAL, and instrumental with her in founding the order of the VISITANDINES.

Freemasonry

Originally a religious fraternity of English masons, perhaps in the twelfth century, under the protection of John the Baptist, guarding the craft-mysteries. Later concerned with the moral and religious education of its members. Abolished in 1547, it was re-established, and spread to many other countries. In Catholic countries it tended to become associated with Deism and hostile to organized Christianity; in Protestant countries its undogmatic religion co-existed with the Churches, and membership often overlaps. Freemasonry offers a kind of modern mystery religion with initiation into a secret cult by symbolic tests of courage and endurance, and participation in a strictly formulaic ritual. But there is no promise of exclusive salvation. Symbolic association with masonry has been retained, and God is seen as the great Architect. The organization today combines innocent social pleasure, a touch of élitism, a bit of pageantry, a general belief in religion and a certain amount of philanthropy. The official account in Germany describes freemasonry as 'the activity of closely united men who, employing symbolical forms borrowed principally from the mason's trade and from architecture, work for the welfare of mankind, striving morally to ennoble themselves and others, and thereby to bring about a universal league of mankind, which they aspire to exhibit even now on a small scale'. Freemasonry inspired one great work of art, Mozart's THE MAGIC FLUTE.

Friends of God

'Friend of God' is a phrase applied scripturally to Abraham (Exod. 33, 11; Jas 2, 23); more important, Jesus called his disciples 'friends' (Jn 15, 15). Early Christian writers take up these passages: CLEMENT OF ALEXANDRIA and John Chrysostom call the martyrs 'friends of God'. In Islam Abraham is called the Friend of God.

The phrase was widely used by TAULER and other German mystics of the fourteenth century. It does not seem that the *Gottesfreunde* was ever a formally constituted society. The word was applied among themselves to mystics who had attained the highest stage of the contemplative life, and who formed a kind of spiritual élite within the Church. The Friends of God tend to be practical and anti-intellectual, to take a pessimistic view of the world, to stress ascetic practices and complete submission to the will of God. They stand against the libertarian attitudes which they associate with the BRETHREN OF THE FREE SPIRIT. There is a strong element of renunciation in their attitudes. Two stories well illustrate this. One Friend of God in the state of surrender heard a voice, 'Permit me, my beloved child, to share in you and with you all the riches of my divinity, all the passionate love of my humanity, all the joys of the Holy Spirit.' The visionary replied: 'Yes, Lord, I permit you, on condition that you alone shall enjoy it, not I.' In the other story a Friend of God saw his Lord offering him the kiss of Divine Love. The Friend replied: 'I do not want to have it, for the joy of it would flood my heart so that I should lose consciousness, and then I could no longer serve you.'

For a remarkable treatise associated with the Friends see BOOK OF THE NINE ROCKS.

G

Galgani, Gemma
(1878–1903)

Italian ecstatic, born of a simple family. She was refused acceptance as a Passionist nun, but made her own private vows. She was a visionary, sometimes suffering experience of the presence of devils, more frequently enjoying spiritual raptures. In her self-identification with the passion of Christ marks of scourging appeared on her back and she experienced STIGMATIZATION.

Gardeil, Ambroise
(1859–1931)

French Dominican, who worked for a period in West Africa, and subsequently helped to found the *Revue Thomiste*, important not least for his influence on Reginald GARRIGOU-LAGRANGE and for his work *La Structure de l'âme et l'expérience mystique*, the product of a lifetime of spiritual experience.

Garrigou-Lagrange, Réginald
(1877–1964)

Dominican theologian and philosopher, author of an authoritative commentary on the *Summa* of THOMAS AQUINAS, and of a major work, *Dieu, son existence et sa nature* (1915), in which he defended the ontological validity of first principles. He was the author of a number of important spiritual treatises, giving a Thomastic account of the spiritual life, and urging the universal call to holiness and the mystical life. Among the more important of these are *Perfection chrétienne et contemplation* (1923); *Les trois conversions et les trois voies* (1933); *Les trois âges de la intérieure* (1941); *De sanctificatione sacerdotum secundum exigentias temporis nostri* (1947); *De unione sacerdotis cum Christo Sacerdote et Victima* (1948).

Gautama
(*c.* 563–483 BC)

Family name of Indian prince, founder of BUDDHISM, also known by his personal name Siddhartha, or by a nickname Sakyamuni (sage of the Sakyas'). Many legends grew up around his birth and early life. According to one story a sage predicted that he would be a world-ruler or, if he should see a decrepit old man, a diseased man, a dead man and a monk, he would become a homeless wanderer. The king tried to shield him, but he saw his four signs, learned the lesson of the vanity of earthly things and in the Great Renunciation gave up his privileges. He went in search of liberation, but did not find it in the wisdom of sages or the asceticism of eremites. He sat in meditation under a tree. All day he faced one temptation after another and overmastered them. Then in the dark he received enlightenment, became the Buddha, or enlightened one, and attained NIRVANA. He stayed for a period under the Tree of Enlightenment, and then in compassion for mankind for forty-five years travelled through India preaching and making converts. The life he proclaimed is a middle way between sensuality and mortification of the flesh; it includes reverence for all life, the refusal to meet evil with evil, the positive values of love and compassion. Eventually he faced the Great Decease, left his parting words to his disciples ('All compound things are subject to decay: strive with earnestness') and through a

Gautama Buddha. A Chinese Sui (AD 593) dynasty bronze altar group

series of trances attained PARANIRVANA, 'complete *nirvana*', the escape from the weary wheel of birth and death.

George, Stefan
(1868–1933)

German poet, who made extensive use of symbolism, and wrote with deliberate eccentricity. His early verses manifest some mystical poses, not least in his devotion to *die Herrin*, the Mistress of Vision. But George's thought is solidly rooted in the sensible world. In 1895, in *Die Bücher der Hirten- und Preisgedichte*, he has three sections – ancient Greek, mediaeval, oriental: spirit, soul, body. Then in 1901 he met a brilliant, handsome, precocious boy named Maximin, who died three years later. Maximin became for George a symbol. In *Der siebente Ring* (*The Seventh Ring*) (1907) he portrayed Maximin as the harbinger of a new age. There is something Platonic in George's attitude; he starts from *eros*, love for Maximin; but it lifts him to a realm of spiritual vision. But the vision could not bear the weight he placed on it, and his own lyrical springs seemed to dry up. He wrote poems extolling the coming of war, and poems of disillusion with war. Then at last something seems to return, and with it for the first time perhaps a mystical vision. In 'The Man and the Satyr' man's rationality is seen as empty, and the last word is with the Satyr: 'It is through magic alone that life stays awake.' And in the last poem of his last collection, he writes of walking in mystical union with an ideal being, a kind of perfected Maximin:

> You who are pure as flame and slender,
> You shoot from fine strain flowering,
> You like the dawn serene and tender,
> You like a simple, secret spring.
>
> My fellow through the sunlit meadows,
> Thrill round me when eve darkeneth,
> Lighting my path among the shadows,
> You cooling wind, you fiery breath.
>
> You are my longing and my thinking,
> I breathe you in all air that is,
> I sip you when my lips are drinking,
> In every fragrance find your kiss.
>
> You like the dawn serene and tender,
> You like a simple, secret spring,
> You who are pure as flame and slender,
> You shoot from fine strain flowering.
>
> *(tr. C. M. Bowra)*

Gerson, Jean le Charlier de
(1363–1429)

Gerson was born in the Ardennes, and studied in Paris, to which he returned after a spell in Bruges. Later, however, through the hostility of the Duke of Burgundy, he was forced away first to Vienna and finally to Lyons. Living in a turbulent period, he was deeply concerned with the reform of the Church, which he hoped to achieve through spiritual renewal.

His main mystical writings were *The Mountain of Contemplation*, *Mystical Theology*, *The Perfection of the Heart* and commentaries on the Magnificat and *The Song of Songs*. He is a synthesizer rather than an original thinker. According to Gerson there are three kinds of theology, symbolical, natural and mystical; and the last, which depends on inner experiences, affords the greatest certainty. The cognitive power has three faculties: sense-perception, understanding (which bridges the sensible and intelligible worlds), and the intelligence or illumination which comes from God. Corresponding to these are the affective faculties of emotion, rational desire and SYNTERESIS, and the activities of thought, meditation and contemplation. Mystical theology depends on the affective, not on the cognitive faculties; it arises from faith and love and leads to peace of mind. Its means are seven: the call of God, certainty of being called to the contemplative life, freedom from encumbrances, concentration upon God, perseverance, ASCETICISM, withdrawal from sense-perception.

Gertrude 'the Great'
(1256–1301)

One of the great German mystical nuns, who gave herself to a life of contemplation after a vivid experience at the age of twenty-five, and left a record of her revelations in *The Ambassador of Divine Piety* as well as some powerful personal prayers. Her visionary experiences were mostly associated with the offices of the Church. Her devotional life was focused upon the Sacred Heart of Jesus, which was the object of her deepest mystical experiences.

al-Ghazali, Abu Hamid Muhammad ibn Muhammad
(1059–1111)

One of the greatest Islamic scholars, theologian, lawyer and philosopher, he was nicknamed 'The Proof of Islam'. He was for a time a pillar of orthodoxy, but was dissatisfied with his public life, withdrew, studied the Sufis and their approach and was converted to them. In an autobiographical writing he tells how he went as far as he could by intellectual study: 'as for the rest, there was no way of coming to it except by leading the mystical life'. He was surrounded by worldly interests. All, even his teaching, 'seemed unimportant and useless in view of the life hereafter'. He had to renounce the desire for worldly fame, and take refuge with God alone. The rest of his life was that of a mystical ascetic. But the habit of writing was strong with him, and he expounded his new-found mystical faith in a series of works, of which the most celebrated is *The Revival of the Religious Sciences*. This consists of four volumes. The first is concerned with worship: the nature of knowledge and the foundations of belief; an extended section on the spiritual meaning of the Islamic rituals of purification, prayer, almsgiving and pilgrimage; and the devotional duties. The second volume deals with personal behaviour, and passes from practical advice about everyday matters, such as eating, drinking and earning a living, to the elements of mystical training – companionship, character, withdrawal, travel, ECSTASY through works of art, wise counselling, prophetic gifts. Volume three deals with the deadly sins: gluttony and sensuality; the sins of the tongue; anger, malice and envy; setting too much value on worldly goods; riches and avarice; pride in position and hypocrisy; arrogance and conceit; pride. Finally there is al-Ghazali's own exposition of the Sufi road to salvation: conversion; patience and gratitude; fear and hope; poverty and self-denial; belief in the One True God and trust in him; love, yearning, intimacy and satisfaction; resolution, truthfulness and sincerity; contemplation and self-examination; meditation; and reflection on death. He calls the mystical experience an ascent 'from the nadir of metaphor to the zenith of truth'. At the summit the mystics 'see with a direct vision that there is nothing in existence except God the One'. All things except God are of themselves pure Not-Being, but they have an existence which permeates them from the primal reality. For those who have this vision plurality falls away. They are 'drowned in pure solitude'. Nothing is left to them but God. They are spiritual drunkards, in a state of FANA. They are unconscious of themselves, unconscious of their unconsciousness of themselves. They are in a state of union. 'Beyond these truths there are further mysteries which it is not permitted to penetrate.' It is interesting to compare this with al-Qushairi's scheme (outlined under SUFISM) of half a century earlier. The significant points are the same, but al-Ghazali has grouped them in a way which must reflect his own analytical mind, and his own mystical experience as well.

Ghost dance

Religious movement among North American Indians beginning about 1870 in California with a visionary named Wodziwob, who prophesied that the dance would lead to the resurrection of all the dead Indians on a renewed earth, free from death, disease and misery. About 1890 another visionary, Wovoka, was responsible for a fresh wave of interest, though this time on the other side of the Rockies, among the Arapaho, Cheyenne, Pawnee and Sioux. There was a strong nationalist and political element about the revival, which was in part a reaction against white domination; at the same time Wovoka repudiated war and called his followers to live at peace with all men; the power of the dance, not their weapons, would eliminate white power. The notorious Battle of Wounded Knee in 1890 was a massacre of Indians whose leaders were dancing, not fighting. Alexander Lesser eloquently recaptured the mood of the Indians: 'Into this situation of cultural decay and gradual darkness, the Ghost Dance doctrine shone like a bright light. Indian ways were not gone, never to be recovered. Indian ways were coming back. Those who had lived before in the "golden age" were still carrying on the old ceremonies, old dances, old performances, and old games in the beyond. They were coming back; they were bringing the old ways and the buffalo. Dance, dance, dance. The white man would be destroyed by a great wind. The Indian would be left with the buffalo, with his ancestors, with his old friends and his old enemies. Cast aside the white man's ways like an old garment; put on the clothes of the Indian again. Get ready for the new day and the old times.'

Gichtel, Johann Georg
(1638–1710)

German Protestant visionary who lived most of his life in Amsterdam, and published the first complete edition of Jakob BOEHME, being himself deeply influenced by Boehme's thought.

Giotto di Bondone
(*c.* 1266–1337)

Italian artist and architect, a superb draughtsman who broke with the traditions of Byzantine art to tell complex human stories in a visually persuasive way. In this he might seem the most unmystical of artists. But his very gift of humanity in the service of the Christian faith made the meeting of divine and human more powerful. His masterpieces are the frescoes at Assisi portraying the life of FRANCIS and the frescoes in the Cappella degli Scrovegni at Padua showing the life-story first of Mary and then of Jesus. From Assisi we may perhaps pick out *The Driving of the Demons from Arezzo* (in which we are at first arrested by the forceful gesture of the friar but soon realize that the power is through Francis kneeling in prayer behind, as the lines of the picture make clear), *The Miracle of the Spring* (in which Francis rapt in prayer has not noticed the miracle) and the exquisite *Sermon to the Birds*; from Padua, to mention only two, *The Sacrifice of Joachim* (where the firm actuality of the angel shows the incarnational quality of the mystical experience, while the shepherd-boy's upward gaze points the meeting of the eternal and the temporal) and *Noli Me Tangere* (where the wind of resurrection sweeps new life through the dark sky, and Jesus moving towards freedom and light looks back towards Mary as she kneels in ecstasy; their hands reach out to one another without touching, but between them new plants spring up on the same mountain).

Gita

See BHAGAVAD GITA.

Glossolalia

See SPEAKING WITH TONGUES.

Gnosis

Greek term for 'knowledge', applied especially to revealed religious truth. *See* GNOSTICISM, and, for a more explicitly Christian *gnosis*, CLEMENT OF ALEXANDRIA.

Gnosticism

Mystical theosophy emerging in Syria and Egypt in the second century AD. Before that we can discern similar tendencies, but nothing systematic. Gnosticism blends together strands of thought from the East, from Mesopotamia, Persia and even India; from Greece, especially Platonism and some Hellenistic speculation; and from Judaism and Christianity.

Gnosticism is a world-rejecting religion. It espouses a thorough-going dualism. God stands in opposition to the world, which was formed by an anti-god (who is identified with the Old Testament Yahweh). Alongside the God-world dichotomy are three others: spirit-soul (*pneuma-psyche*), light-darkness (deriving from Zoroastrianism), life-death. Gnostic systems commonly have a complex mythology of a cosmic fall, the imprisonment of the soul in matter, and the emergence of a saviour. The soul needs LIBERATION; liberation comes from *gnosis*, certain knowledge, contrasted with *pistis*, mere faith. Liberation requires a liberator; he is often seen as Christ, but because of the evil in matter the Gnostics tend to distinguish between the spiritual Christ and the physical body of Jesus of Nazareth. *Gnosis* comes from revealed knowledge: in this sense Gnosticism is one of the mystery religions.

An intaglio engraved with Gnostic symbols, found at Ephesus

Man is a being with a divine spark, fallen into the world of matter, estranged and needing to be awakened by a divine call so as to be restored to his highest state.

Gnostic systems will be found under BASILIDES, ENCRATITES, MANDAEANS, MANICHAEISM and VALENTINUS; and Gnostic writings under THE GOSPEL OF TRUTH and THE HYMN OF THE PEARL. Other Gnostic sects were associated with the figures of Simon Magus and of Marcion. Hans Jonas has called the Gnostics the first speculative theologians in the new age of religion which superseded classical antiquity.

God

Term used for the Ultimate Being, usually conceived as personal or not less than personal. 'What is God?' asks BERNARD. 'I can think of no better answer than, He who is.' It is difficult to see how it is possible to make meaningful statements about the Ultimate, but characteristic language describes God as infinite, eternal, First Cause, Source, One, almighty or omnipotent, all-wise or omniscient, all-good, all-compassionate. Typical images for God are King, Father (or sometimes Father and Mother), Creator or Architect and (in mystical experience) Bridegroom; among impersonal images, FIRE and LIGHT. Two important concepts for mystical religion are those of God as LOVE and as the Universal Self.

Important distinctions between different beliefs in God are those between *monotheism* (belief in one God, strong in Judaism and Islam), and *polytheism* (belief in many gods, who may however be regarded as different manifestations of the one God, or as subordinate ministers of the God of gods); and between *deism* (belief in a remote creator), *theism* (belief in a personal God at work within his world), PANENTHEISM (belief that everything has its being in God, and that God is immanent within all parts of his creation) and PANTHEISM (belief that God is identical with the universe). Much mystical thought is pantheistic or panentheistic.

Some mystical approaches accept the impossibility of describing the Infinite in finite language, and follow the VIA NEGATIVA: the Universal Self is soundless, formless, intangible, tasteless, odourless, without parts, without actions, without motion. It is in fact 'Not this, not that'.

W. T. Stace has argued that mystical experience requires five minimum characteristics if the Universal Self is to be called God. First, God must be living and conscious; second, He must be capable of serving as the goal of mystical aspiration; third, He must be such as to arouse a sense of holiness, of the numinous; fourth, He must be thought of as the ultimate Source of all values and of all goodness. Fifth, He must be thought of as the source of the world. It will be observed that these are parallel to some of the philosophical arguments for the existence of God. The mystics are however not concerned with philosophical arguments but with direct experience.

Some mystics make an important distinction between the Godhead, God in His eternal nature, and God as revealed to us. A similar distinction is made by Greek Christian mystics between the unknowable Essence of God and His revealed 'energies'.

Not all mystics link their mystical experiences with God. Buddhism is a mystical religion without a personal god. Some nature-mystics are at least vague in their language. Richard JEFFERIES is clear: he does not believe in a god, though he speaks of 'the unutterable existence infinitely higher than duty'. Jefferies is unusual, but he shows that mysticism is not incompatible with atheism.

Godhead

Term used by some mystics to refer to the absolute, unknowable Essence of the Deity, by contrast with the term God which stands for the Deity in His revelation of Himself. ECKHART says, 'God and Godhead are as distinct as heaven and earth. Heaven stands a thousand miles above the earth, and even so the Godhead is above God.'

Gospel According to Thomas, The

A fourth-century Coptic manuscript, discovered near Nag Hammadi in Upper Egypt in 1945, containing 114 sayings of Jesus, showing him as the centre and source of a mystical *gnosis*. The gospel begins: 'These are the secret words which Jesus the living one spoke.' In one episode Jesus, as in the New Testament, asks the disciples who he is. Thomas, in expressing his inability to answer, calls him Master. Jesus answers, 'I am not your Master [they have received his revelation and are one with him] for you have been drinking; you are intoxicated with the bubbling spring which belongs to me and which I have spread abroad.' Then he takes Thomas aside and speaks three secret words to him. These were no doubt *Kaulakau*, *Saulasau* and *Zeesar*, corruptions of the Hebrew of Isaiah 28, 10, and interpreted in Gnostic circles as meaning primal man, mortal man and the Jordan which flows upwards. Another interesting variant on a New Testament story comes when Jesus says, 'Give Caesar what is Caesar's; give God what is God's; and give me what is mine!' This shows that in Thomas 'God' is the creator of the visible world, but not the Ultimate Source of all goodness, of which Jesus is the unique revelation. Jesus in this gospel stresses that the revelation is to the few: 'I tell my mysteries to those who are worthy of my mysteries.' 'Many stand outside the door, but it is only the single ones who enter the bridal chamber.' 'There are many around the opening but no one in the well' (this last said by a disciple). One of the most powerful mystical sayings in the collection is 'Images appear to man, but the light which is in them is hidden in the image of the Father's light. He will reveal himself; his image is concealed by his light.'

Gospel of Truth, The

GNOSTIC scripture, plausibly attributed to VALENTINUS, and discovered at Nag-Hammadi in 1945–6. It begins, 'The gospel of truth is joy to those who have received from the Father of truth the gift of knowing him by the power of the Logos, who has come from the pleroma and who is in the thought and mind of the Father, he it is who is called "the Saviour", since that is the name of the work which he must do for the redemption of those who have now known the Father.' *The Gospel of Truth* is a fairly straightforward reinterpretation of Christian doctrine. Men are drunk in darkness, dreaming nightmares, oblivious of their origin and destiny. Salvation, through knowledge, is offered by Jesus Christ. Error tried to destroy him, but TRUTH and Knowledge cannot be destroyed.

Grail

Holy vessel conferring mystical blessings to those who look on it, sometimes identified with the cup of the Last Supper of Jesus, and an object of mystical quest. It is the theme of many mediaeval romances, but its origins are uncertain. Some authorities suggest that they lie in Celtic folklore, others that the story is a Christianized version of initiation into an ancient Near Eastern mystery-cult. In the prehistory of the Grail it is given by Christ to Joseph of Arimathea and brought to England by one Brons. At some point it becomes mixed up with the Arthurian cycle, and the quest for it belongs to Gawain or Perceval (Wagner's PARSIFAL) or Galahad. It is protected by the Fisher King, and it is one of three symbols or talismans, the others being a sword and spear; associated with the quest is often an awe-inspiring adventure in the Chapel Perilous, whose explanation is part of the 'holy secret' of the Grail (this certainly reads like part of an initiation ceremony). In the oldest versions the Grail was a kind of cornucopia supplying food and drink. Later its powers become spiritual: it separates the pure from the impure with blessings for the former. Even here purity is differently interpreted: in some versions it is ascetic chastity, in others loving charity. But ecclesiastical authority never looked kindly on the story.

Greco, El
(1541–1614)

Domenikos Theotokopoulos, better known as El Greco, 'the Greek', was born in Crete, and trained in Venice; but the years of his greatness lay in Spain. He is the most visionary of painters: the quality shines even from the early *Mt Sinai*. Forty years later he painted *Toledo* on a canvas now in the Metropolitan Museum, New York,

The Burial of Count Orgaz, *painted by El Greco in 1586*

as a visionary cataclysmic eschatological scene. His most remarkable works are those where he sees through from earth to Heaven; these may be exemplified by the superb *Burial of Count Orgaz* of 1586, in Toledo, where realism and vision interact and the human and divine worlds interpenetrate. Little less remarkable is *The Fifth Seal of the Apocalypse*, also in New York, though this has been mutilated: still the figure of John remains one of the most remarkable portrayals of ECSTASY.

Gregory of Nyssa
(*c.* 335–95)

Gregory, whose brother Basil revolutionized Christian monasticism, is the most mystical of the Greek Christian Fathers. In his mysticism we may single out four features. First, his insistence that the outward universe is a symbol of the unseen; that the visible world is the garment and drapery of God. Gregory is a Christian Platonist and he is seeking to express an aspect of Platonic thought in Christian terms. But there are practical conclusions for the contemplative who seeks to find God through the world. Secondly, and also Platonically, he has a magnificent chapter on the ascent to Spiritual Beauty. The object is 'to become oneself as beautiful as the Beauty which he has touched and entered, and to be made bright and luminous oneself in communion with the real Light', to be changed into something better than we are, and so with clearer vision to see God, the archetype of all Beauty. Thirdly, man's essential being is like God. This is associated with an ancient Greek notion that like perceives like and attracts like. The soul is by a strict necessity attracted to the Deity who is its kin, and God grapples to Himself the soul which belongs to Him and drags it out of the material and the irrational (cf. Plato, *Theaet.* 176B). Finally, Gregory gives his Platonism a Christian content in linking the ultimate mystical experience with the sacrament of communion; the divine bread and wine nourish the divine life, so that by communion with Deity mankind may be deified.

Gregory I
(*c.* 540–604)

Gregory 'the Great' was born of rich parents, but sold his property for the poor and became a monk in a monastery of his own foundation. After various responsibilities, including service in Constantinople, he became pope in 590. He made peace with the Lombards, established the temporal power of the Bishop of Rome, challenged the claims of the Constantinople patriarch, sent missionaries to the British ('angels not Angles'), fostered monasticism, engaged in works of charity, proved himself a consummate administrator and wrote unceasingly.

Gregory the Great in his study, painted in 983

Man, fallen as he is, cannot know God in His perfect Being. He can prepare himself by asceticism and good works, but the act of revelation is God's and God's alone. CONTEMPLATION is the gift of God, not the achievement of man; though 'the greatness of contemplation can be given to none but them that love' (Hom. in Ez. 2, 5, 17). The divine Spirit lifts the soul and the intelligence beyond its function of animating the body and above its normal modes of apprehension, to view through love the beauty of the Creator. That beauty is displayed in boundless, infinite LIGHT: this is Gregory's favourite and continual image.

But the human soul is still enslaved by the body, and cannot long stand the dazzling brilliance of the divine Light. It tires and falls back, as if struck by lightning. So it falls back into its mortal life in knowledge of its own unworthiness. But now that human life brings dissatisfaction, a hatred of its imperfections, a yearning for perfection, a dialectic of fear and hope.

How far Gregory was himself a mystic is uncertain. There is only one certainly autobiographical passage: 'My sad mind, labouring under the soreness of its engagements, remembers how it went with me formerly in the monastery, how all perishable things were beneath it, how it rose above all that was transitory, and, though still in the body, went out in contemplation beyond the bars of the flesh' (*Dial.* I Pref.). But though his analysis of mystical contemplation owes something to AUGUSTINE, it is hard not to think that he is analysing experience of his own.

Grignion de Montfort, Louis Marie
(1673–1716)

French Christian mystic noted for his influential *Treatise on True Devotion to the Holy Virgin*, and for his practical work in fostering missions, and the work of education and healing.

Groote, Geert de
(1340–84)

Born in Deventer of wealthy parents, he studied in Paris and taught at Cologne, following a successful worldly career. An unknown FRIEND OF GOD came up to him and said, 'Why are you standing here? You ought to become another man.' A dangerous illness brought Groote face to face with death. In 1379 he went out as a humble preacher, speaking in the vernacular out of personal experience. For five years he drew the people. But his success was a challenge to the establishment, and his licence to preach was withdrawn. He formed communities, simple, spiritual, practical, engaging in education and social service, rooted in personal religious experience – the BRETHREN OF THE COMMON LIFE – and so effectively created the DEVOTIO MODERNA. Groote was not an ecstatic, but he believed from his own life that 'the Holy Spirit inwardly visits, illumines, and changes the heart of a man' and finally 'incorporates the man into himself'. He himself tried to practise the imitation of Christ, and THOMAS À KEMPIS's great work was seemingly based on Groote's notebooks. Groote died, as he lived, in the service of others, contracting the plague from a brother he was nursing.

Grou, Jean
(1731–1803)

French Jesuit, who died in exile at Lulworth. His first major work was a translation of PLATO; later he wrote a succession of works on the inner life, of which the best known is *Maximes Spirituelles, avec des Explications* (*Spiritual Maxims with a Commentary*) and *L'Intérieur de Jésus et de Marie.* (*The Inner Life of Jesus and Mary*). He himself lived a life of humble and prayerful simplicity; and among the more touching and self-revealing passages is his account of 'simple prayer', 'in which the mind has no other object than a confused and general idea of God; the heart no other feeling than a sweet and peaceful taste of God, which nourishes it without any effort, as infants are nourished by milk. The soul then perceives so little of her operations, so subtle are they and delicate, that it seems to her that she is slothful and plunged into a kind of sleep.' He continually stresses the need for the soul which pursues the inner life to repress its natural activity and to abandon itself to God.

Guérinists

See ILLUMINÉS.

Guyon, Madame
(1648–1717)

Jeanne Marie Bouvier de la Mothe was an emotional girl, married at the age of sixteen to a man more than twice her age, Jacques Guyon. Her emotionalism, her husband's invalidism and the unhappiness of her marriage drove her on to her inner resources, and after her husband's death in 1676 she entered a life of religious devotion. Her approach was influenced by MOLINOS. She herself was a voluminous writer; most important among her works are *Brief and very easy means for praying* (1685) and *The Song of Songs* (1688). She was attacked by the great BOSSUET, defended by her disciple FÉNELON, condemned, imprisoned and finally released.

Madame Guyon lived the devotional life in such a way that mystical experience became for her almost a normal occurrence; and even Bossuet never doubted her sincerity. Typical is her declaration that 'My Spirit disenthralled became united with and lost in God. And this was so much the case that I seemed to see and know God only and not myself.' The nature of her QUIETISM is well seen in Cowper's version of her hymn on 'The Acquiescence of Pure Love'.

Love! If Thy destined sacrifice am I,
  Come, slay Thy victim, and prepare
    Thy fires;
Plunged in Thy depths of mercy, let me die
  The death which every soul that loves
    desires!

I watch my hours, and see them fleet away;
  The time is long that I have languished
    here;
Yet all my thoughts Thy purposes obey,
  With no reluctance, cheerful and
    sincere.

To me 'tis equal, whether Love ordain
  My life or death, appoint me pain or
    ease.
My soul perceives no real ill in pain;
  In ease or health no real good she sees.

One Good she covets, and that Good alone;
  To choose Thy will, from selfish bias
    free
And to prefer a cottage to a throne,
  And grief to comfort, if it pleases Thee.

That we should bear the cross is Thy
  command,
  Die to the world, and live to self no
    more;
Suffer unmoved beneath the rudest hand,
  As pleased when shipwrecked as when
    safe on shore.

She taught complete indifference, not merely to the external world, but even to eternal salvation; and the annihilation of all distinctions, even among the revelation of God in the life of Christ. The highest mystical experience she called the 'apostolic state'.

H

Hadewijch
(*c.* 1150–1200)

Prioress of the Premonstratensian convent of Meer in Prussia. Little else is known about her historically. Eleven *Visions* give an account of her mystical experiences, which included the experience of oneness with God. Her letters contain a mystical understanding of God's love. Her poems are among the earliest mediaeval mystic love-lyrics: she uses the images and language of courtly love for the divine Love.

Hafiz, Shams al-Din Muhammad
(*c.* 1326–90)

The greatest of Persian lyric poets, and therefore one of the greatest of all lyric poets. Hafiz came from Shiraz, spent his early days in poverty and sang of wine and love. Hafiz has always been a figure of superstitious respect; and his poems, like the Bible and Vergil, have been used as oracles by being opened at random. Sufis claim that he was a mystical poet, that intoxication represents mystical ecstasy and the Beloved stands for God. Recent European scholarship has tended to take the poems literally. It is important to see that these are not mutually exclusive, and Sufi literature often allows interpretation at various levels. One example must serve: the last line points the deeper level.

> When my Beloved the cup in hand taketh
> The market of lovely ones slack demand
> taketh
>
> I, like a fish, in the ocean am fallen,
> Till me with the hook yonder Friend to
> land taketh.
>
> Every one saith, who her tipsy eye seeth,
> 'Where is a shrieve, that this fair firebrand
> taketh?'
>
> Lo at her feet in lament am I fallen,
> Till the Beloved me by the hand taketh.
>
> Happy his heart who, like Hafiz, a goblet
> Of wine of the Prime Fore-eternal's brand
> taketh.

(tr. J. Payne)

A modern Persian critic has said of him, 'Hafiz's spiritual greatness and mental power proceeded from that mystical consciousness which in him attained perfection.'

Hakuin
(1685–1768)

Japanese ZEN master. He had his first mystical experience at the age of twenty-four, and they thereafter continued through life. He was a great educator: he was also poet, artist, preacher and reformer, and endowed with a winsome personality. He originated the famous *koan* which reads: 'If someone claps both his hands, you hear a sound straightaway. Now listen to the sound of a single hand.' He summed up his philosophy under the three mystical states of the Great Doubt, the Great Enlightenment, the Great Joy.

Hal

Moslem term for a mental condition, 'now', and so ECSTASY, a religious experience interpreted as a direct visitation from the Divinity. Sometimes, at the graves of Moslem saints for example, *hal* takes a violent physical form, in which the body is contorted, and the person may shout, foam at the mouth and dance wildly, and seems impervious to normal injury. Some of the more orthodox frown on these extreme manifestations, but approve of gentler forms of ecstasy.

al-Hallaj, Mansur
(857–922)

Born in Fars, the son of a wool-carder, he early showed himself concerned with spiritual truth. At the age of twenty he emigrated to Basra, where he became a Sufi. He also married, remaining monogamous all his life. He travelled widely to Baghdad and Mecca, and as far as India and Turkestan, laying aside the garb of the Sufi (which had an inhibiting effect on the company), preaching the message that everyone should find God in his own heart, and calling himself 'the carder of consciences'. He is perhaps the supreme example of the 'intoxicated' Sufi. He was utterly dedicated to the will of God. To him are due the concepts of mystical intoxication, irradiation, enclosed solitude, open solitude and others, including BAQA and FANA, whose first identification and definition come from him. On his last pilgrimage he prayed that God should reduce him to nothing, so that all might be God. Because the highest mystical experience lies in reunion with God, he claimed that man may be seen as God and the revelation of God, taking Jesus as his example. He did not claim to be divine himself, but his assertion on his final return to Baghdad, 'Ana 'l Haqq' ('I am the Creative Truth') comes near it: 'If you do not recognize God, at least recognize His signs. I am that Sign. I am the Creative Truth, because through the Truth I am a truth eternally.' He was denounced for claiming mystical union with God, condemned and crucified, identifying himself with Jesus on the cross and foreseeing his resurrection. His last words were, 'All that matters for the ecstatic is that the Unique should reduce him to Unity', followed by *Qur'an* 42, 18.

Hallucination

A perception without objective reality. Such perceptions are not frequent among normally sane people, though it has been suggested that perhaps one person in five experiences a vivid hallucination at some point in his life, sometimes under the pain of internal disease. Hallucinations may be induced by drugs, and possibly also by the physical deprivations of extreme asceticism. Some religious visions may be explicable on these terms; there are others which do not seem to conform with the usual conditions.

Hammarskjöld, Dag
(1905–61)

International statesman from Sweden who became Secretary-General of the United Nations and died mysteriously in a plane crash during the Congo crisis, leaving behind him the manuscript of his personal and intense spiritual diary, kept over more than thirty years. There are three striking features of this diary, subsequently published under the title *Markings*. First, his spiritual experience was at its deepest during his years at the UN: he himself wrote: 'For many of us in this era the road to holiness necessarily passes through the world of action.' Secondly, he had read the mystics. He quotes from THOMAS À KEMPIS and ECKHART and JUAN DE LA CRUZ. He had *The Imitation of Christ* with him at his death. He said of them: 'Love, for them, was a surplus of power which they felt completely fitted them when they began to live in self-forgetfulness.' But, thirdly, his experience was his own. He said: 'There is no formula to teach us how to arrive at maturity, and there is no grammar for the language of the inner life.' And he plainly passed through some great mystical experience without at the time realizing it. But he wrote afterwards: 'I don't know who – or what – put the question. I don't know when it was put. I don't even remember answering. But at some moment I did answer Yes to Someone – or Something – and from that hour I was certain that existence is meaningful and that therefore my life in self-surrender had a goal.'

Hare Krishna Movement

See KRISHNA CONSCIOUSNESS MOVEMENT.

Hashish

A drug derived from dried flowers of hemp, most commonly smoked, but sometimes taken in the form of pills, leading to intoxication and persistent and exalting hallucinations. It has been widely used at all times in Asia: its use in Europe and North America is the subject of current controversy. Its Mexican name is marijuana. The English word 'assassin' is derived from 'hashishi': those who became intoxicated by the drug and committed violent actions.

A 15th-century Persian lady using a hookah to smoke a form of hashish. A miniature illustrating the Persian Kama Sastri

Hasidism

The word *hasid* means 'pious', and the *hasidim* appear in the Jewish *Psalms* as a general term for the righteous; in the Maccabaean period as a group of quietist ascetics whose strong adherence to the Law led them into opposition to Antiochus, but later also to Judas, and who perhaps contributed to the Essene movement. The term recurs from time to time to refer to pietistic groups.

In mediaeval Germany Hasidism was the most important factor in the development of Jewry. The Hasidim were wider in their approach than other Jewish mystics. They combined mystical vision whose object was God's unity, with exegetical speculation, practical ethics, mystical prayer, a system of penitence and a theology of suffering. The end is the true fear and pure love of God, and at the highest level the two coincide. The Hasid is the man who turns his back on the community and his face to God, and so paradoxically becomes a better servant of the community. To the Hasid God is at once the closest and the most distant, manifest and at the same time hidden, transcendent and yet immanent: 'Everything is in Thee, and Thou art in everything; Thou fillest and encompassest everything; when everything was created, Thou wast in everything; before everything was created, Thou wast everything.'

In the middle of the eighteenth century a new Hasidism emerged through the genius of Israel BAAL SHEM. In the last half of the century, through it there appeared a shining cluster of mystical saints. To them was due the wider spread of the Kabbalistic idea of a mystical relationship to God as the highest thing in life; with them the experience of enthusiasm or ecstasy was linked with a popular revival and interpreted in Kabbalistic terms. The leader of each community was known as the *tsaddiq* or righteous one, and was believed to have a special relationship to the divine Spirit, which might take the form of miraculous power. But their distinctive contribution lay in linking mystical experience to ethical value: Martin Buber described Hasidism as 'Kabbalism become ethos'. The exemplar of ethical value lay in the life of the Hasidic saint. This meant a reduced concentration on the *Torah*, and led to charges of antinomianism against the Hasidim. It also meant that the Hasid's life counted for more than his learning. A disciple said of one Hasid: 'I did not go to him to learn Torah from him but to watch him tie up his bootlaces.'

There is a touching story of the inheritance of the Hasidim. When the Baal Shem had a difficult task to face he would go to a particular place in the woods, light a fire, meditate in prayer, and his problem was solved. A generation later the Maggid of Mesentz would go to the same place in the woods, and say, 'We can no longer light the fire but we can pray the prayer', and in that he found his solution. After another generation Rabbi Moshe Leib of Sassov said 'We cannot light the fire; we do not know the secret meditations; but we can go to the place in the woods', and in going there he found his solution. Yet another generation, and Rabbi Israel of Rishin did not leave his seat. He said 'We cannot light the fire; we cannot speak the prayers; we do not know the place; but we can tell the story.' In that verbal re-enactment of the mystic's experience he too found the answer.

Heat

The idea of mystical heat is found in Vedic texts, and is important both in YOGA and TANTRA. The heat is induced by techniques of holding the breath, and by the transmutation of sexual energy. One initiatory ordeal consists in the capacity of a candidate to dry wet sheets on his naked body during a water storm. Mystical heat is part of the mastery over fire possessed by the SHAMANS. But in some parts of the world, in Malaysia for example, such heat is the province of black magic only.

See also FIRE.

Heaven

In theistic religion, the dwelling-place of God or the gods; in mystical religion, the ultimate destination of the righteous, or those initiated to salvation. In the 'three-tier' universe Heaven is generally identified with the sky (hence ASCENSION); though in some mystery religions the blessed are envisaged as living below the earth or on the surface of the earth, e.g. in the Isles of the Blessed; and Heaven is reserved for the gods. With greater sophistication Heaven is regarded less spatially. Heaven is wherever God is, not just 'up there'. As *The Cloud of Unknowing* puts it, 'heaven ghostly is as nigh down as up, and up as down; behind as before, before as behind, on one side as other'. Introspective mysticism finds Heaven within the soul, just as Milton's Satan cries 'Which way I fly is hell; myself am hell.' Heaven is in fact not a place but a state or condition, the state of union with God or at least of life lived in God's continual presence. Benjamin Whichcote, father of the CAMBRIDGE PLATONISTS, succeeds in having it both ways: 'Heaven is *first* a Temper, and *then* a Place.' The Buddhist NIRVANA is often regarded as equivalent to Heaven. It is picturesquely described as the opposite bank of a river, but the picture melts away into a condition of blissful liberation.

Hegel, Georg Wilhelm Friedrich

(1770–1831)

German philosopher of Absolute Idealism, voluminous and difficult. He held that 'the real is the rational and the rational is the real' and offered an evolutionary view of the universe progressing as a thesis is challenged by an antithesis, and out of the conflict emerges a higher synthesis, which in turn becomes the thesis of a new stage of dialectic. He is thus a philosopher of BECOMING. But in the end all is submerged in the ABSOLUTE, which is (as one critic put it) 'the lion's den to which all footprints tend and from which none return'. For Hegel only the Whole is real. Hegel applied his dialectic to religion. Oriental religion is pantheistic, God is everything, man nothing. Greek religion is naturalistic, man is everything, and the gods are human beings writ large. Christianity, centring on the God-man Christ, and finding the infinite in the finite, offers the synthesis. But Christianity in turn is only a stage in the eternal progress of the Idea, which Hegel

Georg Friedrich Hegel in his study

thought had come to a full consciousness in his own philosophy, which he thus saw as a kind of mystical revelation.

Heiler, Friedrich
(1892–)

German Christian, converted from Catholicism to Lutheranism, much influenced by von HÜGEL, and author of a major work on prayer, *Das Gebet* (1918), which covers all forms of prayer from inarticulate incantation to mystic union.

Hekhaloth

See MERKABAH.

Heraclitus
(*c*. 544–484 BC)

Ancient Greek mystical philosopher, noted in antiquity for his gnomic obscurity ('He was fond of concealing his metaphysics in the language of the Mysteries' – CLEMENT OF ALEXANDRIA). Interpretation is controversial, but he seems to have propounded a dialectical philosophy by which there is a unity through a conflict of opposites: 'Things taken together are whole and not whole, something which is being brought together and brought apart, which is in harmony and discord. Out of all things comes a unity, and out of a unity all things.' 'God is day and night, winter and summer, war and peace, satiety and hunger.' Everything is in a state of flux, as the waters of a river are always changing. But there is a principle of balance, the sort of power of tension we find in a bow or lyre, unseen but real. There is, he seems to say, an underlying rationality, for which he uses the word LOGOS. Heraclitus's philosophy is a religious philosophy. There is a continual interaction by which immortals become mortals, and mortals immortals. Gods are everywhere: he was once sitting in the kitchen and invited visitors in, saying, 'Here too are gods.' Real understanding is to be found only in the divine nature, which Heraclitus equated with FIRE. Fire would judge the world. A man's guardian divinity was his own character, and the best soul was the 'driest', the one nearest to fire. The virtuous soul would be finally absorbed in the cosmic fire. Heraclitus is something of a pessimist, critical of conventional religion, critical of contemporary politicians, contemptuous of human illusions.

Herbert, George
(1593–1633)

Christian pastor and poet, whose posthumous volume *The Temple: Sacred Poems and Private Ejaculations* affected all subsequent mystical verse in England. In 'The Elixer' he holds, as firmly as Brother LAWRENCE, to the practice of the presence of God:

> Teach me, my God and King,
> In all things Thee to see.

In 'Love Bade Me Welcome' there is a conceit of the type Herbert loved, an unexpressed pun on 'host'. Love is the 'host' at the EUCHARIST. Above all, his poems express a continuing dialogue with Christ.

Hermeticism

From Egypt there have survived eighteen tractates, generally known as the *Corpus Hermeticum*, the scriptures of a small mystic sect which honoured the Egyptian god Thoth identified with the Greek Hermes under the title Trismegistos 'Thrice-Greatest'. They date from the first centuries AD. They bring together wisdom from Egypt, Greece and Asia. Two of the tractates, the first, *Poimandres* (*Shepherd of Men*), and the thirteenth, *The Secret Discourse on the Mountain*, are of special importance. All are concerned to declare a divine revelation. Initiation began with a call to repentance: this is what the seventh tractate is about. So in *Poimandres*: 'Repent, you who have journeyed with error and joined company with ignorance; rid yourselves of darkness and grasp light; forsake corruption and partake of immortality.' Then came personal instruction. The initiate was required to turn away from ignorance, grief, intemperance, sensuality, injustice, avarice, folly, envy, deceit, anger, impetuosity and malice, and to embrace knowledge of God, joy, self-control, continence, righteousness, generosity, truth, goodness, life and light. This involved ascetic self-discipline. 'It is not possible, my son, to attach yourself both to things mortal and to things divine. There are two sorts of things, the corporeal and the incorporeal; that which is mortal is of one sort, and that which is divine is the other sort; and he who wills to make his choice is left free to choose the one or the other.' From this discipline the initiate passed to silent meditation: 'Do not speak, but keep solemn silence; so will the mercy come down on us from God.' 'Then only will you see the vision, when you cannot speak of it, for the knowledge of it is deep silence, and suppression of all the senses.' The climax was an ecstatic vision of LIGHT, delightful and joyous: that Light is described as 'the first God'. 'This alone, the knowledge of God, is man's salvation; this is the ascent to Olympus; by this alone can a soul become good.' The experience is one of rebirth. 'I can tell you nothing but this; I see that by God's mercy there has come to be in me a form which is not fashioned out of matter, and I have passed out of myself and entered into an immortal body! I am not now the man I was; I have been born again in spirit, and the bodily shape which was mine before has been put away from me. I am no longer an object coloured and tangible, a thing of special dimensions; I am now alien to all this, and to all that you perceive when you gaze with bodily eyesight. To such eyes as yours, my son, I am not now visible.' The result of this rebirth is a sense of identity with all creation, with earth, water and air, animals and plants. More, it is to enter into God. 'We must not be frightened of affirming that a man on earth is a mortal god, and that a god in heaven is an immortal man.'

Hesychasm

The word means precisely QUIETISM and is applied to a system of Christian mysticism evolved within the Orthodox Church by the monks of Mt Athos in the fourteenth century. A hesychast is 'one who in silence devotes himself to inner recollection and private prayer'. The movement claimed as its father SYMEON OF STUDION, 'the new theologian'. The object was the vision of the Divine Light, the Energy not the Essence of the Godhead, and the method ascetic practices, complete quiet of mind and body, breathing and posture directed to quietude (somewhat as in YOGA), and repetition of the formula 'Lord Jesus Christ, Son of God, have mercy upon me.' The movement was involved in controversy partly because of its claim that God's Essence was inaccessible and was not the subject of the BEATIFIC VISION, partly for its replacement of the authority of tradition by inner illumination. Its greatest exponent was Gregory PALAMAS.

Hildegarde of Bingen
(1098–1179)

Benedictine nun, the first great mystic of Germany. She was a visionary, and says of her visions, 'These visions which I saw, I beheld neither in sleep, nor in dream, nor in madness, nor with the eyes of the body, nor with physical ears, nor in hidden places, but wakeful, alert, with the eyes of the spirit and with inward ears, I perceived them in open view and according to the will of God.' She speaks of a blazing red light: 'From my infancy up to the present time, I now being more than seventy years of age, I have always seen this light, in my spirit and not with external eyes, nor with any thoughts of my heart, nor with help from my senses. But my outward eyes remain open and the other corporeal senses retain their activity. The light which I see is not located, but yet it is more brilliant than the sun, nor can I examine its height, length or breadth, and I name it "the cloud of the living light". . . . But sometimes I behold within this light another light which I name "the living light itself". And when I look upon it every sadness and pain vanishes from my memory, so that I am again as a simple maid and not as an old woman.' Hildegarde was an ecstatic with healing power; she was also a woman of high intelligence and practical competence. She was something of a scientist, something of a theologian, something of a poet. Her correspondents included popes and emperors. No less a person than BERNARD OF CLAIRVAUX commended her visions and prayed for her intercession: 'I trust that when you are united to God in the Spirit you will be able to help and profit us much.'

Hildegarde of Bingen with Volmer, her secretary. A 12th-century German illustration in a book recording her visions

Hilton, Walter
(d. 1396)

Little is known for sure of Hilton's life. He was ordained to the priesthood, studied at Cambridge, had a short period as a solitary eremite, and became an Augustinian canon. His masterpiece is *The Scale of Perfection* or (better) *The Ladder of Perfection*.

Book I is specific to a particular disciple. It begins with a contrast between the lives of action and contemplation, speaks of the central virtues of humility, faith and love, gives an account of different forms of prayer, analyses the difficulties and dangers which beset the path of the would-be contemplative and gives some guidance as to moral and ascetic discipline. Book II is general. It falls into four main sections. The first is an examination of regeneration in faith and feeling within the sacramental life of the Christian Church. The second is an allegorical depiction of the contemplative's progress in terms of a pilgrimage to Jerusalem. The third is an account of the relationship between God and the soul in mystical experience, in which all comes from

God. The fourth expounds more fully the gifts of the contemplative life in knowledge and love.

Essential to Hilton's thought is the idea of the image, taken from PAUL. This is linked with the idea of regeneration. We are formed in the image of the earthly man; through regeneration we need to be reformed in the image of the heavenly. God is best known when he is discerned in the soul which he has reformed after his image. Mystical experience involves self-effacing love ('I am nought. I have nought. I coveite nought bot on' [i.e. 'but one']. All is of God: 'luf informed, that is God himself, is cause of al this knowynge. He is both the gifer and the gifte, and makith us than bi that gifte for to knowen and lufen him.') Hilton's explicit expressions are naturally couched in Christian language; he speaks for example of the name of Jesu; but he goes on to make clear that he does not mean a kind of magical combination of letters, but 'al goodnesse, endles wisdom, luf and swetnesse, thi joye, thi wurschip, and thin ay lastende blis, thi God, thi Lord, and thi salvation'.

Hilton's religion is not élitist; he continually insists that mystical experience is not reserved for the select few, but is part of the normal growth of the Christian life.

The first printed edition calls his work 'This hevenly boke more precyous than golde'.

Hinduism

Predominant religion of India. Sir Charles Eliot said of it, 'Hinduism has not been made but has grown. It is a jungle, not a building.' Consequently it is possible to find within Hinduism the proliferation of rites and images; and the rejection of all externals; animal and even human sacrifice, and the prohibition of taking the life even of an insect; an extreme polytheism and a high monotheism. The oldest books, The *Vedas*, show a polytheistic system with various gods. Mystical teaching becomes very strong in the UPANISHADS and the BHAGAVAD GITA, in popular legends and devotional groups, and (in very different ways) in the philosophical systems of SANKARA and RAMANUJA. The meditative practices of YOGA, and the personal devotion of BHAKTI grew up within Hinduism.

Hippie

The derivation of the word is uncertain; perhaps a variant on the swinging 'hep-cat' of the 1930s, whose derivation is equally unknown. Used in the 1950s to describe a group in America, mainly middle-class or upper-class, mainly young, who were seeking an alternative way of life to that offered in contemporary American society. Some retreated to country wilds; others formed urban communities, as in Haight-Ashbury, San Francisco. Yablonsky reckoned in the late 1960s that of the true hippies up to 15 per cent were priests or full initiates, about 35 per cent novices, and the rest hangers-on of various kinds, including drug addicts. The true hippie is not a drug addict, but uses marijuana and LSD 'sacramentally' in pursuit of new levels of religious or spiritual experience. A broad characterization of hippie philosophy would include a search for God in man through drugs; a strong belief in the power of love, which comes as a consequence of finding all people and all nature as one with oneself and God; an uninhibited but not promiscuous attitude to sex; and the conviction that 'You can't change anyone else – you can only change yourself.' Religious attitudes are often an amalgam of New Testament Christianity (but a rejection of the twentieth-century Church), ZEN Buddhism, Hindu mysticism and Chinese philosophy.

Hitlahavut

Jewish term for the burning or ardour of ECSTASY, climax of the mystical experience of the HASIDIM. *Hitlahavut* is not a state, but an ascent, which takes its possessor above nature, time and thought. The past and future become present. He discerns the meaning of life. The world is to him only the strength and glory of the Creator. He is in holiness. He moves from strength to strength upward and upward until he comes to the root of all teaching and all command, to the I of God, the simple unity and boundlessness. Then he becomes detached from all being. He can no longer become inflamed; he is all FIRE.

Hölderlin, Johann Christian Friedrich
(1770–1843)

German lyric poet of erratic but undoubted genius. His poetry has been described as 'the record of a unique spiritual experience of a profoundly religious character'. Love played a part in this: he had an unhappy love for Suzette Gontard, wife of a Frankfurt banker. So did his admiration for the ancient Greeks, whose ideal harmony (as he saw it) he yearned to restore but knew he could not. So did an almost mystical sense of incompleteness, seen clearly in his verse play *Empedocles*, itself unfinished. He was mentally unstable, but at the same time something of a visionary, and his later poems, especially 'Patmos', show the vision of an earth renewed and restored:

> Too long, too long already
> Has the glory of the Blessed been viewless.
> For almost must they guide
> Our fingers for us, and basely
> A mighty force teareth our heart from us.
> For each of the Blessed demand sacrifice.
> Yet if one were passed over
> Ne'er did it bring about good.
> We have served the earth our mother
> And of late we have served
> The light of the sun
> Unwittingly, but the Father who rules over
> all

Loves best that the constant Letter be
  fostered,
And enduring existence
Interpreted well. With this is accordant
The song of my people.

(tr. R. F. C. Hull)

With Hölderlin, one feels more than with any other poet, that a craftsmanship which is his own is allied to an inspiration from without. It has been said of him that 'the finest of his odes were certainly written at a time when his contact with reality was strained'. It depends on what you mean by reality; he might have claimed the reverse.

Holy insecurity

Term coined by Martin Buber for one aspect of genuine religious experience which 'comes when our existence becomes incomprehensible and uncanny, when all security is shattered through the mystery'. This is associated with the fear of God which leads to the love of God. Buber contrasts the state of holy insecurity with the defensive position of those who grasp at an infallible book, an infallible Church, or who in other ways try to make of God a kind of private possession; this is to run from insecurity into a more paralysing fear. The open man has no ready-made answers, but in making his insecurity holy, he comes to terms with it.

Holy Spirit

The spirit of God is important in the Old Testament, moving on the face of the waters in *Genesis*, inspiring prophets and men of action, the source of holiness, moral purity and wisdom, the power of life. In the New Testament, the Spirit is seen to descend on Jesus at his baptism. Jesus promises the disciples the gift of the Spirit. At Pentecost the disciples had an ecstatic experience which they associated with the coming of the Spirit. Through the book of *Acts* and the theology of PAUL, the Spirit, called the Holy Spirit, the Spirit of God, or the Spirit of Christ, appears as the active and inspiring presence of God, sometimes manifested through ecstatic utterance or unusual powers. After this the sense of the presence of the Spirit becomes dimmer, though it was revived by the MONTANISTS. Towards the end of the fourth century a group known as the Pneumatomachi or Macedonians denied the divinity of the Spirit. The descent of the Spirit is celebrated on Whit Sunday: numerous hymns for that day begin with 'Come'. John WESLEY was particularly insistent on regeneration through the power of the Holy Spirit and on the need for the continued presence of the Spirit for right living. In the PENTECOSTAL churches there is an ecstatic awareness of the Spirit.

Gerard Manley Hopkins aged 15. A watercolour portrait painted by a member of his family

Hopkins, Gerard Manley
(1844–89)

Jesuit, scholar and religious poet whose intensity of passion is linked with precise observation and matched by originality of vocabulary and rhythmic structure. His most ambitious poem 'The Wreck of the Deutschland', occasioned by a shipwreck in which five nuns were drowned, begins

Thou mastering me
God! giver of breath and bread;
World's strand, sway of the sea . . .

He describes himself there as 'soft sift in an hourglass'. He sees God, or Christ, or man's spirit, in and through all nature; the falcon hovering in the wind, the harvest under the silk-sack clouds, the dare-gale skylark, the moonrise, the starlight night with its circle-citadels, the very air we breathe, speak to him of things ultimate. He praises God for all dappled things.

The world is charged with the grandeur of
  God.
    It will flame out, like shining from shook
      foil . . .

And Nature is never spent

Because the Holy Ghost over the bent
    World broods with warm breast and
      with ah! bright wings.

But Hopkins is not only a nature-mystic, as we see in 'The Habit of Perfection':

Elected Silence, sing to me
And beat upon my whorlèd ear . . .

He called on his fellows to give God glory alike in prayer and work: 'He is so great that all things give him glory if you mean they should. So then, my brethren, live.'

Hua-yen

See KEGON

Hügel, Baron Friedrich von
(1852–1925)

The son of an Austrian statesman and a Scottish mother converted from Presbyterianism to Catholicism, von Hügel was brought up in Florence, Brussels and Torquay by an Anglican governess, a Lutheran tutor and a Catholic scholar. He lived most of his life in England, though travelling widely. In early life he experienced a religious crisis; he later acknowledged his debt to the Jesuits in bringing him back to faith. He was associated with the Modernist movement, but escaped the official censure which others suffered. In 1908 he published his great study *The Mystical Element of Religion as studied in St Catherine of Genoa and her Friends*. But, while sympathetic to mysticism, he was suspicious of MONISM in any form, as destructive of man's sense of God's transcendence and his own utter dependence. The three aspects of religion, the Mystical, the Intellectual and the Institutional, are all 'necessary parts of the whole'.

Hugh of St Victor
(*c.* 1096–1141)

Founder of the school of contemplatives at the abbey of St Victor in Paris. He has a vivid description of his own experiences: 'Suddenly I feel myself transformed and changed; it is joy unspeakable. My mind is exhilarated; I lose the memory of past trials; my intelligence is clarified; my desires are satisfied. I grasp something inwardly as with the embracement of love.' Like BERNARD OF CLAIRVAUX he fostered reading, meditation, prayer, contemplation and action conjointly and in proportion. He speaks of three grades of knowledge: cogitation, when the image of a thing arises suddenly through senses or from the memory; MEDITATION, which is the attempt to penetrate the hidden; CONTEMPLATION, in which the hidden has become manifest and can be comprehended and enjoyed. Contemplation is of two kinds: one, 'for beginners', considers creatures; the higher contemplates the Creator. Hugh's greatest follower was RICHARD OF ST VICTOR.

Hui Hai
(8th century AD)

Chinese ZEN Master, known as 'the Great Pearl'. It was in dialogue with an earlier Master, Ma Tsu, that he 'realized his mind'. He composed a treatise on SUDDEN ILLUMINATION which led the older man, punning upon his disciple's former name Chu, to say 'In Yueh Chou there is now a great pearl; its lustre penetrates everywhere freely and without obstruction.' Hui Hai is notable for his use of dialogue in exposition, and for his care to relate his own advanced mysticism to traditional Buddhist scriptures.

Hui-Neng
(638–713)

Hui-neng came from a poor home in southern China and, moved by hearing the Diamond Sutra, went north in search of enlightenment. He was given the work of pounding rice for the Buddhist brotherhood. The mastership was to pass to the man who could best prove his mastery of the religion. The most brilliant of the brotherhood, Shen-hsiu, proclaimed:

This body is the Bodhi-tree,
The soul is like a bright mirror;
Take care to keep it always clean
And do not let dust collect on it.

But the simple rice-pounder capped this:

The Bodhi is not like a tree;
There is no brightly shining mirror;
As there is nothing from the first,
Where can the dust collect?

This showed a much more profound grasp, and Hui-neng became the Zen master. He is often regarded as the real founder of Chinese Buddhism for he approached it as a Chinese, not as an Indian. For him Zen was 'seeing into one's own nature'. This had practical consequences for his mystical approach. He was for example no great believer in long periods of withdrawn meditation; better, so to speak, to catch the self in the act. Hence some of the intuitive abruptness of his teaching. He did not use metaphysical or traditional mystical language. On the contrary, like Jesus, he used immediately familiar terminology, which it is easier to grasp than to explicate. For example a monk asked him for instruction: his reply was 'Show me your original face before you were born.' The answer is easy to grasp, impossible to explain.

Curiously, one of his major contributions was to see the mind as the mirror of reality; for this he was named 'Zen Master of the Great Mirror'. It follows that the mind must be removed from reflecting the material world; then it will shine with primal purity. The mind in its true nature is enlightened: 'The enlightenment is your real nature. Originally it was utterly pure. Only avail yourselves of this mind, and you will immediately become a Buddha.' This requires the elimination of passions and material images. The enlightened nature may be compared to the Void, or to space. Another distinctive doctrine of Hui-neng is his rejection of gradualism and his assertion of sudden enlightenment. So contemplation does not precede WISDOM; they are inseparable, like light and a lamp.

Hui Shih
(fourth century BC)

Chinese philosopher belonging to the Dialecticians or School of Forms and Names. Hui Shih was responsible for formulating ten mystical paradoxes:

1 The greatest has nothing beyond itself and is called the Great Unit, the smallest has nothing within itself and is called the Little Unit.
2 That which has no thickness cannot be increased in thickness, yet in extent it may cover a thousand miles.
3 The heavens are as low as the earth; mountains are on the same level as marshes.
4 The sun at noon is the sun declining; the creature born is the creature dying.
5 A great similarity differs from a little similarity. This is called the little similarity-and-difference. All things are in one way all similar, in another way all different. This is called the great similarity-and-difference.
6 The south has no limit and has a limit.
7 I go to the state of Yüeh today and arrived there yesterday.
8 Connected rings can be separated.
9 I know the centre of the world; it is north of Yen (in the north) and south of Yüeh (in the south).
10 Love all things equally; the universe is one.

Hui-Yüan
(334–416)

Chinese Buddhist, a convert from Taoism, who established a famous monastery at Lu-shan in south China, used Confucian and Taoist concepts and language in the exposition of Buddhism, and founded the PURE LAND school.

Hululis

Followers of al-HALLAJ who believe in a doctrine of personal deification through an 'infusion' (*hulul*) of the Divine Spirit, and who were repudiated alike by the orthodox Moslems and by the Sufis.

Hurufism

Mystic pantheistic doctrine which emerged in Azerbaijan in the late fourteenth century: the name is derived from *huruf*, meaning 'letters'. Hurufism was founded by Fazlullah Naimi (d. 1394). Its distinctive doctrine was that letters form the divine basis on the universal. In one way they can be treated as numerals (there is here a parallel with the Greek Pythagoras); in another they are the elements from which words are built; words and thoughts are not to be dissociated, and thoughts are the essence of things. The holy QUR'AN is formed of words and so of letters. In scripture God expresses Himself in words.

Hurufism went further. Man is the true revelation of the universe. The letters of the alphabet, holy scripture, God, are all to be discerned in the face of man. The great Hurufi poet Imadeddin Nasimi writes in the first person; but only as he himself sums up all humanity and all divinity: 'Supreme God is himself humanity's son.' 'The thirty-two immortal letters am I; no partner, no equal, no substitute have I.' 'To see my face you need an eye that can perceive the true God.'

> Since my ending is eternal and my being primordial,
> primordially and eternally I am the Supreme Being.

Nasimi treated love as the essence of religious commitment, and the physical union of love as Heaven on earth; he did not look for fulfilment beyond the grave. Immortality is here and now.

> Call me a man who has immortal life,
> for I am immortal and alive for ever.

Nasimi died in taking the place of a young disciple accused of heresy. One of his inquisitors said to him as he was flayed alive: 'You say you are God. Then why do you grow pale as your blood drains away?' Nasimi answered: 'I am the sun of love on the horizon of eternity. The sun always grows pale at sunset.'

Huxley, Aldous
(1894–1963)

English writer and thinker, grandson of Thomas Henry Huxley and brother of Julian Huxley, he made his name as a writer of satirical fiction, only later turning to non-fictional studies.

In *The Perennial Philosophy* (a title taken from Leibniz) Huxley draws together an anthology and commentary on 'the metaphysics that recognizes a divine Reality substantial to the world of things and lives and minds; the psychology that finds in the soul something similar to, or even identical with, divine Reality; the ethic that places man's final end in the knowledge of the immanent and transcendent Ground of all being'.

In *The Doors of Perception* Huxley records his experiences with MESCALIN. His sense of colour was heightened and natural objects took on an enhanced significance. Space and time became irrelevant. He uses the language and categories of Hindu and Buddhist mysticism to describe his experience. He understood *Sat Chit Ananda*, the BEATIFIC VISION of Being-Awareness-Bliss. He recognized that the Dharma-Body of the Buddha was, in the ZEN paradox, indeed the hedge at the bottom of the garden. He contemplated a bamboo chair, and became one with it, 'being by Not-self in the Not-self which was the chair'.

Aldous Huxley

Huxley claims that his experiences with mescalin revealed to him 'contemplation at its height' though 'not yet in its fullness'. Huxley's claims were put to critical examination by R. C. Zaehner in *Mysticism Sacred and Profane*.

Hymn of the Pearl, The

Also known as *The Hymn of the Robe of Glory*, or *The Hymn of the Soul*.

The most immediately charming of all GNOSTIC writing, perhaps dating from the early third century AD. It begins:

When I was a little child,
and dwelt in the kingdom of my Father's house,
and took joy in the wealth
and glory of my upbringing,
my parents gave me provisions and sent me out
from our homeland in the East.

They take off his glorious robes and send him down to Egypt to fetch the Pearl, which is guarded by a snake. On arrival there, he puts on the Egyptians' clothes, but they drug him into forgetting his past and his mission. His father sends him a letter to awaken him. He charms the snake, seizes the Pearl, puts off the filthy and impure clothes he is wearing. His parents send his robe to greet him.

Suddenly, as I looked straight at it,
the robe seemed like a mirror-image of myself,
I saw myself entire in it,
in looking at it I was looking at myself.

So he returns, and does obeisance to his Father, who promises him that he shall enter with his pearl the presence of the King of Kings.

This is plainly an allegory. The king's son is the Saviour, the Pearl is as usual the Soul, Egypt is the world of matter and the Egyptian clothes are the body. The glorious robe is the true Self. But the allegory is, perhaps deliberately, ambiguous, because we are plainly meant in some sense to identify ourselves with the king's son, so that the Prince and the Pearl are overlapping concepts. We need to return to our Father and to find our true self in the spiritual world.

I

Iamblichus
(d. *c.* 330)

Neo-Platonist philosopher from Syria, important for his exaltation of the Ultimate, placing a higher One, beyond PLOTINUS's One, beyond the Good, beyond everything except Oneness; for his insistence on 'the law of mean terms', that two unlike entities must be connected by an intermediary like one in one respect and the other in another; for his introduction of theosophical fantasy and magical theurgy into Plotinus's system; and for his insistence that we have an innate impulse to the Good and an immediate knowledge of the gods.

Ibn al-Farid
(1182–1235)

Mystical poet of Cairo, with a great gift for combining fantasy and realism. His greatest poem is the *Ta'iyya* (rhyming on the letter 't') in which he recounts the different phases of mystical experience through which he passed before attaining union with God and seeks to convey something of that ultimate bliss. The imagery is that of a love-song, and God is symbolized as the Beloved. He is a difficult poet, enigmatic and obscure, abounding in word-play, intellectual conceits and fantastic imagery. He must have acquired a disciplined and practised control of words, since his close friends record that he would dictate his poems on emerging from a mystical trance which might last as long as ten days. Sometimes his mystical experience takes the form of union with the spirit of the Prophet, but in at least one passage he seems to claim such union with God that he appears as God incarnate, and as the *élan vital* of the universe.

> My spirit is a spirit to all the spirits; and all visible beauty in the universe flows from my nature.
> Ascribe to me alone the knowledge with which I alone was endowed before my visible appearance, while amongst created beings my friends did not recognize me.

Ibn ʿArabi, Muhyi al-Din
(1165–1240)

A monumental writer, from whom some two hundred works survive and perhaps the same number have failed to survive, who effectively provided a compendium of mysticism for the Arabic world. He travelled widely over the Mediterranean basin, 'scattering' Sufi wisdom. Arberry has summed up his system under nine heads (here somewhat adapted):

1 God is Absolute Being; in Him Being and Existence are inseparable; He is the source of all existence.
2 The universe possesses relative being; in God's knowledge it has eternal existence, but, being external to God, it has temporal non-existence.
3 God is both transcendent and immanent. 'The Reality of whom transcendence is asserted is the same as the Creation of whom immanence is asserted, although the Creator is distinguished from the created.'
4 Being, apart from God, exists by virtue of God's Will. His agents are the Divine Names, the Platonic Forms.
5 Before coming into existence material objects were latent in the Mind of God (as Platonic Forms); these Platonic Forms are thus intermediary between the One and the Many.
6 There is no such thing as becoming one with God; there is the realization that the mystic is already one with God.
7 The creative, animating and rational principle of the universe, the primary Nous or Intellect, is the Reality or Form of Muhammad, and finds its full manifestation in the Perfect Man. (This is adapted from Plotinus.)
8 Every prophet is *a* Logos of God, Muhammad is *the* Logos, and all the others are unity in the Form of Muhammad.
9 The Perfect Man is a miniature of Reality, a microcosm who reflects all the perfect attributes of the macrocosm. He is the epiphany of God's desire to be known; he alone knows God, loves God and is loved by God.

Ibn ʿArabi used the Ka'ba, the sacred building at Mecca, as a central theme for mystical meditation. 'Behold the secret building before it is too late, and you will see how it takes on life through those who circle round it and walk round its stones.' The eye of the heart sees through the attributes to the essence, through the dead stones to the living God, so that to kiss the Black Stone is to kiss God's right hand.

Ibn ʿArabi wrote a collection of love-poems, *The Interpreter of Dreams*. These must be read at two levels. They are straightforward love poems, and we know something of the girl, Nizam, to whom they are addressed. But they are also the poems of a mystic, who, Platonically, looks behind the face of a girl to the eternal Beauty.

> The ordinary lover loves an appearance, a
> second-best,
> I love the Real.

In one poem, shocking to orthodoxy, his creed rings clear:

> My heart is capable of every form:
> A cloister for the monk, a fane for idols,
> A pasture for gazelles, the votary's Ka'ba,
> The tables of the Torah, the Quran.
> Love is the creed I hold: wherever turn
> His camels, Love is still my creed and faith.
>
> *(tr. R. A. Nicholson)*

Ibn 'Arabi was accused of PANTHEISM, but despite orthodox hostility his influence was immense both on Islamic and Christian mysticism. He was called the Greatest Sheikh.

Ibrahim ben Adham
(d. 777)

Celebrated noble of Balkh, who, like an earlier ruler, GAUTAMA the Buddha, was converted to an ascetic mysticism. His conversion took place while he was hunting and heard a voice saying 'It is not for this that you were created; it was not this that you were charged to do.' He immediately gave his horse to a shepherd in exchange for the shepherd's woollen cloak, so becoming literally and symbolically a SUFI. He became a wanderer, earning his living by manual work. He learned GNOSIS from a Christian monk named Simeon, who taught him to do without, to endure the labour of an hour for the glory of ETERNITY. His mystical ASCETICISM depended on three pillars, self-denial, silent meditation and, above all, a life completely centred on God. 'The beginning of service is meditation and silence, save for speaking the name of God.' His prayer is noteworthy, like that of Rabia later: 'O God, Thou knowest that Paradise weighs not with me so much as the wing of a gnat. If Thou befriendest me by Thy recollection, and sustainest me with Thy love, and makest it easy for me to obey Thee, then give Thou Paradise to whomsoever Thou wilt.'

I Ching

The Chinese *Book of Changes* dating perhaps from the beginning of the Chou dynasty, say early in the first millennium BC, though not taking its present form till the Han period a thousand years or so later. It contains a cosmology depending on a primeval unity manifested in the two complementary forces of YIN and YANG. From their interaction come the changes and transformation of the universe. But *I Ching* offers also a way for a man in harmony with the cosmic process. *I Ching* was much used for purposes of divination, on the basis of its eight trigrams, symbolizing among other things, heaven, earth, mountains, marshes, wind, fire, water, thunder. There are ten appendices, known as the Ten Wings, traditionally but falsely ascribed to Confucius.

Ignatius Loyola
(*c.* 1491–1556)

A soldier who while recovering from a wound was converted to becoming a soldier of Christ. In 1534 he founded the Society of Jesus, which was officially sanctioned in 1540. His aim was the reform of the Church from within, missionary evangelism and the combatting of heresy. During a formative period at Manresa in 1522–3 when he was engaged in prayer and ascetic discipline, he enjoyed mystical experiences which deeply affected him, and led him to the first draft of his famous meditations, called *The Spiritual Exercises.* These are intended to last over four weeks. The aim is 'to prepare and dispose the soul to rid itself of all inordinate affections, and, when it has rid itself, to seek and find the Divine will in the disposition of one's life, for one's soul's salvation'. The first week is the reformation of the deformed, and comprises meditations on sin and its consequences; this corresponds to the PURGATIVE WAY. The second is the conformation of the reformed, and is a series of meditations on the Kingdom of Christ. The third is the confirmation of the conformed,

Detail of The Miracle of St Ignatius of Loyola, *from Rubens's altarpiece in the Jesuit church in Antwerp*

a meditation on the passion of Christ. The fourth is the transformation of the confirmed, a meditation on his risen glory. The climax is the prayer 'Take, Lord, and keep, all my freedom, my memory, my understanding and all my will, whatsoever I have and possess. Thou hast given all these things to me; to Thee, O Lord, I restore them. All are Thine, dispose of them according to Thy will. Give me Thy love and Thy grace: that is enough for me.' Ignatius has a remarkably practical understanding of ascetic discipline, a power to appeal to the imagination as well as to the intellect, and an ultimate vision which springs from his own experience. As one critic put it, 'the entire book was *lived* before being written'.

Ikhnaton

See AKHENATEN

Ikkyu
(1394–1481)

Japanese ZEN Master, of noble and perhaps royal blood, whose conversion came through hearing a crow in the dark. Ikkyu opposed conventional religion. Many Buddhists hoped for Paradise. Ikkyu said 'If a person purifies the ground of his own mind and beholds his own nature, there remains no Pure Land for which to hope, no hell to fear, no passions to overcome, no duality of good and evil. He is free from the cycle of rebirths. He will be born in every life as his mind wishes.' He mixed with all sorts and conditions of men, a lovable eccentric.

Illuminati

A group of religious enthusiasts in Bavaria, formed by Adam Weishaupt on 1 May 1776, to propagate a new religion of enlightened reason, reason open to the direct action of the Divine Reason and not dependent on the authority of Church or State, aiming at a peaceable and democratic world-order. The *Illuminati* were a kind of mystic closed sect who were to be the 'creative minority' in this. The organization of the order was based on FREEMASONRY.

Illuminative way

In Christian mysticism the second stage of the spiritual life, in which after purgation or purification the soul receives illumination to prepare it for union.

Illuminés, Les

A mystical Christian group appearing in southern France in 1623, similar to and perhaps developing from the ALUMBRADOS, and claiming direct inspiration from the HOLY SPIRIT. They were strengthened in 1634 by the accession of Pierre Guérin whose dynamic leadership led to the nickname Guérinists. The movement was regarded as heretical, and suppressed.

Illuminism

General term for any doctrine that professes the enlightenment or illumination of the human mind, whether by immediate divine revelation or through the inspired use of reason. The term is applied particularly to the mystical groups of the ALUMBRADOS and ILLUMINÉS, as well as to the very different philosophy of the eighteenth-century Enlightenment, whose religious expression is exemplified in the Bavarian ILLUMINATI.

Imitation of Christ, The

Mystical work usually attributed to THOMAS A KEMPIS, but actually constructively edited by him from pre-existing material, perhaps going back to the notebooks of Geert de GROOTE.

The work begins with the quotation 'He who follows me does not walk in darkness' (Jn 8, 12). But to follow does not mean a slavish, lifeless copy. It requires constant meditation upon the life of Jesus Christ; more, only those who receive the Spirit of Christ can conform their lives to the life of Christ (1, 1). Further the life that follows Christ will find its fruits in practical action. It is no use knowing the Bible by heart if you do not know the love of God (1, 1). When the day of judgment comes, we shall be examined not on what we have read but on what we have done, not on the eloquence of our words but on the holiness of our lives (1, 3). Love is the mainspring: 'To love much is to do much. To do a thing well is to do much. To serve the community rather than one's own will is to do well' (1, 15). So 'Never be entirely idle; be always reading or writing or praying or meditating or engaged in some useful work for the common good' (1, 19). Thomas puts magnificently our involvement with others: 'If you would be carried, carry another yourself' (2, 3).

Thomas takes a pessimistic view of this life. We are exiles from our native home, strangers and pilgrims with no real concern for the business, the cares or the pleasures of this wretched world. All is vain vision, deceitful shadows. Man is a worm. Death lies round the corner. 'Blessed is the man who always has the hour of his death before his eyes and daily prepares himself to die' (1, 23). So Thomas calls us to the renunciation of this world. You cannot obtain perfect liberty unless you wholly renounce yourself (3, 32). 'A man ought to rise above all finite things, and completely forsake himself, and stand in a trance, and see that You, the Creator of all things, hast nothing amongst creatures like Yourself' (3, 31). 'Let go all, and you shall find all; abandon desire and you shall find rest' (3, 32). There is a formidable indictment of nature, crafty, ambitious, selfish, lazy, luxurious, worldly, covetous, complaining, unreliable (3, 51). There is a long exposition of the theme that it is misery to live on earth (1, 22). Thackeray did not like the book for this reason: it 'would make the world the most wretched, useless, dreary, doting place of sojourn. There would be no manhood, no love, no tender ties of mother and child, no use of intellect, no trade or science – a set of selfish beings, crawling about, avoiding one another, and howling a perpetual Miserere!' That is of course unjust to the positive message of *The Imitation*. For, firstly, to Thomas, it is we who are wrong, not the world. Peace of mind comes from within. There are four ways to it: doing the will of another not our own; choosing less rather than more; seeking the lower place; being desirous for the will of God to be realized in us (3, 23). External things are not evil, it is our selfish will that is evil. 'If your heart were right, then every creature would be a mirror of life and a book of holy doctrine to you.' And, secondly, Thomas's rejection of the world is set against his immeasurable sense of the power of love. 'Nothing is sweeter than love, nothing stronger, nothing higher, nothing wider, nothing more pleasant, nothing fuller or better in heaven or on earth. . . . A lover flies, runs, rejoices. . . . Love often knows no limits, but is fervent beyond measure. Love feels no burden, thinks nothing of labours, attempts what is above its strength, pleads no excuse of impossibility. . . . Though wearied, it is not tired; though pressed, it is not straitened; though alarmed, it is not confounded; but as a lively flame and burning torch, it forces its way upwards, and passes securely through all' (3, 4).

This springs from the life of meditation and devotion. 'Seek a convenient time to retire into yourself, and meditate often upon God's acts of love' (1, 20). It depends upon the inward life, meditation on the Most High, directly or indirectly through the passion of Christ (2, 1). It depends on the practice of the presence of Christ. 'When Jesus is present, all is good and nothing seems difficult; but when Jesus is absent, all is hard' (2, 8). 'Love all for Jesus, but Jesus for himself' (2, 8). Thomas has a striking meditation on the Cross: 'The Cross is always ready, everywhere in wait for you. You cannot escape it wherever you run, for wherever you go, you carry yourself with you and will always find yourself. Turn yourself upwards, turn yourself downwards, turn yourself outwards, turn yourself inwards – everywhere you will find the Cross, everywhere you must hold tight to patience, if you will have inward peace and earn an everlasting crown' (2, 12). Above all, Thomas, as an orthodox Christian, sees the point of union with Christ in the sacrament of the EUCHARIST, and devotes his last book to this.

This exquisite book, with its melodious rhythms, appears in some of our manuscripts under the title *Ecclesiastical Music*. In the Christian world it has had an influence second only to the Bible.

Immanence

Presence in the world of sense-perception of the Ultimate Principle or Principles, opposed to TRANSCENDENCE. A strong belief in immanence readily goes along with some forms of NATURE-MYSTICISM.

Infused contemplation

Stage of non-verbal mental prayer reached through direct divine action on the soul, as opposed to ACQUIRED CONTEMPLATION.

Inge, William Ralph
(1860–1954)

Inge had a brilliant academic record at Eton and Cambridge. As he grew up he was influenced by the Tractarians, and this no doubt contributed to his sensitive understanding of mystical thought; later in life he was a leader of the Modern Churchmen's Union. The world at large knew him for his weekly scarifying articles in *The Evening Standard*, written as Dean of St Paul's, 'the gloomy dean'. His lasting reputation rests on his contributions to the understanding of mystical religion, from his Bampton lectures of 1899 on *Christian Mysticism* to his Gifford Lectures of 1917–18 on *The Philosophy of Plotinus*. Inge was persuaded that it was vital for theology to grasp the nature of religious experience, and that mysticism presents this in its purest form. His own mature creed is found in 'Confessio Fidei' in the second volume of *Outspoken Essays*. He does not claim mystical experience himself, but writes, 'Formless and vague and fleeting as it is, the mystical experience is the bedrock of religious faith. In it the soul, acting as a unity with all its faculties, rises above itself and becomes spirit; it asserts its claim to be a citizen of heaven.'

Initiation

It is probably true to say that initiation ceremonies originate in what van Gennep has taught us to call '*rites de passage*', the dangerous period of transition from one stage of life with its own presiding spiritual powers to another. Such are birth, puberty, marriage and death. Initiation into closed societies of various kinds is analogous to such a passage, but it is perhaps most closely parable to initiation into full membership of a tribe. Such societies may be primarily social, though over most of human history social and religious are not to be separated from one another; they may be religious. Even in the latter, initiation may be into a religion or into a small group within a religion possessing a higher truth or means of salvation. Initiation ceremonies may also be associated with entry into a particular office.

Initiation ceremonies are likely to contain some or all of the following: purification (often including fasting), preparation, vows of secrecy, a real or symbolic ordeal, an act of renunciation of the old life and of entry upon the new, a revelation (sometimes verbal, often visual) and instruction.

Thus in Hinduism initiation is known as *diksa*. A *guru* or teacher is essential to initiation. First comes the period of preparation; the initiate's devotion, intentions, insight and mastery of ritual are tested over several months. The *guru* also conducts the initiation. This may be consecration by touching or speaking or seeing. In the first the touch of blessing produces union with Siva; in the second the spoken word conveys the divine presence; in the third the *guru* closes his eyes and concentrates the highest Principle in them and then conveys the divine Presence by his gaze. The initiate is now led into a hut with four doors opening to the four points of the compass, and a great jar in the centre; this is the world, with God at the centre, and the initiate is blindfolded, led round the hut, then into it, and allowed to look at the jar. He receives a MANTRA which represents his own share of the divine Wisdom, and is sacred and secret; he will have to recite this daily. He receives a new name, and is expected to lead a new life. The *guru* will continue to watch over his progress, and will decide when he is ripe for a higher initiation. As darkness, having reached dawn, disappears quickly, so man, having reached *diksa*, is liberated from good and evil. As water which is poured out into water, and as milk which is added to milk, so the man who through *diksa* knows his *mantra* turns to mystic union.

Fasting is a common preparation for initiation. It was insisted on at ELEUSIS: Lucius had to fast before his initiation into the mysteries of ISIS; fasting was the precondition of the shaman's mystical experiences; a number of early Christian writers mention fasting as necessary for one or two days before Christian baptism.

The place of ordeal in initiation may well be exemplified by the SHUGENDO rite in which the initiate had his hands bound and was placed on the scale-pan of a gigantic balance, counterweighted with a boulder, and swung out over a precipice, there to confess his sins. We know that in MITHRAISM initiation to the several grades was accompanied by ordeals; we hear of scourgings and ritual deaths.

The act of dying to the old life is well exemplified in the initiation of Lucius into the mysteries of Isis in Apuleius's novel: 'I approached the border of death and stepped into the gateway of Proserpina.' Similarly with Christian baptism. Although all baptism has no doubt an element of lustration, the washing away of sin, Christian baptism symbolizes death. Just as Jesus saw his death as baptism or the entry into new life (Lk. 12, 50), so Paul sees baptism as death to the old life (Rom. 6, 3–4). 'Do you know that all of us who have been baptized into Christ Jesus were baptized into his death, so that as Christ was raised from the dead by the glory of the Father, we too might walk in newness of life.' In the Mithraic temple at Carrawburgh there is a shallow oblong pit; it is hard not to think that this is a symbolical grave in which the initiate had to lie as if in death. In Sufi initiation the candidate has to pass through three deaths, White Death, Green Death and Black Death; each is preceded by social activity specified by the Sheikh or Master, and leads to a rebirth or transformation.

Instruction is naturally associated with initiation. A good example is the HERMETIC tracts which represent part of the didactic side of initiation into a minor sect. Jewish and Christian catechisms are part of a similar process, and Josephus tells us that a two-year process of instruction preceded initiation into the ESSENES. This instruction may come as part of the preparation for initiation; but it is also regularly found as part of the revealed secret of the mysteries and the working out of a new way of life.

Mircea Eliade has rightly emphasized the anthropological importance of initiation: it is an indispensable factor in the process by which men really become human beings. Only by initiation does a man become a real, full, spiritual man, understanding the different dimensions of human life. Closed sects are often the province of a social minority or of a socially underprivileged group. It is common for them to honour a founder-figure who is for them in some sense a liberator. The privilege of esoteric mystical knowledge is a compensation for the lack of worldly power. Initiation thus becomes a jealously reserved privilege, and the mysterious revelations are the private province of a relatively small number, and within that number betrayal of the mysteries is severely punished. Among the initiates themselves there is commonly a hierarchy, and often

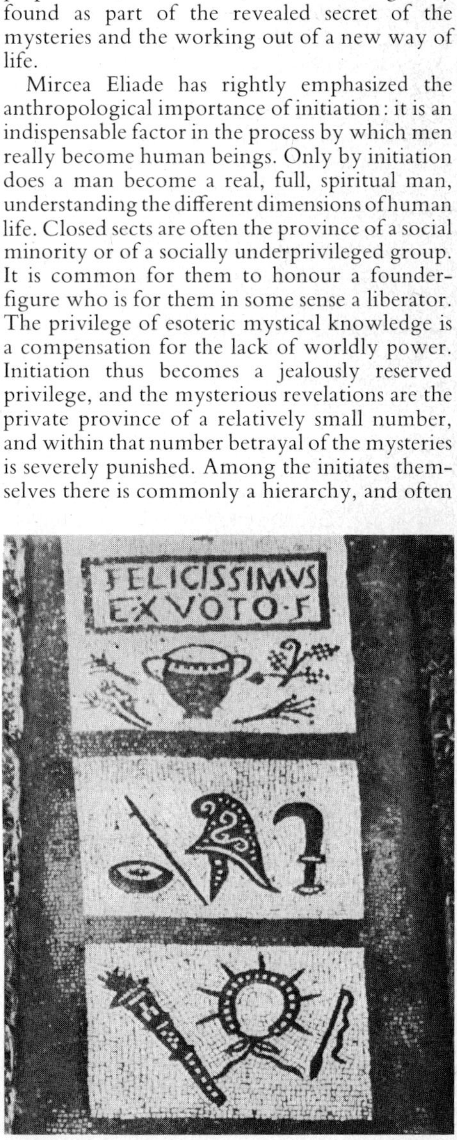

Representation of three of the grades of Mithraism in a mosaic floor of the 3rd century at Ostia.

a whole series of grades (the SHUGENDO and MITHRAISM offer good examples from different parts of the world), sometimes involving a whole series of consecutive initiations, as Lucius went through three initiations into the mysteries of ISIS AND OSIRIS. But the very intensity of esoteric belief also leads to the formation of sub-groups, divisions and heresies. In general the social psychology of initiation has been well expressed by C. G. JUNG: 'All esoteric teachings are seeking to grasp that which is unfolding in the psyche without which it is impossible to have any insight, and all esoteric systems claim the supreme authority for themselves.'

Inner Light

Modern phrase for that which George FOX and the SOCIETY OF FRIENDS tend to call the Inward Light, which they identified with the Spirit of Christ in every heart. So Fox recalled his own enlightenment: 'Now the Lord God hath opened to me by His invisible power how that every man was enlightened by the divine Light of Christ; and I saw it shine through all. . . . This I saw in the pure openings of the Light, without the help of any man.' Friends are insistent that the Inner Light and the Light of the World seen in Jesus cannot run counter to one another, and that for individuals to open their lives to the Inner Light cannot lead to faction and anarchy, for the Light is One and leads men to do that which is right not in their own eyes but in God's. Fox indeed affirms that the Light 'was before Time and is in Time'. Further, it is with power. 'I saw . . . there was an ocean of darkness and death, but an infinite ocean of light and love which flowed over the ocean of darkness.' 'Mind the Light and dwell in it and it will keep you a-top of all the world.' Sometimes he calls the Light the Topstone. All have the Light in a measure, and are called to be faithful to the measure they have received, and then they will be led to a greater measure of the TRUTH. For example Quakers believe war to be un-Christian. But one whose conscience calls him to fight must be faithful to the measure of Light he has received. If he remains open and sensitive, sooner or later he will make his own stand against war. So the Light is not to be identified with conscience. Conscience may reflect the measure of Light we have received, but it is also conditioned by our social upbringing. The Light illumines conscience and seeks to transform it. And the Light is universal. It has been given to all men everywhere from the beginning of time.

Introspective mysticism

See TWO WAYS.

Introversion

See TWO WAYS.

Isaac of Nineveh
(7th century)

Christian Bishop of Nineveh, who resigned after five months to become a contemplative among the hills and who wrote a series of *Mystical Treatises*, which are influenced by the Christian NEO-PLATONISM of DIONYSIUS and THE BOOK OF THE HOLY HIEROTHEOS. Isaac does not much speculate on the nature of God. He is the only real Being, the First Cause, Perfect Goodness. It follows that in Him the soul will find its true being, that it naturally seeks to be united with its origin, and that the means will be the purification from all that is not good. So ASCETICISM is the mother of saintliness and Isaac elaborates on the renunciation of the world (not merely of sin, but of all which is not God and does not minister to the love of God), on solitude (which is the liberation of the soul), on vigils, on the love of God (Isaac regards love of the neighbour as commendable, but inferior) nourished by prayer. Prayer is intercourse with God; its purest form is mental prayer, and beyond that lies ecstasy; prayer is the seed, contemplation the harvest. The mystic will find God in himself as in a mirror; this is insight without sight; and in the vision the soul is one with God.

Isis and Osiris

In Egypt the Great Mother was found in the form of Isis. She was sister and consort of King Osiris, who was murdered and dismembered by the evil Set. Isis recovered the body, except for the phallus, which she replaced by a gold model, and reassembled it. Osiris was resurrected as king of the dead, and recreated in his son Horus. Isis is the earth, the land of Egypt, waiting for the fertilizing moisture from her consort. Set is the power of drought, Osiris the waters of the Nile, which recede in summer, autumn and winter, and then as the snows melt far to the south, flood over the land in spring: Isis was called 'the bride of the Nile'. But Osiris was also the corn, and effigies made of vegetable mould and stuffed with corn were buried in graves or placed

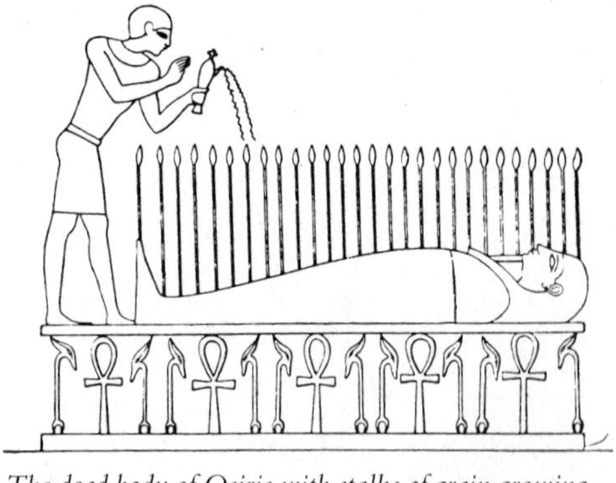

The dead body of Osiris with stalks of grain growing from it. Detail of a line-drawing made from a relief at Philai

between the legs of mummies. In a representation at Philae we see the dead body of Osiris with stalks of corn springing from it, watered by a priest. There is an inscription: 'This is the form of him whom one may not name, Osiris of the mysteries, who springs from the returning waters.' A religion then of the earth and its fertility; but at the same time, a promise of resurrection for the dead. The dead man may even be addressed as Osiris and called to resurrection: 'Raise yourself to life: you do not die!' 'Osiris, live! stand up, unhappy one, lying there! I am Isis, I am Nephthys.'

The evidence for such beliefs goes back to the third millennium BC. By the Hellenistic and Roman periods Isis was making universal claims. Her worship spread from Dura-Europos on the Euphrates to York. She was called 'the one who is all things', the goddess of ten thousand names, the first of the heavenly beings, the single appearance of the gods and goddesses. She was the great inventress, the discoverer of hieroglyphics, patron of the arts, originator of navigation, goddess of agriculture, healer of the sick, giver of law and government. In this period the traditional gods of Egypt had added to them Serapis, a fusion of Osiris and the sacred bull Apis, seemingly invented as a universal symbol of the new age. He did not oust Osiris; he came in alongside him.

In a hymn of praise Isis says, 'I have revealed to mankind mystic initiations.' In the Hellespont she was known as Mystis, Lady of the Mysteries. She had her own mysteries in which the sufferings of Osiris, and her own trials and sorrows, were re-enacted, so that others, through her sympathetic power, could learn to overcome difficulties and put on immortality. It happens that in Apuleius's novel *The Metamorphoses* (or *The Golden Ass*), we have an account of initiation. The hero, Lucius, has been delivered by Isis. He frequents her temple; she appears to him in dreams and urges him to be ordained. The priest will not let him undergo initiation hastily, but he is eventually accepted. He is shown sacred hieroglyphs, baptized and purified, and entrusted with mystical secrets. He then fasts for ten days. Then comes the initiation; he does not reveal the full mysteries, but he died to his former life, had an ecstatic vision of the cosmos, and entered the presence of the gods with a brilliant illuminating light in the darkness. He emerges in the morning clad in twelve stoles and a cloak embroidered with fantastic animals, wearing a wreath of flowers with palm leaves arranged like the rays of the sun, and carrying a lighted torch; so he makes his epiphany before the people, for the initiate is now one with the divine power. This is his re-birthday; there is public banqueting, but also a religious communion which is the climax of the initiation. Later, Lucius, continually inspired by dreams and nightly visions, undergoes further initiation into the mysteries of Osiris and the college of priests.

What initiation meant can be seen clearly in the magnificent remains from the temple at Beneventum in Italy. The Emperor Domitian was an initiate, and he appears as 'Domitian, living for ever'. So the promise from Isis to Lucius is: 'You shall live in blessing, you shall live glorious in my protection; and when you have fulfilled your allotted span of life and descend to the underworld, there too, you shall see me, as you see me now, shining amid the darkness of Acheron and ruling in the depths of Hades, you shall live in the field of Elysium and constantly honour me for my favour towards you. And if you show yourself obedient to my divinity by regular observance of religious duties and persistent chastity, you will know that I alone have permitted you to extend your life beyond the time allocated by your destiny.' As truly as Osiris lives, he also shall live; as truly as Osiris is not dead, shall he not die; as truly as Osiris is not annihilated shall he not be annihilated. As an aretalogy of Isis puts it 'I overcome Fate.'

Islam

World-religion founded by MUHAMMAD in the seventh century AD. Muhammad himself was a visionary, who stressed the need for asceticism, and the five Pillars of the Faith of Islam include both prayer and FASTING. Islam centres upon the absolute power of God, who is at the same time compassionate, merciful and forgiving; and the absolute dependence of man. There is thus a great abyss between the absolute God and His creatures. But at the same time man is set apart from the rest of creation because he is capable of receiving the divine revelation; and THE QUR'AN does allow for the approach of man to the presence of God. It speaks of 'those who have near access to God' (3, 40), and declares that 'God will guide to Himself one who turns to Him' (13, 27). For man's essence is his heart, which contains his conscience (*sirr*); he was created with a divine spark within. The Prophet's original companions included men noted for asceticism and quietism. But the main mystical movement in Islam came rather later, with the rise of SUFISM.

J

Jacopone da Todi
(*c.* 1230–1306)

Italian poet and mystic, who found the object of his adoration in the 'Love that gives all things form'. He sought his goal through asceticism, but found that it led only to indigestion, insomnia and colds in the head. Jacopone was a Franciscan convert, whose poetry, once he had freed himself from the tyranny of the flesh, reflects his master's joy.

Ineffable Love Divine,
Sweetness unformed, yet bright,
Measureless, endless Light,
Flame in this heart of mine.

(tr. Mrs Theodore Beck)

There are three heavens, and we must climb, spurred on by LOVE, from one to the next. The first is the starry heaven of multiplicity, in which darkness is spangled with points of light. The second is the crystalline heaven of contemplation; the soul finds harmony with the divine, and through love has a dim apprehension of God. The third he calls 'the hidden heaven'. Jacopone's vision of the hidden heaven, when 'ineffable love, imageless goodness, measureless light' dawned on him, led him to realize the inadequacy of all his previous concepts. 'I thought I knew Thee, tasted Thee, saw Thee under image; believing I held Thee in Thy completeness I was filled with delight and unmeasured love. But now I see I was mistaken – Thou art not as I thought and firmly held.' In the hidden heaven he found himself entering 'into possession of all that is God'.

When the mind's very being is gone,
   Sunk in a conscious sleep,
In a rapture divine and deep,
   Itself in the Godhead lost:
It is conquered, ravished and won!
   Set in Eternity's sweep,
   Gazing back on the sleep,
Knowing not how it was crossed,
To a new world now it is tossed,
   Drawn from its former state
   To another, measureless, great,
Where Love is drowned in the Sea.

(tr. Mrs Theodore Beck)

Jainism

A religion of India, which rejected the Hindu system involving caste and sacrifice and sought through ASCETICISM liberation from the cycle of reincarnation. The great legendary teachers were called *Tirthankaras*, 'ford-makers', who crossed the stream of reincarnation. The last of these, Mahavira, was a contemporary of the Buddha. At the age of twenty-eight he renounced his family, and spent twelve years in silent meditation and stern asceticism, not even wearing a loin-cloth. In the thirteenth year after a long fast he achieved perfect knowledge, and with it liberation. Fundamentally, this is a means of escape from the tyranny of *karma*, the wrong and misdirected action which obstructs our freedom. He spent the rest of his life preaching his gospel of liberation and organizing his followers. Salvation comes from right faith (an enlightened understanding of the nature of the soul) and right conduct (non-violence, truthfulness, non-stealing, chastity, non-attachment, together with fasting, charitable aid to others and spiritual meditation on the true nature of the self). There is no belief in a saving deity – there are temples without gods – but it is believed that the *Tirthankaras* or *Jains* have in compassion opened a door for others to follow. There are fewer than two million Jains today; but (like the English Quakers) they have had an influence out of proportion to their numbers.

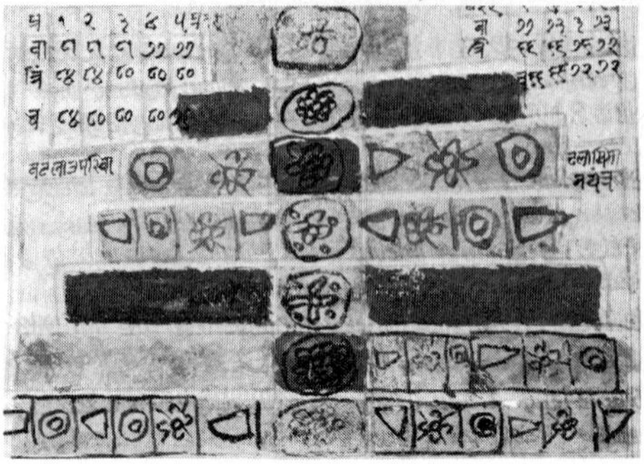

A Jain diagram of the successive levels of the world tree from an 18th-century Indian painting

James, William
(1842–1910)

American philosopher and psychologist, brother of the novelist Henry James. Philosophically, James was known as an exponent of pragmatism. His book *The Varieties of Religious Experience* (1902) is important as a careful philosophical and psychological study of mystical and other religious experience; he concludes that 'higher powers exist and are at work to save the world on ideal lines similar to our own'.

Jami, Nur al-Din ʿAbd al-Rahman
(1414–92)

Jami, scholar and mystic, was the last great Persian poet of the classical age. In *Seven Thrones* he links seven long poems, including two love stories, allegories of the mystic's search for God. His voluminous prose works include *Effulgences*, a mystical treatise, *The Alexandrian Book of Wisdom*, a demonstration of the unity of tradition between Greek and Sufi mysticism, *Breaths of Friendship*, biographies of some hundreds of saints. Some of his sayings on love are especially memorable: 'Ordinary human love is capable of raising man to the experience of real love', and

Love becomes perfect only when it transcends itself –
Becoming One with its object,
Producing Unity of Being.

The flowers of human beauty are only blossoms on the tree of Absolute Beauty. Beauty and Love are as body and soul. Beauty is the mind and Love the gem. The eternal Love is the expression of the eternal Beauty.

Jeanne D'Arc
(*c.* 1412–31)

French visionary, born at Domrémy. When she was aged about thirteen she began to hear voices, which she identified as those of the saints Michael, Catherine and Margaret, accompanied by a blaze of light. These called her to a mission to save France from the English. She won acceptance with the court, claiming direct revelation; flouted military opinion, at first with success, relieving Orléans, but failing before Compiègne; and was taken prisoner, and condemned for sorcery and heresy, despite her shrewd and witty defence and her firm belief in the genuineness of her experiences. Faced with the stake she at first recanted, and then withdrew her recantation.

Jefferies, Richard
(1848–87)

English naturalist and mystic. Born near Swindon and largely self-educated, he had a deep love for the countryside. At first sight he seems a typical nature-mystic: 'Through every grass blade in the thousand, thousand grasses; through the million leaves, veined and edge-cut, on bush and tree; through the song-notes and the marked feathers of the birds; through the insects' hum and the colour of the butterflies; through the soft warm air, the flecks of clouds dissolving – I used them all for prayer.' He has a powerful sense of the Beyond breaking through in sun and sky, earth and sea. Where Jefferies is unusual is that this mysticism is combined with atheism. He does not believe in creation, design or providence. God is an 'invisible idol'. The mind demands 'something higher than a god'. Man has 'wrested from the unknown' the three ideas: 'the existence of the soul, immortality, the deity'. He must go beyond. These are stepping-stones to a fourth idea, or rather a whole uncharted ocean of ideas. 'By the Beyond,' he wrote in his notebook, 'I mean the idea of the *whole*: that would fill the sky.' He speaks of prayer, but it is an aspiration of his whole being, not a conversation with a personal God. He prays by all that is most powerful, and by his own soul, and he prays that 'I may have something from each of these, that I may gather a flower from them, that I may have in myself the secret and meaning of the earth, the golden sun, the light, the foam-flecked sea.'

Jehudah of Worms
(d. 1217)

Jehudah was one of the most notable of the HASIDIM, and it is his teachings which lie at the root of mediaeval German Hasidism. He stands to Jewish thought of the period much as FRANCIS OF ASSISI stands to Christian thought. Jehudah was something of a saint, who combined mystical devotion and practical service. Noteworthy in his thought is an element of 'realized eschatology': the mystic here and now experiences that which is appropriate to the Messianic kingdom. Notable too is his doctrine of a twofold glory (*Kavod*). The inner glory is one with the SHEKHINAH; it is without form but has a voice; it is the Holy Spirit, the will of God. It is not possible to see God; but it is possible to 'connect oneself with the glory'. As well as the inner glory, there is the visible glory; it is this which is seen in the vision of the prophets, and which confirms that the vision comes from God. A contemporary said of Jehudah, 'If he had lived in the time of the prophets he would have been a prophet.'

Jesus of Nazareth
(d. *c.* 33)

Jesus was born to a Galilean family; his mother Mary was married to a village carpenter named Joseph. As a boy he seems to have had an unusual sense of divine destiny. But Joseph died while Jesus was still young, and as the family breadwinner he took his father's trade. At the age of thirty he embarked on a ministry of preaching ('Change your lives, for the Kingdom of Heaven is at hand') and healing, the latter being a sign of the power of God and the coming of a new age. He was baptized, and the baptism coincided with a mystical experience, a vision of a power descending from the sky, and the sound of a divine voice. He then went off alone for six weeks to wrestle with his destiny. Through the story of the next three years he showed himself a magnetic personality, a winsome speaker (but also a formidable controversialist), a man endowed with a rare healing gift and utterly

The Resurrection of Jesus. *Detail from a painting by Matthias Grünewald, 1515*

dependent on a dedicated life of prayer. From time to time the records tell of individuals glimpsing in him a kind of superhuman authority. There was a second major mystical experience, shared by three of his closest followers, and generally called the Transfiguration, in which he appeared transformed by divine LIGHT. In orthodox Christendom this sense of Jesus as the vehicle of the divine glory is very strong.

One at least of Jesus's twelve closest associates – perhaps more – was a member of the freedom-fighters of the day. When the leader of the disciples, Simon Peter, called him the Messiah (Christ or Anointed), who was expected to lead the movement for liberation and establish an independent theocracy, he did not disown the title. But he refused a military uprising and was arrested and executed for rebellion by the Romans while continuing to proclaim and practise a life of nonviolent love. Two days later his disciples became convinced that he was still alive and with them, that love was stronger than death. They went out to proclaim Jesus and the Resurrection, and in so doing formed the new religion of Christianity, which started as a reformist movement within Judaism and became a universal faith.

As the Christians reflected on Jesus they saw in him a human being in the fullest sense, hungry, thirsty, tired, compassionate, angry, subject to pain and death: any denial of this was a heresy, Docetism. But they also saw a life uniquely one with God. He was 'son of man' and 'son of God'; the phrases hardly mean more than wholly and utterly human, and wholly and utterly divine. He himself spoke of God in close personal terms as 'Father', and had declared 'I and the Father are one.' Alongside the two great moments of mystical revelation he had a continual sense of his oneness with the Father, broken only momentarily, and perhaps not even that, in the cry of desolation from the Cross. One strand of Christian thought brought in the Greek concept of the LOGOS to speak of Jesus as God's revelation of Himself.

Christian mysticism, seeing in Jesus the perfect revelation of the eternal nature of the God who is LOVE, has tended to stress union with Christ as the goal of mystical experience. In one saying preserved outside the New Testament he seems to promise this: 'Wherever there are two, they are not without God, and where there is one alone, I say, I am with him. Raise the stone and there you will find me; cleave the wood and there I am.' The last words have been taken pantheistically, but may only refer to the crucifixion and resurrection. The promise of his continued presence is amply paralleled.

Jesus-Prayer

Diadochus of Photice in the middle of the fifth century AD, and John Climacus in the early seventh century recommended the continual repetition of the name of Jesus in prayer, rather as the eastern meditation on the syllable OM. Later the formula was developed into 'Lord Jesus Christ, Son of God, have mercy on me', and HESYCHASM in particular used the prayer, associated (as in YOGA) with a particular bodily posture (head bowed, chin on chest, eyes fixed on the place of the heart) and controlled breathing, as a means to concentration. There is a notable exposition of the prayer by Bishop Brianchaninov.

al-Jili, Abdu 'l-Karim ibn Ibrahim
(*c.* 1365–1412)

Sufi mystic, of whom little is known, except that he came from south of the Caspian and travelled in India. He wrote numerous mystical treatises, of which the best known is *The Perfect Man (Insanu 'l kamil)*, more fully *The Man Perfect in knowledge of the first and last things*. His theme is God, His names, attributes and essence. God's Essence is pure Being; it is the 'dark mist'. Absolute BEING descends from Oneness, through 'He-ness', to 'I-ness', thus becoming both the subject and object of thought. The created world is the outward aspect of that whose inward aspect is God. Man is the cosmic thought taking flesh; he is the bridge between Absolute Being and the world of nature. The three stages of mystical illumination correspond to the three stages of the descent of Absolute Being: they are (in reverse order of course) the Illumination of the Names, the Illumination of the Attributes and the Illumination of the Essence.

Jiriki

Japanese term for one own's strength, contrasting with TARIKI, another's strength; though in mystical terms the two ultimately coincide.

Joachim da Fiore
(*c.* 1131–1202)

Cistercian mystical prophet. We know little of his life. He left three books: *Harmony of the Old and New Testaments*, *Commentary on the Apocalypse* and *The Psalter with Ten Strings*. Joachim took the doctrine of the Trinity as the basis of an historical analysis. In the first age, symbolized by the nettle, or brass, or water, or starlight, the Father worked through the patriarchs by the Law; in the second, symbolized by the rose, or silver, or wine, or dawn, the Son worked through the Apostles by grace; in the third, symbolized by the lily, or gold, or oil, or daylight, the Spirit will work through the religious by liberty. Joachim's prophetic visions were immensely influential throughout the Middle Ages: DANTE praised him as one endowed with the spirit of prophecy.

Joan of Arc

See JEANNE D'ARC.

Jodo

PURE LAND Buddhist sect in Japan.

John of Lycopolis
(d. *c.* 394)

Early Christian mystic, author of the mystical treatise *The Spiritual State of the Soul*. John stresses the need for asceticism and discipline of mind and body as essential preparation for mystical union. The things of this world are, he says, contrary to the Way of Christ, and hide the Way of Christ from us. But the love of Christ acts on the soul as fire on iron, burning away impurities, and enabling the iron to take on the colour and semblance of the fire. 'When the soul is purified and made serene, and the knowledge of Christ the Lord dawns upon it, its mind ascends and beholds the Majesty of God, and sees Him to be Incomprehensible and Infinite. When it looks on high, it sees Him as at first, and when it looks within itself, it sees Him there. When the mind floats on the sea of the Majesty of God and His Incomprehensibility, it is amazed and lost in wonder at the serene majesty of God. And forthwith the soul becomes humble, so that if it were possible, when the effulgence of God's Majesty envelops it, it would take its place below the whole creation, because of its awe and wondering amazement at the Majesty of God, ineffable, incomprehensible as it is, beyond the penetration and seeking out of His servants.'

John of the Cross

See JUAN DE LA CRUZ.

John the Evangelist

In *According to John*, the fourth Gospel, a mystical understanding of the life of Christ becomes most prominent. At the outset the evangelist asserts the creative power of God through the LOGOS, in Greek thought the reason at the heart of the universe, in Hebrew thought the word or utterance through which God expresses Himself. He goes on to say that the divine Logos became flesh in Jesus, and 'we beheld his glory'. In a number of passages of John (8, 24; 8, 28; 8, 58; 13, 19; 18, 5–6), Jesus speaks of himself under the divine name I AM. John stresses the unity of the Father (God in His eternal nature) and the Son (God as revealed in Jesus).

John uses several images to express the mystical relation of Jesus to his followers. One is the vine: he is the vine, they are the branches, and their life comes from him. Another is the bread: 'I am the bread of life.' The image of life is altogether important. Jesus says 'I am the Resurrection and the Life', and the story of the raising of Lazarus symbolizes this. At the outset it is said that life is to be found in the Logos. Then another image supervenes, that of light, a light shining in the darkness which the darkness cannot put out. An important image is that of the new birth: 'Unless a man be born again, he cannot see the Kingdom of God.' And it is John's Gospel which contains the image which links to the mysteries of ELEUSIS and Egypt: 'In truth, in very truth I tell you, a grain of wheat remains a solitary grain unless it falls into the ground and dies, but if it dies it bears a rich harvest' (12, 24).

Joseph, Father

See LECLERC DU TREMBLAY

Juan de la Cruz (John of the Cross)
(1542–91)

Juan de Yepes y Alvarez was born in Old Castile into a family of ecclesiastics and businessmen, who repudiated his father for a marriage of which they disapproved. Juan grew up in poverty. At twenty-one he joined the Carmelite order, and studied at the University of Salamanca, reading and being impressed by 'DIONYSIUS THE AREOPAGITE'; he practised FASTING, self-flagellation and all-night vigils. Then came the turning-point of his life, contact with TERESA DE JESUS, now a woman in her fifties, who took him with her to Avila. She appreciated his scholarship – he was her 'little Seneca' – and his gift of contemplation. He was all that she in theory believed in; in practice he sometimes irritated her strong practicality. She once said: 'If one tries to talk to Padre Fray Juan de la Cruz about God, he falls into a trance and you along with him.' He was confessor to the nuns at Avila and to

Teresa among them, and their mystical experiences complemented and played upon one another.

Teresa's reforms had aroused jealousy. Counter-action was taken and Juan was put in prison. Here his self-examination and his agonizing doubts were more fearful than his physical sufferings: they are reflected later in *The Dark Night of the Soul* and *The Ascent of Mount Carmel*. He experienced 'great interior afflictions and dryness', but seems also to have been consoled by ecstatic mystical experiences, and wrote some of his *Spiritual Canticle*. Then the chance came to escape, and he took it; he felt like Jonah delivered from the whale. He spent eight happy months at the hermitage at El Calvario. By now the reformists were coming back into favour, and Juan was appointed in 1579 rector of the new Carmelite college at Baeza. Then after a brief encounter with Teresa, their last, in 1582 he was moved to new work in Granada.

In prison he had begun to write, and it was at Granada that he composed *The Dark Night of the Soul* and *The Ascent of Mount Carmel* and his great poems 'On a night of darkness' and 'Living flame of love'. For the rest his life was simple. He chose the smallest cell; his food was plain; much of his life was spent in prayer; there were simple relaxations, story-telling and walks in the country. He himself described the life of the order as 'a great harshness of life, poverty and deprivation, much mortification and self-denial and a negation of all the creatures'.

His influence grew. He became Vicar Provincial of Andalusia, and one of the senior people in the order. But he was at odds with the Vicar General, a former Genoese businessman named Doria, able and austere, but no contemplative and lacking the grace of humility. Doria eased him out of authority, then had him disgraced. On 14 December 1591 he died uttering the words 'Tonight I shall sing matins in heaven.'

Juan's lasting fascination lies in his combination of mystical experiences with a supreme gift for lyric poetry. In this last he fuses the poetic technique of the Castilian soldier-poet Garcilaso de la Vega, the language and imagery of the Bible (especially *The Song of Songs*) and his own experience. When he writes

> I entered – where I knew not.
> I stayed uncomprehending,
> passing beyond all knowledge

we cannot doubt that he has himself made this transcendental journey. But his writings show deliberate skill as well as inspiration. A good nun asked him whether the words of his *Canticle* were given him by God; he answered, not without wit, 'Sometimes God gave them to me, at others I had to find them for myself.'

Juan's great image is that of the DARK NIGHT OF THE SOUL: he took it from Garcilaso. It appears as the title of one of his prose treatises. This, together with *The Ascent of Mount Carmel*, which is really the first part of the same treatise, deals with sensitivity and at the same time with analytical rigour, with the lower steps of mysticism, the purgation of the lower self; in *The Ascent* by active means, in *The Dark Night* by passive. The general theme is splendidly expressed in the verses from *The Ascent* which T. S. Eliot used in *East Coker*:

> In order to arrive at pleasure in everything,
> you must seek pleasure in nothing.
> In order to arrive at possessing everything,
> you must seek to possess nothing.
> In order to arrive at being everything, you must seek to be nothing.

S. Juan de la Cruz. *Portrait by Joaquin Canedo (1795)*

In order to arrive at knowing everything, you must seek to know nothing.
In order to arrive at that in which you find no pleasure, you must go by a way in which there is no pleasure.
In order to arrive at that which you do not know, you must go by a way you do not know.
In order to arrive at that which you do not possess, you must go by a way of dispossession.
In order to arrive at what you are not, you must go by a way in which you are not.

(tr. G. Brenan)

The soul can soar only if it cuts the guy-ropes and sheds the weights that anchor it to earth. So one aspect of the Dark Night is the emptying of the self in silence, solitude, poverty, deprivation and the stripping of all attachments. But there is another aspect which he describes as 'horrendous and terrifying'. This is the period of dryness, of doubt, of fear of being forsaken; it arises from intensity of love, and corresponds to an earthly lover's fears and jealousies. Juan says that 'the very bones seem to be dried up, the natural powers to be fading away, their warmth and strength to be perishing through the intensity of that thirst of love'.

Yet, because it is part of the freedom from earthly bonds, and because it is the precondition of union with God, the Dark Night is peaceful and joyous. He headed his verses 'On a night of darkness' with the words 'Songs of the soul that rejoices at having reached the high state of perfection, which is union with God, by the path of spiritual negation.'

On a night of darkness,
In love's anxiety of longing kindled,
O blessed chance!
I left by none beheld,
My house in sleep and silence stilled . . .

O night, you were the guide!
O night more desirable than dawn!
O dark of night you joined
Belovèd with belov'd one,
Belov'd one in Belovèd now transformed!

(tr. Lydia Nicholson)

So another poem, based on another key-image, a 'song of the soul that delights in knowing God by faith', begins:

How well I know the spring that brims and flows,
Although by night.

(tr. Lydia Nicholson)

A third great image, based on *The Song of Songs*, and of course found in 'On a night of darkness', is that of love. This is worked out in detail in Juan's most difficult poem, *The Spiritual Canticle*, which is a dialogue between lover and beloved. The stages of seeking, courtship, consummation represent purgation, illumination and union; and at the end the BEATIFIC VISION is revealed in lines which move from the imagery of love to the imagery of nature:

The breathing of the air,
The sweet nightingale's song,
The grove and its loveliness
In the calm night,
With flame which devours without pain.

The recurrence of the image of night in the Beatific Vision is notable. One of Juan's finest poems will provide an example of the image of love expressing the stage of union:

O living flame of love,
How tenderly you wound
And sear my soul's most inward centre!
No longer so elusive,
Now, if you will, conclude
And rend the veil from this most sweet encounter.

O cautery that heals!
O consummating wound!
O soothing hand! O touch so fine and light
That savours of eternity
And satisfies all dues!
Slaying, you have converted death to life.

O lamps of burning fire
In whose translucent glow
The mind's profoundest caverns shine with splendour
Before in blindness and obscure,
With unearthly beauty now
Regale their love with heat and light together.

With what love and sweetness
You waken in my breast
Where in secrecy and solitude you move:
Suffused with joy and goodness
In the fragrance of your breath,
How delicately you kindle me with love!

(tr. Lydia Nicholson)

Juan de Los Angeles
(1536–1609)

Spanish Franciscan mystic, unusual in his awareness of the mystical tradition from north of the Pyrenees. In *The Manual of the Perfect Life* he deals with ascetic practices; in *The Spiritual Strife* he presents 'the greatness and the triumphs of love', not ignoring its wounds and sufferings; in *The Conquest of the Kingdom of God* there is an account of what Fray Juan calls the 'intimacy' of the soul, and others have called 'the apex of the spirit': that divine portion of the soul which is raised above all created things in unity with God and in the illumination of the eternal uncreated LIGHT; in *The Triumphs of the Love of God* he starts from an account of the nature and aspiration of the soul, and its fulfilment through LOVE, and passes to the mystic's love of God, and the course of mental prayer which leads to union and transformation.

Juan of Avila
(1500–69)

Spanish Christian mystic, friend of TERESA, noted for his powerful preaching, his fearless attacks on the power and dangers of wealth, his austere self-discipline and the courage with which he met continual pain. 'Let us love,' he wrote, 'and we shall live.'

Judaism

See HASIDISM, KABBALAH

Julian of Norwich
(*c.* 1342–1420)

One of the greatest of the English mystics; a Benedictine nun of Conisford near Norwich, who describes herself as 'a simple creature that could no letter'. She herself records in *Revelations of Divine Love*, one of the great classics of mysticism, the visions she received at the age of thirty. She had prayed for three gifts: a bodily sign of Christ's passion; to have a bodily illness at the age of thirty; to have, of God's gift, three wounds – contrition, suffering with Christ and yearning for God. The second not unnaturally came. In her illness, in gazing at a crucifix she seemed to experience the crucifixion afresh. This was the beginning of her visions.

She records these visions or 'shewings' with considerable objectivity, vividly and simply. She realizes that though she has the impression of a physical manifestation, others do not, and that her perception is in fact spiritual. A good example of spiritual perception may be seen in one of her most famous experiences: 'He showed me a little thing, the size of a hazel nut. I looked at it with the eye of my understanding, and thought "What may this be?" and received the general answer "It is all that is made".' Further she does not regard all the 'shewings' as God-given, and makes distinction between them.

Julian is one of the most joyous of the mystics. A refrain recurs through her work: 'All shall be well, and all shall be well, and all manner of thing shall be well.' She is gently concerned about evil. The revelation she receives is that God, out of the Fall, brings atonement again through Christ's death, 'and since I have made well the most harm, it is my will that thou know thereby that I shall make well all that is less'. 'Shame shall be turned to worship and more joy.' She was troubled by the idea of God's wrath. Her answer is that this is a human idea: 'I saw no wrath but on man's part, and that He forgives in us. For wrath is nothing but a frowardness and contrariness to peace and love; and either it comes from failing of might, or from failing of wisdom, or from failing of goodness – where failing is not in God, but on our part.' God was revealed to her in Life, Love and Light, which added up to one single Goodness: 'And at the end of woe, suddenly our eyes shall be opened, and in clearness of light our sight shall be full; which Light is God, our Maker and Holy Ghost, in Christ Jesus our Saviour. Thus I saw and understood that our faith is our light in our night; which light is God, our endless day.'

The ending of her book is of great beauty. From time to time she tried to discern the meaning of her visions. 'Fifteen years after and more, I was answered in ghostly understanding, saying thus "Wouldst thou learn thy Lord's meaning in this thing? Learn it well: Love was His meaning. Who showed it thee? Love. What showed He thee? Love. Wherefore showed it He? For Love. Hold thee therein and thou shalt learn and know more in the same. But thou shalt never know nor learn therein other thing without end." Thus was I learned that Love was our Lord's meaning. And I saw full clearly that ere God made us He loved us; which love was never slacked, nor ever shall be. And in this love He hath done all His works; and in this love He hath made all things profitable to us; and in this love our life is everlasting. In our making we had beginning; but the love wherein He made us was in Him from without beginning; in which love we have our beginning. And all this shall we see in God, without end.'

Julianus Pomerius
(*c.* 500)

Author of a book *On the Contemplative Life*. There are four approaches to contemplation: knowledge of future things, abstention from worldly business, the study of sacred writings, and the vision of God. Julianus is important because of his sense that true contemplation leads to practical service, and is not true contemplation unless it does so. The fusion of Mary and Martha, of the vision glorious and social responsibility, is one of the profoundest of all insights.

al-Junaid, Abu 'l-Qasim
(d. 910)

Al-Junaid was a pupil of AL-MUHASIBI in Baghdad. He was perhaps the subtlest and most systematic of the Sufi mystics; he was nicknamed 'The Crown of the Mystics'. He starts from the separation of the Eternal from that which was originated in time. Man's separate existence is part of God's plan. At the same time God wills to break down this separateness by the gift of His own BEING. The story of Man is the story of his quest to return to the state in which he was before he was – before the Creation, the time when there was only God. But he cannot do this of himself; it is the gift of God; and the means are FANA, the dying-to-self, the death of self which is life in God. Yet the mystic does not wholly cease to exist as an individual. Rather his individuality is given a new dimension by being taken up in God. And in the flesh he is still separated. God grants him freedom from this world while in union with Himself, but then separates him and restores him to this world again. So al-Junaid, like RABIA and DHU'L-NUN, uses the language of love, of the lover yearning for the Beloved. He also uses the language of NATURE-MYSTICISM, for the separated mystic will seek the Creator through His creation, through 'verdant pastures, beautiful vistas and fresh green gardens'. Al-Junaid spoke of this rhythm of separation and union in a poem:

> Now I have known, O Lord,
> What lies within my heart;
> In secret, from the world apart,
> My tongue hath talked with my Adored.
>
> So in a manner we
> United are, and One;
> Yet otherwise disunion
> Is our estate eternally.
>
> Though from Thy gaze profound
> Deep awe hath hid Thy Face,
> In wondrous and ecstatic Grace
> I feel Thee touch my inmost ground.

Jung, Carl Gustav
(1875–1961)

Swiss psychiatrist, who took his medical degree at Basel, and worked principally at Zürich. He studied under Pierre Janet, and was friendly with Freud, whose theories he at first supported but later criticized. Jung is well known for his theory of psychological types and to him we owe the distinction between introverted and extraverted attitudes, combined with distinctions of functional emphasis between sensation, thinking, feeling and intuition. Intuition is defined as perception via the unconscious; introverted intuition may produce fantastical cranks, but it also produces the mystical dreamer and the seer. It is important to say that it is rarely if ever that we find an absolutely pure type.

One of Jung's other major contributions was to identify archetypes of the collective unconscious, images held in common by different people at different times and in different places, and appearing for example in dreams. It was the study of the archetypes of the collective unconscious which led Jung to the conclusion that man possesses a religious function, and he went so far as to say that it was the prime task of all education to convey the archetype of the God-image to the conscious mind. Now for Jung the God-image is an archetype of the self, and the relation of God to the inner man, and the finding of the self in God and God in the self, are important aspects of mysticism. Further, Jung found certain recurrent symbols, notably the MANDALA, which he regards as symbols of the self, and which have historically appeared as religious symbols. He found an unexpected affinity between dream symbolism and the concepts of ALCHEMY. Jung came to hold that wholeness, whether achieved in normal development or as recovery from mental illness, comes through the 'individuation' process, which might simply be described as the full experience of the archetype of the self, or the finding of the God within, and he found the whole process exemplified in the Chinese mystical treatise THE SECRET OF THE GOLDEN FLOWER.

K

Kabbalah

The root meaning is 'received'. In Judaism the *Kabbalah* is the received (i.e. revealed and handed down as a mystical secret) inspired tradition of mystical understanding of God and the universe. References to such secret lore are found in the Hellenistic age, and it certainly influenced the growth of APOCALYPTIC and GNOSTICISM. We can trace its growth through the Talmudic period into the Middle Ages, and the production of the major mystical work of the mediaeval Kabbalists, THE ZOHAR, and through Isaac LURIA to its influence on HASIDISM.

The Jews were rigid monotheists. How could a single transcendent God create and govern the material world? To provide an answer Jewish esoteric mysticism went to three sources. The first was their own scriptures, which had however to be interpreted allegorically. The second was Platonic, and particularly Neo-Platonic, philosophy, which offered an unchanging real world in contrast to the mutability of the physical world, and in its doctrine of emanation brought the two worlds into relationship. The third strand came from farther east. In Persia they found an antithesis between light and dark, good and evil; this is the source of the Kabbalistic 'tree' whose right side represented light and purity, and whose left side darkness and impurity, and of Kabbalistic dualism generally. They also found a host of intermediate divine beings forming a bridge between the Ultimate and Absolute God and humanity. It is from this source that the belief in angels and archangels and all the company of Heaven and in the demonic powers and hosts of darkness is drawn; from here too that the SHEKHINAH and WISDOM come in as intermediate powers, philosophically interpreted as manifestations of, or emanations from the Almighty. From the east too came a linking of all this with cosmogonical speculations and with a theosophy of astral powers.

The mystic literature shows three important elements. The first is theosophic, and based in part upon ecstatic visions. Even God Himself in the early period is sometimes represented in human form, but immeasurable. In the higher mysticism He is inconceivable to man in Himself, being pure spirit, but creates a being with form and dimensions so as to communicate with His world. In one strand of theosophy primal man, Adam Kadmon, is a bisexual being ninety-six miles tall and ninety-four miles broad, who is split in two, the masculine part becoming the MESSIAH, and the feminine the Holy Spirit. Also important to this theosophy is the description of the seven halls of Heaven or *Hekaloth* and the mysteries of nature. This leads to the second element, the cosmological. Here we encounter a variety of spectacular views. Typical are the emergence of visible matter from a primal substance, normally water; the concept that God wrapped Himself in light to reveal Himself; the discovery of the origin of evil in the disobedience of the water, and its subsequent division into the masculine water of the heavens and the feminine waters of the earth. The third element is theurgy, the practical control of divine powers, through mystic names and formulae.

Typical of early speculative Kabbalistic philosophy may be taken the system whereby there are five intermediate beings between God and matter: the will of God, an emanation from His Being manifested in creative power; universal form and matter (the philosophy at once Platonic and Aristotelian: this makes possible a chain of being); the universal spirit; the thinking animate and vegetative souls; physical nature. In another scheme there are nine primal substances: the One; Intellect; the World-Soul; Primal Matter; Active Nature; Secondary Matter; the World of the Spheres; the Elements; the Physical World.

In the later Kabbalism the same problems remain. God is Absolute, *En-sof* (the Infinite); we know what God is not, not what He is. But if nothing exists outside God, how is the

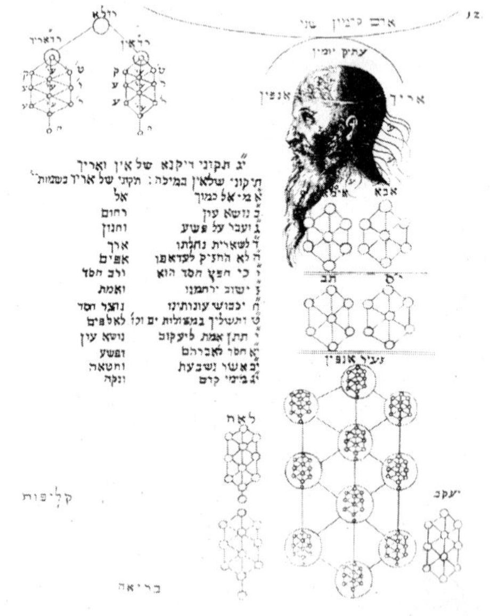

'The Ancient of Days' or 'The Great Head of the Zohar'. An illustration from a 17th-century Kabbalist treatise

Universe to be explained? We must see God as the First Cause, and the universe as an emanation from His Will or WISDOM. The finite has no existence except in the light of the Infinite, which contracted so that the finite might be. Essential here is the doctrine of the SEFIROTH, in whom God is immanent though His Being transcends man. There are four worlds, the world of the *Sefiroth*, the world of creative ideas, the world of creative formations and the world of creative matter, each with its own spiritual beings: they correspond to the spiritual, teleological, organic and mechanistic, but even the lowest has its basis in a higher world. Man is the highest point of the created world, and his soul contains animal and moral elements, but also an element of pure spirit, which in the righteous ascends to God.

Notable techniques of mystical interpretation among the Kabbalists include *Gematria*, the assignment of numerical values to words and the exploration of their relationship to other words of the same value; *Notarikon*, the interpretation of a word by means of a sentence of which its letters provide the acronym; *Temurah*, the interchange of letters according to fixed principles.

One curious feature of the relative freedom of interpretation allowed by such methods is the fact that the Kabbalists vary from the stringent conservative to the radical revolutionary. This was realized at the time; as Isaac Hacohen of Soria said in the thirteenth century, there are two signs of authority, to receive tradition from the past or to be granted the grace of divine inspiration.

But though Kabbalistic literature shows an extraordinary welter of speculation, the aim of the Kabbalists is not intellectual comprehension but spiritual union. The Kabbalists place themselves in contrast with the Talmudists, who engage in fruitless study; they themselves seek results. The method is in general meditation and contemplation, and prayer in particular; and the sexual imagery of marriage is often used to describe the ultimate union. Even the use of alphabetical and numerical mysticism is primarily designed not for intellectual understanding but for the production of spiritual ecstasy.

An anonymous treatise written in Palestine in 1295 and called *The Gates of Justice* expounds well the basis of prophetic Kabbalism. There are three roads of spiritual expansion. The first, the vulgar way, lies through asceticism and concentration on the exclusion of natural forms and images. The second is philosophic, and for the intellectual is winningly attractive. It passes from the study of the material world to the study of the principle which lies behind it, from natural science to theology, and culminates in contemplation; but it is so attractive that it is hard to get beyond the intellectual. The third is the Kabbalistic way, which starts indeed from the natural sciences and the literal meaning of the *Torah*, but then reaches out beyond the finite forms, through the spiritual interpretation of names and numbers, to the infinite Truth, to a force which the seeker cannot control, but which controls the seeker. Such a spiritual ascent starts from the cleansing of the body, then the cleansing of the emotions, then the cleansing of the soul from material. The author recommends isolation in an environment of fresh green colours, prayer, psalm-singing and the study of the *Torah*, imaginative concentration on the principles behind the world, *Temurah*, abstract meditation, until the seeker reaches the point that is beyond thought and beyond words, and then beyond that through the power of imagination he can contemplate his utmost being as in a mirror.

Kabir

(*c*. 1440–1518)

Indian mystical poet, important because (like MECHTILDE in Germany and Richard ROLLE in England) he turned to the vernacular in singing of the divine Love. He was influenced by VAISHNAVISM and by Islamic mysticism, but held that God is directly accessible without the need for religious observances whether Hindu or Moslem. As with many mystics, his universe has three orders, Becoming, Being, God. Kabir is a pantheist: 'The Lord is in me, the Lord is in you, seek for Him within you.' God is revealed in beauty: 'How shall I find words for the beauty of my Beloved? For He is merged in all beauty.' He is revealed in life: 'If you merge your life in the Ocean of Life, you will find life in the Supreme Land of Bliss.' He is revealed above all in love: 'One Love it is that pervades the whole world, few there are who know it fully.'

> How could the love between Thee and me sever?
> As the leaf of the lotus abides on the water:
> so Thou art my Lord and I am Thy servant,
> As the night-bird Chakar gazes all night at the moon:
> so Thou art my Lord and I am Thy servant.
>
> *(tr. Rabindranath Tagore)*

The final mystical experience is that of absorption.

> Subtle is the path of love!
> Therein is no asking and no not-asking,
> There one loses one's self at His feet,
> There one is immersed in the joy of seeking:
> plunged in the deeps of love as the fish in the water.
>
> *(tr. Rabindranath Tagore)*

Kandinsky, Vassily

(1866–1944)

Russian painter, born in Moscow, the pioneer in modern abstract art. After the revolution he was for a period involved in art administration; but his ideas were not acceptable to the Bolsheviks, and in 1921 he left, and in the following year joined the Bauhaus at Weimar. The advent of the Nazis forced him to leave in 1933, and he spent the rest of his life in Paris.

Kandinsky has told how he came to abstraction. In 1910 he was looking at his canvases in a darkened studio, and saw them as formal patterns, not as representations of objects. He made his first watercolour experiment in the same year. In 1912 he expressed an aesthetic mystique in his book *On the Spiritual in Art*, in which he speaks constantly of spirit, soul, life and cosmos. The essence of a work of art is 'inner necessity' which makes it 'a subject breathing spiritually'. So 'creation of a work is creation of a world', a cosmic event. He regarded abstract art as beyond space and time, 'pure realism', renouncing contact with the material world but expressing a deeper reality. He saw his art as a mystery: 'To discuss mysteries by means of the mysterious – is not that the meaning?'

Kant, Immanuel
(1724–1804)

German philosopher of immense influence. Kant held that all knowledge is a synthesis between thought and its object. The world is not an objective fact independent of us; it is the product of the laws of our understanding. In this way he cut away traditional metaphysics and the familiar proofs of the existence of God. We know the phenomenal world; we cannot know the noumenal world. Yet he did not cut at the roots of religion, and himself said: 'I had to deny knowledge of God, freedom, and immortality, so as to make room for faith', and in stating: 'Two things fill the mind with ever-increasing awe, the starry heavens above, and the moral law within', gave a basis for a mystical apprehension of the Ultimate.

Kavanah

In Jewish Hasidic mysticism, the purposeful direction of the whole being in accordance with some feeling springing from the depths of one's nature, the concentration of the soul on a single aim, ultimately the redemption of the world. It is regarded as a gift, or rather as a ray from the LIGHT of God. Redemption involves entering the state of nothingness, 'the form of the intermediate'; only so is transformation possible.

Kegon

Japanese name (Chinese Hua-yen) for a metaphysical Buddhist school emphasizing difference in sameness and sameness in difference. Kegon metaphysics were taken over by the ZEN Masters.

Kelpius, Johannes
(*c.* 1673–1708)

German who moved to America and settled in Pennsylvania, where he lived as an ascetic in the wilderness, attracting to himself disciples and followers. Kelpius was influenced by BOEHME and the PHILADELPHIANS. His book *A Short Essay and Comprehensive Method of Prayer* is one of the finest English post-Reformation mystical treatises. Internal prayer is the only means to attain perfection and to kindle pure love, because it brings us to union with the Will of God. The true inward prayer, which never ends, is an everyday inclination of the heart to God, flowing from that LOVE which draws the presence of God into us: it is as natural as breathing. All it requires by way of preliminary is the practice of the presence of God, and a resigned dedication to His will; all else is Peace and Silence. If, as may happen, we ourselves are 'dry and scattered', God will still act within us if we are faithful. This is the Mystical Way.

Kempe, Margery
(*c.* 1373–1440)

Margery Kempe was born at Lynn in Norfolk; was married at the age of twenty to a worthy citizen named John Kempe, to whom she bore fourteen children; had an extended nervous breakdown after her first childbirth; received a vision of Christ; lived for a while in a mixture of worldliness and devotion; gradually moved to a life of devotion; visited JULIAN OF NORWICH; made pilgrimage to Palestine and a journey to the Baltic. Her autobiography is her claim on posterity, and includes the record of voices and visions, including a spiritual marriage to the Godhead in Rome. She was undoubtedly for long periods conscious of a sense of close communion with Christ, and had a deep sense of gratitude for his love. 'Jesus has been long dead,' she said to one priest. 'Sir, His death is as fresh to me as if He had died this same day, and so, methinketh, it ought to be to you and to all Christian people.' She received too the gift of tears, and an overpowering compassion for the sins of the world. She would 'cry, roar, weep' and 'fall down with boisterous sobbings'. But of all the mystics she is one of the least satisfactory. Her piety and good works are beyond doubt, but so are a vivid imagination, and a tendency to hysterical exhibitionism, and we cannot gain from her any deep spiritual wisdom.

Khidr

The unseen guide for some Sufis, known as the Green One or Master of Saints, and sometimes identified with Elijah, or the unnamed Guide to Moses in THE QUR'AN, or St George. He is liable to appear at any time to help or save or with a revelation, and to be swept away with a rushing sound in the air.

Kingdom of God

Judaic and New Testament concept. The word 'Kingdom' (*basileia*) is better rendered 'kingship'. It does not necessarily refer to an organization or institution, but rather to a state of affairs where God is King. In Matthew the expression 'the kingdom of heaven' is used, indicating a sovereignty which comes down from Heaven to earth; it thus cannot be achieved by human effort. The believer sees, encounters, receives, inherits, dwells in or enters into the kingdom of God; he does not build it or produce it. In early Christian centuries the concept develops in two rather different ways. It may be ethical: righteousness is the condition of entry into the kingdom. In Egypt this was associated with an ascetic dualism. Or it may be eschatological, so that the sovereignty of God is revealed and asserted in a cosmic catastrophe. Both strands have their roots in Judaic prophetic and apocalyptic literature and in the New Testament.

In one passage (Lk. 17, 20–1) Jesus says 'The kingdom of God is *entos humon*'. The Greek is ambiguous between 'among you' and 'within you', and interpreters have differed; but two of the most influential translations, the English Authorized and Luther's, took the latter view, which helped to internalize the concept and make it a matter of personal rather than cosmic mysticism.

In some mystics, such as BOEHME and LAW, the kingdom of Heaven appears as Eternal NATURE. This is influenced by Platonic philosophy by which there are eternal Forms of all things in the natural world. Sometimes it appears as a Platonic interpretation of the heaven of heavens of Psalm 115, 16. For Boehme it is a fourth element additional to the Trinity, the uncreated Heaven or Unapproachable Light, the Jewish SHEKHINAH.

Koan

A *koan* is defined as 'a public document setting up a standard of judgment'; it is a test of the understanding. Typical examples are: 'What is the Buddha? – Three measures of flax.' 'What is the meaning of the first patriarch's Visit to China? – The cypress tree in the front courtyard.' The answers were always provided by the master appropriately to the stage of the pupil's development. It was, so to say, a sign of grace in the pupil to ask the question in the first place. The answer at one and the same time is a check on the way the intellect is working and a demonstration of the limitations of intellect. The object is to make the student question a commonsense materialist view of life with a subject-object structure, and to open his mind to the possibility of new dimensions of experience, e.g. 'What is the sound of one hand clapping?'

T'ui-yin makes ten points on the *koan*.

1 Do not calculate according to your imagination.
2 Do not let your attention be distracted by the Master raising his eyebrows or having a twinkle in his eyes.
3 Do not try to extract meaning from the exact wording of the *koan*.
4 Do not try to exact a demonstration out of the words.
5 Do not think that the sense of the *koan* is to be grasped at the point where it makes contact with the intellect.
6 Do not take Zen for a state of passivity.
7 Do not judge the *koan* by the criteria of Yes and No.
8 Do not take the *koan* as indicating absolute emptiness.
9 Do not ratiocinate about the *koan*.
10 Do not keep your mind in the attitude of waiting for *satori* to turn up.

Krishna

God incarnate in the BHAGAVAD GITA and an Avatar in Hindu epic and legend. The appearance of the Eternal Spirit in human form introduces into Indian religion the element of BHAKTI or personal devotion.

Krishna Consciousness Movement

A widespread incursion of Hinduism into the western world, introduced into the US in 1966 by Swami A. C. Bhaktivedanta. Its adherents are vegetarian and teetotal, devoted to prayer, and dressed in saffron robes. To them the Lord KRISHNA is the 'sweetest' god, and their repetitive cry 'Hare Krishna' is familiar.

Kumarajiva
(343–413)

Indian Buddhist who studied for twenty years, and went to China as a missionary translating some 300 sacred texts, and introducing the MADHYAMIKA or Middle Path. He was an upright, warm and attractive person.

Kuo Hsiang
(d. 312)

Commentator on CHUANG TZU, who denied the existence of a Creator and saw in nature the only reality, and each thing in nature acting according to its own principles. 'If we differentiate things according to their differences, everything is different from the other. If we consider things similar according to their points of similarity, there is nothing which is not the same.'

Kundalini Yoga

Special form of YOGA in which the human body is pictured as a reflection of the whole cosmos, with the spinal column as the *Axis Mundi*. The serpent Kundalini lies in sleep at the base of this column, identified with the power of life (with strong elements of sexuality). The aim of the meditation is to awaken the sleeping power of life and cause it to rise up a twofold spiralling path through the several spiritual centres; at the point where the paths cross there is a release of tension and a breakthrough in consciousness. Eventually the life-force passes out into freedom through the thousand-petalled lotus at the top of the head.

L

La Combe, François
(1643–1712)

Barnabite visionary, spiritual director of Madame GUYON. La Combe was a simple, earnest man, swept off his feet by the theories of MOLINOS. He went with Madame Guyon to Paris, where their QUIETIST views caused him to be confined to the Bastille. In prison he became more and more absorbed in God and in silent prayer. He died in an asylum in Charentes.

Lallemant, Louis
(1587–1635)

French Jesuit, whose instructions on the spiritual life were collected after his death. He insisted on purity of heart and openness to the Holy Spirit, and laid down spiritual exercises to make possible discernment of the will of God. The highest point of prayer is union with Christ. Action should lead to prayer, prayer should prepare for action. 'The final point of the highest perfection in this world is zeal for souls.' J. J. SURIN was his disciple.

Lao-Tzu
(6th century BC)

Legendary Chinese sage, older contemporary of Confucius, putative author of TAO-TE-CHING. A later anecdote records Confucius as saying 'I know that a bird can fly, a fish can swim, and an animal can run. But the dragon's ascent to heaven on the wind and the clouds is something which is beyond my knowledge. Today I have seen Lao-Tzu, who is rather like a dragon.' The story well exemplifies the difference between the down-to-earth middle-of-the-road reformer and the mystical genius. In fact we know virtually nothing about the historical Lao-Tzu, and some scholars have doubted his existence. But some of *Tao-Te-Ching* could well belong to the sixth or fifth century, and there is no particular reason to doubt that it derives from an individual of exceptional mystical insight.

In *Tao-Te-Ching* there seems little to suggest that the writer has had personal mystical experience. Perhaps one section only points to this (48):

> The student learns by daily increment
> The Way is gained by daily loss,
> Loss upon loss until
> At last comes rest.
>
> By letting go, it all gets done;
> The world is won by those who let it go!
> But when you try and try,
> The world is then beyond the winning.

There we seem to have the voice of experience describing the emptying of images from the self.

Lao-Tzu. An early Chinese painting on silk

There is a story told of Lao-Tzu in extreme old age. He asked a disciple to look in his mouth. 'What do you see?' 'Nothing.' 'No teeth?' 'No, no teeth. But I do see a tongue.' This was Lao-Tzu's dying lesson that the sharp, hard, brittle things disappear; the things which are soft and yielding remain.

Laredo, Bernardino de
(1482–1540)

Spanish Franciscan, noted for his austere asceticism and his practical concern for the ill; author of a mystical work *Subida del Monte Sion por la via contemplativa*, which out of humility he published anonymously.

Latifa

Term of Moslem mysticism, often rendered 'subtlety', but referring to the points of faculties of illumination within the individual. It is the task of the Sheikh or Master to develop the sensitivity of these areas through physical and spiritual exercises. The five primary *lataif* are Heart, Spirit (located at the corresponding point of the body on the other side), the Secret *latifa* half-way between, the Mysterious *latifa* in the forehead, the Deeply Hidden *latifa* in the brain. Beyond these is the Self, the total personality, associated with the navel; the seventh and final *latifa* is a mystery accessible only to the Master or Adept.

Law, William
(1686–1761)

Law's father was a Northamptonshire tradesman. The son became a Fellow of Emmanuel College, Cambridge, but withdrew from his fellowship as a Non-juror. The next period of his life is obscure. He emerges from time to time as a writer: we do not know what else he was doing. In 1727 he became tutor to Edward Gibbon, father of the historian, and this brought him in touch with the Wesleys, with whom he had an ambivalent relationship. At this period he wrote his best-known work, *A Serious Call to a Devout and Holy Life*, a trumpet-call against Laodicean tepidity in religion. In 1740 he returned to Northamptonshire with two wealthy and ageing ladies as his devotees. He lived quietly there till his death.

Already at Cambridge he had become interested in Malebranche's view that 'we see all things in God'. Later he was influenced by the mystical writings of Jakob BOEHME. He was not afraid to be dubbed an enthusiast: 'Enthusiasm is as common, as universal, as essential to human nature as love is.' 'Every man, as such, has an open gate to God in his soul. . . . Every Christian, as such, has the first fruits of the Spirit, a seed of life, which is his call and qualification to be always in a state of inward prayer, faith and holy intercourse with God.' Here is the essence of Law's mysticism.

Law's mystical understanding has its outcome in love. In *The Grounds and Reasons of Christian Regeneration* he wrote, 'God is love, yea, all love, and so all love that nothing but love can come from him.' There is no wrath on God's side; it is all on ours; in this last affirmation Law is close to JULIAN OF NORWICH. In his most attractive work, *The Spirit of Love*, he makes the same affirmation. God is 'only an eternal Will to all goodness'. In the same work he says that body and spirit are not two separate independent things but 'only the inward and outward conditions of one and the same being'. This thought comes from Boehme. He also gives his own Christian expression to the idea of a heavenly spark innate in each soul. 'If Christ was to raise a new life like His own in every man, then every man must have had originally in the inmost spirit of his life, a seed of Christ, or Christ as a seed of heaven, lying there as in a state of insensibility or death, out of which it could not arise, but by the mediatorial power of Christ.' And Christ cannot appear in anyone save as love, a love which shows itself in life. For this we must die to ourselves: this is the experience of the Cross. And all this is in the deepest sense natural. 'There is nothing that is supernatural, but God alone.'

Lawrence, Brother
(*c.* 1605–91)

Nicolas Herman was a soldier who became a hermit, and in 1649 joined the Carmelite community in Paris as a lay brother in charge of the kitchen. His maxims were collected after his death by the Abbé de Beaufort. Brother Lawrence practised a simple but profound mysticism which consisted in 'the practice of the presence of God' at all times, in all places and in all activities. His prayer was simply 'a sense of the presence of God'. At the beginning of the day he prayed to continue in the presence of God as he worked. During the day he talked with God as he went about the duties of the kitchen. At the end of the day 'he examined himself how he had discharged his duty'. If he felt he had failed, 'without being discouraged, he set his mind right again, and continued his exercise of the presence of God as if he had never deviated from it'. 'The time of business,' he would say, 'does not with me differ from the time of prayer; and in the noise and clutter of my kitchen, while several persons are at the same time calling for different things, I possess God in as great tranquillity as if I were upon my knees at the Blessed Sacrament.'

Leclerc du Tremblay, Joseph
(1577–1638)

François Leclerc du Tremblay received an excellent education, travelled in Italy, and became a soldier and a diplomat, having the court title of Baron de Mafflier. Then in 1599, after coming under the influence of the circle of BÉRULLE, Mme ACARIE and BENET of Canfield, he renounced the world to become a Capuchin friar with the name of Joseph. He was an ardent contemplative, preacher, reformer and missionary. In 1606 he was one of the founders of the Daughters of Calvary, for whom he wrote a manual of devotion. His dream of a new crusade against the Turks brought him back into politics, and for a quarter of a century he was at Richelieu's side as *l'Eminence grise*; through all his career as diplomat and as minister he practised austere self-discipline and the contemplative life. In 1638 he was about to receive the rank of cardinal when he died. Aldous HUXLEY wrote an understanding account of him in *Grey Eminence*.

Lee, Ann
(1736–84)

See SHAKERS.

Leon, Moses de
(d. 1305)

Spanish Jewish mystic, to whom THE ZOHAR has been plausibly attributed. He also left a number of writings in Hebrew. He started as a follower of the philosopher Maimonides, and only in middle life became absorbed by Kabbalistic speculation. He wrote in a style which, although over-elaborate and in some ways harsh, is of conscious artistry. His great themes are the mystery of the Being of God, and a mystical approach to morality. A typical passage will give an impression of the man and his thought:

'Everything is linked with everything else down to the lowest ring on the chain, and the true essence of God is above as well as below, in the heavens and on the earth, and nothing exists outside Him. And this is what the sages mean when they say: When God gave the Torah to Israel, He opened the seven heavens to them, and they saw that nothing was there in reality but His Glory; He opened the seven worlds to them and they saw that nothing was there but His Glory; he opened the seven abysses before their eyes, and they saw that nothing was there but His Glory. Meditate on these things and you will understand that God's essence is linked and connected with all worlds, and that all forms of existence are linked and connected with each other, but derived from His existence and essence.'

Lévi, Eliphas
(1810–75)

Pen-name of Alphonse Louis Constant, nineteenth-century philosopher of the occult. In Lévi's philosophy there is a medium through which spiritual truth is communicated, which he calls Astral Light. To appreciate this and be illuminated by it requires the development of the powers of the will. Essential to the operation of will is the understanding of analogy, which he calls 'the last word of science and the first word of faith', 'the sole possible mediator between the visible and the invisible, between the finite and the infinite'. Lévi's system is closer to magic than to mystical religion. Yet he hovers between the two. 'Too deep a study of the mysteries of nature may estrange from God the careless investigator, in whom mental fatigue paralyses the ardours of the heart.' He held in fact that piety and magic lead to the same end.

Levitation

Various stories are told of saints in ECSTASY being raised above the ground. Sometimes the evidence is suspect, either because it is late or because it is not corroborated by those who know the central figure best. But with some the evidence is strong. TERESA has left her own account of the experience of rapture which forced the body off the ground no matter how she struggled against it. Bishop Yepes once saw her struggling in ecstasy not to be swept up, clutching an iron grille and crying 'Lord, for a thing of so little consequence as is my being deprived of this favour of yours, do not permit a creature so vile as I am to be mistaken for a holy woman.' There is also, deposited under oath by Sister Anne of the Incarnation, an eye-witness account of Teresa lifted a foot and a half off the ground for the space of half an hour. PHILIP NERI too left his own record orally to Father Gallonio of the experience of being swept off his feet and into the air; it is clear from eye-witness accounts that he resisted it. With Joseph of Cupertino there are over a hundred eye-witness accounts. Nor does the evidence relate solely to a more or less remote past. There is twentieth-century evidence in the cases of Gemma GALGANI and Maria della Passione. It is perhaps important to say that evidence of levitation is not decisive for beatification or canonization. Naturally the evidence in all cases must be carefully – perhaps sceptically – scrutinized. But (without pronouncing either way on such 'secular' instances of levitation as that of D. D. Home) there does appear to be evidence of the physical body behaving in very unusual ways in conditions of spiritual ecstasy.

Liberation

Seen from the side of man's present state, liberation suggests a pessimistic or unfavourable attitude to this world; it is illusion, or a vale of tears, or a prison. At the same time liberation is release into something better and greater. Sometimes as among the Buddhists, and some strands of Hindu mysticism, concentration is on the state of the liberated soul. Sometimes, as in Christian and Moslem mysticism, it is a stage in the journey towards union with a personal God.

Lieh-Tzu

One of the three classics of TAOISM, attributed to a mythical philosopher, Lieh-Tzu. It is the least important and latest of the three, but like the others has as its message the essential unity of all things in the Tao, the futility of human effort and the call to relax in harmony with the universe. The book shows some preoccupation with death and the desire to conquer death.

Ligature of the Faculties

A condition in which, during mystic union, activity such as verbal prayer is impossible.

Light

The origins of light-mysticism are partly traditional and partly arise from direct experience. The imagery is strong in the Bible. It is strong in other parts of the eastern Mediterranean. It is powerful in Persia with the warfare of Light and DARKNESS, in all the astrological religions which depend on sun, moon and stars, in Egypt with the exaltation of Ra and the Aten, in the Hellenistic mysteries where illumination might

Tantric diagram illustrating the strengthening of the spirit towards liberation

be expressed in a blaze of light, or in the release of the initiate from a blindfold into the light.

On the other hand the mystics seem to have had direct experiences which they can describe only under the image of light. Mother Isabel Daurelle says, 'The light which has filled my soul has come not from books but from the Holy Spirit.' Hildegarde of Bingen offers a particularly good example. She was a visionary who saw all her visions through a dazzling light. 'From my infancy,' she says, 'I have always seen this light, in my spirit . . . more brilliant than the sun.' She calls God *Lux vivens*, living Light, and Reality she calls Cloud of the Living Light. She illustrated her writings and the illustrations show a group of shimmering points of light, moving as waves. Her vision of the *Zelus Dei*, the Zeal of God, combines brilliant light with violent, terrifying motion. She describes the falling angels: 'I saw a great star, most splendid and beautiful, and with it an exceeding multitude of falling sparks which with the star followed southwards.' When she was over seventy she wrote 'Sometimes I behold within this light [of the visible world] another light which I name the "living light itself".'

For some mystics light seems of the essence of their experience. To Augustine contemplation aims at 'a kind of spiritual contact with the unchanging light', to Gregory (with whom light-imagery is very strong) it is 'the endeavour to fix the eye of the heart on the very ray of unencompassed light'. For Angela of Foligno the sacrament would shine more brilliantly than the sun. When Sadhu Sundar Singh was converted to Christianity he thought that the room was on fire.

Indian mystical philosophy makes much of light as the manifestation of pure being. The *Brihadaranyaka Upanishad* has a triple equation: 'from non-being lead me to being, from darkness lead me to light, from death lead me to immortality'. And the *Chandogya Upanishad* asserts that this light, which shines in the highest worlds beyond which there are none higher, is the very light that shines within the heart of man. So theophanies are expressed in terms of light. KRISHNA appears to Arjuna like the simultaneous effulgence of a thousand suns, blazing like fire, utterly dazzling. In *The Mahabharata* Vishnu appears in a lightning-flash as bright as the light

Vishnu-Krishna in his cosmic form. An 18th-century Indian painting

of a thousand suns, and it is said that 'by penetrating this light mortals skilled in Yoga attain final deliverance'. So too at the moment of illumination the Buddha perceives the Pure Clear Light of the Universal void, colourless, without spot or shadow, the light of the dawn sky, and this symbolizes the Buddha-state. In general the object of mysticism is to realize the Pure super-cosmic Light within the heart. Eliade has said well that 'for Indian thought the Light mystically perceived denotes transcendence of this world, of profane and conditioned existence, and the attainment of another existential plane – that of pure being, of the divine, of supreme knowledge and absolute freedom. It is a certain sign of the revelation of ultimate reality – of reality devoid of all attributes. That is why it is experienced as a dazzling white Light, into which one gazes blinded and into which one finally disappears, dissolving and leaving no trace. . . . One who reaches the Light and recognizes himself in it reaches a mode of transcendent being beyond the reach of the imagination.'

Among the Eskimo shamans clairvoyance is the result of *qaumeneq*, which means 'lightning' or 'illumination'. It is a mysterious light which the shaman suddenly feels in his body, inside his head, within the brain, enabling him to see in the dark, both literally and metaphorically speaking, for he can now, even with closed eyes, see through darkness and perceive things and coming events which are hidden from others. With the experience of the light goes a feeling of ascension, distant vision, clairvoyance, the perception of invisible entities and foreknowledge of the future. There is an interesting parallel, despite differences, in the initiation of Australian medicine-men, who go through a ritual death, and are filled with solidified light in the form of rock-crystals; on returning to life they have similar powers of clairvoyance and extra-sensory perception.

In THE QUR'AN (24, 35–42) the 'Light verse' which starts from the thought of God as Light has been a constant source of inspiration to Moslem mystics. 'God is the Light of the Heavens and of the Earth. His Light is like a niche with a lamp in it, the lamp encased in glass, the glass as it were a shining star. It is lighted from a blessed tree, the olive which belongs neither to East nor West, whose oil would almost blaze forth, even without the touch of fire. It is light upon light. God guides to His light whom He will. . . . If God does not grant a man light, that man is utterly without light.' This was the starting-point of AL-GHAZALI's great meditation *A Niche for Lights.*

In Islam in the account of the BEATIFIC VISION by al-Arabi (d. 1240) the Vision impregnates the elect with divine light, which pervades their very beings, and radiates from them, as if reflected from mirrors. The direct Light of the Vision is too great for them to enjoy, but in the reflected light they find joy. In general Moslem mystics express their experience through the imagery of light. For example at one stage of the mystical journey seven coloured lights appear successively to the inward eye, and in the deepest experience 'the fires of the *dhikr* never go out, and its lights never fade. . . . You always see some lights ascending and some descending; the fires around you are bright, very hot and flaming.'

This is parallel to the experience of the Orthodox Greek Christian mystics. For Gregory PALAMAS 'the divine Light is a prerequisite of mystical experience'. 'He who shares the divine energy . . . becomes himself in some sort light; he is joined to the Light, and with the Light he sees in full consciousness all that is hidden from those who have not received this grace.' So Symeon the New Theologian saw a light like dawn shining from above, growing brighter and brighter, and himself at the centre of the light; he saw the light permeating his physical being, and turning him completely to fire and light, destroying for him all awareness of the shape, position, bulk and appearance of his body. Palamas built a whole mystical theology round the light of Tabor.

Sometimes mystics at the height of their experience seem to be bathed in streaming light. A good example is the transfiguration of Jesus. THOMAS À KEMPIS, writing as a contemporary of Lidwina of Schiedam, says, 'Apart from her mental illumination . . . she was discovered by her companions to be surrounded by so great a divine brightness that, seeing the splendour and struck with considerable fear, they dared not approach near her. And although she always lay in darkness and material light was unbearable to her eyes, nevertheless, the divine light was very agreeable to her, and her cell was often so wonderfully flooded with this by night that to the watchers the cell itself appeared full of material lamps or fires.' Again, we have an eyewitness, one Jerome da Silva, who gives an account of breaking in on Francis Suarez at his devotions: 'I pushed aside the curtain and entered the inner apartment. Then I perceived that a blinding light was coming from the crucifix, so intense that it was like the reflection of the sun from glass windows, and I felt that I could not have remained looking at it without being completely dazzled.' A disciple of SERAPHIM OF SAROV found his being at the moment of illumination so bright that it was impossible to look at him: 'Father, I can't look at you, your eyes flash lightnings, your face is more dazzling than the sun, and it hurts my eyes to look at you.'

Leuba, in *The Psychology of Religious Mysticism*, has examined a number of such experiences and decided that they are 'uncontestably wholly physiological in origin'. 'The perceptual quality of the experience cannot be doubted.' Clearly drugs like MESCALIN and LSD do occasion a similar experience of brilliance.

The image or symbol of light is also common. RUYSBROECK furnishes a good example. The contemplative must learn to lose himself in darkness, and in the abyss of darkness he begins to find

God: 'For in this darkness there shines and is born an incomprehensible Light, which is the Son of God, in whom we behold eternal life. And in this Light one becomes seeing; and this Divine Light is given to the simple sight of the spirit, where the spirit receives the brightness which is God Himself . . . and where it receives immediately the brightness of God, and is changed without interruption into that brightness which it receives. Behold, this mysterious brightness, in which one sees everything that one can desire according to the emptiness of the spirit: this brightness is so great that the loving contemplative, in his ground wherein he rests, sees and feels nothing but an incomprehensible Light; and through that Simple Nudity which enfolds all things, he finds himself, and feels himself, to be that same Light by which he sees, and nothing else. And this is the first condition by which one becomes seeing in the Divine Light. Blessed are the eyes which are this seeing, for they possess eternal life' (*The Adornment of the Spiritual Marriage* cl).

Lin-chi
(tenth century)

Chinese ZEN Master, who used shouting and beating to lead people to enlightenment. He said that there were four kinds of shout – the sword, the crouching lion, the fisherman's pole and weeds, and the shout that is not really a shout, representing keenness, power in reserve, the power which reveals itself in ordinary life, and paradox. Lin-chi was a man of strong personality and keen dialectical mind. The sect named after him was the most lastingly significant of the FIVE HOUSES.

Little Book of Eternal Wisdom, The

Mystical treatise by SUSO.

Little Gidding

Manor in Huntingdonshire where Nicholas FERRAR and his extended family and household lived a life of communal devotion and activity. The house has gone but the church is still standing. J. H. Shorthouse's novel *John Inglesant* gives a generally persuasive picture of the life of the community. T. S. Eliot used Little Gidding as title and theme for the last of his *Four Quartets*.

Loa

Spirits in the VOODOO cult of Haiti, which possess their subject. There are two main groups, *rada* and *petro*. The *loa* are represented by symbolic drawings called *vèvè*.

Logos

Greek term, which can mean both 'speech' and 'thought', and in mathematics 'proportion' or 'balance'. In HERACLITUS it seems to be a principle of stability in a world of flux; perhaps 'balance', perhaps an underlying rationality; it is also the seer's own words and the inspiration behind them. The STOICS took it over from Heraclitus to mean the Reason behind the universe, which they called God. In the eclectic mood of the late Hellenistic Age this began to coalesce with PLATO's emphasis on reason as the essential part of the human soul. At the same period the Jewish thinkers began to fill the gap between God and man with WISDOM, and sometimes with the Memra or Word of God: in Genesis God speaks and it is done; His Word is His self-expression, and it is with power. Jews in Alexandria, of whom PHILO is the best known, desirous of bringing together Greek and Jewish insights, equated this with the Logos. The Christian Evangelist JOHN took this up, and used it as the basis of a mystical view of Jesus; his opening words are 'In the beginning was the Logos', and he goes on to claim that the divine Logos was incarnate in Jesus. This is also the basis of the mystical philosophy of CLEMENT. The Logos appears in several GNOSTIC systems, and in later Christian mysticism. In some ways the concept of the Logos approximates to that of the TAO; it is the principle behind the Universe, and the Stoic idea that we must live according to the Logos (sometimes misleadingly rendered 'according to reason') is close to Taoist philosophy; Chinese Christians render the opening of John 'In the beginning was the Tao.'

Lorenzo Monaco
(d. 1425)

Piero di Giovanni, better known as Lorenzo Monaco, was a member of the CAMALDOLESE contemplatives, one of a group of illuminators associated with the monastery. His style is Gothic, as can be seen in the *Adoration of the Magi* in the Uffizi: the debt to GIOTTO and the Sienese may be seen in various versions of *The Coronation of the Virgin* (one in the National Gallery, London). He influenced Fra ANGELICO.

Louis de Blois
(16th century)

Abbot of Liessies in the Spanish Netherlands, author of a *Book of Spiritual Instruction*. According to Louis, in the centre of the soul there is an 'abyss', a divine temple from which God never departs and which is constantly irradiated by the uncreated Lights; so that the omnipresent God dwells in the human soul 'in a very special way'.

Love

George Eliot once said that love is a word of all work. We talk of loving God, loving our parents or children, loving our neighbour as ourselves, loving a husband or wife, loving mountain scenery, loving our jobs and so on. Discounting the extension of the word to inanimate objects there are in classical Greek, to which much of the European tradition is indebted, four separate words to express different aspects of the experience of Love. *Storge* means natural affection. *Philia* means friendship or mutual love. *Eros* means sexual desire. *Agape* is the New Testament word for love, and the noun had virtually to be invented to express it; the verb was used, among other things, for the patient seeking of another's well-being, no matter whether they respond.

In religious mysticism friendship may play some part. In the Christian tradition Jesus in the Upper Room called his disciples 'not slaves but friends', and, although the word used is *agape*, when John in his first *Letter* writes 'We love because he first loved us' (4, 19), he records an experience not inappropriately called *philia*. Hence the mediaeval mystics who called themselves FRIENDS OF GOD, and the later SOCIETY OF FRIENDS. So too friendship is one of the five degrees of BHAKTI.

But the two great words for love have been *agape* and *eros*. The Platonic tradition in particular took *eros* as the aspiration towards God, a kind of sublimation of sexual desire, a direction of the libido towards the spiritual; and PLOTINUS actually dared to coin the phrase 'God is *eros*.' This may be no more than a counterblast to the Christian 'God is *agape*', but he may also be saying that the very aspiration towards God is itself God. Anders Nygren in a famous book tabulates the antithesis between *eros* and *agape*:

Eros is acquisitive desire and longing.	Agape is sacrificial giving.
Eros is an upward movement.	Agape comes down.
Eros is man's way to God.	Agape is God's way to man.
Eros is man's effort: it assumes that man's salvation is his own work.	Agape is God's grace: salvation is the work of divine love.
Eros is egocentric love, a form of self-assertion of the highest, noblest, sublimest kind.	Agape is unselfish love, it 'seeketh not its own', it gives itself away.
Eros seeks to gain its life, a life divine, immortalized.	Agape lives the life of God, therefore dares to 'lose' it.
Eros is the will to get and possess which depends on want and need.	Agape is freedom in giving, which depends on wealth and plenty.
Eros is primarily *man's* love; God is the *object* of Eros. Even when it is attributed to God, Eros is patterned on human love.	Agape is primarily *God's* love: 'God *is* Agape'. Even when it is attributed to man, Agape is patterned on Divine love.
Eros is determined by the quality, the beauty and worth, of its object; it is not spontaneous, but 'evoked', 'motivated'.	Agape is sovereign in relation to its object, and is directed to both 'the evil and the good'; it is spontaneous, 'overflowing', 'unmotivated'.
Eros *recognizes value* in its object and loves it.	Agape loves – and *creates value* in its object.

Nygren insists that his aim is to bring out a difference in type, not a difference in value, but it is hard not to feel that there are implications of the latter. Further, Nygren makes a distinction between mysticism, with the symbolism of the heavenly ladder, and the emphasis on ASCETICISM, deification, natural immortality, ECSTASY, vision and beatitude, all of which belong to the world of *eros*; and revelation, which requires nothing but faith, and which comes from *agape*.

Subsequent interpreters, while recognizing the value of Nygren's work, have felt that the dichotomy is less absolute. In the Christian tradition, as Nygren admits and regrets, *agape* and *eros* are closely intertwined and virtually impossible to disentangle. Other languages than Greek do not possess or have not developed the verbal and conceptual distinctions implied. Or sometimes the conceptual distinction is there but not the verbal one. The Sufi poet RABIA makes clear that love towards God is qualitatively different from any other kind of love. The fact that Sufi poetry has to be read at two levels itself implies a difference as well as a similarity. More, if the libido is understood in the widest sense as the drive, urge or energy of the personality, not merely must *agape* in man be seen as an expression of that libido, but so must the faith which Nygren contrasts with *eros* as the necessary response to revelation. And within Nygren's own Christian tradition, if man is made in the image of God, that which makes God 'tick' (so to speak), i.e., *agape*, cannot be alien to that which makes man 'tick', i.e., in the sense defined, his libido. The dichotomy cannot be absolute.

Eastern mystics of all traditions, but particularly the Sufis, use the language and imagery of sexual love in their expression of the experience of union. Even within this explicit form of expression there is often the sense that to strive towards the Bridegroom is fruitless and that the soul must wait for the Bridegroom to come; it can prepare for him, but cannot compel him. But the idea of love is much wider than this might imply. Thus the essence of Sufi teaching is that love conquers self because it looks away from self. So RUMI, 'Love is the remedy of our pride and self-conceit, the physician of all our infirmities. Only he whose garment is rent by love becomes entirely unselfish.' He calls love 'the astrolabe of the mysteries of God'. Hindu *bhakti* is akin to Christian *agape*. There is a constant witness that love to God is not genuine unless it is shown in love to man, and an occasional witness that (as a Hindu proverb has it) 'Love of man leads to love of God'. Further, love is all-powerful. The motto of the All-India Jaina Association is 'Love conquers all.' The Chinese sage Mencius says

'Love cannot be outnumbered.' 'Love', says *Tao-Te-Ching* (67), 'is triumphant in attack and invulnerable in defence.'

In Christian thought the identification of God with Love goes back to the New Testament (1 Jn 4, 9). Ruysbroeck identifies Love with the Holy Spirit, born of the interaction of the Father and His Eternal Wisdom. ECKHART takes up the same thought. 'The best masters say that the love wherewith we love is the Holy Spirit. Some deny it. But this is always true: all those motives by which we are moved to love, in these is nothing else than the Holy Spirit.' But if God is Love, Love is also God. In one of the finest passages in *The Mirror of Simple Souls* we read '"I am God," says Love, "for Love is God and God is Love. And this soul is God by condition of love: but I am God by Divine Nature. . . . This soul is the eagle that flies high, so right high and yet more high than any other bird, for she is feathered with fine love." So Love transforms the soul.' TRAHERNE puts this finely: 'Love is so divine and perfect a thing, that it is worthy to be the very end and being of the Deity. It is His goodness, and it is His glory. We therefore so vastly delight in Love, because all these excellencies and all other whatsoever lie within it. By Loving it does dilate and magnify itself. By Loving it does enlarge and delight itself. By Loving also it delighteth others, as by Loving it doth honour and enrich itself. But above all by Loving it does attain itself. Love also being the end of souls, which are never perfect till they are in act what they are in power. They were made to love, and are dark and vain and comfortless till they do it.' He goes on: 'God is present by Love alone. By Love alone He is great and glorious. By Love alone He liveth and feeleth in other persons. By Love alone He enjoyeth all the creatures, by Love alone He is pleasing to Himself, by Love alone He is rich and blessed. O why dost thou not by Love alone seek to achieve all these, by Love alone attain another self, by Love alone live in others, by Love attain thy glory? The soul is shrivelled up and buried in a grave that does not Love. But that which does love wisely and truly is the joy and end of all the world, the King of Heaven, and the Friend of God, the shining Light and Temple of Eternity: the Brother of Christ Jesus, and one Spirit with the Holy Ghost.'

The Jewish mystics, although they speak of love towards God, think of it as the love of a child for his father. Unlike the Christians, they did not interpret '*The Song of Songs*' in terms of the love of God for the soul. To these there is one exception. The SHEKHINAH is thought of as a feminine principle, and the mystics are continually speaking of the love of God for His Shekhinah. For the Platonic element in Kabbalism required every earthly manifestation to have its perfect counterpart in the world of the Infinite, and this sacred union between the King and the Queen, the divine I and the divine You, gives meaning to human love and indeed to human existence. In one astonishing passage Moses's experience in encountering God is actually described as intercourse with the Shekhinah; this is unique.

Love is the means of purification. 'Love', said al-Shibli, 'is a fire in the heart consuming all save the Will of the Beloved.' 'Love', said Abu 'Abd Allah al-Qurashi, 'means giving all you have to Him Whom you love, so that nothing remains to you of your own.' 'Love', said JUAN DE LA CRUZ, 'has set the soul on fire and transmuted it into love, has annihilated and destroyed it to all that is not love.'

Love leads us ever onwards and upwards. 'Love,' said ISAAC OF NINEVEH, 'of which God is the cause, is as a spring welling from the depths, whose current will never cease. For He alone is the source of love whose supply does not fail.' 'Love,' said CLEMENT OF ALEXANDRIA, 'goes with us into the fullness of God, and increases the more when perfection has been granted.' 'Love', said RABIA, 'has come from Eternity and passes into want of love.'

Love is an experience of joy. 'Love to God', said AL-MUHASIBI, 'is the kindling of the heart with joy because of the proximity of the Beloved.' 'Love', said ISAAC OF NINEVEH, 'is the wine that gladdens the heart of man.'

Love leads to knowledge: it is indeed a form of knowledge. So William LAW said 'Love is infallible; it has no errors, for all errors are the want of love.'

But there is another aspect of Love. It does seemingly imply a distinction between the Lover and the Beloved. So the Christian Neo-Platonist treatise *The Book of the Holy Hierotheos* says, 'Love is the pure and holy communion which binds divinely, and wondrously encircles that which loves unification; but those in this condition are very far from unification. For, you see, the very name of Love is a sign of distinction, for Love is not established by one but by two, by the lover and by that which he loves.'

See also SEX, SPIRITUAL MARRIAGE.

LSD

Short for lysergic acid diethylamide, a drug which overstimulates a section of the brain and so distorts responses. The result may be that familiar objects become of extreme beauty and colours appear of rare brilliance, some of the effects being close to those of mystical religion. Time sense is affected, and past, present and future become one. The senses interact and music, for example, may produce visual experiences or bodily vibrations: there is synaesthesia. Logical categories fall away, and opposites unite. One experimenter records a flash of illumination in which he saw himself as a 'minute and miserable microcosm, containing but the barest hint of the infinitely more complex and enormously vast macrocosmic Mind of God'. He was filled with awe and love of God, and felt that every object was touched by God's presence. Dr Leary also emphasizes its capacity to produce an expanded sexual consciousness and expanded sexual energy. But also it can produce fear and horror, or again an illusion of impregnability, and it has been known to lead to insanity, suicide and attempted murder.

'Lucie-Christine'
(1858–1916)

Pen-name of a French mystic. Outwardly she led an ordinary life in the enjoyment of her children and their friends. But in solitude, she wrote, 'my soul found itself transported into the Infinity of God; not merely as into some new region, but as if, having lost its own life, it was living in the Infinite itself'. She was an ordinary orthodox Catholic; she had never read anything about the great mystics. She was in her late twenties when she suddenly had a vision of the words GOD ALONE, and with it 'a Light, an Attraction and a Power. A Light which showed me how I could belong completely to God alone in this world; an Attraction, by which my heart was subdued and delighted; a Power which inspired me with a generous resolution, and in some way placed in my hands the means of carrying it out.' From this, though there were periods of darkness and desolation, she came to a vigorous, joyous sense of the presence of God. Her spiritual experiences centre on Christ, but they range also into the 'absolutely other', the timeless and eternal, the Ultimate. Her *Spiritual Journal* is one of the most important mystical documents of this century. One quotation will convey something of it: 'My way is very simple. My soul lives on God, by a glance of love between Him and myself. By this glance God gives Himself to me, and I give myself to Him. This is my habitual state, that in which God has placed me. I neither can nor should turn myself from it on account of suffering. This I accept as inseparable from love here below. Love suffers as the voice sings.'

Luis de Granada
(1504–88)

Luis de Sarria was born in Granada. He was a profound scholar, and a brilliant preacher, who held high office in the Dominican order, but rejected worldly ambition, and lived a long untroubled life. Among Spanish mystics he is unusual for his NATURE-MYSTICISM. He approaches God through the night sky, through the rebirth of life in spring, the subtle varieties of sea-shells, through the marvellous reproductive power of fish, through whale or through frog. He writes also of the mystic life, the need for humility and perseverance, the way in which a glimpse of God makes the soul hunger for more, the ultimate aim 'to give up all but God and to be joined in spirit with Him in continual and most ardent love', 'the transformation of the soul in God himself', though this, he says, is but for the few. In his *Libro de la Oracion* he offers an introduction to the practice of meditation with particular insistence on the preparation of the heart, offering a simple method suitable for tyros. His mystical writings were suppressed by the Inquisition but were restored to favour and influenced FRANÇOIS DE SALES.

Luis de Leon
(1528–91)

Spanish mystic, scholar and poet, member of the Augustinian order, and professor in the University of Salamanca. His life was stormy; he was quarrelsome with his colleagues and ran foul of the Inquisition. After four years in prison he resumed duties to a crowded lecture-hall, and began 'As we were saying yesterday . . .'

Luis is a nature-mystic, who found Christ in the fields:

When I behold the sky
With stars innumerable spangled bright,
And then the Earth descry
Encompassèd with night,
Buried in sleep, oblivion infinite,

Sorrow and love arise
And with a burning fever fill my breast,
And ever from my eyes
The tears flow without rest
Till my tongue speaks at last, with grief
oppressed:

O dwelling of great might,
Temple of lovely light incomparable,
My soul that to thy height
At birth aspired, what spell
Doth in this dark, low prison-house compel?

(tr. A. F. G. Bell)

Luis is no ascetic; he delights in all the joys of life. But he has the genuine mystic's experience of 'the birth of Christ in the soul', 'the glories of contemplation' and 'the ecstasies of the spirit', and there is something more than a little touching in the great controversialist's resting in Christ as Prince of Peace.

Lull, Ramon
(*c.* 1232–1315)

Spanish Christian mystic and missionary, follower of FRANCIS. In youth he was gay and worldly. One story tells how he was pursuing a girl. She took him to one side, and uncovered her breast which was foul and cancerous. 'Ramon,' she said, 'see the foulness of this body which has won your affection. Better to have set your love on Jesus Christ, of whom you may have an eternal reward.' Even this did not change him. But suddenly while writing love poetry he saw before him Jesus on the Cross. Five times the vision came and constrained him to give up his worldly life. He set himself to bring the love of Christ to Islam. He learned Arabic; he also learned something of Sufic mysticism. To this end he travelled through North Africa and through Asia as far as India.

Ramon Lull

Ramon Lull was a voluminous writer. In *Blanquerna* he wrote a novel about a boy who became Pope and then laid down office to spend his last days in contemplation. *Blanquerna* contains a kind of inset, *The Book of the Lover and the Beloved*, which contains Lull's profoundest mystical writing. It tells of the relation between the Lover, 'the faithful and devout Christian', and the Beloved, God, Creator and Redeemer, transcendent and immanent: 'Thou, O my Beloved, art so great a Whole, that Thou canst abound and be wholly of each one who gives himself to Thee.' As intermediary between these two is Love; he stands between them, so that the Lover cannot reach the Beloved without passing through Love. He sustains and inspires the Lover. The end is the Lover's surrender ('I would give Thee all of myself that I may have all of Thee, and Thou all of me') and a union in which 'whether they are near or far is all one; for their love mingles as water mingles with wine. They are linked as heat with light, they agree and are united as Essence and Being.'

Much of the attraction of the book lies in a form of NATURE-MYSTICISM. The sun rising and setting, shining in a clear sky or rimming the clouds with splendour, mountain and valley, leaf and flower and fruit, the gentle breeze and the storm wind, lucent spring and tossing ocean, and always, above all, the song of the birds, speak of the God who is Love. Lull's spiritual vision has two poles: the love of God in nature, and the love of God in Christ, and in one wonderful passage, Christ becomes identified with the Lover, and the two visions come together: 'The birds hymned the dawn, and the Lover, who is the dawn, awakened. And the birds ended their song, and the Lover died in the dawn for his Beloved.'

Luria, Isaac
(1534–72)

Isaac Luria was the creative force in the Jewish mystical movement centring on Safed in Palestine. He left no writings. He was first and foremost a visionary, who became a legend in his own lifetime. Luria's theory of creation is that the existence of the universe is made possible by the withdrawal or concentration (*tsimtsum*) of God. The first act of the cosmic drama is God's self-limitation. Only then does He send out LIGHT. But now there is a two-way process: the light flows out from God and back to Him, and He has to continue to withhold Himself, to limit Himself.

Two other important ideas of Luria are the 'breaking of the vessels', which is an attempt to answer the problem of evil: the vessels holding the divine light were broken, and the light either flowed back to its source or became diffused, and formed the lower worlds. Hence the cosmic drama. But with evil came Luria's other concept, redemption or mending (*tikkun*), which is the work of God, who leaves some part of it to man. The Jew, through obedience to the *Torah* and through prayer (Luria has a complex theory of mystical prayer), can share in the work of restoration, which will have its culmination in the appearance of the Messiah.

Isaac Luria's theosophy is thus a cosmic myth of exile and return, and deeply linked with the experiences of the Jewish people.

M

Macarius
(*c.* 300–390)

An Egyptian monk celebrated for his sanctity and miracles. The name means 'Blessed'. Known as Macarius of Egypt, Macarius the Elder or Macarius the Citizen. Some fifty homilies attributed to him are of uncertain authorship. They smack of Constantinople rather than Egypt, and seem to be influenced by Messalian ideas. They are mystical in tone and incorporate the experiences of non-Christians as well as of Christians: 'If you seek God in the depth, you find Him there; if you seek in the water, there you find Him, if you seek Him in the fire, you will find Him there also. He is everywhere.' The homilies use the familiar images of fire working on metal, of Light within light, of the heavenly Bridegroom and the perfected bride. Of Macarius himself it was said that 'he was at all times in a state of wonder at some divine Vision, and he used to become like a drunken man because of some hidden vision, and his mind was more often exalted to God than it was concerned with earthly and sublunary things'.

Madhyamika

The Middle Path of Mahayana Buddhism expounded by NAGARJUNA, by which through contradictions the disciple learns to comprehend the unreal.

Magdalena de la Cruz
(1487–1564)

Franciscan of Cordova, three times abbess of her monastery, who according to her own testimony was inspired by the Devil to seek a reputation for sainthood out of vanity; she had visionary experiences which were terrifying, not exalting; she devised for herself the marks of the STIGMATA, pretended to a fast she was not practising, and showed other signs of supernatural powers. For thirty-eight years she deceived theologians, Church leaders and the common people; then in 1543 in a grave illness repented and confessed; regretted her repentance, and was subjected to exorcism, and ended her days in another convent.

Magic Flute, The

Opera by Mozart to a libretto by Schikaneder, first performed in 1791. The drama started from a fairy story. The hero meets the fairy queen, who gives him a portrait of her daughter, who is to be rescued from a wicked magician with the aid of a magic flute. But Mozart changed the libretto round into a glorification of mystic religion, associated with FREEMASONRY and the ancient Egyptian mysteries of ISIS AND OSIRIS. So the wicked magician turns out a beneficent guide, in whose realm vengeance has no place, and sin is neither glorious nor damned, but is dismissed by the beams of the sun; the hero and heroine, Tamino and Pamina, are initiated through silence, self-knowledge, despair and the dark night of the soul, and march together in love through ordeals of fire and water. To most people this is Mozart's musical masterpiece, and the fantasies of the story should not distract us from the fact that this opera contains what the rationalistic Bernard Shaw described as 'the only music yet written fit for the mouth of God'.

Mahayana

See BUDDHISM.

Maithuna

In TANTRA the ritual union of a male devotee with a woman who is an incarnation of Sakti. The union is a mystical union and does not include the ejaculation of semen. During union the couple attain nirvanic consciousness which forms at the top of the head, and fills the sexual organs with a fivefold light: the creative power of the man thus becomes one with the creative power in the universe.

Papageno overcomes Monostatos with the aid of his magic bells. A late 18th-century illustration of a scene from Mozart's The Magic Flute

Stéphane Mallarmé. *A portrait etching by Paul Gauguin*

Mallarmé, Stéphane
(1842–98)

French symbolist poet, one of the apostles of 'art for art's sake'. Mallarmé did not believe that science could reveal truth. Nor did he believe that similes or analogies susceptible of intellectual analysis lead to illumination. Instead he used his symbols directly, expressing the idea that reality is one. So too he constructed his poems to avoid the predominance of individual words in a line or lines in a poem, and used ambiguous syntax to create a sense of unbroken flow; again the One is supervening on the many. Mallarmé was as opposed to religion as he was to science – he writes of 'This old and malicious plumage, overthrown, fortunately, God' – but he passed through the DARK NIGHT OF THE SOUL to illumination, as he himself records: 'after finding *Nothingness* I have found *Beauty*'.

Malon de Chaide, Pedro
(*c.* 1530–89)

Spanish poet and prose-writer, whose work *The Conversion of the Magdalen* is an essay in popular mysticism, treating in dramatic form the all-sufficiency of LOVE, God as the Universal centre, and the experience of Union with God. From the contrast between the sinless, suffering Jesus and the weak, sinful Magdalen we see the sinner become a saint, and ultimately attain to the vision of the celestial city, where life is true life, glory is absolute glory, where they have one wish, one will, one counsel: 'They love one thing, desire one thing, contemplate one thing, and are united with one thing: yes, that one thing – that is the one thing needful.'

Mana

Melanesian word for a power found in material objects and in spirits of the dead.

Mandaeans

GNOSTIC sect, more properly called Nasoreans, which can first be traced in Palestine in the late first or early second century AD. The Mandaeans appear to have emerged in the Christian period, and to have been influenced by Christian ideas and paid some veneration to John the Baptist, though later they became hostile to Christianity. The major writings come from the seventh or eighth century. The Mandaean GNOSIS has been summarized under ten heads:

1 A supreme Being, without form, producing spiritual powers and worlds from its own being.
2 Among these emanations are creator gods, including archetypal man, who produces the universe we know.
3 A dualism of light and darkness.
4 A world of Platonic forms.
5 The soul is an exile, her home being in the supreme Being.
6 Astrology.
7 A saviour to help the soul to the world of light.
8 A cult-language.
9 Ritual mysteries.
10 Secrecy.

The dualism is basic: 'Behold and learn that between darkness and light there can be no union or pact: on the contrary, hatred, enmity and dissension. . . . For darkness is the adversary of light. They are Right and Left, soul and spirit, moreover they are called Adam and Eve.' The principle of creation is divided between male and female, non-matter and matter, sky and earth, with the same correspondences; creation is not possible without union between them. There is a horror of the body, and of the world of matter (though, paradoxically, a great delight in natural beauty): 'Who has made me dwell on earth, who has cast me into the physical body which has no hands or feet and does not know how it will walk? It lies there and crawls!' The object is escape, and there is a splendid image of the soul as a silk worm wrapped in the cocoon of the body and emerging as a winged moth. A beautiful hymn recited at baptism tells of the final union.

In the name of Life!
What did your Father do for you, Soul,
The great day on which you were raised up?

He called the faltering soul, and went before her up the mountain, through the fire and into the sea.

'He entered the sea before me;
He cried aloud that I might hear,
That I might hear he cried aloud,
"If there is strength in you, Soul, come!"

"If I go into the sea I shall sink,
I shall be overturned and perish from the world!"

To heaven I lifted my eye,
And my soul waited upon the House of Life.
I went into the sea and was not drowned,
I came and found the life of my Self.'

Yea, Life! Lo, Life!
Life has triumphed over this world
And Life is victorious.

(tr. E. S. Drower; altered)

The Mandaean sect survives in the Baghdad area to this day.

Mandala

Sanskrit word for a magic circle, which may be applied to a variety of concentric figures. In Eastern religions the *mandala* is used as a help to contemplation, and as a symbol of the deity. JUNG found the *mandala* recurring in his patients' dreams and visions, often divided into four segments, symbolizing the striving of the Self to achieve wholeness and total unity.

Tibetan tantric mandala. An 18th-century painting on cloth

Mande, Hendrik

(*c.* 1360–1431)

Known as the 'Ruysbroeck of the North', he was a follower of GROOTE and one of the BRETHREN OF THE COMMON LIFE. In the monastery of Windesheim he had a number of visionary and mystical experiences: the fruits of these were embodied in twelve tracts which he composed on mysticism in Flemish.

Manichaeism

Mani seems to have been born in Persia in the early third century AD, and was greatly influenced by Zoroastrian dualism. His own originality of speculation drove the Zoroastrians into opposition and he was exiled to India. He returned, and for a period enjoyed imperial support but in the end died a martyr's death. Mani was the originator of a characteristic GNOSTIC system, but was unusual in that his purpose was to found a world religion, not an esoteric sect.

Mani's system is a rigid dualism: 'Before the existence of heaven and earth and everything in them there were two natures, the one good and the other evil. Both are separate each from the other. The good principle dwells in the place of Light and is called "Father of Greatness". Outside him dwell his five Powers: Intelligence, Knowledge, Thought, Deliberation, Resolution. The evil principle is called "King of Darkness", and he dwells in his land of Darkness surrounded by his five Æons, the Æons of Smoke, Fire, Wind, Water and Darkness. The world of Light borders on the world of Darkness with no dividing-wall between.'

DARKNESS rises up against LIGHT, and this stirs the world of Light, which is too peaceable to resist, to create a saviour, Primal Man. Primal Man is defeated, and the soul is taken as booty and fettered in impurity. Primal Man regains consciousness and calls on the Father. This results in the second creation, producing the Living Spirit who releases Primal Man. Soul is still imprisoned, but this pre-liberation is the guarantee of salvation. The Living Spirit now creates the cosmos, but out of the remains of the powers of evil. The world is an embodiment of the Arch Power of Darkness, and a prison for all the powers of Darkness, and only a small portion of Light is left within it. But it is the scene of the Soul's purification. Now the Father performs His third act of creation, the Messenger, who is to be liberator and saviour. He forms plants and animals. The King of Darkness counters by forming Adam and Eve as a prison for the soul; the human body is thus designed by the powers of darkness. The powers of Light send Jesus, who is an emanation of the Messenger. Jesus makes Adam eat from the Tree of Knowledge (the Jewish myth is turned on its head), and reveals himself as the personification of all the Light imprisoned in matter, the suffering form of Primal Man, who 'every day is born, suffers and dies', who 'hangs from every tree', who is thus redeemer and redeemed.

I am in everything, I bear the skies, I am the foundation, I support the earths, I am the Light that shines forth, that gives joy to the souls.

I am the life of the world: I am the milk that is in all trees: I am the sweet water that is beneath the sons of matter . . .
I bore these things until I had fulfilled the will of my Father; the First Man is my father whose will I have carried out . . .
O soul, raise your eyes to the height and contemplate your bond . . . look, your Fathers are calling you.

Escape comes from mortifying the body, through an extreme asceticism, including vegetarianism and abstinence from sex. We have a prayer of confession: 'My Lord! We are full of defects and sins, we are deep in guilt; because of the unsatiable shameless demon of greed we always and incessantly, in thought, word and deed, and in seeing with our eyes, in hearing with our ears, in speaking with our mouths, in grasping with our hands, and in walking with our feet, torment the Light of the Five Gods, the dry and the wet earth, the five kinds of animals, the five kinds of herbs and trees.' Such extreme asceticism was not for all, and the Manichaeans divided mankind into the Elect, who lived ascetically and after death entered the Paradise of Light; the Soldiers or Hearers (a touch of PLATO and Pythagoras here), the mass of believers, who return to the world and its terrors until they are ready to join the Elect; and sinners, who fall into Hell.

AUGUSTINE was at one time much affected by Manichaeism, and its dualism and rejection of the world of matter have recurred at various times in religious history.

Manitou

Algonquin word for a spiritual force manifested in a material object.

Mantra

A prescribed sacred formula in Indian mystical religion, often passed down from a *guru* (teacher) to a pupil for private meditation. A famous story tells how RAMANUJA ignored the usual secrecy and shouted his *mantra* from the roof of a temple, because if it had any relevance it had to be relevant to the whole world. Sri AUROBINDO describes the *mantra* as 'a direct and most heightened, an intensest and most divinely burdened rhythmic word which embodies an intuitive and revelatory inspiration and ensouls the reality of things and with its truth and with the divine soul-forms of it, the Godheads which are born from the living truth', or again as 'a supreme rhythmic language which seizes hold upon all that is finite and brings into each the light and voice of its own infinite'. For a type of Christian *mantra* see JESUS-PRAYER. The most famous of all *mantras* is the syllable OM.

Margaret Mary Alacoque
(1647–80)

Illness and family opposition made Margaret's childhood in provincial France unhappy. In 1671 she entered the Convent of the Visitation at Paray-le-Monial. She had a passion for humiliation, suffering, penance, MORTIFICATION, which her superiors found it wise to curb. Two years later her visions of the Sacred Heart began – 'a pictured expression of one of the deepest intuitions of the human soul, caught up to the contemplation of God's love' (Evelyn Underhill) – and continued for a year and a half. Her superiors treated her visions as delusory, but her sincerity and devotion won their way. From the visions emerged the pattern of devotion to the Sacred Heart of Jesus, which centred upon the sacrament of the EUCHARIST in reparation for all the wrongs committed against the divine Love. The observances were not authorized till seventy-five years after her death.

Maria de Jesus
(1602–65)

Mary of Agreda, as she is often called, was foundress and first abbess of the Franciscan Recollects at Agreda. The account of revelations she claimed to receive was published in *La mistica ciudad de Dios*. This work came in for severe criticism: BOSSUET described it as 'an impious impertinence and a trick of the devil'. That was undoubtedly too severe, and her critics accept that she had genuine experience of rapture and that her virtues were 'heroic'. One unusual feature of her raptures was that her superiors could recall her from them by a mental order given at a distance. The revelations she professed to receive were a curious amalgam. They included physical facts about dates and distances which do not accord with the evidence (as that the earth's radius is 1,251 miles); they include an affirmation of her own infallibility; they include prodigies attributed to the Virgin Mary, which may have arisen from imagination and reading, combined with a desire to exalt the Virgin: they include also experiences which bear the hallmark of positive illumination. Mary's revelations have their supporters and detractors; the sanctity of her life is widely admired.

Maria Magdalena de' Pazzi
(1566–1607)

Florentine of noble birth who entered a Carmelite convent, of which she later became subprioress. After a period of spiritual darkness, and a dangerous illness, from 1584 she experienced a succession of ecstasies, out of which she would deliver spiritual advice which others recorded. She particularly stressed the value of suffering for spiritual development. Her spiritual approach is strongly Eucharistic. Her experiences gained her the sobriquet of the Ecstatic Saint.

Marijuana

See HASHISH.

Marquart of Lindau
(d. 1342)

The greatest of the Franciscan mystics, indebted also to ECKHART and TAULER. Marquart is particularly interesting for his Platonism. Ideas or Ideal Forms are the prototypes of everything on earth, the causes of all created things, the source of all human knowledge, 'flowing rivers of divine sweetness' which bring to the blessed their bliss. All past and all future are present in the Ideas. But although the Ideas might seem to offer a kind of *gnosis*, Marquart ranks will above knowledge: martyrs are superior to confessors. The will 'penetrates the unity of the highest will and the power of love and becomes one with the pure and only Good, eternally united'.

Martyn, Henry
(1781–1812)

English evangelical missionary, influenced by John WESLEY and Charles Simeon. Martyn, an outstanding academic, abandoned the university to serve as a missionary in India and Persia. He did major work in translating the New Testament into Hindustani, Arabic and Persian. He was at the same time a man of great simplicity who loved children and animals. His declared aim was to have his whole soul swallowed up in the will of God, and observers spoke of the light which seemed to shine through him. In Persia he talked with Sufis and found them kindred spirits: he described them as 'the Methodists of the East' and told them what he had learned of 'the very recesses of the sanctuary', and though his preaching was uncompromisingly Christian, they too recognized him as one of them. He died at Tokat.

Mary of Agreda

See MARIA DE JESUS.

Ma Tsu
(707–86)

Chinese ZEN Master, who used violent methods, shouting and even physical violence, 'striding about like a bull and staring like a tiger', to shake his followers. He did not believe that meditation was the only means to enlightenment. He held the identity of the mind with the Buddha. He was a master of paradox.

Maximus the Confessor
(*c.* 580–662)

Maximus was a nobleman who held the office of Imperial Secretary at Constantinople under Heraclius, before turning to the monastic life. He was the leader of the orthodox party against monothelitism (the doctrine of a single will in the God-man Jesus Christ). He had a turbulent life, was exiled for a period and, at the age of eighty, mutilated. He was a voluminous writer on a variety of subjects. His most important mystical works are his paraphrases of DIONYSIUS, and his *Mystagogia*, a mystical treatment of the liturgy. His central doctrine is that the Incarnation of the Word of God leads to the deification of man, the restoration of the original image, which man corrupted by his desire for pleasure, the reunion of God and man through love in a life prepared by ascetic discipline. Maximus's mysticism thus centres on the Incarnate Word. But it is associated with his whole concept of God; he describes the saints as those who express the Holy Trinity in themselves, and shows the identity of will between the believer who lives by love, and God, when he writes 'God and those who are worthy of God have the same energy.'

Maya

Hindu term for unreality, the flux of phenomena, sometimes rendered 'illusion'. It is also used for the power whereby BRAHMAN created the world, and so an intermediary between Brahman and the world, or mythologically his wife. As the self in its ultimate essence is one with Brahman, the soul will find its true self in separation from MAYA.

Mazdaism

The worship of AHURA MAZDA.
See ZOROASTRIANISM

Mechthilde of Magdeburg
(1217–82)

German mystic and creative writer, who wrote in both prose and verse of her visions and revelations in *The Book of the Flowing Light of the Godhead*. She was twelve when she experienced her first ecstasy. Her visions extended over more than thirty years with extraordinary vividness; it was as if she could see her guardian angel, and even God Himself. Not merely did she have a strong sense of spiritual sight, but also an intense capacity for spiritual feeling which led her to share the sufferings of Jesus.

In one of her most characteristic productions we begin with a spiritual love-romance, in which the virgin soul adorns herself for her bridegroom; she goes to the forest where she hears nightingales singing of union with God. Her bridegroom sends his messengers to dance for her, and encourage her to dance. This she will not, and he comes himself and rebukes her. She replies

> Unless you lead me, Lord, I cannot dance.
> Would you have me leap and spring,
> you yourself, dear Lord, must sing,
> so shall I spring into your love,

from your love to understanding,
from understanding to delight.
Then soaring far above
all human thought, there circling will I stay
and taste encircling love.

So their union is prepared. Now having put her message in clear dramatic terms, Mechthilde intellectualizes it in a dialogue betwen soul and senses. Finally in the climax of the work the soul repudiates the cautious advice of the senses that she will not bear the fire of God's presence.

The fish in the water cannot drown,
the bird in the air cannot sink down,
gold in the fire cannot decay
but shines more brilliant every way.
God grants to every creature
to live by its own nature.
How can I bind my nature's wings?
I must speed to my God before all things.
My God, by His nature my Father above,
my Brother in his humanity,
my Bridegroom in his ardent love,
and I his from eternity.
Do you think that his Fire will consume my soul?
He knows how to burn, and then to gently cool.

'And so did the utterly loved go in to the utterly lovely, into the Secret Chamber of the Pure Divinity. And there she found the resting-place of love, and the home of love, and the Divine Humanity that awaited her.'

Lord God, I am now a naked soul,
and you arrayed all gloriously:
we are Two in One, we have reached the goal,
immortal rapture that cannot die.
Now a blessed silence flows
over us. Both have willed it.
He is given to her and she to him.
What now will happen the soul well knows
And therefore I am comforted.

Meditation

In mysticism meditation is a half-way house between thought and CONTEMPLATION. It is important as a lead-in to the mystical experience, not as the experience itself. It begins very much in this world. TERESA DE JESUS would say to her disciples: 'I do not require of you to form great and curious considerations in your understanding: I require of you no more than to *look*.'

Really to look involves concentration: that itself is a guard against distraction. It leads to the process which Teresa calls RECOLLECTION.

Mencius

See MENG TZU

Meng Tzu

(372–289 BC)

Chinese Confucian philosopher, known in the west as Mencius, who built his ethical ideals on the essential goodness of human nature and supported ethical principle against utilitarianism. Meng Tzu has a strong mystical streak. All things are complete within us; we seem to be separated from the universe but the condition of sincerity is the breaking of the barriers. He speaks of a powerful moving force, which is transcendental, but becomes immanent in steadfast righteousness. So 'Wherever the Superior Man passes, transformation follows, wherever he stays, there is a spiritualizing influence. This flows abroad above and below together with Heaven and Earth.'

Merkabah

The throne-chariot of Ezekiel 10, a major topic of Jewish mysticism; the throne-world is seen as the true centre of all mystical contemplation. The throne-world is divided by mystics into seven halls or palaces (*hekhaloth*), in the last of which the divine Glory appears. A number of mystical tracts describe these halls and the ascetic and mystical practices necessary to attain them, and the angelic beings who inhabit and guard them. Of special importance are *The Lesser Hekhaloth*, which speaks, in common with most mysticism, of the ascent of the soul, and *The Greater Hekhaloth*, which speaks paradoxically of the descent of the soul to the *Merkabah*;

Seven tantric symbols used as aids to meditation

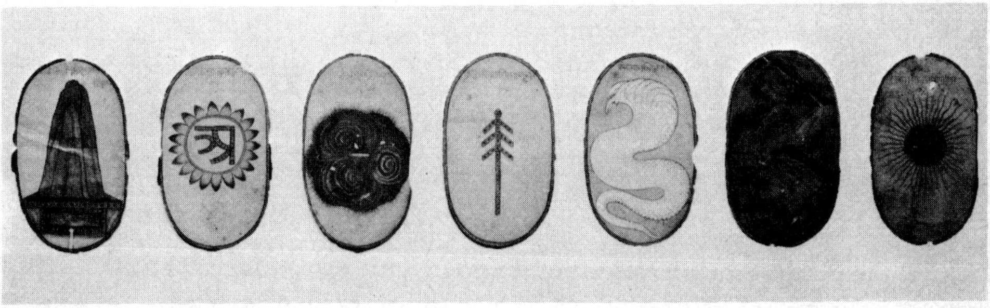

the mystics associated with this last treatise are *Yorde Merkabah*, Descenders to the Throne. *The Greater Hekhaloth* contains an alphabetical hymn of praise – here slightly modified to show the alphabetical approach (there are twenty-two lines in the original).

Adornment and permanence – are His who lives for ever
Blessing and understanding – are His who lives for ever
Crown and glory – are His who lives for ever
Dignity and majesty – are His who lives for ever
Exaltation and righteousness – are His who lives for ever
Faithfulness and excellence – are His who lives for ever
Grandeur and greatness – are His who lives for ever
Hymn and song – are His who lives for ever
Invocation and holiness – are His who lives for ever
Knowledge and expression – are His who lives for ever
Lustre and brilliance – are His who lives for ever
Might and meekness – are His who lives for ever
Nobility and exultation – are His who lives for ever
Omnipotence and omniscience – are His who lives for ever
Precept and practice – are His who lives for ever
Rule and sovereignty – are His who lives for ever
Splendour and wonder – are His who lives for ever
Tenderness and power – are His who lives for ever
Unity and honour – are His who lives for ever
Veneration and goodness – are His who lives for ever
Wisdom and mystery – are His who lives for ever.

Merswin, Rulman
(*c.* 1307–82)

Merswin is a fascinating figure, a rich Strasbourg banker who was converted by TAULER to the mystical approach of the FRIENDS OF GOD, and in 1367 formed a retreat on the Green Isle in the River Ill. Attributed to Merswin are five tracts, though in three of these, notably the important BOOK OF THE NINE ROCKS, he is adapting the work of others. In addition there are sixteen tracts ascribed to 'The Friend of God from the Oberland'. The authorship of these has occasioned stormy debate, but it seems likely that they were written by Merswin. They are an account of the way the ideal Friend of God is prepared for his work in life. They include a picture of the spiritual ladder, and the way the Holy Spirit helps the believer to climb to his origin where he experiences an ecstasy of love. Even more interesting is *The Spark in the Soul*. The Spark is almost smothered by the ashes of worldliness. But if the believer will die to himself the Holy Spirit blows the Spark into flame. If he persists in contemplation of the sufferings of Christ, the flame will blaze up. The third stage is a period of darkness and temptation. The believer must stand fast and wait with patience; the flame will blaze hotter yet. In the fourth stage he is bathed in joy and gladness through the practice of virtue; in the fifth, streams of divine Light surround him; in the sixth they shine actually from him; in the seventh his love for others reaches white heat and he knows the blessedness of eternal life.

In *The Story of the First Four Years of his Life* (the new life he entered on conversion) Merswin describes his first ecstasy. He was walking in a garden, meditating on the love of God when a radiant light swept round him, and he felt an experience of levitation. He practised an extreme and brutal asceticism; he suffered severe temptations; but experienced a countervailing joy, especially in the EUCHARIST, and had frequent ecstasies. In the fourth year the storms receded, peace and calm supervened, and he had the mystical experience of full union. The danger now was spiritual pride, which he overcame in the service of others.

Merton, Thomas
(1915–68)

American contemplative, born in France of an English father and American mother. Merton was converted to Roman Catholicism in 1938 and became a Trappist monk in 1941. His account of his progress to conversion, *The Seven Story Mountain*, was a best-seller. From then on his writings were widely and deeply influential. Merton found fulfilment in the contemplative life, but at the same time was actively involved in concern for his fellow-men in an unpeaceful world, and worked actively for peace and civil rights. He deplored the identification of Christianity with western power politics, and became increasingly interested in eastern religious experience. He died while following this line of study at Bangkok; his body was flown back to the United States with the bodies of soldiers killed in a war of which he disapproved. Merton wrote poetry, devotional books, autobiography and scholarly studies. Among his other important works related to mysticism are *Seeds of Contemplation* and *Mystics and Zen Masters*.

Mescalin

Mescalin is the principal alkaloid ($C_{12}H_{47}NO_7$) in mescal, the peyote cactus. Interest in the drug and its capacity for producing hallucination has been strong since Aldous HUXLEY experimented with it in his search for the BEATIFIC VISION. There is some unanimity of experience but not of response. The sense of time is lost. Visual experience is generally effected; colours glow brilliantly and blaze, shimmer and revolve, shapes change and melt into one another. Huxley wrote: 'I became aware of a slow dance of golden lights. A little later there were sumptuous red surfaces swelling and expanding from bright rods of energy that vibrated with a continuously changing, patterned life. At another time, the closing of my eyes revealed a complex of grey structures, within which pale bluish spheres kept emerging into intense solidity.' Trivial objects, a trouser-leg, a stucco wall, a shelf of books, a chair-leg, the creases in clothes, take on the beauty of a mystical revelation. On the other hand, things which usually evoke sensations of beauty lose their effect. There is a tendency to break into mocking laughter; there are sudden onsets of panic. So that where Huxley claimed to understand the Beatific Vision, Raymond Mortimer, following in his steps, found his own experience horrifying. Mescalin is used sacramentally in the liturgy of the Native American Church.

Messalians

The name (from Syriac: Greek Euchites) means 'People of Prayer'. A pietistic Christian sect which originated in Mesopotamia in the fourth century AD and spread round the Fertile Crescent into the Balkans and Egypt. They believed that because of Adam's sin everyone had an evil spirit attached to him, which could be driven out only by unceasing prayer supported by asceticism and the consequent elimination of all desire and passion. Those who in this way attained perfection received an immediate vision of the Holy Trinity.

Messiaen, Olivier
(b. 1908)

French musical composer with a strong mystical strain. Technically he is important for relating twelve-tone techniques to principles of strict rhythmic organization. Himself a devout Catholic, whose music owes something to plain-song, he has also studied Hindu music. His first published work was the organ piece *Le Banquet Céleste* (1928); his first major work and perhaps his best-known was the symphonic *L'Ascension* (1933–4). But his most important expressions in music of mystical experience are the superb *Quatuor pour le Fin du Temps* (1941) and the monumental set of piano pieces *Vingt Regards sur l'Enfant Jésus* (1944). In the 1950s Messiaen turned to a kind of musical nature-mysticism and expressed his mystical philosophy through a series of major works based on a close study of bird calls. Messiaen holds that the subject-matter of music should be lofty sentiments, and religious sentiments in particular. The method of communication should be the excitement of delicate, voluptuous pleasures; music should be iridescent. The listener will succumb to charm and be led 'gently towards that theological rainbow which is the ultimate goal of all music'.

Messiah

The Hebrew word means 'anointed', and is the equivalent, through the Greek, of 'Christ'. In Jewish thought the Messiah is the divinely appointed liberator of Israel, and many prophetic visions centre upon him and the kingdom of peace and justice which he inaugurates. Christians in general identify the Messiah with Jesus but tend to see the work of liberation as carried out by suffering and service in his passion and resurrection. Both Jewish and Christian scriptures however look forward to a final coming of the Messiah in judgment and glory.

Metempsychosis

See REINCARNATION.

Michelangelo di Lodovico Buonarotti Simone
(1475–1564)

Italian poet and artist, much influenced by NEOPLATONISM. It rings from his poetry, even (as with the Persian Sufi lyricists) from his love poetry.

> I cannot now see in things doomed to die
> Your eternal light, without a deep desire.

There is the contrast between the transitory material world and the permeating powers of eternity; and the deep desire, Eros, love, the aspiration towards the Divine. Even the beauty of the beloved Vittoria Colonna will fade. But Beauty will *not* fade.

> The beauty which you see is indeed hers
> but grows as it mounts to a better place.
> passing through mortal eyes to the soul.
> It becomes divine, noble, beautiful,
> for one immortal seeks others like it.
> This, nothing else, is your vision's goal.

FICINO had spoken of the soul as 'falling, at the beginning of our lives, from the purity with which it was created, and being imprisoned in the gaol of a dark, earthly, mortal body'. Michelangelo wrought some statues of slaves or prisoners for the tomb of Pope Julius II, though he later eliminated all terrestrial symbolism. They are allegories of the soul, fettered by its own sensuality. On one of the statues can be seen a sketch of an ape in the unfinished stone, man's animal nature.

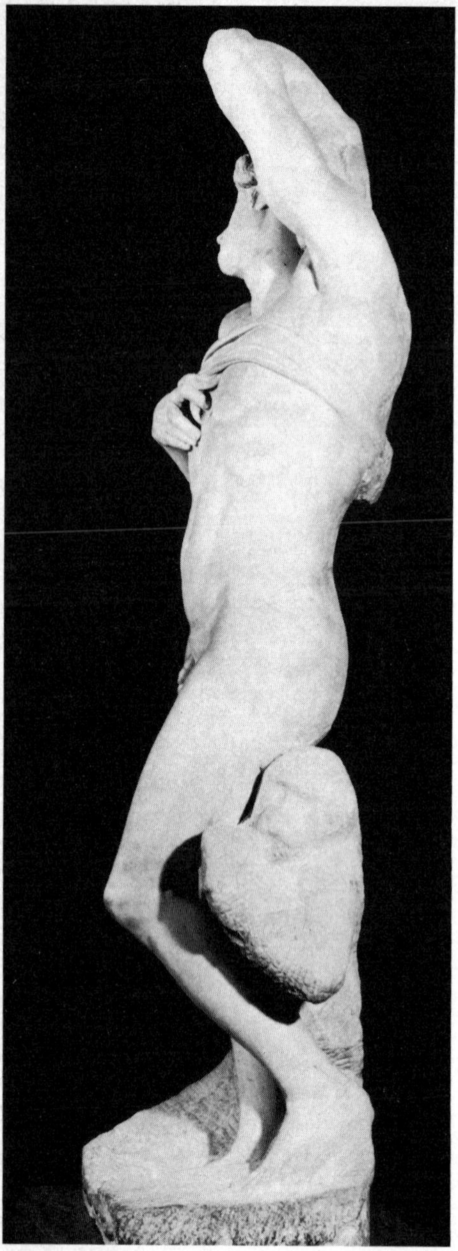

Michelangelo's The Dying Captive, *showing the ape as symbol of man's lower nature*

When some poor slave, chained in a savage
fetter
lies for long periods a prisoner to hopelessness,
he grows accustomed to his wretchedness
and freedom hardly seems to him any better.

Indeed in the unfinished state of the work we feel that the slave is imprisoned in the stone. Neo-Platonism in fact has touched the whole concept of the creative process.

Milarepa, Jetsun
(1052–1135)

Tibetan mystic, whose life was written by his disciple Rechung. As a boy he was orphaned and brought up by harsh relatives, and turned to the practice of black magic in search of revenge. But he became restless, longing for a true knowledge and true faith, and went to a Lama named Marpa who imposed on him a period of frustrating trials, after which he was ready for initiation and teaching. Next he was sent into the mountains to meditate. He renounced the world; he showed patience where he had once been vengeful. He turned to ascetic exercises and 'began to experience a state of calmness and clarity of vision that is above the physical plane'. He received Transcendent Knowledge, and began to comprehend the Oneness of the All. NIRVANA and MAYA, he saw, were only relative terms: there was nothing but Mind, with no distinction or separateness. From this he developed the power of dissociation of soul from body, first in sleep and then in waking vision, so that he had the sensation of flying. He kept his mind on the divine fire of the Vital Force. Even in death on the funeral pyre, he appeared seated with the flames like a lotus-flower enveloping him, and gave Rechung final injunctions to 'think of past, future and the present all as one: . . . beyond this there is no more Truth'.

Miracle plays

See MYSTERY PLAYS.

Mirror of Simple Souls, The

Anonymous mystical treatise produced in Flanders under Franciscan influence about the year 1300. It is long, daring and often profound. A fine passage for example shows how the pursuit of the virtues, which is a necessary part of the PURGATIVE WAY, may itself become a bondage, so that the soul has to say 'Virtues, I take leave of you for evermore!' Another fine passage describes the soul soaring like an eagle on the wings of LOVE, one with God, for God is Love and Love is God. The experience is one of gladness and joy. 'This soul, says Love, swims in the sea of joy: that is, in the sea of delight, the current of divine influences.' The Ultimate is ineffable. 'There is none other God but He that none may know, which may not be known. No, soothly, no! Without fail, No . . .He only is my God that none can one word of say, nor all they of Paradise one only point attain nor understand, for all the knowing that they have of Him.'

Reasons have recently been found for attributing the book to a BÉGUINE named Marguérite Porete, who was burned for heresy in 1310.

Mithraism

In the Zoroastrian religion of Persia life is a battle between the forces of light, headed by the great god of light, Ahura-Mazda or Ormuzd; and the forces of darkness, headed by Angra-Mainyu or Ahriman. In that encounter each commander has his staff-officers. Among those on the side of light is the Sun, and also Mithra or Mithras, perhaps a power of the upper air, associated with truth and the oath. But somehow, somewhere, he became the central deity as a saviour-god in an almost new religion. Ahura-Mazda remains the great god, but devotion is offered to Mithras.

Associated with the new religion is a myth. Mithras was born from the rock. Ahura-Mazda's first creation had been a wild bull. Mithras wrestled with it and carried it to a cave. The bull escaped. Mithras's ally, the Sun, sent his messenger, the Raven to espy it. Mithras followed it with his faithful hound, pulled back its head, and plunged a dagger into its throat. From the blood flowed life. On the reliefs can be seen animals, the dog, the ant, the snake and scorpion seeking to lap up the blood. The Sun now knelt before Mithras, acknowledging his supremacy, received a crown from him, and made a covenant with him. In other stories Mithras saves mankind from flood and drought. Finally he took leave of the Sun in a ceremonial banquet.

Mithraism spread through the Roman Empire, through soldiers, traders and finance-officials, as a mystery-cult. Only men were admitted, but there were fraternal relations with the cult of CYBELE. There were seven grades of initiate arranged in two groups. The lower, the servitors, comprised the Raven, Bridegroom and Soldier; the upper, the Participants, comprised Lion, Persian, Courier of the Sun, and Father. INITIATION at all stages involved real or symbolic tests of endurance. The Soldier was offered a crown across a sword. He had to win this and then renounce it, saying 'Mithras is my crown.' The Lion had his tongue and hands purified with honey. At Carrawburgh in the Roman Wall there is a 'grave' for a ritual death and resurrection. At Capua we can see painted scenes of initiation. In one the initiate, blindfolded and naked, is being pushed uncertainly forward by a *mystagogus*. In another he is kneeling blindfold while a priest approaches with a staff or sword. In a third he is kneeling on one knee with his hands tied behind him and a sword on the ground at his side. There are others where he is lying on the ground in a symbolic death; kneeling, and about to be pushed over, but caught in the nick of time; kneeling, with the *mystagogus* holding him firm with his foot, and pushing him towards the garland and sword which he must refuse. Some of the ordeals were genuine and tough, including fasting and physical endurance. There was a regular routine of public worship, with fire kept perpetually burning, and daily offices. Gatherings for worship were held in underground chapels called 'caves'. Such may be well seen in Rome under S. Clemente, in ancient Ostia, or in Britain at Carrawburgh, reconstructed in the University Museum in Newcastle. A relief of Mithras killing the bull was the focus of the worshipper's attention. The initiates wore costumes appropriate to their grades. There was a communion meal in commemoration of the farewell banquet of Mithras and the Sun, with the drinking of communion wine, and the eating of something which (in the Konjica relief) looks uncommonly like hot cross buns.

The central mystery relates to the journey of the soul. The soul is immortal, and its period on earth is a time of trial. At birth it descends from the home of light through the gate of Cancer, passing through the seven planetary spheres, and accumulating impurity, ambition from Jupiter,

Mithras slaying the wild bull, a 3rd-century Roman relief

lust from Venus, greed for gain from Mercury, sloth from Saturn, anger from Mars. On earth the soul has the chance to shake off the weight of these impurities by a combination of moral striving and revealed knowledge. After death the spirits of light and darkness struggle for the soul, with Mithras as arbiter. If the good qualities outweigh the bad, the soul ascends again through the gate of Capricorn, shedding its impurities. It meets divine officials called 'Customs-Officers' who must be cajoled or intimidated into letting it pass into the realms of light. In all this there is much astral symbolism, as we see also in the mysterious figures of Cautes and Cautopates who flank the bull-slaying relief, one with his torch upwards, symbolizing sunrise and spring, the other with his torch down, symbolizing sunset and winter. In the end this is what it is about, the battle of light and darkness, good and evil, summer and winter, day and night. The Mithraist was, or hoped to be, in the most solemn sense on the side of the angels.

A curious magical papyrus from Egypt, dating from about AD 300 shows a blend of Mithraism with some rather crude other elements. But it demonstrates that Mithraism is about rebirth; there is a continual contrast between physical birth and spiritual rebirth, and the final prayer runs: 'O Lord! I have been born again and pass away in exaltation. In exaltation I die. Birth that produces life brings me into being and frees me for death. I go my way as thou hast ordered, as thou hast established the law and ordained the sacrament.'

Mixed liquids

Image used by mystical writers of the union of the soul with God, as a drop of water mingles with wine. It is used by BERNARD in *De diligendo Deo* of man's ultimate state, and often thereafter. The language is ambiguous as to whether the water *seems* to disappear or *is seen* to disappear. When it was applied to mystical experience during an individual's lifetime without Bernard's careful *videtur*, it tended to pantheism and was discouraged by ecclesiastical authority.

Moksa

In Hindu theology, the word for release or LIBERATION.

Molinos, Miguel de
(*c.* 1640–97)

Spanish priest and mystic, who came to Rome about 1670, and published five years later a mystical treatise called *Spiritual Guide*. Molinos distinguished two ways towards the knowledge of God. The exterior road is MEDITATION, helpful to beginners, but not leading all the way. The interior road is CONTEMPLATION or pure faith, annihilation of self, utter resignation to God's will, so that 'we sink and lose ourselves in the immeasurable sea of God's infinite goodness, and rest there steadfast and immovable'. CONTEMPLATION is supported by prayer, obedience, the EUCHARIST and inner mortification. The best prayer is silent; silent prayer may depend on words, or desires, or thought; and the last is best, for there God speaks to the soul.

The book caused something of a sensation, and he developed his teaching in correspondence, reaching the position that perfection is found only in the perpetual union of the soul with God, or indeed the transformation of the soul into God. External observances of all kinds were a hindrance to this, not a help. Perfection involved the annihilation of the will. The novice should begin in devotion to the Church, then pass to devotion to Jesus, and rise finally to devotion to God in His absolute BEING.

Under the influence of his teaching nuns began to abandon their normal spiritual exercises and discipline, and in 1685 Molinos was condemned to prison for the rest of his life. In prison he showed a supreme tranquillity of spirit.

Mondo

'Question-and-answer' in ZEN.

Mondrian, Piet
(1872–1944)

Dutch painter, who began with traditional sombre landscapes, changed to a more brilliant palette and more stylized treatment. In 1909 his interest in fundamental questions led him to join the Dutch Theosophical Society; he is said to have kept a portrait of Madame Blavatsky in his studio. In the same year he moved to Paris and the impact of Cubism liberated his original genius; he changed from colouristic Expressionism to a sternly disciplined linear technique. From 1908–13 he was much engaged in painting pictures of a single tree, in which he seems to pass from a single observed tree to the essence of treeness, the Platonic Form of tree. His saying, 'The emotion of beauty is always obstructed by the appearance of the "object"; therefore the object must be eliminated from the picture', is not far from ECKHART's 'To find nature herself all her likenesses have to be shattered; and the further in, the nearer the actual thing.' From then on he is concerned with the vertical and horizontal, almost the primal pair YIN and YANG, and the 'dynamic equilibrium' between them. The curved line became an intrusion. He declared his inability to see 'squares' in his pictures, but his language sometimes suggests the symbolism of the cross as a meeting-point of Heaven and earth. One critic has written of his 'obsession with spiritual faith'. Mondrian called his later art Neo-Plasticism; he was the leading figure in the group which took its name from the magazine *De Stijl*.

Monism

Philosophy that all is one, expressed in Hinduism by the term ADVAITA, non-dualism. But the idea that all reality is ultimately one does not necessarily imply an undifferentiated Monism and may take different forms. For some Monists the One is the Ultimate and the only real Being, and is manifested in the many in different ways and different degrees. Or again, some would say that the One has many centres of BEING. But all would say the unity and continuity among the apparent plurality of things derives from the ultimate One. Some thinkers have espoused a materialistic monism, some have seen the ultimate One in terms of Mind or Spirit; some twentieth-century Anglo-American philosophers (including William JAMES) tried to espouse a 'mental Monism' in which the ultimate was, in the narrow sense, neither purely physical nor purely mental. Among Western philosophers PLOTINUS, SPINOZA, HEGEL and BRADLEY are obvious examples of Monists. Most, though not all, mystics tend towards Monism in some form. It is very strong in the East, and in ECKHART.

Montague, Margaret Prescott
(1878–1955)

American mystic. This remarkable woman who suffered from progressive blindness from an early age, and almost total deafness later, and grievous suffering of other sorts, proclaimed 'If the world be shut without, I'll sail the hidden seas within', and communicated her courage and her experience in many writings under her own name and the pen-name Jane Steger. In *Twenty Minutes of Reality* (1917) she describes an intense mystical experience. She was recovering from an operation, and had been in a state of acute mental depression, having come to a sense that there was no God, or else an indifferent one. Her bed was wheeled out into the open. It was March; there was no trace of spring; but the wind blowing made an impact on her imagination. As she lay there, for the first time in her life she 'caught a glimpse of the ecstatic beauty of reality'. The experience was so overwhelming that she could not afterwards remember whether it was gradual or sudden. 'I saw no new thing, but I saw all the usual things in a miraculous new light – in what I believe is their true light. I saw for the first time how wildly beautiful and joyous, beyond any words of mine to describe, is the whole of life. Every human being moving across that porch, every sparrow that flew, every branch tossing in the wind, was caught in and was part of the whole mad ecstasy of loveliness, of joy, of importance, of intoxication of life.' A gleam of sunshine catching the hair of a nurse was a vision of eternal beauty, a sparrow chirping was one of the sons of God shouting for joy. The experience was one of falling in love with all around her.

Montanists

Ecstatic Christian sect, prominent in the second half of the second century AD, initiated by a Phrygian convert to Christianity named Montanus, and two women, Prisca and Maximilla. Some have seen it as an attempt to restore the simplicity, purity and openness to the Spirit shown by the early Christians, others as one of the first appearances of an ecstatic, prophetic group within the Church. There is some evidence of a mystical identification with the Divine (though the evidence is that of the orthodox looking for heresy): Montanus is recorded as saying, 'I am the Father, the Word, and the Advocate', Maximilla, 'I am the Word, the Spirit and Power.' It seems also as if the inspiration of Montanus was thought to begin a new era. Certainly the Montanists felt that the inspiration of the spirit-men (*pneumatici*) set them in a different class from the animal-men (*psychici*). Along with ecstatic prophecy went ascetic behaviour. The spread of the sect to Africa won a notable convert and propagandist in Tertullian, but by the third century the sect had been largely condemned by the orthodox. In Phrygia it persisted till the fifth century.

Moravians

The oldest of the Protestant sects, dating from 1457, the first to produce a hymn book (in the Czech language in 1505), and a Church with notable missionary activity. Its alternative name, *Unitas Fratrum*, expresses well the solidity of its fellowship. The Church, after a period of decay, was revived through the work of ZINZENDORF, who brought them into the PIETIST tradition, and one of their number, Peter Bohler, influenced John WESLEY. Moravians are expected to have a personal experience of the saving work of Christ.

More, Dame Gertrude
(1606–33)

Gertrude More was a descendant of Thomas More and a pupil of Augustine BAKER. She had a high reputation for sanctity, and was nearly appointed abbess of her Benedictine convent at the age of twenty-three. She died young, of smallpox, leaving the fruits of her mystical experiences, her meditations and prayers in two volumes. Her mysticism was a mysticism of love: 'O my God, let me walk in the way of love which knoweth not how to seek self in anything whatsoever. O sight to be wished, desired and longed for, because once to have seen Thee is to have learned all things! Nothing can bring us to this sight but love. O Lord, give this love into my soul, that I may never more live nor breathe, but out of a pure love of Thee, my all and only Good.'

More, Henry
(1614–87)

See CAMBRIDGE PLATONISTS.

Mortification

The compassing of the death of the old self so that the true self may live in its place. 'Who hinders you more than the unmortified affections of your own breast?' asks THE IMITATION OF CHRIST, and declares that 'if we were perfectly dead to ourselves and not entangled within our own breasts, then we should be able to taste divine things, and to have some experience of heavenly contemplation'. This is the passage through death to life 'In the truest death of all created things, the sweetest and most natural life is hidden', says TAULER.

Mortification is a temporary phase in the mystic's journey. He reaches the stage described by JACOPONE DA TODI

The war has reached its ending.
In the battle of virtues,
in the labours of the mind,
there is no more contending.

So SUSO after sixteen years of self-torture saw a heavenly messenger who told him to stop. So CATHERINE OF GENOA, after four years of constant mortification which could not remove her obsession with sin, found that 'all thought of such mortifications was in an instant taken from her mind'.

Muggletonians

Sect founded by John Reeve (1608–58) and Ludowicke Muggleton (1609–98). Muggleton received 'motional voices' and visions concerned with Heaven and Hell, between April 1651 and January 1652, and Reeve was in a state of sustained visionary ecstasy at the end of January and beginning of February 1652, as a result of which he wrote *A Transcendant Spiritual Treatise*. They seem at first to have been more concerned with damning their opponents than with positive doctrine; but the work of Jakob BOEHME, recently translated, offered them a theology. They proclaimed the unity of God; the eternity of matter; the mortality of the soul; and through a dualistic myth the division of mankind into cursed and blessed. They claimed to be the repositories of the message of salvation. The sect survived till the 1870s.

Muhammad
(*c.* 570–632)

Founder of Islam (which should however never be called Mohammedanism, since Muhammad is the Prophet, last and culminating figure in a great line of prophets, not himself divine). An able businessman, happily married to a widow named Khadija, he was forty when he received a vision of the archangel Gabriel who called him to recite.

Recite in the name of your Lord who created,
Created man from clots of blood.
Recite. For your Lord is most beneficent,

Episode from Muhammad's Night Journey. From the Khamseh of Nizami. India, 16th century

Who has taught the use of the pen,
Has taught man that which he does not know.

Muhammad was at first terrified; but Khadija encouraged him, and the angel appeared again, declaring, 'You are God's Prophet.' There seems now to have been an interval in the visions; then they began again; and the Prophet was called to warn men of judgment, to break idolatry and honour the one God, Allah. Muhammad acquired followers and provoked opposition. In 622 he withdrew from Mecca to Medina to return successfully with the cry 'God is great' (*Allahu akbar*) eight years later.

Muhammad is one of the great shapers of history, visionary and man of action. 'There is one God and Muhammad is his Apostle.' He was himself devout and ascetic and stressed in his teaching the importance of prayer and FASTING.

The story known as Muhammad's Night Journey played some part in Islamic mysticism; the story, which is variously told, is an account of his descent into Hell, and his ascent from Mecca to Paradise.

al-Muhasibi, al-Harith Ben Asad
(781–837)

Sufi teacher, born in Basra, but teaching in Baghdad. His name means 'self-examination'; and self-discipline was his key to the discovery of God. In one work he wrote eloquently of LOVE, the love which cannot be separated from faith. This love is the gift of God, and he who is self-satisfied about it loses it. So love is yearning, aspiration. His *Kitab al-Tawahhum* culminates in a terrifying vision of the Last Judgment finally overbalanced by the glories of the BEATIFIC VISION.

Muso Kokushi
(1275–1351)

Japanese ZEN Master, whose main work expounded Zen in question-and-answer form in terms readily understood by the Japanese. 'Not to trust the transient things of the world, but to seek rather the Way of the Buddha, that is to awaken the mind which seeks the Way and believes in the Noble Law.' Muso was an artist, famed for his brush-writing. But his great achievement lay in gardens planned to express symbolically yet naturally the essential mystical message of Zen, with water rising from a spring as the human spirit rises, or varieties of moss expressing the various approaches to truth. He was particularly associated with the new temple of Tenryuji.

Mystery

From the Greek word *myein* 'to keep one's mouth shut', hence a secret revealed to initiates, and generally not to be disclosed to others, though sometimes a truth not understood until revealed.

Mystery plays

Early Christian repudiation of the licentious theatre of the early Roman Empire faded with the disappearance of the theatre. By the ninth century AD Ethelwold speaks of the 'praiseworthy custom' of celebrating the death and resurrection of Christ with action and dialogue in church in the course of or after the completion of the liturgy. It was probably from this that the mystery plays or miracle plays emerged – literally emerged, since they were commonly performed in the open air – though some have argued that they had an independent origin in individual compositions from the Bible and other sources. It has been argued by some that the miracle play was in origin a drama based on the lives of the saints, drawing on material from outside the Bible. But the terms are loosely used, and in England the term 'miracle' predominates for Biblical and non-Biblical material. French sources speak of *les mystères*, though it is hard to be sure just what the term refers to; and one noted cycle was known as *Les Miracles de Notre Dame*. In Italy they were simply called *sacre rappresentazioni*. With the Reformation they declined, but through the example of the Oberammergau Passion Play (vowed for deliverance from plague), the last century has seen a revival.

Mystery Religion

Term applied to cults in the Graeco-Roman world; these cults were generally practised by closed societies; there were initiatory rites, and proceedings were secret. Many came from the east. Christianity has affinities with the mystery religions.

See also CYBELE, DIONYSUS, ELEUSIS, HERMETICISM, ISIS AND OSIRIS, MITHRAISM, ORPHISM, SAMOTHRACE.

Mystery theology

A theological approach developed in twentieth-century Catholic Christianity by O. Casel and I. Herwegen, concerned with the relationship between the mystery of Christ's saving presence in the sacrament, and the total concept of salvation, and bringing together in a single system the primordial mystery of God's eternal decree, the mystery of iniquity, the Christ-mystery of the Cross and the cultic mystery of the sacraments. Mystery theology aroused considerable criticism but made a significant contribution to liturgical revival as well as to theological thinking.

Mystic

'We apply the word mystic to those supernatural acts or states which our own industry is powerless to produce, *even in a low degree, even momentarily*' – R. P. A. Poulain. Of people the term 'mystic' is properly applied to those who have mystical experience.

Mystical state

In *The Varieties of Religious Experience* William JAMES identifies four marks of the mystical state, of which the first two are essential. These are *ineffability* (which he calls a negative mark) and *noetic quality* (the association of the mystical experience with a revelation of knowledge). The other two, less sharply marked but usually found, are *transiency* and *passivity*. TERESA DE JESUS insists that the special quality of the mystical state (which she calls 'supernatural') is that though we can and should prepare for it, no effort of ours can enable us to attain to it. Poulain claims that in the mystical states 'God is not satisfied merely to help us to *think* of Him and to *remind* us of His presence: He gives us an experimental, intellectual knowledge of His presence. In a word He makes us feel that we really enter into communication with Him.' In the lower mystical states this is only obscurely experienced, and becomes more distinct in the higher states.

See also MYSTIC UNION.

Mystical theology

The Franciscan thinkers, such as BONAVENTURE, divided theology into three: '*symbolic* theology, by which we deal correctly with sensible things, theology *proper*, by which we deal correctly with intelligible things, and *mystical* theology, by which we are caught up into ecstasies which transcend the mind'. Jean Gerson developed this distinction at book length, emphasizing the fact that as the other two theologies take their start from external effects, mystical theology starts from actual but internal experiences. He called mystical theology 'an experiential knowledge of God received through the union of spiritual affection with him'. Similarly Ven. John of Saint-Samson said in his *Maxims*: 'Mystical theology, taken in its essence, is nothing other than God ineffably perceived.' Again, Ribet: 'Mystical theology . . .: a passive, supernatural attraction of the soul to God, deriving from an internal illumination and embrace, anticipating reflection, surpassing human effort, and capable of exercising a wonderful, irresistible hold on the body.'

Mystical Theology is also the title of an earlier work by DIONYSIUS THE AREOPAGITE.

Mysticism

Attempts to define mysticism have been very various. One group concentrates on union with God. Thus THOMAS AQUINAS speaks of 'the knowledge of God through experience'. Pfleiderer defines mysticism as 'the immediate feeling of the unity of the self with God', Arberry as a 'constant and unvarying phenomenon of the universal yearning of the human spirit for personal communion with God'. Rufus Jones as 'the type of religion which puts the emphasis on immediate relation with God, on direct and intimate consciousness of the Divine Presence', Edward Caird as 'religion in its most concentrated and exclusive form . . . that attitude of mind in which all other relations are swallowed up in the relation of the soul to God'. This however is not true of all mysticism; among the Hindus or Buddhists the emphasis is on release from our present state, rather than on attachment to a personal God.

Some accounts of mysticism emphasize the element of feeling rather than of rationality. This is true of Pfleiderer's definition; he goes on to speak of 'God-intoxication'. So too Goethe: 'Mysticism is the scholastic of the heart, the dialectic of the feelings.' Those who are sceptical of mystical pretensions often take some such view. Victor Cousin writes, 'Mysticism consists in substituting direct inspiration for indirect, ecstasy for reason, rapture for philosophy.' But this does not do justice to the element of the intelligence in the approach of the mystics, many of whom do not so much renounce the intelligence as use it in a particular way. Bonchitté put it wisely: 'Mysticism consists in giving to the spontaneity of the intelligence a larger part than to the other faculties.'

Récéjac tried to define mysticism by its use of symbols: 'Mysticism is the tendency to approach the Absolute morally, by means of symbols.' So R. L. Nettleship: 'True mysticism is the consciousness that everything that we experience is an element and only an element in fact; i.e., that in being what it is, it is symbolic of something more.' This is an exceptionally interesting approach in its concentration on methodology. But unless the idea of the symbol is very widely understood, this hardly does justice to the VIA NEGATIVA.

Probably a broad definition is best, like Evelyn Underhill's 'Mysticism is the art of union with Reality. The mystic is a person who has attained that union in a greater or less degree; or who aims at and believes in such attainment', or the anonymous and succinct 'Mysticism is to possess the infinite in the finite.' Aldous HUXLEY had something similar in mind when he said, 'The technique of mysticism properly practised, may result in the direct intuition of, and union with, an ultimate spiritual reality that is perceived as simultaneously beyond the self and in some way within it.' Pringle-Pattison was more complex, and more personal, but still general: 'Mysticism appears in connection with the endeavour of the human mind to grasp the divine essence or the ultimate reality of things, and to enjoy the blessedness of actual communion with the highest. The first is the philosophical side of mysticism, the second is its religious side. God ceases to be an object and becomes an experience.' The trouble with all such definitions is that they are so broad that they are not very informative.

How is 'genuine' mystical experience to be identified as opposed to experience that is consciously or unconsciously simulated?

Elmer O'Brien has suggested three criteria. First, the experience should be contrary to the subject's fundamental world-view. (Here O'Brien surely underestimates the power of the unconscious in throwing up those things which we have suppressed or repressed precisely because they are contrary to our world-view.) Second, the mystic should be reluctant, so that the experience is not mere wish-fulfilment. (But again the wish may be repressed; and it would be hard to deny the genuineness of some experiences willingly entered into; in other words if reluctance is a test of genuineness, still willingness should not be taken as a test of falsity.) Third, the experience alone gives meaning and consistency to the mystic's doctrines. (This would seem to suggest that only systematic thinkers can have genuine mystical experience.) Many others, including some of the greater mystics, have claimed that true experience is distinguishable from false by its fruits. In truth there is no infallible test. But it is important to see that if all mystical experience is in fact illusory, there are different levels of illusion, and CATHERINE OF GENOA and TERESA DE JESUS knew perfectly well the difference between mere hysteria and other sorts of experience.

E. G. Browne has spoken eloquently of the unity of mystical experience: 'There is hardly any soil, be it ever so barren, where Mysticism will not strike root; hardly any creed, however formal, round which it will not twine itself. . . . Wonderfully uniform, too, is its tenor: in all ages, in all countries, in all creeds, whether it come from the Brahmin sage, the Persian poet, or the Christian quietist, it is in essence an enunciation more or less clear, more or less eloquent, of the aspiration of the soul to cease altogether from self and to be at one with God.' Others, like Zaehner (who writes as a committed Christian), stress the differences rather than the resemblances, distinguishing the theistic mysticism of unity from the pantheistic mysticism of identity.

We can make certain generalizations about mysticism, which will be found to be widely if not universally true. First, mystics believe that there is an Ultimate Being, a dimension of existence beyond that experienced through the senses. This Ultimate Reality is Absolute BEING. It is often, though not invariably, conceived in personal terms, and called God. It is the Source and Ground of all that is. Secondly, mystics claim that the Ultimate can in some sense be known or apprehended. God is not wholly other, not utterly withdrawn. He is a God who hides Himself, but he is also a God who reveals Himself. Thirdly, the soul perceives the Ultimate through inward sense. 'It is a spiritual sense opening inwardly,' says R. W. Trine in his once popular book *In Tune with the Infinite*, 'as the physical senses open outwardly, and because it has the capacity to perceive, grasp and know the truth at first hand, independent of all external sources of information, we call it intuition.' To put it differently, mysticism denies that knowledge is limited to sense-perception, the intellect and the normal processes of consciousness. Fourthly, it would be widely held among mystics that there is an element in the soul akin to the Ultimate, a divine spark, 'a fragment of himself' (as Seneca puts it), a holy spirit within. In this way to find God is to find one's true self. God is recognized as 'the foundation of the soul's being, and the soul's perception of its own essence is, in fact, the perception of its unity with the Divine nature'. Fifthly, mysticism has as its zenith the experience of union with the Ultimate. 'Mysticism,' writes Margaret Smith, 'going beyond religion, aspires to intimate union with the Divine, to a penetration of the Divine within the soul and to a disappearance of the individuality, with all its modes of acting, thinking and feeling, in the Divine substance. The mystic seeks to pass out of all that is merely phenomenal, out of all lower forms of reality, to become Being itself.'

There would also be wide agreement about the way in which union can be approached from man's side. Christian mysticism, with its analytical precision, has spoken of three ways or stages on the road, the Purgative, the Illuminative and the Unitive. Something similar is found in most mystical systems. For example, in SUFISM one teacher speaks of the need to begin by renouncing that which is unlawful, to go on to renounce that which is lawful, and finally to renounce everything except God. This corresponds well with the three ways. In the first the soul is separated from what Paul of Tarsus calls the 'flesh', from the ties of the lower self, from vice and sin. Often this stage includes ascetic discipline, as a means to 'self-loss'. 'Who shall ascend to the hill of the Lord? or who shall stand in his holy place?' sang the Jewish poet. 'Even he that has clean hands and a pure heart.' 'Purity is the characteristic of the lovers of God, who are like suns without shade,' said the Sufi al-Hujwiri. 'Only when all images of earth are hushed and the clamour of the senses is stilled and the soul has passed beyond thought of self,' wrote Margaret Smith, 'can the Eternal Wisdom be revealed to the mystic who seeks that high communion with the Unseen.'

In the second stage the external life has ceased to be a stumbling-block. The inner life must be now brought into accord with the divine Will. This is (says Evelyn Underhill) 'the complete surrender of man's personal striving to the overruling Will of God and thus the linking up of all the successive acts of life with the Abiding'. The presence of God now becomes an experienced reality, though not yet a union which absorbs the soul, and is often felt as Light. The final stage is that of complete union.

The aspiration to the Ultimate is generally called LOVE. So RUYSBROECK: 'When Love has carried us above all things . . . we receive in peace the Incomprehensible Light.' In mystical love the two great strands of *agape* and *eros* come together, the former the love spoken of in the New Testament, the love revealed in Jesus, the love which gives freely no matter how unworthy the recipient, the other the love spoken of by PLATO and PLOTINUS, the desire to possess, aspiration, the sublimation of our sexual desires, an image which is often used by the mystics of Islam.

For different varieties of mystical approach see, further, TWO WAYS and TYPOLOGY.

Mystic union

The state of the soul in union with God through CONTEMPLATION. The ascent to the state is through quietude and prayer into the ECSTASY where the presence of God is experienced directly and immediately. Mystic union is often symbolized by SPIRITUAL MARRIAGE. TERESA DE JESUS identifies four stages or degrees of mystic union: (a) the incomplete mystic union or prayer of quiet, (b) the prayer of union, (c) ecstasy, (d) the spiritual marriage of deifying union. Of the experience of union in the second stage she writes 'God visits the soul in a manner which prevents it doubting, when returning to itself, that He was within it and that it dwells in Him'; of the fourth stage 'Unless the soul first deserts God, I believe He will never fail to make her sensible of His presence.'

In Poulain's masterful analysis twelve features of mystic union are identified:

1 It consists in an experimental knowledge of the presence of God.
2 The knowledge is the result of a spiritual sensation of a special kind, parallel on the spiritual plane to physical sensations.
3 It does not depend upon our will: Teresa constantly insists on this. We cannot bring it about, we cannot foresee it, we cannot intensify it.
4 The knowledge of God is obscure; it is often compared to darkness rather than light. Dionysius writes 'If anyone, when he has seen God, understands what he has seen, it is never God that he has seen, but some one of those things of His which exist and are known' (*letter* 1).
5 Similarly the mode of communication is partially incomprehensible.
6 The union is not produced by reasonings, by the consideration of created things, or by interior images of the outside world. It is the Night of the Senses. So Dionysius tells Timothy to leave behind sensible perceptions and intellectual efforts, and all objects of sense and intelligence, and all things not being and being. John of the Cross writes 'This interior wisdom, so simple, general, and spiritual, does not enter into an intellect entangled and covered over by any forms or images subject to sense.'
7 It varies continually in intensity. As Teresa puts it, the rapture is not continuous, it comes and goes.
8 It requires less effort than meditation. We might think that it requires no effort at all, and this is true of the higher stages, but in the first stage an effort of the will may be needed to avert distractions and to overcome weariness.
9 It is accompanied by sentiments of love, of repose, of pleasure and often of suffering.
10 It is accompanied by an impulsion towards the different virtues. Perhaps the primary sense is one of humility. Thus Angela of Foligno tells how she heard the voice of God: 'I will work in you great things in the sight of the people,' and consequently felt in herself more humility than she had ever felt before. But Teresa goes further and says that to have enjoyed mystic union seems intolerable, unless the soul employ herself in doing something for God, and will not allow mystical experience to justify contemplatives in indifference to practical service.
11 The experience of mystic union acts on the body. In ecstasy for example, normally (there are exceptions) the senses cease to act, the limbs become immobile, pulse and respiration are almost arrested and vital heat seems to disappear. Extreme physical effects are levitation and stigmatization.
12 Mystic union causes a ligature of the faculties, an impediment of normal activity. Mystics have found in the experience of union difficulty or impossibility in rational meditation or verbal prayer.

Mystics of St Victor

General name for the group of mystics associated with the Abbey of St Victor outside Paris in the twelfth and thirteenth centuries; they include HUGH OF ST VICTOR, Peter the Lombard, Adam of St Victor, and RICHARD OF ST VICTOR.

N

Nagarjuna
(second century AD)

Indian Buddhist who taught the Madhyamika or Middle Path between existence and non-existence. 'Nothing comes into existence, nor does anything disappear. Nothing is eternal, nor has anything an end. Nothing is identical, nor is anything differentiated. Nothing moves in one direction, nor in any other.' Through these paradoxes and contradictions we learn to comprehend the void (*Sunyata*) and so find wisdom (*prajna*).

Nanak, Guru
(*c.* 1469–1539)

Founder of SIKHISM. Guru Nanak grew up in the Punjab, but somewhere about 1500 became a wandering ascetic, and travelled widely in India and outside. His thought is indebted both to theistic developments in Hinduism in northern India, and to the mystical tradition within Islam (he declared, 'There is no Hindu and no Muslim'), but he had a distinctive vision of his own which he expressed with magnetic clarity. Guru Nanak's religion is founded on his concept of God, One, transcendent, formless, eternal, ineffable. How then can man know God? In His eternal nature he cannot. But man can know God through His creation. For the transcendent God is immanent in His creation, 'everywhere present', and visible to the spiritually illuminated eye. And the God who is present in all creation is peculiarly present in the human heart, and is to be found through inward meditation. Man is the enemy of his own salvation, for he will not loose his grip from the illusion (MAYA) of worldly values. But God in His grace reveals Himself in three ways. *Nam*, the divine Name, and *shabad*, the divine Word, represent God's self-expression or revelation; any affirmation about Him is part of this revelation. The *guru*, the divine teacher, is the inner voice speaking to the heart. The *hukam*, the divine order, is the revelation of God through the order of the universe, with which man must seek to be in harmony. To reach this harmony man must submit himself to spiritual discipline, an inward not an outward observance. Repetition of the divine Name may help, but it is only a means to meditation on the divine Name, to a complete opening of one's whole being to the divine Name, and so to the ultimate harmony or union. Guru Nanak speaks of five stages of growth of which the highest is the Realm of TRUTH, the mystical union with God, which frees the soul from the wheel of truth and death for the eternal bliss of the BEATIFIC VISION:

> Love the Lord, o my soul . . .
> A well without water, a cow without milk,
> a shrine in darkness –
> so are you without him, o my soul.

Nan-ch'üan
(748–834)

Chinese ZEN Master, disciple of MA-TSU, who like him held the identity of the mind and the Buddha. A classic story tells how the Master held up a cat. He would kill it unless someone found the right thing to say. No one did; the cat was killed. In the evening his favourite disciple Chao-chou arrived. 'What would you have said?' Chao-chou took off his sandals, put them on his head and walked out. 'If you had been here,' said Nan-ch'üan, 'the cat would have been saved.' His meaningless action transcended affirmation and negation.

Nasoreans

See MANDAEANS.

Nasrudin

A fictitious character, known all over the Middle East, the subject of innumerable jokes and anecdotes collected in *The Subtleties of the Incomparable Nasrudin*. Many of the stories are very funny, and they are enjoyed for their own sakes; others are dull to Western taste. But they also form a part of Sufi teaching and many of them can be interpreted at a variety of levels. Here are some examples.

A story about the limitations of intellectualism: Nasrudin was ferrying an academic across some rough water. 'Have you ever studied grammar?' asked the scholar. 'No.' 'Then half your life has been wasted.' A few minutes later Nasrudin rejoined, 'Have you ever learned to swim?' 'No.' 'Then all your life is wasted. We're sinking.'

A story about our failure to see the truth which is close at hand: Nasrudin used to take his donkey across a frontier each day, its panniers laden with straw. He boasted openly that he was smuggling, and grew more wealthy, but the customs officers could never find anything. Years later, one of them asked him to come clean. 'What *were* you smuggling?' 'Donkeys,' said Nasrudin.

A story about the way we search for enlightenment in the wrong places: Nasrudin was down on his knees in the street looking for something. A neighbour asked, 'What have you lost?' 'My key.' 'Where did you drop it?' 'At home.' 'Then why, for heaven's sake, are you looking here?' 'There's more light here.'

A story of the relation of the visible example to the Platonic Form: Nasrudin was discussing this theme. A disciple said, 'Show me something practical – an apple from Paradise, say.' Nasrudin handed him an ordinary apple. 'But this apple is half bad – surely a heavenly apple would be perfect.' 'A heavenly apple would be perfect, but as far as you are able to judge it, and with your present faculties, this is as near to a heavenly apple as you will ever get.'

A story with a meaning which calls for technical explication: Nasrudin is taking a heavy load of salt to market. The donkey finds in crossing a stream that if he lets the panniers into the water the salt is washed away and his load lighter. Nasrudin teaches him a lesson by loading the panniers with wool. Here the donkey is man. Salt is a pun on the word for practical virtue. Man lightens himself of the burden of good living, but in fact loses, because there is no money for his fodder. Wool is a pun on SUFISM. In loading himself with mystical wisdom he increases his burden, but does better in the end.

Another example: A tyrant said to Nasrudin, 'I shall have you hanged if you do not prove that you have the deep perceptions attributed to you.' Nasrudin said promptly, 'I can see a golden bird in the sky and demons below the earth.' 'But how can you do this?' 'All you need is – fear.' Here fear is also a technical Sufi term for the faculty of conscience, the SYNTERESIS, which produces mystical vision.

Nasrudin is the mirror in which we see ourselves. Idries Shah compares him to the Cup of Jamshi, into which the Sufis gaze to see the world. Some of the stories have the paradoxicality of ZEN teaching. It is said that the mystical effect of seven Nasrudin stories, properly studied, will prepare an individual for enlightenment.

Nature

In Western thought, nature, the creation, is contrasted with God, the creator; natural is opposed to supernatural or divine. Man is opposed to nature; and we speak of conquering nature, conquering Mt Everest, conquering space. But the creation cannot be opposed to the creator in essence, and man is a part of nature. In Eastern thought there is more likely to be a sense of man's oneness with nature, and of co-operation with nature. This is very strong in TAOISM and in ZEN.

See also NATURE-MYSTICISM.

Nature-Mysticism

Nature-mysticism has been well defined by Rudolf OTTO as 'the sense of being immersed in the oneness of nature, so that man feels all the individuality, all the peculiarity of natural things in himself. He dances with the motes of dust and radiates with the sun; he rises with the dawn, surges with the wave, is fragrant in the rose, rapt with the nightingale: he knows and is all being, all strength, all joy, all desire, all pain in all things, inseparably.' Meister ECKHART says that in the experience 'all blades of grass, wood, and stone, all things are One'. So too Jakob BOEHME: 'In this light my spirit saw through all things and into all creatures, and I recognized God in grass and plants.' The borderline between nature-mysticism, properly so-called, and natural religion in a wider sense is impossible to define precisely. FRANCIS OF ASSISI saw all created things, birds and beasts and flowers, sun and moon, yes and death herself, as children of God and his brothers and sisters in Christ. SUSO writes of the inspiration of spring and adds 'O tender God, if Thou art so loving in Thy creatures, how fair and lovely must Thou be in Thyself.' FRANÇOIS DE SALES and FÉNELON write of the footprints of the Divine Wisdom in the world around us. There is a magnificent passage in GREGORY OF NYSSA: 'Travelling through the creation, the virtuous man is led to the apprehension of a Master of the creation; . . . when he observes the beauty of this material sunlight, he grasps by analogy the beauty of the real sunlight; . . . look at an ear of corn, a bunch of grapes, at the growing grass, . . . at the springs of water, the rivers, and the sea, and suchlike sights, and how can the eye of reason fail to find in them, all that our education for true realities requires?' So too John SMITH: 'There is a twofold meaning in every creature, a literal and a mystical, and the one is but the ground of the other.' In all these it is hard to say how far the believer is experiencing the power of God through the world, and how far he is arguing to God from the world. Some interpreters make a distinction on the other side, between nature-mysticism, and the Unitive Vision which approaches the One, in whom all stone and wood and blades of grass, even all grass-spiders are One, through the world of nature. None of these distinctions is absolute.

In nature-mysticism the 'trigger' for mystical experience is the natural world, sun and stars, land and sea, mountains and trees and flowers and birds and animals. As one absorbs this scene, the distinction between subject and object begins to fall away. The experience is well conveyed in a passage from Forrest Reid's novel *Following Darkness* (London 1902, p. 42): 'It was as if I had never realized how lovely the world was. I lay down on my back in the warm, dry moss and listened to the skylark singing as it mounted up from the fields near the sea into the dark clear sky. No other music gave me the same pleasure as that passionate joyous singing. It was a kind of leaping, exultant ecstasy, a bright, flame-like sound, rejoicing in itself. And then a curious experience befell me. It was as if everything that had seemed to be external and around me were suddenly within me. The whole world seemed to be within me. It was within me that the trees waved their green branches, it was within me that the skylark was singing, it was within me that the hot sun shone, and that the shade was cool. A cloud rose in the sky, and passed in a light shower that pattered on the leaves, and I felt its freshness dropping into my soul, and I felt in all my being the delicious fragrance of the earth and the grass and the plants and the rich brown soil. I could have sobbed for joy.'

It will be noticed that it is the beauty of nature which acts as the trigger: nature is not seen as 'red in tooth and claw'. It is doubtful how far mountains could act as a trigger in an age when they were regarded as sprawling wastes rather than objects of beauty and awesomeness.

Nature-mysticism has a tendency towards PANTHEISM, as in these verses of RUMI:

I am the dust in the sunlight, I am the ball
of the sun,
To the dust I say: Remain. And to the
sun: Roll on.

I am the mist of morning. I am the breath
of evening,
I am the rustling of the grove, the singing
wave of the sea.

I am the mast, the rudder, the steersman
and the ship.
I am the coral reef on which it founders.

I am the tree of life and the parrot in its
branches,
Silence, thought, tongue and voice.

I am the breath of the flute, the spirit of
man,
I am the spark in the stone, the gleam of
gold in the metal,

The candle and the moth fluttering
round it,
The rose and the nightingale drunk with
its fragrance.

I am the chain of being, the circle of the
spheres,
The scale of creation, the rise and the fall.

I am what is and is not. I am – O you
who know,
Jaluladdin, O say it – I am the soul in all.

Some early Christian writers held a form of nature-mysticism without pantheism by their doctrine of creation. Thus Tertullian: 'I offer you a rose; you will not scorn its creator.' This is very strong in AUGUSTINE. In *The Confessions* he seeks for God in the world of nature, but all nature cries, 'Not us, not us, but Him who made us'.

One of the finest expositions of nature-mysticism is found in the Cambridge Platonist, John Smith (1618–52): 'God made the universe and all the creatures contained therein as so many glasses wherein He might reflect His own glory. He hath copied forth Himself in the creation; and in this outward world we may read the lovely characters of the Divine goodness, power and wisdom. . . . But how to find God here, and feelingly to converse with Him, and being affected with the sense of Divine glory shining out upon the creation, how to pass out of the sensible world into the intellectual, is not so effectually taught by that philosophy which professed it most, as by true religion. That which knits and unites God and the soul together can best teach it how to ascend and descend upon those golden links that unite, as it were, the world to God. That Divine Wisdom, that contrived and beautified this glorious structure, can best explain her own arts, and carry up the soul back again in these reflected beams to Him who is the Fountain of them . . . good men may easily find every creature pointing out to that Being whose image and superscription it bears, and climb up from those darker resemblances of the Divine wisdom and goodness, shining out in different degrees upon several creatures, till they sweetly repose themselves in the bosom of the Divinity; and while they are thus conversing with this lower world . . . they find God many times secretly flowing into their souls, and leading them silently out of the court of the temple into the Holy Place . . . true religion never finds itself out of the infinite sphere of the Divinity . . . it beholds itself everywhere in the midst of that glorious unbounded Being who is indivisibly everywhere.'

For other nature-mystics *see* JEFFERIES, WORDSWORTH.

Negative way

See VIA NEGATIVA.

Neo-Pentecostalism

Movement of PENTECOSTALISM within the Roman Catholic Church.

Neo-Platonism

Revival of the philosophy of PLATO, which became the dominant philosophy of the Greek works about AD 250–500. Its founder was PLOTINUS, and his most important successors PORPHYRY, IAMBLICHUS and PROCLUS. Fundamentally Neo-Platonism centres on the One, the absolutely transcendent God, and all else consists of emanations from this ultimate first cause. Through DIONYSIUS THE AREOPAGITE Neo-Platonism affected the traditions of religious mysticism in Christianity and Islam. It was revived at the Renaissance by PICO DELLA MIRANDOLA and Marsilio FICINO.

See also NEO-PLATONISM IN ART.

Neo-Platonism in art

It has been amply shown by Ernst Gombrich and Erwin Panofsky that there are strong elements of NEO-PLATONISM in Italian art of the Renaissance. Sandro Botticelli (1444–1510) offers some particularly good examples. His *Primavera* was commissioned by Lorenzo de Pierfrancesco de' Medici, a pupil of FICINO. It is a complex Neo-Platonic allegory, drawing on some verses by

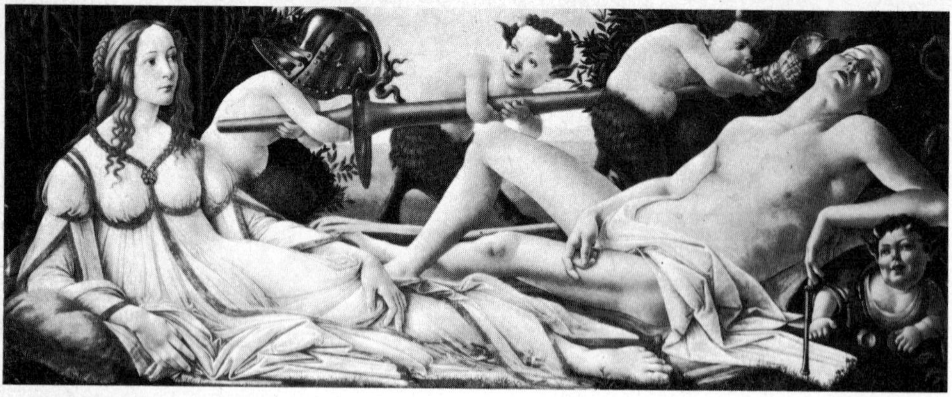

Sandro Botticelli, Mars and Venus

Politian. Mercury, who is Reason, is plucking fruit from a tree: so young Lorenzo's reason will come to fruition if united with humane culture. The Three Graces are dancing: they are Splendour, Youth, Happiness, or Grace, Beauty, Faith. Their threeness speaks of Christian mystery. At the same time they are associated with Venus; Pico speaks of the division of the unity of Venus into the Three Graces. Over Venus's head Cupid aims at these three; they too must aspire to God through love. On the other side Zephyrus, the West Wind, comes from the sun's setting with the nymph Flora, who is transformed into the serene goddess with the flowery dress. A picture of spring, then, but symbolizing the awakening of the love of God through humane culture. Another Botticelli, *The Birth of Venus*, has its scenario from Politian, but is dependent on Ficino for its interpretation: it is an allegory of the birth of Beauty alike in the very being of the universe and in the world of matter. In the myth Saturn castrated Heaven and threw his testicles into the sea; from the agitated foam Venus was born. This is the potential fecundity latent in the first principle. The divine spirit pours this into the soul and matter ('which is called sea'). The soul thus fertilized creates Beauty within itself. But just as Botticelli introduces a Christian reference into *Primavera*, so too he baptizes Venus by grouping the figures round her as in traditional representations of the baptism of Christ. In yet another picture, *Mars and Venus*, we have to think of astrology. Mars stands for violence, Venus for peace, beauty and creativity. Ficino says, 'Mars is outstanding in strength among planets because he makes men stronger, but Venus masters him. Mars never masters Venus. The clearest sign of love's unrivalled strength is that all things obey love. Love obeys no-one. Gods love, animals love, all creatures love, men love, wise men, brave men, rich men, rulers. . . . Love yields to no-one. Love is free. It rises in the free will, which not even God can force since he willed it to be free. Love rules over all and submits to none.'

Titian's portrayal of the common Aphrodite clothed and the open, honest, nude Heavenly Aphrodite, both good, but nullifying unless you rise from the first to the second, from sensual love to spiritual love, is another Neo-Platonic allegory. There is one Cupid between the two of them: they are aspects of the same principle. They are by a classical sarcophagus from which water is flowing, life from the place of death.

MICHELANGELO is another strongly Neo-Platonic artist.

Neo-Pythagoreanism

Revival of PYTHAGOREANISM in the first century BC, which maintained the dualism of soul and body and the ascetic and dietary discipline, blended together elements from PLATO, ARISTOTLE and the STOICS and from oriental religions, e.g. astrology, together with an exalted mysticism which pointed the way to PLOTINUS and NEO-PLATONISM.

Neumann, Theresa
(1898–1962)

See FASTING.

Nicholas of Cusa
(1401–64)

German philosopher who rose to be cardinal in 1448 and Bishop of Brixen in 1450. His thought has affinities with NEO-PLATONISM, and he was influenced by AUGUSTINE and DIONYSIUS, as well as by mediaeval mystical thinkers like BONAVENTURA and ECKHART. He holds that the vision of God in mystical theology can only take place 'in a fog of coincidence' which is infinity; it is therefore an entering into infinity in which contradictions coexist and in which there is no end. We can know nothing with the intellect; our highest state is educated ignorance: SOCRATES would agree! Truth is one, simple and absolute;

what we call knowledge is multiple, complex and approximate. We must seek the Truth beyond reason in intuition. God is not one or three, but three in one. The divine attributes, which are many, coincide in the divine Essence. God is both infinitely great and infinitely small, the centre and the circumference, everywhere and nowhere. To apprehend him we must pass from intelligence through faith to vision under the power of love. Knowledge and love move hand in hand and are united only in the experience of ultimate union. That experience is one of indescribable delight. But it can be translated into the work of the world; for in Christ, the Mediator between God and man, contemplation becomes action.

Nicholson, Reynold Alleyne
(1868–1945)

British orientalist, fellow of Trinity College, Cambridge, whose studies in SUFISM are the greatest made by any European scholar, and whose own translations show a sensitive poetic gift and spiritual understanding.

Night of the Soul

JUAN DE LA CRUZ identifies two Nights of the Soul, two stages in prayerful contemplation of God.

The first, which he calls the Night of the Senses, is an experience of spiritual dryness, usually painful, which leads to the simple direction of the soul towards God with the single desire to possess God more fully. Spiritual dryness brings restlessness, distractions, doubts and temptations, and the unsatisfied spiritual thirst can be agonizing. At the same time as the soul turns to God there is a sense of peace and joy, and the suffering and joy may be experienced simultaneously.

The second, which he calls the Night of the Spirit, is the continuing sense of darkness in all mystic states except the highest. He characterizes it as 'infused contemplation'. The soul is passive, aware of its own poverty, aware of God without understanding so that the rays of divine Light become darkness, and natural perceptions are eliminated without anything to take their place, and it is subjected to often painful change. Suffering and joy here too are commingled.

Nikolaus von Flüe
(1417–87)

Swiss ascetic. Bruder Klaus, as he came to be known, lived a normal secular life for fifty years as soldier, judge, husband and father. At the age of fifty he retired to become a hermit in the mountains, where he acquired a high reputation for sanctity. Tradition claims that he lived for nineteen years with no food except the EUCHARIST: certainly he provides one of the more remarkable instances of sustained FASTING.

Nirvana

The haven of the Buddhists, beyond all heavens, a state of ineffable peace, free from the world of space and time, free from contingent being, free from the craving to become and the craving for what becomes, free from the weary cycle of birth and death and rebirth, free from the senses, free from illusion, free from all kinds of passion, free from all that is transient. It is a state of liberation, spiritual freedom, true health, immersion in cosmic consciousness. Analogies are found in the scent of a flower or a country scene of even charm.

Nirvana, in Nagasena's words, is 'uncompounded; it is made of nothing at all. One cannot say of Nirvana that it arises or that it does not arise or that it is to be produced or that it is past or present or future, or that it is cognizable by the eye, the ear, nose, tongue or physical touch.' Or as it is said in *Udana* (81), 'There is, monks, an unborn, not become, not made, uncompounded, and were it not, monks, for this unborn, not become, not made, uncompounded, no escape could be shown here for what is born, has become, is made, is compounded. But because, monks, there is an unborn, not become, not made, uncompounded, therefore an escape can be shown for what is born, has become, is made, is compounded.'

Nirvana can be attained in this life, and the Buddha lived in it after his enlightenment. *Nirvana* also passes beyond death. This is the escape. But, as the *Lankavatra Sutra* has it, 'If they only realized it, they are already in Nirvana, for, in Noble Wisdom, all things are in Nirvana from the beginning.'

Even beyond *Nirvana* lies PARANIRVANA, beyond the Beyond. *Nirvana* is our human goal; *Paranirvana* lies beyond that.

No-mind

A ZEN doctrine which goes back at least to HUI-NENG and his assertion 'From the first not a thing is.' Hui-neng insisted that the object of Zen is 'seeing into one's own self-nature' which thus becomes 'seeing into nothingness'. To see into nothingness requires no-mind. It is in its way a doctrine of the unconscious, but not in either a psycho-analytical or a metaphysical sense. One of Hui-Neng's followers produced a dialogue which begins:

Q. I have left my home to become a monk and my aspiration is to attain Buddhahood. How should I use my mind?

A. Buddhahood is attained when there is no mind which is to be used for the task.

Q. When there is no mind to be used for the task, who can ever attain Buddhahood?

A. By no-mind the task is accomplished by itself. Buddha too has no mind.

Q. The Buddha has wonderful ways and knows how to deliver all beings. If he had no mind, who would ever deliver all beings?

A. To have no mind means to deliver all beings. If he sees any being who is to be delivered, he has a mind, and so is surely subject to birth and death.

There is an excellent story of Yao-Shan sitting cross-legged in meditation. A monk asked him: 'In this immovable position what are you thinking?' He replied: 'Thinking of that which is beyond thinking.' The monk went on: 'How do you go on with thinking that which is beyond thinking?' 'By not thinking.'

Non-attachment

Phrase coined by Aldous HUXLEY to describe the ideal man of the free philosophers, the mystics, the founders of religions. The ideal man is non-attached to bodily sensations and lusts, to craving for power and possessions, to the objects of these various desires, to anger and hatred, to exclusive loves, to wealth, fame, social position, even to science, art, speculation, philanthropy. Non-attachment is negative only in name: it involves charity, courage, intelligence, generosity and disinterestedness. Non-attachment is found in the Hindu identification of the flux and multiplicity of the material world as MAYA or illusion, or the similar Buddhist doctrine of SAMSARA. In Greece the followers of HERACLITUS saw the material world as in a state of constant movement or flow, and PLATO, who studied with one of them extended this in his teaching that true reality is to be found in the immaterial changeless 'forms' and that the philosopher must learn through mathematics and dialectic to detach himself from the relativities of the material world and concentrate his mind upon unchanging reality. The leading thinkers of the Hellenistic age all in their different ways were fostering *autarkeia* ('self-sufficiency', but well translated 'non-attachment'). The most extreme was Diogenes the 'Dog', founder of the Cynics, who taught himself to do without anything except a jar for shelter, a satchel and in old age a staff. He inured himself to hardship by lying in summer in the torrid sand under the open sun, and in winter by night embracing a marble statue in the snow.

Such non-attachment is equally strong in later mysticism. Thus RICHARD OF ST VICTOR speaks of the need to 'forget all outward things'. THOMAS À KEMPIS writes 'Learn to turn from worldly things, and give yourself to spiritual things, and you will see the Kingdom of God come within you.' Walter HILTON sees the pre-condition of self-knowledge, and with it knowledge of the spiritual world, as the detachment of the soul 'from all earthly preoccupations and from the influence of the senses, so that it understands itself as it is in its own nature, taking no account of the body'. JUAN DE LA CRUZ even recommends to this end concentration upon the worst of temporal things rather than the best, so as to lead to detachment from them. ECKHART sums up the whole position well: 'Three things prevent a man from knowing God at all. The first is time, the second corporality, and the third is multiplicity or plurality. As long as these three things are in me God is not in me nor is he genuinely at work in me.'

Nothing

Some religions (as Judaism and Christianity) speak of creation out of nothing. For many adherents this is simply non-existence. But for many mystics, e.g. DIONYSIUS THE AREOPAGITE, John Scotus ERIGENA or the Kabbalist David Ben Abraham Ha-Laban, this Nothing is infinitely more real than all other reality. Creation out of Nothing is creation out of the Ultimate, out of God, and to know reality the soul must strip itself of all encumbrances and of all seemingly positive but actually limiting thought, and descend into the depths of Nothing to encounter the Divine.

Novalis
(1772–1801)

Pseudonym of Friedrich Leopold Freiherr von Hardenburg, romantic poet and prose-writer with a strong mystical strain. In *Selected Thoughts* he touches on his mystical philosophy: 'The spirit world is in fact revealed to us; it is always open. Could we suddenly become as sensitive as is necessary, we should perceive ourselves to be in its midst.' So in *Thoughts on Religion*: 'What is Mysticism? What must be mystically treated? Religion, Love, Nature, the State. – All that is select is related to mysticism. If all men were a pair of lovers, the distinction between mysticism and no-mysticism would fall away.' Novalis regards mysticism as essential to human development: 'Mystical faith in what has actual existence, as in the old and known, and mystical hope of all that is to come, or of the new and unknown, are two important characteristics of the humanity of the past.' Two great unfinished prose romances express his mysticism even more clearly than his verse. *The Disciples at Sais* has a particularly exquisite passage in which the Master learns and demonstrates the interrelation of all things. He has one disciple who seems dull and incapable of finding the crystals and flowers to form patterns of beauty. One day he returns singing, with an ugly little pebble. The Master places it at a key-point. 'It was as though we had transitorily caught into our souls a clear vision of this wondrous world.' In *Heinrich von Ofterdingen* there is an account of the search for the blue flower, which symbolizes the mystical Ultimate.

Numinous

Term coined by Rudolf OTTO to express the idea of holiness or awesomeness which he regarded as the essence of religion.

O

Oahspe

Title of a new scripture written 'under spiritual guidance' in America by Dr John B. Newbrough in 1881, *A sacred History of the Dominion of the Higher and Lower Heavens on the Earth for the next Twenty-four Thousand Years.* This work, which claims that since 1848 the world has entered a new era, is still going into new editions.

Odour of Sanctity

PAUL (2 Cor. 2, 15) writes 'we are the good odour of Christ to God', and it may be that the idea of the odour of sanctity has been affected by a too literal reading of that passage. But there are records throughout history of the association of fragrance with religious experience. It is found in some accounts of early Christian martyrs, such as Polycarp. A good example, though at second hand and therefore to be treated with caution, comes from TERESA DE JESUS's account of Catalina de Cardona: 'All our nuns assured me that there was about her a fragrance as that of relics, so strong that it moved them to give thanks to our Lord; it clung even to her habit and her girdle which she left behind, for they took her habit from her and gave her another; and the nearer they came to her the more strongly did they perceive it, though her dress, owing to the heat which then prevailed, was of a kind to be offensive rather than otherwise. I know they would not say anything which was not in every way true.' A particularly interesting example is Sister Giovanna Maria della Croce of Roveredo (d. 1673). She experienced a mystic espousal to Jesus, and from that point her finger began to exude fragrance, which was passed on to others by touch.

Olier, Jean-Jacques
(1608–57)

French mystic, influenced by VINCENT DE PAUL and Charles de CONDREN, notable for his foundation of the Society and seminary of Saint-Sulpice in 1642. Olier, in his early twenties, was suddenly struck blind, and it was his cure which directed him away from worldly ambition to a deeper spirituality; we could rightly say that the loss of outward sight led him to interior vision. His spirituality is reflected in the SULPICIAN METHOD developed by his successors from his insights.

Om

In Hindu mysticism, a syllable for meditation. The *Mandukya Upanishad* divides it (as AUM) into A, the state of waking consciousness, U, the state of dreaming consciousness, and M, the state

A stylized depiction of the mantra *Om. The largest figure is Brahman, transcendent and immanent universal Spirit*

of sleeping consciousness. The silence following the utterance of the whole syllable is the awakened life of supreme consciousness. OM, the Eternal Word, thus is the ATMAN or Self, and 'he who knows this with his self enters the Self'. OM is the whole world, past, present and future. Meditation upon OM thus leads to deliverance, to union with BRAHMAN and to immortality. In the *Taittriya Upanishad* it is written: 'AUM is Brahman. AUM is this all. AUM, this, in truth is compliance. On uttering "recite", they recite. With AUM they sing the *saman* chants. With AUM, SOM they recite the prayers. With AUM the Adhvaryu priest utters the response. With AUM the Brahman priest speaks the introductory ascription. With AUM there is assent to the offering to fire. With AUM a Brahmana begins to recite "May I obtain Brahman", in the wish he does indeed obtain Brahman.'

Omar Khayyam
(d. *c.* 1122)

Persian Sufi poet and philosopher, much misunderstood in the West because of Edward

Fitzgerald's beguiling but misleading version of some of his quatrains: a more accurate version will be found in Swami Govinda Tirtha, *The Nectar of Grace* (1941). His verses are in fact incomprehensible without a knowledge of SUFISM.

> The secret must be kept from all non-people:
> The mystery must be hidden from all idiots.
> See what you do to people –
> The Eye has to be hidden from all men.

Omar has been granted the vision of the TRUTH.

> When the Original Cause determined my being
> I was given the first lesson of love.
> It was then that the fragment of my heart was made
> The Key to the Treasury of Pearls of mystical meaning.

So when we read of wine in Omar, as we often do –

> I cannot live without wine,
> Without the cup's draught I cannot carry my body.
> I am the slave of that breath in which the Saki says
> 'Take one more cup' – and I cannot do so –

we are to think of the Sufi doctrine of spiritual intoxication as the ecstatic experience which leads to *gnosis*. And when has the *via negativa* been more clearly put that in the line 'O ignorant ones – the Road is neither this nor that!'?

Omar, in addition to his mystical poetry, was a great mathematician.

One

Term for the Ultimate or God in many mystical religions and philosophies.

Opium

Drug extracted from the poppy. The active principle, morphine, is medically important as a pain-killer. It can create illusions of a mystical kind; it can also lead to dangerous addiction.

Orenda

Iroquois word for a power inherent in material objects; it is not far from our term 'energy'. It is associated with the notion of will or desire, but differs from MANITOU in not involving the concept of animation by a personal spirit.

Orison

Term sometimes used for mystical prayer by contrast with other forms of prayer.

Ormuzd

In ZOROASTRIANISM Spenta Mainyu, the Good Spirit, becomes assimilated to AHURA MAZDA, and the opponents in the battle of light and darkness are called Ormuzd and Ahriman.

Orozco, Alfonso de

(1500–91)

Spanish Augustinian who began writing in response to a vision of the Virgin Mary who spoke to him the single word 'Write'. He was a voluminous writer, a court preacher and man of affairs as well as an austere contemplative, who proclaims it a great thing that the soul while still in mortal flesh may be caught up so as to behold God in His Essence, without use of the senses, but warns those who follow him that the man who would face the supreme Wrestler, God, must first have wrestled with himself.

Orphic mysteries

Orpheus was a legendary singer in Greek myth, a kind of double of DIONYSUS, who was musician to the Argonauts, could charm animals and stones and trees by his song, rescued his wife Eurydice from death by his music (the story of his last-minute failure is a later addition), and was himself torn to pieces by Maenads, though his head continued to sing after death. He was thus a natural figure for a mystery-religion promising life after death and the inspiration of divine power. We meet Orphics in Sicily and Greece in the fifth century BC. We may be reasonably supposed to meet them (though Zuntz has recently argued to the contrary) in buried gold tablets giving instructions to the soul on its movements after death:

> You will find to the left of the House of Hades a spring,
> And by its side a white cypress standing.
> Do not approach near this spring.
> You will find another, with cold water flowing
> from the Lake of Memory, and sentinels in front of it.
> Say 'I am a child of Earth and starry Heaven,
> but my race is of Heaven. You know this already.
> But I am parched and perishing of thirst. Give me quickly
> the cold water flowing from the Lake of Memory.'
> Then they will freely let you drink from the holy spring,
> and thereafter you will have lordship with the other heroes.

One recurrent phrase in these tablets is 'A kid, I have fallen into milk.' In one the soul is greeted with the words 'You have become god from man.' We meet them also in a cult-society of the Roman age, perhaps from Pergamum, which has left behind a series of some eighty-odd hymns, addressed to various deities. They certainly do belong to a mystery cult, and use all the language of initiation, promising to the initiates a blameless life and a blessed end.

Associated with the Orphics was a myth. Dionysus was killed and devoured by the Titans; his heart was rescued and a new Dionysus born from it. The Titans were destroyed by Zeus' thunderbolt, and mankind formed from their ashes. Man is thus compounded of a Titanic element, the body, and a Dionysiac element, the soul, and his aim is to purify himself of his Titanic element. This requires religious observance, asceticism including vegetarianism, and moral probity. There was a doctrine of reincarnation and 'a sorrowful, weary circle' of death and rebirth, from which initiates enjoy an accelerated escape till they hear the words 'Happy and blessed one, you have become divine instead of mortal.'

We have some remarkable bowls associated with the Orphic cult, and datable to the third century AD or thereabouts. On one bowl – it was found at an undisclosed site in the Mediterranean zone in the 1860s – the outside seems to be a representation of the cosmos, round, and supported on twenty-four columns. The circles on the base represent the movement of the spheres. Four nude figures blowing trumpets are the four winds. Inscribed on the base in not very good Greek are four quotations from Orphic hymns. Within the bowl a winged snake in the centre twines round the cosmic egg, which is protected by flames of fire. Around are sixteen nude worshippers, nine female, seven male. They gesticulate with various combinations of gesture, one or the other hand being raised, or at the side, or to the breast, navel or genitals. Plainly here is a scene of revelation: the ultimate mystery of life, and creation, rebirth from fire (like the phoenix), the rebirth of the snake which sloughs its skin. To receive the illumination we must strip off all external trappings. This is a sacramental bowl: we may suppose that the wine was drunk from it, and when it was consumed the mystery would be revealed.

Another bowl was found near Pietrosa in Rumania in 1837; this has since been destroyed for its gold, but records of it survive. Interpretation is controversial. In the centre a goddess is seated on a vine-encircled throne, with a chalice in her hand. She must be in some guise the Great Mother, and she is offering the sacrament of life. Immediately around her are animals together with one human figure. Then, more elaborately portrayed, are sixteen figures. Dominating the scene, straight in front of the goddess is a seated figure with a lyre, and an animal at his feet. This is Orpheus in one of his aspects. He looks to his right: all that comes leads up to him: this is the end and culmination and glory. Next on his left is Orpheus as a fisherman, with rod, net and fish. Here Orpheus draws the initiate to him, and we follow him in his journey round to the vision glorious. We see him with the raven of death in attendance carrying the pine-cone of life and the torch of light. He passes reverently before Demeter and Kore, the powers of life and death, and is blessed by the powers of fortune. We see him next with a begging bowl, stripped of all his possessions, and ready to pass before two torturers with whips: the raven is there: this is the symbolic death. But now comes the resurrection, and with the staff of wisdom and the basket of abundance he is welcomed into the presence of the rejuvenated and enthroned Orpheus.

Osiris

See ISIS AND OSIRIS.

Osuna, Francisco de
(d. *c.* 1540)

Spanish mystic, whose work *The Third Spiritual Alphabet* deeply influenced TERESA DE JESUS. Little is known of his life. His book is profound but incoherent. He writes for those 'who in purity of spirit would attain to God'. He guides the beginner through the need for vigilant meekness to the practice of the prayer of recollection. 'It is the coming of the Lord to the soul. . . . It is the friendship or the opening of the devout heart to Christ. . . . It is a spiritual ascension with Christ. . . . It is the third heaven to which the contemplative soul is caught up.' He is insistent that the eyes must ever be fixed on the goal: 'Desire your Beloved always.' 'He is the end of all your works and desires.' God then becomes the guide to life. 'Then shall He be always with you as the Star was with the Magi and the North with the sailor.' Osuna is a man of tenderness, deeply concerned to help those who are on the road. Of the actual experience of union he does not have much to say; it is 'the summit of contemplation, where striving is no more but all is rest'.

Otto, Rudolf
(1869–1937)

German Protestant theologian, with a wide knowledge and deep appreciation both of Western science and Eastern religion, professor successively at Breslau and Marburg. His book *Das Heilige* (1917) identified the essence of religion with the Holy or the NUMINOUS; *West-östliche Mystik* (1926) is a fascinating comparison of ECKHART and SANKARA.

Ouroboros

Snake devouring its own tail; an important mystical symbol. Analytical psychology suggests that this is a primal image, in which male and female, positive and negative, conscious and unconscious elements and elements hostile to consciousness are intertwined. Others have seen in it a representation of the universe as cyclic.

P

Palamas, Gregory

(*c.* 1296–1359)

Palamas was born to a noble and devout family. In 1318 he went to the sacred mountain of Athos and became an adept of the system of HESYCHASM. In defence of this he became involved in controversy with a Calabrian monk named Barlaam. His career went through many vicissitudes, but within ten years of his death he was established as a 'Father and Doctor of the Church'.

Gregory held that man is a single whole, body and soul, and the whole man is made in the image of God, the whole man prays to God, and the whole man is redeemed. Christ through the Incarnation 'made the flesh an inexhaustible source of sanctification. Man cannot know the invisible, incommunicable Divine Essence. He can know the energies or activities of God. God is not a being, for he is above all beings. Nothing created can have communion with the supreme nature. But through his energies God communicates himself to man, and because God is Light, he communicates himself in the form of Light, not physical light, but uncreated light.' Gregory thus is able to maintain his doctrine of God's IMMANENCE and His mystical revelation without becoming involved in PANTHEISM.

Panentheism

Term coined by K. C. F. Krause (1781–1832) to describe the doctrine that God is immanent in all things but also transcendent, so that every part of the universe has its existence in God; but He is more than the sum total of those parts.

Pantheism

Term coined by John Toland (1670–1722) to describe the doctrine that God and the universe are identical. Much Hindu mystical thought is pantheistic, and there are elements of PANTHEISM in such Christian mystics as DIONYSIUS, ERIGENA, NICHOLAS OF CUSA, ECKHART and BOEHME. There is an excellent example of a pantheistic hymn in the *Svetasvatara Upanishad:*

That is the fire,
That is the sun,
That is the air,
That is the moon,
That is the pure,
That is Brahman,
That is the waters –
That is the creator of all.

You are woman, you are man,
You are the youth, you are the maiden.
You are the old man, tottering with his staff.
Once born you face everywhere.

You are the dark blue butterfly,
You are the green parrot with red eyes,
You are the thunder-cloud, the seasons, the seas.
You are without beginning,
You pervade all things,
And from you all beings were born.

(tr. E. G. Parrinder)

So too in the BHAGAVAD GITA the Lord KRISHNA declares that he is the thread on which the pearls of the universe are strung, the taste of water, the radiance of the sun, life in all beings, the intellect of the intelligence, the prowess of the powerful (7). He is the Self existing in the heart of all beings; the beginning, middle and end of beings (10). Western philosophers of pantheism have included SPINOZA (whose pantheistic formula *Deus sive Natura* made the terms God and nature interchangeable), and HEGEL.

Paracelsus

(1493–1541)

Self-adopted name of Theophrastus Bombastus von Hohenheim, indicating that in his own view he was greater than the Graeco-Roman medical writer Celsus. Paracelsus was a doctor's son, himself a doctor and alchemist, a restless traveller who acquired an amazing stock of miscellaneous and secret lore. He called himself 'the Monarch of Arcana', a son of God, born of nature. 'Of her I am born; her I follow. She knows me, and I know her. The light which is in her I have beheld in her; outside, too, I have proved the same in the figure of the microcosm, and found it in that universe.' Paracelsus was an alchemist, but he was not primarily concerned with the search for transmutation into gold, but with the power of healing. He believed that sickness and health are controlled by astral powers, and saw nature as a kind of world-alchemist with whom the healer must co-operate. Paracelsus's mystical theosophy had its roots in NEO-PLATONISM: he believed that we knew God only in so far as we are God.

Paradise

Originally a Persian term meaning a garden or park, it was applied to the scene of primal innocence in Genesis and in Jewish literature came to mean a state of blessedness, or place of blessedness. The concept passed over to the

A contemporary woodcut portrait of Paracelsus

Christians and Muslims; a similar concept is found among the Zoroastrians, where it is called 'the Abode of Song'. Mystical experience may be expressed as an experience of Paradise.

Paradox

Ronald Knox, in *Enthusiasm* (pp. 250 ff.), identifies the Seven Paradoxes of Mysticism: (a) The mystic has a sense of being carried away by a force stronger than himself, yet he can merit by his prayer. (b) The contemplative's apprehension of God, in becoming more direct, becomes less distinct. (c) In trying to love God more, the soul makes less use of its affections. (d) The will becomes more and more the centre of our prayer, yet its acts become less and less perceptible. (e) Some contemplatives find that the more they pray, the less they ask for. (f) The more the soul enters into itself, the less it is self-conscious. (g) The soul, as it advances in contemplation, becomes less, not more conscious of living virtuously.

A major paradox has been called the vacuum-plenum paradox. It can be tabulated as follows:

The Universal Self

Positive (Plenum)	*Negative (Vacuum)*
has qualities	has no qualities
is personal	is impersonal
is dynamic, active,	is static, inactive,
creative.	motionless.

The paradox is excellently put in the *Isa Upanishad*: 'The One, the Self, though never stirring, is swifter than thought. . . . Though standing still, it overtakes those who are running. . . . It stirs and it does not stir.' Another not dissimilar paradox arises from the thought that God is all, and yet that all is not God. Similar to this again is the paradox of union and separateness. For God and the soul to unite they must be separate, otherwise they are already one. But how can two different entities become one?

A particularly good example of mystical paradox will be found in Buddhism; Heinrich Zimmer has called it 'bold and stunning'. NIRVANA is the disappearance of all distinction between *nirvana* and SAMSARA, between ETERNITY and TIME. In other words *nirvana* and *samsara* are both nothingness; there is no such thing as *nirvana*. This paradox is expounded in the dialogues known as *Prajna paramita* or *Transcendental Wisdom*. 'Thus, O Sariputa, all things, having the nature of emptiness, have no beginning and no ending. They are neither faultless nor not faultless; they are neither perfect nor imperfect. In emptiness there is no form, no sensation, no perception, no discrimination, no consciousness. There is no eye, no ear, no nose, no smell, no taste, no touch, no mental process, no object, no knowledge, no ignorance. There is no destruction of objects, there is no cessation of knowledge, no cessation of ignorance. There are no Noble Fourfold Truths; no pain, no cause of pain, no cessation of pain, no Noble Path leading to the cessation of pain. There is no decay and no death, and no destruction of the motion of decay and death. There is no knowledge of Nirvana, there is no obtaining of Nirvana, there is no not obtaining of Nirvana.'

T. S. Eliot, in *East Coker*, made magnificent poetry out of a mystical paradox in JUAN DE LA CRUZ.

In order to arrive at what you do not know
    You must go by a way which is the way of ignorance. . . .
In order to arrive at what you are not
    You must go through the way in which you are not.
And what you do not know is the only thing you know
And what you own is what you do not own
And where you are is where you are not.

Much mystical teaching is done through paradox. The Zen KOAN offers some particularly good examples. Part of the object is to startle the disciple into looking below the surface. In a Sufi catechism we find 'How can *The Qur'an* be the eyebrow of a mistress?' 'How can *The Qur'an* be marks made by carbon and gum on pieces of paper with wood from a swamp?'

Paramita

In Buddhism, 'perfection', a means of crossing to the farther shore, that is of entering NIRVANA. There are six: the *silaparamita* (observing the precepts), the *ksantiparamita* (perfect forbearance), the *viryaparamita* (steadfast zeal), the *dhyanaparamita* (concentration in meditation), the *prajnaparamita* (wisdom) and the *danaparamita* (relinquishing). In the end all depend on the last, since they themselves must be relinquished.

Paranirvana

Complete NIRVANA, escape from the cycle of birth and death.

Parenhenic mysticism

Term used by R. C. Zaehner for the more familiar NATURE-MYSTICISM.

Parmenides

(*c*. 512–445 BC)

Greek philosopher who seems to have been a dissident PYTHAGOREAN. Parmenides wrote a poem with the force of a religious revelation. In the prologue he is carried, like a shaman, by a heavenly chariot out of darkness into light, and is brought into the presence of 'the golden', who is unnamed, but who is the source of his revelation. The revelation depends on the impossibility of the existence of Not-Being or any intermediate state between BEING and Not-Being: coming into being, or 'becoming', is an impossibility, for it involves a passage from Not-Being to Being. All we can say is 'It is'. Parmenides can only compare reality to a sphere, equally balanced in every direction from the centre. It follows naturally that sense-perception and the divisions of the seeming world are all illusory. All that exists is the One.

Parsifal

Opera by Richard Wagner (1813–83) produced in 1882. The story is a version of the GRAIL legend, with which Parsifal or Perceval, originally the hero of an independent cycle, had become associated. The Knights of the Holy Grail guard it and the Sacred Spear, but the latter is lost to a magician, Klingsor; and the young guardian the prince Amfortas has been wounded. Parsifal comes as deliverer, even to the temptress Kundry, rescues the spear, baptizes Kundry, heals Amfortas and uncovers the Grail. It was on Good Friday in 1867 that Wagner heard 'that

Parsifal as imagined by the 19th-century French artist Jean Delville

sigh of profound pity which of old has resounded from the Cross at Golgotha, and which, on this occasion escaped from his own breast', and began his first sketch. The opera, which has been described as 'Buddhist renunciation clothed in the garb of Christian sacrament', is complementary to *Tristan und Isolde* with its exaltation of erotic love; it is hard not to think that the Grail and spear are symbols of sex. The opera is noteworthy for the mysticism of its final scene when the glory of the Grail is revealed. Wagner uses for the Grail music advanced techniques of modalism.

Pascal, Blaise

(1623–62)

French mathematician, theologian and man of letters, whose *Thoughts*, a discursive vindication of Christianity, has been greatly influential. For Pascal, religion, though it may be supported by reason, is in the end a matter of faith. We have to place our bets, and the heart has its reasons, of which reason knows nothing. He himself places his bets on Jesus, and *The Mystery of Jesus* is a powerful testimony of personal devotion. At one point Jesus says to him, 'Comfort yourself; you would never have sought me if you had not already found me.'

After his death there was found stitched into his clothes a rough drawing of a flaming cross and the verbal record of a mystical experience.

> In the year of grace 1654 Monday, 23 November, the day of St Clement, Pope and Martyr, and others in the Martyrology;

the eve of St Chrysogonus, Martyr, and others;
from about half-past ten in the evening till about half an hour after midnight

FIRE

God of Abraham, God of Isaac, God of Jacob,
Not of the philosophers and the learned.
Certitude. Joy. Certitude. Emotion. Sight. Joy.
Forgetfulness of the world and of all outside God.
The world hath not known Thee, but I have known Thee.
Joy! Joy! Joy! Tears of joy.
My God, wilt Thou leave me?
Let me not be separated from Thee for ever.

Patmore, Coventry Kersey Dighton
(1823–96)

English mystical poet, technically important for his innovations in prosody. He was once known for *The Angel in the House* (1854–6), a poem extolling married love in a way that is all too easy to parody, though it has felicitous touches. But *The Unknown Eros* (1877) and a final book of prose meditations *Rod, Root, and Flower* (1895), though uneven, show a great depth of mystical intuition. He destroyed an earlier prose work, *Sponsa Dei*, because it betrayed the mysteries. Patmore has elements of NATURE-MYSTICISM, but mostly his is a sexual mysticism.

In the arithmetic of life
The smallest unit is a pair.

For Patmore the body is 'Creation's and Creator's crowning good', the rapture of the sense and the rapture of the spirit are one, and Love – Eros – operates under the 'full Moon of deific vision bright'. A. E. Housman spoke scornfully of Patmore's 'nasty mixture of poetry and concupiscence' but added 'Nobody admires his best poetry enough.'

Paul
(d. *c.* AD 65)

Saul was a Jew from Tarsus, brought up a Pharisee, who became a Christian convert as a result of a cataclysmic vision of Christ. A long solitary spell in the deserts of Arabia prepared him for his work as a Christian leader. After preaching in Caesarea, Syria, Cilicia and Cyprus, he undertook three great 'missionary journeys' through Asia Minor, and down through Greece as well. Rejection by the Jews led him to preach increasingly to Gentiles, and he used his Roman name, Paul. He was arrested and taken to Rome. An early tradition suggests that he was released and visited Spain, to return and be martyred under the Neronian persecutions.

In his letters to his converts Paul laid down the ground-plan of Christian theology, and his teaching on justification by faith; the power of divine grace; the new era of the Spirit brought in through the life, death and resurrection of Jesus Christ; the Church as the body of which Christ is the head, a single united organism; the way of love, joy, peace; and much else, proved enormously influential.

Paul is sometimes claimed as the first Christian mystic. The vision of Christ on the road to Damascus (reflecting the vision of Stephen at the moment of his lynching) has some of the elements of mystical experience, such as the sense of a blazing light. At the same time the experience still involved sensuous imagery. It is very different from his own description of a later experience, seemingly autobiographical (2 Cor. 12, 2): 'I know a Christian man who fourteen years ago (whether in the body or out of it, I do not know – God knows) was caught up as far as the third heaven. And I know that this same man (whether in the body or out of it, I do not know – God knows) was caught up into paradise, and heard words so secret that human lips may not repeat them.' He is prepared to boast upon that experience, because it came wholly from God and not at all from his own efforts.

His concept of 'being in Christ' or 'Christ in you' (Col. 1, 27) is important here. 'The life I now live is not my life, but the life which Christ lives in me' (Gal. 2, 20); 'I bear in my body the marks of the Lord Jesus' (Gal. 6, 17); 'We are transformed into the image of the Lord by the Spirit of the Lord' (2 Cor. 3, 18); 'We are always bearing about in the body the dying of the Lord Jesus that the life also of Jesus may be seen in our body' (2 Cor. 4, 10); 'Our inward self is renewed day by day' (2 Cor. 4, 16); 'For me to live is Christ' (Phil. 1, 21).

Important too is the contrast between life according to the flesh, and life in the Spirit. 'The flesh' does not mean the material world, but man's lower nature. 'Those who live on the level of our lower nature have their outlook formed by it, and that spells death; but those who live on the level of the spirit have the spiritual outlook, and that is life and peace' (Rom. 8, 5). This is the Purgative Way of the later mystics. Paul calls on his readers to let their minds be remade and their whole natures thus transformed (Rom. 12, 2).

Paul is in fact not afraid to use the language of the mystery-religions in speaking of the revelation of God in Christ. He tells the Corinthians that he speaks the wisdom of God in a mystery (1 Cor. 2, 7). It is a mystery that we shall not all sleep but shall all be transformed (1 Cor. 15, 51). To Colossians (2, 2) he writes of the mystery of God, and the Father and Christ; to Ephesians of the mystery of Christ revealed to him (3, 3–4) and the mystery by which marriage symbolizes the relation of Christ to the Church (5, 32). And he is for ever speaking of the mystery of the Gospel.

Peers, Edgar Allison
(1891–1952)

English scholar, for many years Professor of Spanish in Liverpool, whose translations of LULL, TERESA and JUAN DE LA CRUZ, and whose many studies of Spanish mysticism, have done more than anything to make this known and appreciated in the twentieth century. Peers also wrote two important studies of the civic universities under the pseudonym Bruce Truscot.

Péladan, Joséphin
(1859–1918)

Sâr Péladan (as he called himself) set up in Paris in 1882 as art critic and *littérateur*, giving as his creed 'I believe in the Ideal, in Tradition, in Hierarchy.' Stanislas de Guaita, an occultist with whom he soon fell out, influenced him in the direction of ROSICRUCIANISM; he was further affected by Wagner's PARSIFAL; but remained an accepted Catholic. In 1892 he established the Salon de la Rose + Croix, rejecting realism, historic and patriotic painting, landscapes and seascapes, and the picturesque, and fostering Mysticism, Allegory and Dream. Péladan, a bearded guru, was something of a *poseur*, but the Salon was important in fostering Symbolist artists, not least from other countries, like the Swiss Hodler and the Dutch Toorop. Notable exhibitors from France included Bourdelle and Rouault. Péladan wrote a once familiar novel *La Vice Suprème*.

Penington, Isaac
(1616–79)

Son of a Lord Mayor, and himself a man of learning, he was convinced by FOX's preaching in 1657 and became a Quaker, the first adherent from the upper classes. His numerous writings combine clarity and charity. He is insistent that 'the immediate Word of the Lord' may be spoken by any man. It is for Friends 'a great comfort and sweet refreshment' to find in the Bible outward testimony to those things of which they have inward certainty, and would have had even if nothing had ever been written about them. Penington, with all his learning, is certain that the intellect may be an obstruction to the divine working. He has a powerful account of the value of the silent Meeting: the concept of a living fellowship and the watching for the stirrings of the Spirit: 'the ministry of the Spirit and life is more close and immediate when without words than when with words'.

Pentecostalism

Twentieth-century revival within Christianity, originating in America at about the turn of the century. It represents an attempt to recapture the experience of the Christians at Pentecost (Acts 2) as the authentic seal of Christian experience, and arose in reaction to the spiritual dustiness of many of the organized churches. Pentecostalism stresses 'the baptism in the Spirit', attested by SPEAKING WITH TONGUES and forming a second conversion to a life of Christian holiness. Worship in the Pentecostal churches is spontaneous and informal. The Bible is the sole doctrinal authority, and the approach is generally literalist. Some churches practise foot-washing, and spiritual healing is common. The churches are loosely knit together, and have held a series of world conferences at Stockholm (1939), Zurich (1947), Paris (1949) and elsewhere. The largest single grouping is the Assemblies of God. The Pentecostal churches are the predominant example of Christian ENTHUSIASM in the present world.

Percussion

Percussive sound is common in virtually all shamanistic cults as a means of communication with the spirit-world, whether to induce the spirits or to repel them. It has been argued that this may originate in the use of a coffin-log; it has been argued that psychologically percussive rhythms subtly handled help to create a crisis of dissociation; and it has been argued that culturally percussion is associated with *rites de passage*, and therefore with the transition from the spirit-world to the world of living men and back again.

Perennial philosophy

The phrase *philosophia perennis* was coined by Leibniz to refer, in Aldous HUXLEY's words, to 'the metaphysic that recognizes a divine Reality substantial to the world of things and lives and minds; the psychology that finds in the soul something similar to, or even identical with, divine Reality; the ethic that places man's final end in the knowledge of the immanent and transcendent ground of all being'. Huxley comments that rudiments of the Perennial Philosophy may be found among the traditionary lore of primitive peoples in every region of the world, and in its fully developed forms it has a place in every one of the higher religions. His anthology and commentary *The Perennial Philosophy* is a good introduction to the thought pattern involved.

Perfect man

A Sufi concept. The Perfect Man is the being through whom God's consciousness is manifested to Himself. He is the one who, endowed with divine attributes, is unconscious of them. He is a man who has fully realized his essential oneness with the divine Being in whose likeness he is made. He is the one who has received full illumination. He is the mediator between God and man. Such have been the great prophets from Adam to MUHAMMAD, and the elect among the Sufis.

See also al-JILI.

Peter Damian
(1007–72)

Born at Ravenna, a poor swineherd, whose intellectual ability won him recognition, he became a Benedictine in 1035, and was for a period Cardinal Bishop of Ostia. He was a notable reformer, standing for a high Christian morality. Personally he was a man of stern austerity, with a vision of the monastic life as a piece of Heaven on earth.

Peter of Alcantara
(1499–1562)

Pedro Garavito was a Spanish Franciscan, an austere ascetic, much admired by TERESA DE JESUS ('The world cannot suffer such perfection'). He occupied a cell four and a half feet long, fasted two days out of three, and confined his sleep to an hour and a half. His *Treatise on Prayer and Meditation* (the authorship has been questioned) has proved of immeasurable influence. In it he outlines the Alcantaran method of meditation, with its six stages: Preparation (choice of place, posture, control of imagination, confession, preparatory prayer); Reading (careful conning of a short passage); Meditation (intellectual or imaginative, the latter being very tiring); Thanksgiving (particular or general, making use of the *Benedicite* or *Psalm* 103); Oblation (offering oneself and the merits of Christ); Petition (for others and for oneself). Much of the advice is sane and practical. Study, for example, should not be over-intellectual or it will become arid. Meditation should not be predetermined, and we should be ready to pass from one theme to another. We should persevere in prayer even if we do not experience 'sweetness of devotion' and it seems empty and meaningless.

The strength of Peter's mystical devotion is seen in a prayer, which if it is not his, he has made his own. 'O sweetness of my heart! O life of my soul, joyous resting-place of my spirit! O bright and beautiful day of eternity, serene light deep within me! Flowering paradise of my heart! . . . When shall I be wholly Thine? When shall I cease to be my own? When shall nothing but Thyself live in me? When shall I love Thee with the fullest ardour? When shall I be wholly enkindled by the flame of Thy love? . . .'

Petersen, Gerlac
(1378–1411)

Author of *The Fiery soliloquy with God* an attractive exposition of mystical Christian Platonism, the culmination of whose vision is the realization that 'Thou art in me and I am Thee, joined together as one and the selfsame thing.'

Peyotism

The most widespread contemporary religion among Indians in the United States, Peyotism is a fusion of Christian theology, ethics and eschatology with Indian culture. It can be traced back to about 1885. There is an all-night ceremony, divisions being marked by ritual song, and centring on the sacramental eating of peyote, a spineless cactus (*Lophophora williamsi*) containing MESCALIN, which may be consumed fresh, or in the form of the dried button from the top, or infused in water and drunk. It is regarded as possessing healing powers, and as conveying spiritual GNOSIS through a generally heightened awareness, revelatory visions and mystical experience. Peyotists claim that where others read, they experience, where others talk about Jesus, they talk to Jesus. And its resources are inexhaustible: 'You can use Peyote all your life, but you'll never get to the end of what there is to be known from Peyote. Peyote is always teaching you something new.'

Philadelphians

Group of Christian mystics, flourishing about the year 1700 in London, Germany and Holland. They were indebted to Jakob BOEHME and the CAMBRIDGE PLATONISTS for much of their thought. Among their leaders was a visionary named Jane Leade (1623–1704), who from about 1670 began to experience divine revelations. Her revelations gradually showed a spiritual world of increasing complexity: she declared that there were in fact eight worlds, of which ours is the lowest, and ETERNITY the highest and source of all. She spiritualized the Ten Commandments, and declared that it was possible in this life to hold direct communion with Christ and his saints, on condition of passing through spiritual death. The Philadelphians claimed direct illumination by the Holy Spirit, but did not long outlive Mrs Leade. Johannes KELPIUS was an important member of the fraternity.

Philip Neri
(1515–95)

A gentle, courteous Florentine, he left a business career for the religious life, moving to Rome. He would spend nights of prayer in the catacombs, where in 1544 he had an ecstatic experience, through which his heart is said to have been enlarged; he was thereafter subject to curious palpitations and sudden sensations of overpowering HEAT. He was one of those responsible for founding the Confraternity of the Holy Trinity; even more important, the Congregation of the Oratory arose directly from his work. Philip Neri's gift was to combine a profound inward experience with what Faber called 'practical commonplaceness'. He had a rich sense of humour and insisted that cheerfulness was a more Christian attitude than melancholy. He bears, not without desert, the sobriquet of 'the Apostle of Rome'.

Philo
(c. 30 BC–AD 50)

Philo was a Jew of the Dispersion, living in Alexandria, where he rose to a position of eminence, leading the deputation to the Emperor Gaius in AD 40. Philo is important for bringing together the strands of Judaic religion and Hellenic philosophy, especially that of PLATO and the STOICS.

Philo's God is infinitely above man. 'His nature is entirely perfect, or rather God is himself the perfection and completion and boundary of happiness, sharing in nothing else by which he can be rendered better.' God is above all attributes. But He is the source and consummation of all that is good: 'The active cause is . . . better than virtue and better than knowledge and better than the good itself and the beautiful itself.'

But, paradoxically, although God is far above humanity, man is not far away from Divinity. Man is a duality, soul and body, the body fashioned of earth, the soul a fragment of the Divine. CONTEMPLATION is the means to the knowledge of God, and this depends on God giving Himself and seizing the soul out of the relativities of this world. From the human side this means preparation through the conquest of the lower passions and a purpose directed to the service of others. 'When I perceive myself to be but dust and ashes, and what is even more despicable, then I have the courage to meet Thee, having become humble, cast down to the ground.' 'If you seek God, O my mind, go forth out of yourself, and seek for him. But if you remain in the substance of the body, or in the vain opinions of the mind, you are then without any real wish to search into divine things, even if you do put on the appearance and pretence of seeking them.' From the divine side it means revelation through the LOGOS (here Philo brings together the Jewish concept of the *Memra* or Word through which God expresses Himself with power and the Greek belief in a divine Reason). 'God', says Philo, 'can be grasped only by means of the powers which accompany and follow him.' Philo remains certain that God is incomprehensible: 'When the soul that loves God searches into the nature of the Existent, it enters into an invisible search, from which the chief benefit which accrues to it is to comprehend that God is incomprehensible and to see that he is invisible.'

What man may have is an ecstatic apprehension of the Divine, uncontrolled by reason or the will. 'The ecstasy of the spirit is a deep sleep which falls upon it. It becomes ecstatic when it ceases to busy itself with the ideas which impinge upon it, and when it does not exercise activity upon them it slumbers.' Philo gives an illustration from his own experience. 'I am not ashamed to recount my own experience. At times, when I proposed to enter upon my familiar task of writing on philosophical theories with precise knowledge of the materials which were to be put together, I have had to leave off without any work accomplished. . . . But at other times when I had come empty, all of a sudden I was filled with thoughts showered down and sown upon me unseen from above, so that by divine possession I fell into a rapture and became ignorant of everything, the place, those present, myself and what was spoken or written. For I received . . . the most vividly distinct view of the matter before me such as might be received through the eyes from the most luminous presentation.' So he says to his own soul: 'Go out from yourself filled with a divine frenzy like those possessed in the mystical rites of the Corybantes, and possessed by the deity after the manner of prophetic inspiration. For when the mind is no longer self-contained but rapt and frenzied with a heavenly passion, . . . this is your inheritance.'

A 9th-century manuscript illumination portrait of Philo

Photism

Technical term for the appearance of a subjective but quasi-physical light, which is sometimes associated with mystical experience. Some philosophers accept it as genuine, but explicable in terms of molecular rearrangement in the brain.

Pico della Mirandola, Giovanni
(1463–94)

Renaissance Neo-Platonist philosopher, deeply imbued with the theosophy of the KABBALAH, with FICINO's NEO-PLATONISM and with Savonarola's charismatic Puritanism. Ficino's writings are turgid and full of intellectual fantasy. At the top of his universe stands the Godhead, One, Perfect. From the Godhead created worlds emerge as emanations. The highest of these is the realm of Mind, devoted to the eternal contemplation of the divine Being. The second is the celestial world. The third is the sublunary world in which we live. The fourth is man himself, the microcosm. But this fourth world can contain the other three. Man stands between the material world and God. 'God therefore took man as a creature of indeterminate nature and, assigning him a place in the middle of the world, addressed him thus: "Adam, we have not given you a fixed abode, or a form which is yours and yours only, or a function particular to yourself."' So in *The Oration* he expresses the dignity of man; man's dignity is that he can know God, know God as you know a friend rather than know a fact. So Pico says, 'Philosophy seeks the truth, theology finds it, religion possesses it', and 'We may more easily love God than comprehend Him or speak of Him.'

Pierrepont, Sarah
(1710–58)

American mystic, wife of Jonathan Edwards. She was only thirteen when he wrote of her: 'There are certain seasons when this Great Being, in some way or other invisible, comes to her and fills her mind with exceeding sweet delight so that she hardly cares for anything except to meditate on him . . . she is to dwell with him, and to be ravished with his love and delight forever. . . . She loves to be alone, walking in the fields and groves, and seems to have someone invisible always conversing with her.' She herself wrote later: 'I seemed to myself to perceive a glow of divine love come down from the heart of Christ into my heart in a constant stream, or pencil of light. What I felt each minute of this time was worth more than all the outward comforts or pleasures which I had enjoyed in my whole life put together.' Edwards himself, though *The Song of Songs* might sweep him up into a dream-world, had no real mystical experience, and recognized in his wife something he knew he did not possess.

Pietism

Movement started in German Lutheranism by Philip Jakob Spener (1635–1705), who in 1675 wrote *Pia Desideria* with its six 'simple proposals', of which the first, renewed Bible-study directed to personal devotion, played a major part in deepening spiritual life. The others were the spiritual priesthood of the laity: practical works of love; charity in controversy; reform of theological studies; revival of preaching. In the following century Pietism affected ZINZENDORF and later WESLEY.

Plato
(427–347 BC)

Athenian philosopher. SOCRATES taught him to search for ethical definitions, disciples of HERACLITUS that the world of our senses is in a condition of constant change, disciples of PARMENIDES that true reality cannot change. Contact with PYTHAGOREANS in Magna Graecia showed him that in geometry we deal in propositions which are never more than approximately true of the visible world, but are absolutely and immutably true of the triangles and circles we can perceive with our minds. So he came to his Theory of Forms (or 'Ideas'). True reality is unchanging, and is perceived with the mind. The perfect Triangle is imperfectly materialized in the physical triangle, the perfect Table in the tangible table, perfect Beauty in beautiful objects, perfect Justice in human actions. The things of this world may 'imitate' or 'participate in' the perfect Forms, but they are never more than shadows or reflections. 'Plato,' said Diogenes 'the Dog', 'I see tables and cups but not Tableness and Cupness.' 'Precisely,' said Plato, 'because you need eyes to perceive tables and cups, and you have those; you need intelligence to perceive Tableness and Cupness, and that you do not possess.' In *The Republic* he compares mankind with prisoners in an underground cave, watching shadows on a wall. The philosopher is the man who is released into the daylight. At first he is blinded by the brilliance, but gradually his eyes grow accustomed to the light and he sees objects, not shadows, and knows the shadows for what they are. If he then goes back into the cave and tells the prisoners that they are living in a world of illusion they will mock him. Nonetheless, go back he must.

The soul which knows the Forms must itself be immortal since they are eternal and only like can know like. Plato put forward in *Meno* and *Phaedo* a doctrine of RECOLLECTION. The soul has known the Forms before birth, but 'our birth is but a sleep and a forgetting' and material objects may serve for us as a reminder of eternal truths. Plato took from the Pythagoreans the doctrines of transmigration and reincarnation. He expounded the immortality of the soul in mythical form at the end of *Phaedo* and *The Republic*. But the soul itself has a rational and an irrational element, and it seems that ultimately the rational alone survives.

The aspiration of the soul to things higher is called *Eros*, LOVE. Plato gives an account of it in *Phaedrus* and *The Symposium*. In the latter the ultimate vision is one of Beauty. It was a passage which gripped the imagination of Shelley: 'He who has been instructed thus far in the science of Love, and has been led to see beautiful things in their due order and rank, when he comes toward the end of his discipline, will suddenly catch sight of a wondrous thing, beautiful with the absolute Beauty . . . he will see a Beauty eternal, not growing or decaying, not waxing nor waning; nor will it be fair here and foul there, nor depending on time or circumstance or place, as if fair to some, and foul to others; nor shall Beauty appear to him in the likeness of a face or hand, nor embodied in any sort of form whatever . . . whether of heaven or of earth; but Beauty absolute, separate, simple, and everlasting; which lending of its virtue to all beautiful things that we see born to decay, itself suffers neither increase nor diminution, nor any other change. . . . O think you . . . that it would be an ignoble life for a man to be ever looking thither and with his proper faculty contemplating the absolute Beauty, and to be living in its presence? Are you not rather convinced that he who thus sees Beauty as only it can be seen, will be specially fortuned? and that, since he is in contact not with images but with realities, he will give birth not to images, but to very Truth itself? And being thus the parent and nurse of true virtue it will be his lot to become a friend of God, and so far as any man can be, immortal and absolute.' (Symp. 210E–212A tr. R. Bridges.)

In *The Republic* the ultimate is the Form of the Good, Good not in a merely ethical sense, but representing the source of all value and all excellence. As the Forms are Reality, and are contrasted with the material world as Being to Becoming, the Form of the Good is said to be 'beyond reality' or 'beyond being'. It is the source of knowledge: as the sun enables the eye to see and objects to be seen, so the Form of the Good enables the mind to know and the Forms to be known. Scholars have argued whether Plato identifies the Form of the Good with God. Certainly he does not explicitly do so.

In *Theaetetus* (176 A–B) Plato wrote that because of the imperfections of earth we ought to try to escape as speedily as possible to the place of the gods. To escape means so far as possible to become like God; and that means to combine righteousness and holiness with wisdom. This concept of 'likeness to God' is frequently quoted by later writers.

Plato's most influential work on subsequent religious thought was *Timaeus*, a kind of hymn of creation. The divine Craftsman is good and desires all things to be like himself. So he brings order out of chaos and fashions a world-soul; the cosmos is thus a living creature endowed with life and intelligence. The material universe includes fire and earth to make it visible and tangible, and the other elements to give it proportion. The Father creates the divine heavenly bodies, the visible gods; and entrusts to them the fashioning of the mortal part of man; he himself creates, from what is left over from the creation of the world-soul, souls equal in number to the stars. Physical objects are produced by the imprint of the Forms on matter within the Receptacle of space. The vital aspect of the cosmology of *Timaeus* is that soul bridges the worlds of BEING and of BECOMING.

Plato is somewhere at the root of nearly all Western mystical philosophy.

Pleroma

GNOSTIC term for the fullness of the Godhead, in which all love and joy and harmony and praise is to be found. In the system of VALENTINUS the *pleroma* consists of fifteen pairs of spiritual powers.

Plotinus

(205–70)

Plotinus was born in Egypt, studied in Alexandria, somehow became a friend of emperors, travelled in the East with Gordian, is found in Rome with Gallienus (who invited him to found a colony of philosophers near Naples, Platonopolis, Plato's Republic; nothing came of it) and taught in Rome for a quarter of a century before his death. From his lectures and seminars he produced some fifty-four essays. A student of his named PORPHYRY collected these after his death, arranged them by subject-matter in six groups of nine (hence the name *Enneads*) and published them.

Plotinus's philosophy stands in the direct line of descent from PLATO, and is generally called NEO-PLATONISM. Augustine said of him that he was so like Plato as to tempt a belief in reincarnation. His thought centres on his vision of God, the One, immeasurably beyond the world, ultimate Being; he applies to the One Plato's language of the Form of the Good, which is 'beyond reality'. Not merely beyond reality, but beyond personality, It rather than He. 'It is this to which all things are attached, and to which all existence aspires, having It as a first principle and needing It. It is without wants, sufficient to Itself, needing nothing, the measure and limit of all things, giving out of itself mind, substance, soul and life, and – as far as concerns mind – activity.' It is beyond thought, beyond definition, beyond utterance, beyond comprehension, beyond reality. We may not predicate any attributes of It, for this would limit It; we may call It 'The Good' but not good. We may not predicate of It essence or being or life, not because It is less than these things but because It is greater. The One cannot be identical with the sum of individual things, for It is their source and principle, distinct from them and logically prior to them. If It were identical with them, they would be identical with one another, which is not so. 'Thus the One cannot be any existing thing but is prior to all existents.'

The higher produces the lower by a process of efflux, radiation or emanation: this is a kind of half-way house between theism and PANTHEISM. This is not a deliberate act of creation, but an unconscious product of the divine Contemplation. The first emanation is Mind or *Nous*, the divine Craftsman of Plato's *Timaeus* and Form of Beauty in *The Symposium*. In *Nous* the Platonic Forms of classes and individuals exist: multiplicity supervenes on the essential unity. The Forms of individuals is a noteworthy concept: Plotinus is rare among the great mystics in his respect for individuality. From *Nous* proceeds Soul, the World-Soul of *Timaeus*, and the link between the sensible and supra-sensible worlds. In the Trinity of the One, Mind and Soul, Plotinus has produced a philosophical counterblast to the Christian Trinity of Father, LOGOS and Spirit. Soul is found in two stages, the higher in contact with *Nous*, the lower with nature. To be materialized the Forms have to pass down through the two levels of soul as 'generative thoughts'. This enables Plotinus to say that though matter is evil, the material world is not; the material world stands between matter and the Ideal World. Plotinus rebukes the Gnostics for their disparagement of creator and creation. No good man will despise the world and all the beauty in it. To love God is to love the world that emanates from Him; to love the beauty of the world is to be led to love its cause and origin. Even matter, the principle of evil, proceeds ultimately from the One, though it is so far that we can call it the deprivation of good, as darkness is the deprivation of light. It is in fact not-being, 'the image and phantom of mass, a bare aspiration towards substantial existence'.

The highest life is the ascent of the soul to God. The impulse to this is *eros*, love considered as aspiration. Love is 'an activity of the soul desiring the Good'. It may start from the love of physical beauty, but, as in Plato, that is the first step only. The true object of our love lies beyond; it is possible to grasp it, live with it and really possess it, since no envelope of flesh separates it from us. Love is a spirit intermediate between man and God. But at one point Plotinus goes further, and says of God, 'He is worthy to be loved, and is Love as well, that is Love of Himself, inasmuch as He is beautiful only from Himself and in Himself.' If this is more than a counterblast to the Christian assertion 'God is *agape*', it is a profoundly mystical belief that we experience the Ultimate in the aspiration towards it; indeed in some sense, the Ultimate is the aspiration.

There are stages in the soul's ladder of ascent. The first includes purification, the freeing of the soul from the body, and the practice of the cardinal virtues. In the second the soul rises above sense-perception to *Nous* through CONTEMPLATION. A third and higher stage, already ineffable, leads to union with *Nous*. Finally there is the climax of the whole ascent in mystical and ecstatic union with the One. 'He will lapse again from the vision: but let him again awaken the virtue which is in him, again know himself made perfect in splendour; and he shall be again lightened of his burden, ascending through virtue to *Nous*, and thence through wisdom to the Supreme. This is the life of gods, and of the godlike and blessed among men, a quittance from things alien and earthly, a life beyond pleasure, a flight of the alone to the Alone.' 'This is the true end of the soul, to come into contact with this light, and to behold Him through it, not by the light of another thing, but to perceive that very thing itself through which it sees.' Plotinus had experienced this at first hand. His disciple Porphyry records that four times during their association Plotinus enjoyed the vision glorious. Plotinus himself says: 'Many times it has happened. Lifted out of the body into myself; becoming external to all other things and self-centred; beholding a marvellous beauty; then, more than ever assured of community with the loftiest order, enacting the noblest life; acquiring identity with the divine.'

He died, perhaps of cancer of the throat, greeting a friend with the words, 'I was waiting for you, before the divine in me joins the divine in the universe.'

Poimandres

See HERMETICISM

Poiret, Pierre
(1646–1719)

Poiret was a painter manqué, preacher, philosopher, theologian and popular writer. His most important work was *L'économie divine*, in seven volumes, an interpretation of the work of the visionary Antoinette BOURIGNON. Another major work, *Bibliotheca mysticorum*, is the fruit of wide reading down the byways of mysticism. He has valuable teaching on prayer. Continual prayer is not an effort of the mind; it is a spiritual conversation with God, which continues through working, eating, drinking, writing, even sleeping. We should not seek an intellectual understanding of the mysteries of God, but simply talk with Him: 'All the religions of the world cannot give us union with God: we must find it for ourselves.' Poiret had great influence on the German Romantic mystics; he has himself been described as 'the only mystic of the French Reformed Church'.

Poor Clares

The Poor Clares, or Clarisses, are the second order of FRANCIS OF ASSISI founded by him and Clare in about 1215. The rule of complete poverty, individual and communal, was general but not universal. The majority of convents are contemplative.

Porete, Marguérite

See MIRROR FOR SIMPLE SOULS.

Porphyry
(*c.* 232–305)

Neo-Platonist philosopher, immensely learned, but far less original than his friend and teacher PLOTINUS. The object of philosophy is salvation, and Porphyry was concerned with the religious and practical aspects. The soul must purify itself by turning from lower objects to higher. This means ascetic discipline, celibacy and vegetarianism. It means virtuous living: at the lowest stage in the practice of the social virtues, good works and a healthy relation to one's fellows; at the next in the practice of the cathartic virtues, freeing the soul from sensual desires and so achieving the state of 'likeness towards god' (as in Plato, *Theaet.* 176B); at the third, in turning away from all lower desires to Mind; and, at the highest, in the practice of the 'exemplary' virtues under the influence of Mind. The highest stage of the purification of the soul is the knowledge of God.

Port Royal, Convent of

Port Royal is a site about twenty miles from Paris where a convent of Cistercian nuns was established in 1204. In the early seventeenth century it was transformed by the vigorous abbess Angélique Arnauld (Mère Angélique) (1591–1661), who was converted to a strict religious life by a preaching Capuchin and brought deeper inner spirituality. She was profoundly stirred by the influence of FRANÇOIS DE SALES and sought to join the VISITANDINES, but instead brought something of their spirituality to her own community. Later she and the community came under the influence of the Jansenist leader Jean Duvergier de Hauranne, the Abbé de Saint-Cyran, who was spiritual counsellor of the convent from 1633, whose inner life is reflected in his *Lettres chrétiennes et spirituelles*, and who aimed to counter Protestantism by a reform of the Church in the direction of moral rigorism and utter dependence on God's grace. By now the community had grown and moved into a larger house in the suburbs of Paris. Mère Angélique's sister Agnès (1593–1671) was also leader of the community for a time, a woman of mystic devotion and great inner loveliness; and the community helped the tormented but spiritual genius of Blaise PASCAL. The community in fact attracted members and adherents from all classes and walks of life; its moral rigorism and external austerity were given dynamic and made attractive by the mystical passion which infused its life.

Possession

The belief that supernatural powers may become embodied in a human being temporarily or permanently is widespread, and abnormal behaviour is frequently attributed to this cause.

There is an important distinction made by many interpreters in different terms. This is between negative and positive possession. The former is an unwanted disease; it is an assault by dangerous spirits; and it requires exorcism. The second is the core of mystical experience, a 'joyous Dionysian epiphany', an ecstatic state deliberately sought. The distinction is a useful one, though the two forms of possession cannot be totally separated from one another.

Voluntary possession may be induced by various means: wild dancing is one, found for example among the maenads of DIONYSUS, the Sufi dervishes, or in VOODOO; music, especially percussive music, is sometimes used without dancing, as by some shamans; intoxicant liquor, or the inhalation of smoke, or the consumption of drugs in various forms may be employed; sometimes the blood of a sacrificial victim is drunk; sometimes there is self-laceration with or without the licking of blood; sometimes, as again among the shamans, there are techniques of self-hypnosis, such as gazing steadily at a fixed point of the fire in a darkened room.

The object of all these techniques is to enable the subject to communicate with the spirit-world or with a particular deity. This will foster his spiritual powers and insight, and enable him to foretell the future, to issue oracular truths, to heal disease, to propitiate the spirits, to clear the path for the souls of the dead and so on. The state is not an end in itself, but a means to an end.

One important aspect of possession is that belief in the existence of spirits is an evident factor in encouraging psychic experiences which are interpreted as possession by spirits and which in turn reinforce belief in them. When belief in spirits weakens, the phenomenon of possession tends to disappear.

Practice of the Presence of God

The deliberate cultivation of an awareness of God's presence at all times, in all places and with all activities. HERACLITUS, seated in the kitchen, said, 'Come in, come in, there are gods here too.' So TERESA reminds her 'daughters' that 'the Lord walks among the pots and pans'. The phrase derives from Brother LAWRENCE, but something similar is found in a number of other devotional and mystical writers, such as FRANÇOIS DE SALES and Jeremy TAYLOR. There is a beautiful example of it in some lines from a Persian SUFI poet, Baba Kuhi of Shiraz (d. 1050).

In the market, in the cloister – only God I saw.
In the valley and on the mountain – only God I saw.
Him I have seen beside me oft in tribulation:
In favour and in fortune – only God I saw.
In prayer and fasting, in praise and contemplation,
In the religion of the Prophet – only God I saw.
Neither soul nor body, accident nor substance,
Qualities over causes – only God I saw.
I oped mine eyes and by the light of His face around me
In all the eye discovered – only God I saw.
Like a candle I was melting in His fire:
Amidst the flames outflanking – only God I saw.

Myself with mine own eyes I saw most
clearly,
But when I looked with God's eyes – only
God I saw.
I passed away into nothingness, I vanished,
And lo, I was the All-living – only God I
saw.

(tr. R. A. Nicholson)

Prajna

Buddhist term for intuitive wisdom, or monistic vision, leading to absolute truth in the form of SUNYATA. *Prajnaparamita* is Transcendental Wisdom.

Prayer of quiet

In Christian mysticism the first stage of union with God, when the imagination still retains its liberty. It has been called the prayer of the presence of God. The soul feels great delight at being near God, yet the realization is still conscious; but it is also a prayer of repose in which the outward senses are lulled to rest.

Prayer of the heart

Phrase used by Orthodox Christian theologians. When a person begins to pray he thinks out and verbalizes his prayer. This is a prayer of the intellect and of the lips. But as he perseveres he 'finds the place of the heart', his spirit 'dwells in the heart', his prayer is not a conscious production of his intellect but a spontaneous upsurge of his whole being. This is the prayer of the heart, and it is attained not by man's efforts but by the gift of God.

Prayer, Stages of

TERESA DE JESUS identifies four. The first is recollection, the collection of the mind within itself, a process of concentration. Some achieve this by the use of mental images. Her imagination did not work in this way and she found it helpful to focus her attention on a book or picture, or to take a walk in the country and look at fields, water or flowers. Concentration seems necessary to withdrawal. The second stage is the prayer of quiet. Teresa is emphatic that this cannot be achieved by human effort; the most that the individual can do is to bring the mind to a receptive state. In the prayer of quiet, the mind is open to the Divine; desire for earthly things falls away; and there is experience of joy and peace. The third stage Teresa called tumescence. In it is agony but also delight, 'a glorious bewilderment, a heavenly madness, a pleasurable unrest'. It is a state of wisdom arising from inspiration and capable of finding its fruits in activity (such as the writing of poetry). Finally there is the highest state, of union with the Divine.

But Teresa herself is not wholly consistent, and sometimes, for example, treats the stages of recollection and quiet as one. Other mystics use a different analysis. HILTON has 'three steps of contemplation' – knowing; loving; knowing-and-loving. RICHARD OF ST VICTOR has four landings on the 'steep stairway of love' – betrothal, or awakening to mystical truth; marriage, in which the commitment is taken to God but the soul cannot yet come to him; union; fruitfulness. HUGH OF ST VICTOR, less poetically, identifies: meditation; soliloquy; consideration; rapture. There are many other analyses. It is a mistake to try to draw them into a single system, for experiences and temperaments differ. But there is a considerable measure of agreement as to the nature of mystical prayer, and the fact that there are stages.

Proclus
(410–85)

NEO-PLATONIST in the period of Christian dominance. Born in Constantinople, he lived and worked in Athens. Much of his philosophical work lay in commentaries on PLATO: he once said that, given the power, he would withdraw from human knowledge all ancient books except Plato's *Timaeus* and the sacred oracles. Proclus was not really a mystic, though he believed that he received revelations and indeed was the reincarnation of a NEO-PYTHAGOREAN named Nicomachus; and THEURGY, effectively a kind of magic designed to set up a sympathetic chain-reaction from the world to the Divine, and produce a divine apparition, took the place of Plotinus's mystic union, though he held a theoretical belief in this last. In Proclus's universe all proceeds from the One, first the Units of Henads (still unknowable), then the sphere of Mind (subdivided into Being, Life and Thought), then the sphere of Soul (intermediary between the supersensible and sensible worlds) and finally the physical world. The process of development is threefold: remaining in the principle, proceeding out of the principle, turning back to the principle. The One is unchanged by the process of emanation, and preserves its Essence 'neither transmuted into its consequents nor suffering any diminution'. Evil does not really exist, since all proceeds from the Divine. The soul possesses an imperishable portion of LIGHT which enables it to perceive the Divine, and a unitary faculty which permits union with the One, ascending through LOVE, TRUTH and Faith, the last consisting of mystical silence before the Ultimate. Proclus was something of a universalist, who said that the philosopher should not confine himself to the religious customs of one country but be the common hierophant of the whole world.

Prophetism in Africa

See AFRICAN PROPHETIC CHURCHES.

Prophet

In Judaism, term used to translate *nabi*, which in its original usage means an ecstatic. It is applied particularly to a group whose work has come down to us, the most important being Amos, Hosea and Isaiah in the eighth century BC, and Jeremiah, Ezekiel and the unknown writer often called Deutero-Isaiah or the Second Isaiah, because his work is found in Isaiah 40–59, from the sixth century. It is important to see that the prophet is not one who fore-tells the future, but one who forth-tells or proclaims the Word of God, though this of course does not exclude reference to the future or to the last things. The writings of the prophets include visionary experiences. Good examples are Isaiah's vision, while in the temple, of God high upon a throne (6, 1–13); or Ezekiel's vision of the valley of dry bones (37, 1–14); or this from Jeremiah (4, 23–6):

> I saw the earth, and it was without form
> and void;
> the heavens, and their light was gone.
> I saw the mountains, and they reeled;
> all the hills rocked to and fro.
> I saw, and there was no man,
> and the very birds had taken flight.
> I saw, and the farm-land was wilderness,
> and the towns all razed to the ground,
> before the Lord in his anger.

A different type of visionary experience comes when the prophet is gazing at some ordinary object, and from this springs in a flash the message he has to proclaim. With Amos it is a plumb-line (7, 7–9), or a locust (7, 1–3) or a basket of summer fruit (8, 1–2); with Jeremiah it may be an almond-branch (1, 11–12), or a pot boiling on a stove (1, 13–16). In the last the smoke blown by the north wind gives him the message of disaster from the north. Sometimes there is a verbal pun: the almond-branch (*shaked*) is a sign that Yahweh is alert (*shoked*). These visionary experiences were frequently accompanied by the sense that God had delivered them a message: the familiar 'Thus saith the Lord' just means 'Yahweh said'.

The messages delivered by the prophets were filled with immediate political relevance. Amos proclaims the judgment of God on atrocities committed in wartime (1, 11; 2, 1) and on economic injustice (8, 4–10). Hosea denounces the policy of alliance with great powers (7, 11). Jeremiah calls for non-resistance to Babylonian aggression (21, 8–10; 37, 10–14; 38, 17–18). At the same time there is a strongly eschatological element in the visions, in the coming of the Day of the Lord (Am. 5, 18; Is. 13, 6; Zeph. 1, 14; Obad. 15; Joel 1, 15; Ez. 30, 3 etc.). The two strands come together in the idea of the Remnant (Is. 7, 3–4; 10, 20–2; Mic. 2, 12; Jer. 42, 2–3; Zech. 8, 11), which is faithful in political and social crisis and sees the divine promises fulfilled.

The prophets were the instruments of important religious changes. In Amos, already

An illuminated initial (V) in the 12th-century Winchester Bible showing God inspiring the prophet Jeremiah to speak

Yahweh is seen not as the God of Israel alone, but of all peoples (2, 1; 9, 7), and this universalism finds its way into the vision of a world at peace, with swords beaten into ploughshares, and all nations thronging the hill of Zion (Is. 2, 1–4; Mic. 4, 1–2). In Deutero-Isaiah, Jewish monotheism reaches its zenith (40, 9–31). In Amos, there is already a new ethical dimension, and Jeremiah and Ezekiel (18, 20) insist on individual moral responsibility; Jeremiah indeed proclaims a new, inward covenant to be written in the heart (31, 31–4). Deutero-Isaiah in the Servant-songs produces a vision of redemptive suffering and of life beyond the grave (53, 12).

Jeremiah's is a particularly moving example of the relationship of the prophet to his driving force. At the outset he hears the voice of Yahweh saying that before his birth he had been appointed a prophet to the nations. He protests his incapacity, but Yahweh touches his lips and says, 'I put my words into your mouth. This day I give you authority over nations and over kingdoms, to pull down and to uproot, to destroy and to demolish, to build and to plant' (1, 4–10). Later he tells how he did cry out and proclaim violence and destruction, and was mocked for it. He complains that God has duped him. But:

> Whenever I said, 'I will call him to mind
> no more,
> nor speak in his name again',
> then his word was imprisoned in my body,
> like a fire blazing in my heart,
> and I was weary with holding it under,
> and could endure no more. (20, 9)

JESUS of Nazareth was regarded in his own day as standing in the line of the prophets (e.g. Mt. 16, 13–14; 21, 11; 21, 46; Mk 6, 15; 8, 28; Lk. 7, 16–17; 7, 39; 24, 19; Jn 4, 19; 6, 14; 7, 40; 9, 17; Acts 3, 22–3). He, like them, was conscious of being sent by God, of proclaiming the Word of the Lord; indeed he took up Jeremiah's vision of the new covenant and Deutero-Isaiah's of the Suffering Servant and made them his own. He spoke with an authority which came from beyond himself.

In the Islamic tradition Jesus does indeed stand in the line of the prophets, which has its final culmination in MUHAMMAD, *the* Prophet. And indeed *The Qur'an* does seem to be of the same nature as the Jewish prophetic books. 'Recite thou, in the name of thy Lord who created.' 'Arise and warn.' 'Say: O you unbelievers, I worship not that which you worship.' 'Say: He is God alone.'

Ninian Smart has suggested four distinctions between the prophet and the mystic. First, the mystic looks within, into his own soul and beyond; the prophet, such as Isaiah, sees the Deity standing 'numinously over against him'. Second, mysticism can occur without being interpreted as an experience of a deity or numinous being; prophetic experience cannot. Third, contemplative language is often impersonal; prophetic language is strongly personal and even anthropomorphic. Fourth, much mysticism aims at quietude; the Jewish prophets (and Muhammad) proclaimed a dynamic activism.

Psychedelic

Word used to describe a state of enhanced perception and imagination induced by ecstasy with or without the use of drugs; applied also to drugs (such as HASHISH, LSD, MESCALIN and OPIUM) which help to produce that state, and to the use of abnormally brilliant colours in art and design, which has been fostered by psychedelic experiments.

Psychology of mysticism

Plainly, the psychology of mysticism is an exceedingly controversial matter. It has been treated at length by Leuba; it forms part of wider studies in the psychology of religion in the work of Thouless and others; it has particularly interested Carl Gustav JUNG and his followers. Much attention has properly been paid to the accurate recording of mystical phenomena.

Mystical CONVERSION is typically from a state of piety and good works through a period of dissatisfaction and inner conflict. The period of struggle is often described as the attempt to renounce self-will and submit to the Will of God. It is not just the renunciation of sin in the more obvious sense, but the renunciation of normal standards of living, of the good opinion of one's fellows, even of good works; SUSO indeed felt the desire to lead a life of good, honest piety the subtlest temptation which faced him. It often includes the renunciation of human love; in CATHERINE OF GENOA and Madame GUYON it followed unhappy marriages. So Merswin in his vision of the crucifix, 'lifting his eyes to heaven, solemnly swore that he would utterly surrender his own will, person and goods to the service of God', and PASCAL appends to one copy of his record of mystical vision 'complete submission to Jesus Christ and to my director'. Psychologically speaking, this sort of experience would seem to be 'the redirection of the whole of the libido into the religious sentiment'. The period of struggle is the attempt by conscious effort to divert the libido (the psychic energy in the fullest sense, including but not confined to sexual energy) away from all external things with a view to its redirection towards God: it is thus a largely negative process. The crisis comes when the positive, so to speak, takes over completely from the negative.

The condition of mystical experience often includes visions and voices. CONTEMPLATION, even in its earlier stages, seems to have a strongly involuntary element, and involves the suspension of normal activities and faculties: some contemplatives with practical activities before them have had to take care not to 'slip into' ecstasy. ECSTASY is not a condition qualitatively different from the earlier stages of contemplation, but rather an intensification of them. Psychologically regarded, mystical experience is parallel to other states of introversion. There are close similarities between the phenomena of mysticism and the symptoms of hysteria. Von HÜGEL has analysed this fully with relation to CATHERINE OF GENOA; but Catherine is a particularly difficult object of study, as there were clearly pathological elements in her later experiences (as she herself said), which were not present earlier. The two conditions are similar but not identical. One clear difference is that the libido is directed not, as it were, vaguely 'within', but to an object which the mystics regard as having objective reality. In other words, though the symptoms are similar to those of introversion, the object and therefore nature of the experience is different, and the mystics seem quite free from the regressive introversion of *dementia praecox*.

In many ways the most interesting psychological feature of mystical experience is that at the highest level, the stage which Teresa calls the Spiritual Marriage, and Madame Guyon the apostolic state, there is not an intensification but a transformation. Teresa expresses her surprise 'at seeing that when the soul arrives at this state it does not go into ecstasies except perhaps on rare occasions – even then they are not like the former trances and the flight of the spirit and seldom take place in public as they did before'. Rather is it a state of permanent intellectual vision, accompanied by a marked redirection of energy back to practical activity. It seems that at this stage there is a return to extraversion, and the spiritual growth is now applied within the external world.

Pure Land

Sect of Mahayana Buddhism, established in China by HUI-YÜAN in the fourth century, and in

Japan (where it is known as Jodo) by Honen in the twelfth century. The centre of worship is AMITABHA, who rules over the Pure Land, where the worshipper seeks to be born, and from where there is an easy passage to NIRVANA.

Purgative Way

In Christian mysticism, the first stage of the spiritual life, directed to purifying the soul, to prepare it for illumination and union. Two notable examples of the description of this experience are DANTE's journey up the Mount of Purgation, and the description, attributed to CATHERINE OF GENOA, of the Purgative Way as the burning away of the rust which covers the soul. 'No one,' says the THEOLOGIA GERMANICA, 'can be enlightened unless he is first cleansed or purified or stripped.' 'The essence of purgation', says RICHARD OF ST VICTOR, 'is self-simplification.' 'I saw full surely,' says JULIAN OF NORWICH, 'that it behoveth needs to be that we should be in longing and penance until the time that we be led so deep into God that we verily and truly know our own soul.'

Purification

Almost all mystical systems require of the soul an initial purification. This may take various forms. Sometimes it will involve ritual cleansing. It may involve physical deprivation and self-discipline and ascetic practices. It nearly always is seen as involving moral virtue and acts of loving service; also as involving mental and spiritual self-discipline. These are the prerequisites of any true mystical experience.

Pythagoreanism

Pythagoras is a shadowy figure of whom we know little from any early or reliable source, though we have full-length biographies written nearly a thousand years after his birth. He seems to have been born in Samos in the sixth century BC, to have left for political reasons, perhaps travelled as far as India (there are important links between Hindu and Pythagorean thought), and to have settled in southern Italy and formed a community there, which followed his interests in mathematics, music, mysticism and politics. ARISTOTLE, our principal early source, prefers to speak of the Pythagoreans.

The Pythagoreans were a closed religious community. Their cosmology built the world out of number, one for a point, two for a line, three for a surface, four for a solid. One was the basis, and generated the series of even and odd numbers, and with them the whole universe. Moral qualities were numbers: 4 (2×2 and $2+2$) was justice, equal shares all round. A special number was 10, built up of $1+2+3+4$, and containing the point, line, plane and solid; it was known as the *Tetractys* and the oath not to reveal the mysteries of the society was 'by Him who reveals Himself to our minds in the Tetractys, which contains the source and roots of everlasting nature'. Pythagoras had discovered the mathematical basis of music, and (for instance) the fact that an octave can be expressed by the relation 1:2 (a string stopped at half its length will sound the octave above the full length). So music was involved in all life; and even the planets circling in their courses sounded the music of the spheres. To such a mystical cosmology the discovery of an incommensurable such as $\sqrt{2}$ was a major scandal, a skeleton in the cupboard; and one Hippasus was excommunicated for revealing the secret.

Within this cosmos Pythagoreans believed in the immortality of the soul, and borrowed the Hindu doctrine of reincarnation and transmigration. ('What is the opinion of Pythagoras concerning wildfowl?' 'That the soul of our grandam might haply inhabit a bird.') The body is a tomb to be escaped from, through silence, MEDITATION, purification and ASCETICISM, and virtue, the love of friends and religious devotion. Purification lay in cleansing, baptism and lustration, avoidance of ritual pollution and contact with death or birth, vegetarianism and abstinence from beans and a whole series of general taboos. Membership of this saving sect was open to women as well as to men.

Q

Qadiriyya

Oldest of the surviving Islamic mystical orders, founded in the eleventh century by ʿAbd al-Qadir al-Jilani, whose tomb in Baghdad is still a place of pilgrimage. The Qadiriyya are marked by tolerance and good works, and an absence of fanaticism. There is deep devotion, but no rigid pattern. Typical of Qadiri devotion is the repetition a hundred times, after daily prayers, of 'I ask pardon of Almighty God: Glory to God: May God bless our Master Muhammad, his household and companions: There is no God but Allah.'

Quakers

See SOCIETY OF FRIENDS.

Quietism

A movement which held that the road to perfection consists in suppressing our own direct action and leaving all to God. It has been traced to the thirteenth century, but spread most widely in the seventeenth, when its leading exponents were Miguel de MOLINOS and Madame GUYON. FÉNELON expounded a modified Quietism. The Quietists liked to quote FRANÇOIS DE SALES: 'Desire nothing; refuse nothing.' Prayer thus became a totally passive reception of the presence of God. Outward acts, whether of charity or religious observance, were superfluous, even distracting and offensive to God. Divine action superseded human altogether. The soul became sinless. But the lower part of the soul might still be tempted, and resistance to this temptation would be a distraction from the state of contemplative perfection. These views were condemned by Innocent XI in 1687; other mystics have stressed that even less amoral forms of Quietism are wrong in the total suppression of the will: 'Love cannot be lazy.'

Qur'an, The

Sacred book of Islam, complete and self-sufficient. 'If it is not in the Book it is not true; if it is in the Book it is not necessary.' It consists of 114 chapters or *suras*, and includes the revelations received by MUHAMMAD.

The opening of Surah XIX in a 16th-century Persian manuscript of the Qur'an

R

Rabanus Maurus
(784–856)

Pupil of the great teacher Alcuin, ordained priest in 814, and elected abbot of Fulda in 822. For twenty years he governed the abbey, deepening its intellectual and spiritual life; then retired for five years for study and contemplative prayer. In 847 he became Archbishop of Mainz and was a leading figure in the evangelization of central Europe.

Rabia al-Adawiya
(d. 801)

Islamic woman poet and mystic. We know nothing about her birth or parentage; her home was Basra. To her, God is all in all: all else, even 'gods', are nothing. She explained an illness in terms of the absolute power of God: 'By God, I know of no cause for my illness save that Paradise was revealed to me and in my heart I longed for it. I think that my Lord was jealous for me and this was His rebuke. Only He can make me happy.' So she refused marriage: 'The contract of marriage is for those who have a phenomenal existence. In my case there is not such existence, for I have ceased to exist and have passed out of self. I exist in God. I am His, absolutely. I live in the shadow of his command. The marriage contract must be asked from Him, not from me.' For Rabia the way to God was the purity of love. It was she who really brought the doctrine of Divine LOVE into SUFISM. She expresses this in powerful verse:

> There are two ways of love –
> my selfish way, and Yours above.
> My selfish love is when I find
> I yearn to grasp you in my mind.
> Pure love is when You took
> the veil from my devoted look.
> I cannot glory in either phase.
> Two ways of love – in both be yours the praise!

She declared that her love for God left no room for hatred of any, even of Satan. One of her visions was of a glorious tree with wonderful golden fruits. She was told that the tree was hers and the fruits her praises of God. But some fruits were lying on the ground. She asked if they would not have been better on the tree: 'They would have been there, but that you, when you were praising God, were thinking to yourself, "Is the dough leavened or not?" and so these fruits fell off. The servant who desires to be close to his Lord must possess nothing in this world or the next save Him.' Her prayer, a little reminiscent of that of IBRAHIM BEN ADHAM, is a noteworthy expression of devotion: 'O God! If I worship You in fear of Hell, burn me in Hell. If I worship You in hope of Paradise, shut me out from Paradise. But if I worship You for Your own sake, do not withhold from me Your everlasting beauty!'

Racine, Jean
(1639–99)

French dramatist who grew up in the community at PORT ROYAL, and whose tragedies focus on the inner life of the spirit, and the tyranny of passion unredeemed by grace. In expressing this Racine brought a clear style, fine imagery and classical control.

Radha-Krishna cult

Movement in Hinduism, strong in Bengal, in which *bhakti* or personal devotion is expressed through the imagery of love, and the anguish of the (feminine) soul in separation from God, her

Krishna and Radha. An 18th-century Indian painting

yearning for union and bliss in consummation. For the founders of the movement, men like VALLABHA and CHAITANYA, the language and practice was spiritual. In one sect, the Sahajihas, perhaps under influence from the TANTRA movement, union with God was sought through erotic ecstasy.

Raine, Kathleen
(b. 1908)

The leading contemporary mystical poet in Britain, who has also written a major critical study of William BLAKE. In 'The World' she uses two mystical images of fire and nothingness, and the Platonic contrast of change and eternity:

It burns in the void,
Nothing upholds it.
Still it travels.

Travelling the void
Upheld by burning
Nothing is still.

Burning it travels.
The void upholds it.
Still it is nothing.

Nothing it travels
A burning void
Upheld by stillness.

In 'Exile' she has the vision of eternal love through all created things:

Then, I had no doubt
That snowdrops, violets, all creatures, I
myself
Were lovely, were loved, were love.
Look, they said,
And I had only to look deep into the heart,
Dark, deep into the violet, and there read,
Before I knew of any word for flower or
love,
The flower, the love, the word.

They never wearied of telling their being;
and I
Asked of the rose, only more rose, the violet
More violet untouched by time
No flower withered or flame died,
But poised in its own eternity, until the
looker moved
On to another flower, opening its entity.

Her finest mystical poem is 'Message from Home'. It begins with the Platonic doctrine of recollection, much as in TRAHERNE or VAUGHAN:

Do you remember, when you were first a
child,
Nothing in the world seemed strange to you?

It expands into a mighty vision of the unity of all created things:

Of all created things, the source is one,
Simple, single as love . . .

and the underlying message of the mystic: 'Nothing in that abyss is alien to you.'

So in the last stanza of 'Spell of Creation':

O love, my love, there springs a world,
And on the world there shines a sun
And in the sun there burns a fire,
Within the fire consumes my heart
And in my heart there beats a bird,
And in the bird there wakes an eye,
Within the eye, earth, sea and sky,
Earth, sky and sea within an O
Lie like the seed within the flower.

Ramakrishna Paramahamsa
(1834–86)

Nineteenth-century Hindu mystic who revived Hinduism. Ramakrishna was a joyful ascetic. He was virtually uneducated, and lived in a Kali temple in Calcutta a life of great simplicity and devotion. His meditations were directed indifferently to the revelation of God in divine and prophetic figures of many religions, whether the Great Mother or KRISHNA or JESUS or MUHAMMAD; he taught therefore the essential unity of all religions. His meditations would lead him into a state of trance which on one occasion lasted, with only brief intervals when his friends forced food on him, for six months. He taught simply and directly, using parables: his best-known disciple was Swami VIVEKANANDA.

Ramalinga
(19th century)

South Indian mystic. At the age of nine he was writing religious poetry in Tamil. Later, as he became practised in meditation he had a succession of mystical experiences. He has left an account of an ecstasy in which he experienced the vision of the divine Light: 'O Light of lights! O Self-radiance, the dispeller of the darkness of ignorance, I am fully illumined now. All my doubts and delusions have vanished. I am one with the Divine. I am Absolute Existence, Absolute Knowledge, Absolute Bliss. I enjoy Supreme Bliss. How can I describe it? I have attained Immortality. I behold the One All-Prevailing Self only everywhere. All dualities, distinctions and differences have disappeared. My joy is boundless. I have attained that which is beyond the senses, mind and intellect. I am birthless, decayless, changeless. I am beyond time, space and causation.'

Ramalinga's teaching centred on the INNER LIGHT. He had a voluminous but unsystematic approach. He emphasized the importance of physical health, and gave practical instruction in this. His method of meditation was to concentrate on the space between the eyebrows. The aim was to feel that the whole world is your own self, that all beings are your own self.

Ramalinga disappeared mysteriously, and there is no record of his death.

Ramananda
(*c.* 1370–1440)

Follower of RAMANUJA and inspirer of KABIR, he was an effective impulse behind Hindu mediaeval mysticism. He was an unorthodox thinker, who appealed to the lower castes, from whom his principal followers were drawn. He was a poet who used the vernacular. His mystical philosophy is well expressed in these words:

> Wherever I go, I see water and stone;
> But it is You who had filled them all with Your presence.
> In vain they seek You in the Vedas . . .
> My own true Teacher,
> You have put an end to all my failures and illusions.
> Blessed are You.
> Ramananda is lost in his Master Brahman;
> It is the Teacher's word that breaks all bonds.

Ramanuja
(*c.* 1017–1137)

Hindu philosopher and interpreter of the BHAGAVAD GITA. To Ramanuja the first stage in mystical experience is the realization that the soul in its true nature is not dependent on time or space, and is therefore immortal. Then, in realizing the true nature of the soul in release from the material world, we must learn to see all that is in the light of the soul. This is a godlike state. But it is not union with God or knowledge of God; that is to mistake the drop of water for the ocean, the mustard-seed for Mount Menu. Ramanuja was the first of the Hindu mystics to state clearly that the realization of the ATMAN within, 'the One who dwells within, whose form has not knowable boundaries', is not union with the Ultimate or knowledge of Him, but only the first step. That union, that knowledge, depend on love. To know God is to love Him, and if love is not there, God is not there. Ramanuja was strongly opposed to SANKARA's monistic form of philosophy: Sankara's God was impersonal, Ramanuja's profoundly and warmly personal.

Ramdas
(1608–82)

Indian mystic originally called Narain, who made extensive use of the Rama MANTRA, and preferred to live in the forest, as he found it more conducive to meditation. He devoted his life to the spread of Hinduism, and spent thirty-six years as a wandering preacher. His mystical approach is interesting in its combination of ADVAITA with personal devotion to Rama. It is well summed up in his parting advice to his followers: 'See Lord Rama in all creatures. Love all. Feel his presence always and everywhere. Live for him alone. Serve him in all beings. Make total and unreserved surrender to him. You will always live in him alone. You will attain immortality and eternal life.'

Ranters

Christian sect of the mid-seventeenth century. Their central teaching was that God is in every creature. There is one Spirit in the universe, revealed alike in the tiny ivy leaf and the most glorious angels. They believed that they themselves belonged to the dispensation of the Spirit; that the Second Coming of Christ was a spiritual event in the hearts of men, which they had experienced; that outward observations were shadowy dispensations; and now that Christ, the Morning Star, had shone, men had only to take heed to his appearing in their hearts, and the shadows would flee away. They turned aside from the Bible; there was no need to 'eye or mind a Christ who died at Jerusalem, but rather to eye and mind the Christ in themselves'. With this might go profoundly moving experience. Joseph Salmon tells how, with a sense as sure as hearing or sight, he was stripped of glory and emptied of enjoyment, experienced death with Christ, rose again to new life 'wrapt up in the embraces of such pure love and peace, as that I knew not oft-times whether I were in or out of this fading forme', and experienced the new Jerusalem: 'I appeared to myselfe as one confounded into the abyss of eternitie, nonentitized into the being of beings, my soul spilt and emptied into the fountaine and ocean of divine fulness, expired into the aspires of pure life. In briefe, the Lord so much appeared, that I was little or nothing seen, but walked at an orderly distance from myself, treading and tripping over the pleasant mountains of the heavenly land, where I walked with the Lord and was not.' Unfortunately the Ranters' total abandonment of all else left them with nothing whereby to check the quality of their experience, and led them into a vague PANTHEISM and serious antinomian practice, which won them the opposition not merely of orthodox theologians like Richard Baxter, but other mystics like Gerrard WINSTANLEY and George FOX.

Rapture

A sudden and violent form of ECSTASY. TERESA DE JESUS describes it as 'absolutely irresistible' and says that after a succession of raptures she felt 'almost like a drunk'.

Recollection

In PLATONIC philosophy, the process by which the soul reaches towards knowledge through being reminded of the Forms which it had perceived before birth. WORDSWORTH makes play with this idea in 'Our birth is but a sleep and a forgetting'.

In Christian mysticism it signifies the process of concentrating the mind for prayer by calling together again the thoughts that have scattered and dispersed.

Reincarnation

The passage of the soul after death, from one body to another. The terms 'transmigration' and 'metempsychosis' are used synonymously, though they sometimes include passage into an animal or even vegetable life. 'I have already been a boy and a girl,' said Empedocles, 'a bush, a bird, and a dumb sea fish.' Sometimes reincarnation is believed to take place within a family. Among the Yoruba of West Africa, a child born shortly after the death of a grandparent is likely to be called Babatunde ('Father has returned') or Yetunde ('Mother has returned'). Many mystery-religions and mystical systems are associated with a belief in reincarnation, and offer an escape from 'the weary wheel of birth and death'. The belief is strong in India, and is found in both Hinduism and Buddhism. It was perhaps from India that Pythagoras introduced it into the Greek world, and PLATO took it into his system from the Pythagoreans. Orthodox Christianity has never espoused it, but it has formed a part of some Christian theosophies.

Richard of St Victor

(*c.* 1123–75)

A Scot who made his life at the Abbey of St Victor in Paris. In *Benjamin Minor* he treated the prelude of CONTEMPLATION through LIBERATION from the passions and the world of sense, and concentration through reason on its own invisible images which mirror the beauty of God. Then to the soul which is ready the gift of contemplation comes like the last child of a family. *Benjamin Minor* analyses contemplation itself, which passes from sense-perception through reason to the spiritual process which goes beyond reason. We thus have an upwards movement through six objects of apprehension, (a) material objects, (b) the principles behind them, (c) the invisible world reached through the visible, (d) the invisible world in itself, (e) the divine nature as apprehended, (f) the divine nature in itself; and through six reflections of apprehension, (a) sense-perception *per se*, (b) sense-perception according to reason, (c) reason according to sense-perception, (d) reason *per se*, (e) that which is above reason according to reason, (f) that which is above reason *per se*. It is a highly refined Platonism. There are three 'modes of contemplation': the enlargement of the mind, which depends on human effort; the elevation of the mind, in which divine grace and human effort co-operate; and the alienation or ecstasy of the mind, which depends on divine grace. There are four degrees of contemplation: the love that wounds; the love that binds; the love that weakens (before God's ravishment of the soul); and the love that disappears (in the total glory of God and conformation with Christ). And, as with BERNARD OF CLAIRVAUX, the highest love leads to action. In *The Four Degrees of Passionate Love* he wrote, 'In the first degree God enters into the soul and she turns inward into herself. In the second she ascends above herself and is lifted up to God. In the third the soul, lifted up to God, passes over altogether into Him. In the fourth the soul goes forth on God's behalf and descends below herself.'

Rilke, Rainer Maria

(1875–1926)

German poet, born in Prague, who explored in his poetry the whole of life and death. His early poetry shows a mystical approach.

> What will you do, God, when I die?
> When I, your pitcher, broken lie?
> When I, your drink, go stale or dry?
> I am your garb, the trade you ply,
> you lose your meaning, losing me.
>
> Homeless without me, you will be
> robbed of your welcome, warm and sweet.
> I am your sandals: your tired feet
> will wander bare for want of me.
>
> *(tr. Babette Deutsch)*

By 1902 he was wrestling with the expression of his sense of unity between his inner and outer life.

> When I lift my eyes from the page,
> all is great, nothing strange.
> There is all my life *here*,
> all is limitless, here as there.
> Only I weave myself in more tightly
> when my glance chimes in with things
> and with their shapes' grave simplicity –
> then the earth outgrows itself,
> it seems to embrace the whole sky,
> the first star is as the last house.

In three great poems in 1904 Rilke found symbols to express this vision. Two of them were from Greek mythology, Alcestis and Eurydice, who drew together the worlds of life and death. In the third, 'The Rose-bowl', he uses an image of his own: two fighting boys are the divided world, the opening rose the symbol of unity of opposites, and of the hidden and revealed in one. In 'Experience of Death' Rilke explored further the union of life and death; there is an almost Platonic sense that death is the door to reality: 'green, real green, real sunshine, real forest'. In *Elegies of Duino* the symbol of union is the Angels in whom 'that transformation of the visible into the invisible which we are performing already appears complete'.

Rimbaud, Jean Nicholas Arthur

(1854–91)

French symbolist poet. A precocious boy, who wrote all his poetry before the age of twenty and then gave up writing. His early poem *Le Bateau ivre* is in many ways his finest achievement. The poet and the boat of which he writes are one. Image piles on image as he abandons himself to current and tide. He is on a journey in search of

Arthur Rimbaud. A detail from Fantin-Latour's Un Coin de table

experience, reality. Storm and sunshine, an almost PSYCHEDELIC sense of colour, love and death are all part of the kaleidoscope through which he passes. He wants to escape from the bonds and bounds of self: 'May my keel shatter! May I go to the sea!' But in this poem he does not give himself completely; he comes back. But he comes back to use poetry as a road to reality. The true poet makes himself a seer 'by a long, immense, and deliberate derangement of the senses'. Only so will he receive the direct vision of reality. So in *Les Illuminations* Rimbaud recorded the phantasmagoria of his released imagination, and produced his own world of myth and symbol. But on his own terms, this world, for all his deliberate revision of his writing, was not his own conscious creation, or the mere upwelling of his own subconscious, but a glimpse of the truth. His highest mystical achievement is *Saison en Enfer*, and particularly the ecstatic 'O saisons, ô châteaux!', a great exclamation of joy, expressive of the words he wrote in his letters: 'I is Another'.

> I'll have no more mood of strife:
> HE has taken over my life.

The wood of the poet has become a violin on which the Other plays; it is, he says, the ancient wisdom of the East. Yet the experience was, he sensed, partial only, a vision of purity, not of God. In his own language, he was still in the realm of nature; he knew there was a higher realm of Spirit.

Rinzai

See FIVE HOUSES

Rnyin-ma-pa

'The Ancient Ones', Tibetan Buddhist school, dating from about AD 800, and involving a secret GNOSIS. The Rnyin-ma-pa uses the material body and its lusts and emotions. There are three successive stages of practice: the production of mental images of the hundred tutelary deities; the psychosomatic control of the channels of forces within the body and of the *semen virile* in such a way as to lead to happiness, enlightenment and freedom for thought; a realization that the true being of one's own mind is emptiness. The system of the Rnyin-ma-pa is very involved and incorporates astrology, alchemy and magical practices.

Rolle, Richard
(*c.* 1300–49)

The first mystical writer in English; born in Yorkshire, educated at Oxford, he became a hermit. He wrote extensively in prose and verse, in Latin and English; works which include scholarly commentaries on scripture, spiritual direction to women disciples, works of personal devotion, enhanced by extravagant but not unattractive alliteration. He expresses the stages of his mystical experience through progressive symbols, the opening of the door, sweetness (he uses an image from the nightingale's melody), HEAT ('als wele fele the fyre of lufe byrnand in thaire saule, als thou may fele thi fynger byrn, if thou putt it in the fyre') and song ('A mans hart that verraly es byrnand in the lufe of God . . . hase myrth and joy and melody in angels' song'). Rolle sees contemplation as 'a wonderful joy of Goddes lufe', and indeed joy is the keynote of his mysticism, and 'love-longing' his way of expressing his mystical search. For him mysticism operated through meditation on the holy name of Jesu; this, so to speak, was his OM; and he told how the Name freed him from the temptations of the Devil in the form of a woman. Jesus, he said, is closer to contemplatives than brother or sister or any friend. Rolle is sometimes naïve, but there is no doubt about the intensity and sincerity with which he seeks to convey the vision he has enjoyed.

Romuald
(*c.* 950–1027)

Son of a nobleman from Ravenna, he espoused the monastic life in atonement for his father having killed a man in a duel. The life was insufficiently rigorous for him; he became a hermit, and founded the CAMALDOLESE order on nearly eremitic lines.

Rosicrucian Brotherhood

In 1610 a German named Haselmeyer recorded seeing a manuscript entitled *The Story of the Brotherhood of the Meritorious Order of the Rosy*

The emblem of the Kabbalistic Rose + Croix

Cross. This was published in 1614 and told how one Christian Rosenkreutz (a seemingly mythical figure) two centuries earlier had travelled in Spain, Egypt and the Near East, gathered a store of secret wisdom and founded a brotherhood of four (later doubled) 'to improve mankind by the discovery of the true philosophy'. They spread out in work of helping and healing the needy, meeting once a year. They vowed secrecy for a hundred years, and had their own private language and magical alphabet. Their thinking was much influenced by ALCHEMY: 'They believe that this world and indeed the whole universe is permeated with the essence of the Creator, that every rock is instinct with life, that every plant and every tree is imbued with a sense derived from the Master Mind that caused it to exist, and that each living thing moves, acts and thinks in accordance with the supreme design by which all things were made, by which all things exist, and by which they will continue to function till the end of time.'

The Rosicrucians offer an esoteric mystical GNOSIS. Truth is the Great Architect of the Universe. There are three principles, Salt, Sulphur and Mercury, all contained in primal matter, Phar-Min Adama, represented by a circle encompassed by a square (the earth-heaven symbolism in Taoist art). The circle symbolizes Unity, from which the Quaternary Number results. Other Mystic Figures include the interlaced Equilateral Triangles, and the Blazing Star, the latter standing for 'that subtle Quintessence which penetrates all things in a moment by its moist and temperate fire and so communicates its gnosis'. The catechism from which that phrase is taken goes on: 'Why do you people speak so obscurely? – So that only the Sons of God may understand me.' But the ultimate aim is 'the joy of supplying the needs of men of good report' and 'only to be ignored by the world, only to live for God, Who is the sole aim of our true Brethren'.

Rumi, Jalal al-Din
(d. 1273)

Rumi came from Balkh and migrated to Konia (the ancient Iconium) in Asia Minor, where he formed the Mevlevi order of DERVISHES. Rumi is arguably the greatest mystical poet in any language. In his *Mathnawi* he expounds in verse the whole Sufi system. At the outset he uses the image of the reed-pipe to express the mystic's way to God.

Hearken to this Reed forlorn
Breathing, ever since 'twas torn
From its rusty bed, a strain
Of impassioned love and pain.

The secret of my song, though new,
None can see and none can hear.
Oh, for a friend to know the sign
And mingle all his soul with mine!

'Tis the flame of love that fired me,
'Tis the wine of love inspired me.
Wouldst thou learn how loves bleed,
Hearken, hearken to the Reed!

(tr. R. A. Nicholson)

Love and wine are frequently used as allegories of mystical experience in Rumi's lyrics. But other images are there as well. His association with the Whirling Dervishes leads him to a peculiar emphasis on the power of the rotating wheel, the circling of the heavenly bodies, the mill-wheel and millstone.

The mountain of the sun
I'll fashion to a mill.
And as my waters run,
I'll turn thee at my will.

(tr. A. J. Arberry)

Rumi is also something of a nature-mystic.

Men have argued (but they lied)
That this image does not bide;
One declared we are a tree,
Said another, grass are we.

Yet the rustling of this bough
Proves the breeze is stirring now;
Silent then, O silent be;
That we are, and this are we.

(tr. A. J. Arberry)

Sometimes his absorption with nature takes him in the direction of pantheism: a good example is quoted under NATURE-MYSTICISM. In one poem he speaks of the ascent of the soul to God through progressive incarnations, in which in one sense the soul is always in God, but in another has to ascend from mineral to plant to animal to man to angel and ultimately to God alone.

Sometimes Rumi uses images taken from nature with quite extraordinary delicacy, concision and illumination. Consider this as an account of the soul's search for God.

> I sought a soul in the sea,
> And found a coral there;
> Beneath the foam for me
> An ocean was all laid bare.
>
> Into my heart's night
> Along a narrow way
> I groped; and lo! the light,
> An infinite land of day.
>
> *(tr. A. J. Arberry)*

Or this, as an account of the mystic's relation to the physical universe.

> Happy was I
> In the pearl's heart to lie;
> Till, lashed by life's hurricane,
> Like a tossed wave I ran.
>
> The secret of the sea
> I uttered thunderously;
> Like a spent cloud on the shore
> I slept, and stirred no more.
>
> *(tr. A. J. Arberry)*

Ultimately all power and meaning comes from God.

> We are the flute, the music you,
> the mountain we, which echoes you,
> the chessmen set in line by you,
> to win or lose now moved by you.
> We are the flags embroidered with the lion,
> the unseen wind which ripples us is you.
>
> *(tr. Anon)*

And no one is clearer than Rumi that when we seek God it is because God is seeking us.

Russell, Bertrand Arthur William
(1872–1970)

English mathematical philosopher and free-thinker. He examined the claims of mysticism in *Mysticism and Logic* and *Religion and Science*. He asks the question whether we ought to admit that there is available in support of religion a source of knowledge which lies outside science and may properly be described as revelation, and argues for the neutrality of science on this. The mystic may be certain that he knows, but others who repeat the mystic's experiments do not always receive the mystic's experiences. He takes the unanimity of the mystics on three further propositions, that the universe is a single indivisible unity, that TIME is unreal and that evil is mere appearance, and criticizes these, at the same time showing that on other matters mystics are not unanimous but are limited by their own religious systems. His critique is in general not neutral but negative; on more popular occasions he asked why if we do not believe that the man who drinks too much actually sees snakes we should believe that the man who eats too little sees Heaven. But he accords some value to the mystic emotion, though not to the beliefs and assertions which go with it. 'Breadth and calm and profundity may all have their source in this emotion, in which, for the moment, all self-centred desire is dead, and the mind becomes a mirror for the vastness of the universe.' It is 'the inspirer of whatever is best in man'. The greatest philosophers have felt the need of both science and mysticism, and the union of mystic and man of science is 'the highest eminence . . . that it is possible to achieve in the world of thought'.

Bertrand Russell through the eyes of a contemporary cartoonist

Russell, George William
(1867–1935)

See Æ.

Ruysbroeck, Jan van
(1293–1381)

Ruysbroeck grew up in Brussels, where he served as collegiate chaplain for a quarter of a century. Then at the age of fifty, dissatisfied with the distractions of the city and with ecclesiastical formalism, he joined with an uncle and a friend in forming a community of contemplatives in the peace of the forest. Here for thirty-eight more years he lived in worship and contemplation combined with humble and practical service, a combination he fostered in his numerous writings, of which the best known are *The Adornment of the Spiritual Marriage*, *The Sparkling Stone*, *The Seven Steps of the Ladder of Spiritual Love*, *The Book of Supreme Truth*, *The Mirror of*

Eternal Salvation, The Kingdom of the Lovers of God, The Spiritual Espousals. The titles are enough to show something of his use of symbols. But though his central symbol is the spiritual marriage, and though he speaks of 'the coming of our Bridegroom', and of 'the fire of love', his treatment of the mystical experience is cool and sober rather than passionate and ecstatic.

Ruysbroeck identifies three stages in mystical experience. The first is the active life, the stage of moral PURIFICATION, external works and self-disciplined service. It is important to see that this is not a stage which is left behind. On the contrary, the common or practical life is equally the fruit of the contemplation of God. 'The man who is sent down by God from these heights into the world is full of truth and rich in all virtues.' He possesses a universal life, ready for contemplation or action. None of the great mystics lays greater stress on the need for practical service than Ruysbroeck.

The second stage is the interior life, where vision and thought predominate over action and conduct, the stage of spiritual unity. Ruysbroeck naturally speaks of this stage in Christian language, as he does throughout. Among many images, including inevitably that of LIGHT, he uses particularly the spring of Living Water to describe the interior light. It flows with Pure Simplicity (which leads the mind to what Ruysbroeck calls Nudity, freedom from sensual images), Spiritual Clarity (which leads to the perception of 'the unmeasured loyalty of God to his creation') and Grace (which kindles and strengthens the will). At this stage 'the pure soul feels a constant fire of love, which desires above all things to be one with God, and the more the soul obeys the attraction of God the more it feels it, and the more it feels it, the more it desires to be one with God'. 'Love the love which loves you everlastingly – for the more you love the more you desire to love.' Those who reach this stage are rightly called Friends of God.

The third stage is the 'superessential' life, the union with God, far beyond thought or intention, the life of contemplation, the experience of immediate union, without distinction or difference, an ecstasy of knowledge, love and joy. For the spirit to have this immediate experience of God three conditions are necessary. First, he 'must be perfectly ordered from without in all the virtues, and within must be unencumbered'. Secondly, he 'must inwardly cleave to God, with adhering intention and love, even as a burning and glowing fire which can never more be quenched'. Thirdly, he 'must have lost himself in a Waylessness and in a Darkness, in which all contemplative men wander in fruition and wherein they never again can find themselves in a creaturely way'. 'We expire into the eternal namelessness in which we are lost.' But the distinction between Creator and created is not lost. It is impossible for us to become God and lose our created essence; rather, overwhelmed with love, we are one with God.

Ruysbroeck distinguishes between four religious types. Lowest are the *hirelings*, 'those who love themselves so inordinately that they will not serve God save for their own profit and their own reward'. They live in servitude to their own selfhood. Next come the *faithful servants* who serve God actively, but who have not learned the inward life, the Marthas. Third are the *secret friends* who know the 'upward stirring exercise of love' but view their inwardness as an attribute only. Highest of all are the *hidden sons of God.*

Ruysbroeck is an introspective mystic. He is not one of those who like to use the outer world as the basis for their approach to God. He is not afraid to use allegorical gradations, as in *The Seven Steps of the Ladder of Spiritual Love*. These 'steps' are good will, voluntary poverty, chastity, humility, desire for God's glory, contemplation and transcendence. But essentially he is restoring the introspective approach developed by AUGUSTINE in *The Confessions*. He turns his attention away from the distractions of the sense-world into 'the supersensuous regions beyond thought'.

Ruysbroeck is highly original in his use of the Christian doctrine of the Trinity, interpreted in somewhat Neo-Platonic terms, as an intellectual ground for the interpretation of mystical experience. In the divine life we can see expansion and contraction, flux and reflux. Three in One and One in Three, a divine Unity from which three Persons proceed, three Persons whose essential being is a single Unity. So the three faculties of the soul, memory, intelligence and will, are bound together in the unity of the spirit. Man will find his unity in entering into the divine life. For as he descends into himself he finds the image of God in the depths of his soul. He must associate his soul with the Three in One. The three stages of mystical experience correspond with Spirit, Son and Father, and none of them can ever be left behind. But it is at the highest point of contemplation that the soul experiences the reflux into the divine Unity, and knows a union without distraction. The man who possesses this is the 'enlightened' or 'God-seeing' man.

Ruysbroeck set himself against PANTHEISM, which in his view led the believer to complacency and indolence. Pantheists are 'a fruit of hell, the more dangerous because they counterfeit the true fruit of the Spirit of God'. They 'believe themselves sunk in inward peace; but as a matter of fact they are deep-drowned in error'.

The Church granted Ruysbroeck the title of the Ecstatic Doctor. One day his friends found him in the woods. The tree under which he was sitting was ablaze as if with fire, and Ruysbroeck was at its foot, rapt in contemplation.

S

Sabbatianism

Jewish mystical heresy of the seventeenth and eighteenth centuries. Its leaders were Sabbatai Zevi, who had received a profound experience of illumination in his youth, and claimed to be the Messiah, though he renounced his faith under threat of Turkish execution; Nathan of Gaza, who had a mystical experience in which he 'saw the Merkabah, and saw visions of God all day and all night, and was vouchsafed true prophecy like any other prophet', and whose *Treatise of the Dragons* was a mythical account of Zevi's pilgrimage as Messiah; Abraham Miguel Cardozo, who distinguished between the hidden God and the God of Israel, but was unusual among those who made the distinction in placing all his religious emphasis on the latter; and, later, Jacob Frank, 'the apostle of Poland', an ecstatic and visionary but at the same time a megalomaniac who claimed to be an incarnation of Beauty, one of the SEFIROTH, and to have come to deliver the world from every law and every statute which were in force until now.

Sacrament

Sacramentum originally meant an oath of allegiance. It was used, oddly but brilliantly, in the Latin New Testament to render the Greek *mysterion*. From this derived its particular Christian usage. Augustine defined it as 'a sign of a sacred thing' (so Aquinas 'a sign of a sacred thing in so far as it sanctifies men') or 'the visible form of invisible grace'. The classical definition from the Catechism runs 'an outward and visible sign of an inward and spiritual grace given unto us, ordained by Christ Himself, as a means whereby we receive the same and a pledge to assure us thereof'. Sacraments have thus been variously conceived, and Hugh of St Victor lists thirty. They are normally however reduced to seven: baptism, confirmation, the eucharist, penance, extreme unction, order and matrimony. Orthodox Christian mystics have often found their mystical experience through the EUCHARIST in particular.

Sacrificial mysticism

Term applied by S. N. Dasgupta to the first stage of Indian mysticism in the practices of the priests in Vedic times. To this there are three sides. One is the precise performance of sacrificial ritual as a means to the attainment of mystical powers; this was later looked down upon. The second is a form of nature mysticism, praise of fire and water, wind and sun, all with a deep sense of wonder: 'God made the rivers to flow. They feel no weariness, they do not cease from flowing. They fly swiftly like birds in the air.' The third is at least the germs of a personal religion, as in the celebrated *mantra*, 'Let us meditate on the adorable glory of the Radiant Sun' or the prayer to Varuna, 'Cast our sins away like loosened fetters, and let us be thine own beloved.'

Saʿdi, Musharrif al-Din Ben Muslih
(*c.* 1215–92)

Saʿdi, one of the greatest Persian poets, came from Shiraz, studied in Baghdad, and travelled widely and adventurously (he was captured by Crusaders) before settling back in Shiraz. He is best known for *Bustan* or *The Orchard*, a didactic poem which ranges from practical politics to mystic love, and *Gulistan* or *The Rose-Garden*, a collection of improving anecdotes, often about dervishes, interspersed with verse comments; but he was also a great writer of lyric poetry.

Part of Saʿdi's strength is that his language is straightforward (*Gulistan* is often used as a first reader in Persian); but his thought is such that it can be interpreted at many levels, and Sufi masters find in it the deepest communicable wisdom. His precepts range from the immediately practical to the inexhaustibly profound, and often we find the same precept has both dimensions. Here are two examples:

> Make no friendship with an elephant-keeper
> If you have no room to entertain an elephant.

and

> I fear that you will not reach Mecca, O
> traveller!
> The road you are following leads to
> Turkestan!

Here is a simple but profound expression of mystical wisdom:

> A raindrop dripping from a cloud,
> Was ashamed when it saw the sea.
> 'Who am I where there is a sea?' it said.
> When it saw itself with the eye of humility,
> A shell nurtured it in its embrace.

Saivism

Independent religion within Hinduism, first mentioned directly in the eighth century AD, whose worship centred on the god Siva: 'He is Brahma, he is Siva, he is Indra, he is undecaying, supreme, self-resplendent, he is Vishnu, he is breath, he is the spirit, the Supreme Lord, he is all that has been or that shall be eternal.' In the south among the Tamil, so-called 'pure' Saivism was sceptical of any doctrine of mystical absorption into the Ultimate. Concentration was directed to the divine grace of Siva. 'If you contemplate him as beyond contemplation, even this gives no benefit, as it is a mere fiction. If you contemplate him as yourself, this also is a mere fiction. The only way to know him is by understanding him through his grace.'

In Kashmir Saivism took on a strongly mystical trend. The Ultimate is Reality; it is absolute Unity; it is unanalysable, indescribable, ineffable, undefinable. It may not be spoken of, perceived or apprehended. But it can be realized through spiritual discipline. The Ultimate is both immanent and transcendent. The individual mind is identical with the universal mind. Mind is a self-luminous reflector of external objects, and at the same time self-conscious. The universal mind produces the universe from itself; it is not passive, but wholly active. The philosophy at the root of this bears important similarities to Neo-Platonism, and has been called Realistic Idealism.

Sakyamuni

See GAUTAMA.

Salesian method

See FRANÇOIS DE SALES.

Salon de la Rose + Croix

Salon established by Sâr PÉLADAN in 1892 to foster truth throughout art. Six exhibitions were held in all.

Samadhi

Hindu and Buddhist name for the mystical consciousness, which is the object of YOGA.

Samothrace

Samothrace is an island in the northern Aegean, formidably mountainous, which was in classical times the centre of a mystery-cult associated with the Cabeiri, divine beings, normally but not always two in number, sometimes identified with the Dioscuri, the sons of Zeus, Castor and Pollux. They are depicted with hammers, which makes them divine smiths and volcanic spirits, and spirits of the underworld. The cult was international and classless. Slaves and governors, sailors and businessmen, women and men, all shared in initiation. Initiation took place at night; the initiate wore a crown, carried a lamp and shared in a sacramental meal. After initiation he was marked by an iron ring and purple scarf. There were two grades of initiate, the *mystae* who had received the secret, and the *epoptae* or visionaries who had seen the spectacle; this last was a smaller group, admitted only after a confessional. The spectacle seems likely to have been a mystic marriage; we know that it was accompanied by music and dancing. Such a vision bears with it the promise of life, of protection from death and of life beyond death.

Samsara

Buddhist term for the flux of phenomena.

Sankara

(*c.* 788–820)

Perhaps the greatest of the Indian monistic philosophers, who developed the doctrine of ADVAITA, or 'non-twoness'.

Sankara's central thesis is that Brahman alone is the ultimate reality: everything else is false. Now the essence of illusion is that the characteristics of one object are assigned to another, as when we mistake a rope for a snake. The snake is not absolutely non-existent, for the rope is there; it is an illusion. Sankara suggests that since the universal self is felt through our sensation of I-ness; and since it is immediate in all experience, the non-self and its characteristics may be illusorily imposed on the self. The world of appearance is subjective not objective; it is neither real nor unreal. Falsehood ceases to exist when the reality is known. True perception refers to pure being. Ultimate reality is one, uniform, self-luminous. And the witness is

Sankara

within. 'How can one contest the fact of another possessing the knowledge of Brahman, vouched as it is by his heart's conviction?'

His doctrine of an impersonal Brahman won the opposition of later theistic mystics like RAMANUJA. To him God is indescribable. He speaks of his pure Being. Sankara occasionally allows himself phrases which go beyond this, but they seem emotive, almost liturgical. 'His Being is by nature eternal, pure, wise and free, all-knowing and endowed with omnipotence' (*VS* I, II). 'The eternal, omniscient, omnipresent, complete, eternally pure, wise, free Being . . . Knowledge and Joy . . . the one identical, all-highest eternal spirit' (I, I, 4). 'The eternal pure God' (I, I, 5). 'The eternal, perfect, highest God' (I, I, 20). 'The absolutely real Being, exalted, eternal, all-penetrating as the ether, free from all change, all-sufficient, indivisible, self-luminous' (I, 15, 4).

Sankara's text was 'True Being was this in the beginning, one only, without a second.'

Sariputra
(sixth to fifth century BC)

Buddhist leader, who died shortly before GAUTAMA. He was born of a Brahmin family, early embraced the religious life, and attained full enlightenment within two weeks of his acceptance of the preaching of the Buddha. Sariputra's historic importance is that his analytic mind gave to the Buddha's teaching a shape enabling it to be systematically communicated; in this way he had great influence on the training of the Buddhist monks.

Sat-Chit-Ananda

In Hindu thought Being-Awareness-Bliss.

Satie, Erik Alfred Leslie
(1866–1925)

French composer, who in his early twenties became an enthusiastic devotee of ROSICRUCIANISM, a cult which led him into the study of mediaeval music in general and plain-song in particular. During this period he wrote works of a mysterious unworldliness; perhaps outstanding is the 1895 *Messe des pauvres* for voices and organ, with its fluid plainsong melodies and complex chromatic harmonies. But Satie was always open to new developments; he moved away from the Rosicrucians, and learned from Cubists and Surrealists without becoming their prisoner. At the end of the First World War he returned to a mystical approach, though in a more classical mould, by setting words from three of PLATO's dialogues in his symphonic drama *Socrate*. The element of plain-song is still there, though it is more strongly structured. So is the sense of unworldliness. The harmony is austere and almost ascetic. Indeed, the movement portraying the death of Socrates is perhaps Satie's outstanding musical achievement. Satie was something of an idol for the younger French composers, and exercised an influence beyond the achievement of his own compositions.

Satori

ZEN term for enlightenment. It depends on intuitive grasp rather than logical analysis; it consists in looking at our surroundings from a fresh viewpoint so that we see them in a new light. Insofar as all nature is one to the Zen Master, *satori* may be regarded as (in HUI-NENG's phrase) 'seeing into one's own nature'. *Satori* is beyond reason; it depends on insight. It is a positive vision, an acceptance of the universe, not a denial of it. It is a vision which convinces by its own authority; it cannot be shaken by argument. It is a vision of the Ultimate, not normally conceived in personal terms. There is a partial exception in a poem by Chao-pien:

> Empty of thought I sat quietly at my office-desk,
> my fountain-mind at rest, as calm as water –
> a thunder-roll, the doors of the mind bursting open,
> and, look, there sits the old man in all his homeliness.

But that is hardly to be compared with the personal visions of God in His glory. None the less *satori* is in its way an experience of glory. It comes in a flash and goes as quickly. But the mind is changed and cannot be the same again. D. T. Suzuki has called *satori* in modern terminology 'an insight into the Unconscious', and has identified eight characteristics of it: irrationality, intuitive insight, authoritativeness, affirmation, sense of the beyond, impersonal tone, feeling of exaltation and momentariness.

Scale of Perfection, The

See HILTON, WALTER.

Scheffler, Johann

See ANGELUS SILESIUS.

Schleiermacher, Friedrich Daniel Ernst
(1768–1834)

German theologian, influenced philosophically by Kant, and generally by the Romantic movement.

In Schleiermacher's *Addresses on Religion* (1799) he is basically reasserting against FICHTE and others the religious virtue of humble piety in a quite straightforward and non-mystical way. But in the course of so doing he affirms the importance of the vision of what he calls the 'universum'. The universum means more than the sum total of all existing discrete entities; it means the essential oneness of the whole. So 'religion lives its whole life . . . in the infinite nature of the whole, the One and the All'. The *universum* then is perceived not with the senses, but with the intuitive mind; it is almost the Platonic Form of the World, the norm and principle behind the world, and Schleiermacher does call this Principle 'the high spirit of the universe'. So 'to love the spirit of the universe and behold his work with joy; that is the goal of our religion'.

Twenty years later in his *Dogmatic* Schleiermacher presented the obverse of this coin. He looked not outward but inward, and asserted that by immediate inward experience we are conscious of our 'absolute dependence', so that in the highest sense 'immediate self-consciousness' is, or leads to, knowledge of God. 'The sense of absolute dependence in and of itself is the sense of God set in the consciousness of the self.' The means to this lie not through sense-perception or intellection, but through 'feeling'; 'feeling' is however to be understood not as emotion but as a means of apprehension. 'I have proclaimed nothing but the immediate and primal being of God in us through feeling.'

Schopenhauer, Arthur
(1788–1860)

German philosopher, follower of KANT and opponent of HEGEL. Schopenhauer's philosophy has two pillars, one that the inner essence of human nature is will; the other that life is

Arthur Schopenhauer and his poodle. A contemporary caricature

fundamentally evil. Where then is deliverance to be found? Partly through art and especially music, through which the soul finds momentary release from striving, principally through the complete suppression of the individual will, through sympathy, and the conscious realization of *Tat tvam asi* ('That art Thou') in relation to all things, through the starvation of the impulses and utter resignation. 'Life and its forms now pass before him as a fleeting illusion, as a light morning dream before half waking eyes, the real world already shining through it so that it can no longer deceive; and like this morning dream, they finally vanish altogether, without any violent transition.' This is Schopenhauer's particular brand of *nirvana*, and he did indeed claim that his philosophy was one with the mystics whether Eastern or Western.

An excellent anecdote (reminiscent of one of ABU YAZID) tells how Schopenhauer, wandering in meditation in a park, walked into the middle of a flower-bed, and stood there oblivious. The park-keeper shouted: 'Who do you think you are?' 'Ah!' replied Schopenhauer, 'If only I knew!'

Schwarz, Johann Georg
(1751–84)

Schwarz came from Transylvania, and early became an adherent of BOEHME's mystical theosophy. In 1781 he became a member of the ROSICRUCIAN brotherhood. In 1782 he went to Moscow, and there by this educational work, his association with Nikolai Ivanovitch Novikov, one of the leaders of the Enlightenment, and a series of translations carried out by his students, was more than any other single person responsible for introducing mystical and pietistic thinking into Russian orthodoxy. His unremitting efforts led to an early death through overwork, but his work was carried on by Alexander Feodorovitch Labsin and others.

Scriabin, Alexander
(1872–1915)

Russian musical composer, who from about 1900 was exploring through music the possibility of what he called 'Mystery', an ecstatic state achieved through a synthesis of music, dancing, poetry, scent and colour. Thus Scriabin claims that the finale of his third piano sonata displays 'the intoxicated Soul striving and wrestling in the storm of the unchained elements. From the depths of its being, the voice of the Man-God arises, singing a song of victory.' The critic Ernest Newman said of *Prometheus*: 'Here is music that comes as near as is at present possible to being the pure voice of Nature and the soul themselves . . . the wind that blows through it is the veritable wind of the cosmos itself. The cries of desire and passion and ecstasy are a sort of quintessential sublimation of all the yearning, not merely of humanity, but of all nature, animate and inanimate.' L. Sabaneiev called it the 'poem of the creative spirit which, having already become free, freely creates the world'. Scriabin had a theory of colour-correspondence, and to listen to this work with appropriate light-effects is said to have intensified the mystical experience. Scriabin's claims must be judged by *The Divine Poem*, *The Poem of Ecstasy* and *Prometheus: the Poem of Fire*; the middle of the century denigrated them: there might now be a swing of the pendulum.

Secret of the Golden Flower, The

Neo-Taoist treatise, but drawing on Confucian and Buddhist thought as well.

That which exists through itself is the TAO. This is the one Essence; it is contained in the Light of Heaven. The Light of Heaven cannot be seen. It is contained in the two eyes. We must therefore use the two eyes to look inwards. Meditative exercises with lids closed and rhythmic breathing enable us to discover the Light: 'As soon as one is quiet, the light of the eye begins to blaze up, so that everything before one becomes quite bright as if one were in a cloud. If one opens one's eyes and sees the body, it is not to be found any more.' This illumination is the opening of the Golden Flower, which is the Elixir of Life. There are ten thousand snares on the path. On the other hand there is confirmation in spiritual strength and the visionary transformation of the natural world that the Light has crystallized. This means that the life-forces are rising, the self is freed from the conflict of the opposites and will again become part of the one undivided Tao.

Seed-Syllable

In Hindu mysticism, the most powerful MANTRA, consisting of one syllable only, and ending in a vibrating 'overtone'. The most powerful seed-syllable is OM.

Sect of the New Spirit

See BRETHREN OF THE FREE SPIRIT.

Seekers

Early seventeenth-century Christian sect, simple and quietist, who sought 'an upper room Christianity', abandoned external observances, waited in silence upon the direct inspiration of God, believed that a true minister of Christ would receive an immediate call from Christ, a 'powerful enabling' from the Bridegroom or his Friends (that is, the Apostles), and that his ministry would be marked by miracle.

Sefer Hasidim

Jewish mystical treatise written by Judah the Pious (d. 1217) incorporating mythical legend, mystical thought and homiletical exposition, with a strongly penitential character.

Sefer Ha-Zohar

See ZOHAR.

Sefer Yesira

Jewish mystical treatise, perhaps going back to the second century BC though incorporating later material. According to the *Sefer Yesira* all that exists emanates from the One God, as the flame from the candle. All multiplicity originates in One Unity. All has come from God and must return to God. God is revealed in and through His universe. He is immanent and at the same time transcendent. The book gives an account of the ten SEFIROTH or divine powers, which emanate from God, but keeps to strict monotheism: 'The last of the Sefiroth unites itself to its first just as a flame is united with the candle, for God is one and there is no second.'

Sefiroth

Kabbalistic term for the 'regions' or 'spheres', the spirit, air, water, fire, the four cardinal points of the compass, height and depth. These ten are all emanations from God: the crown, the wis-

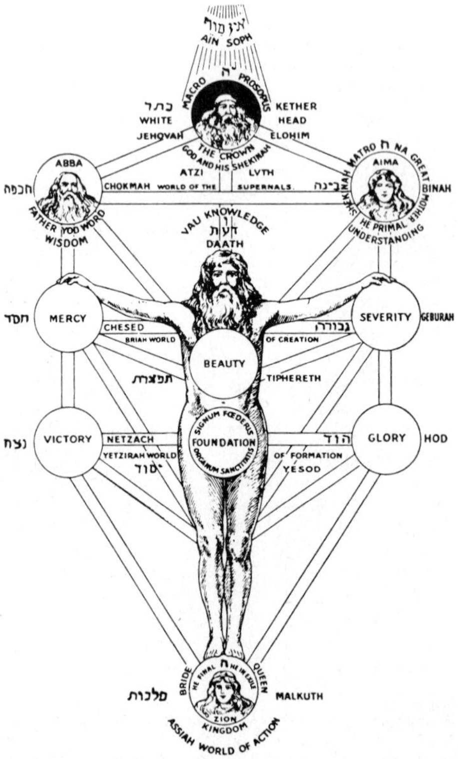

The sacred tree of the Sefiroth

dom, the intelligence, the love, the power, the compassion, the steadfastness, the majesty, the foundation and the kingdom. They are linked together as a vital organism, like a tree whose root is the Infinite, with the kingdom as the trunk, the foundation as the point from which the branches begin to spread, the compassion (or beauty) at the centre and the crown at the top. They are the names which God gave to Himself and which make up the one great Name.

Self

It is the constant witness of the mystics that Self is a barrier to the highest. So Kabir: 'When the I, the Me, and the Mine are dead, the work of the Lord is done.' So *The Cloud of Unknowing*: 'Feel sin a lump, thou wollest never what, but none other thing than *thyself*.' So the *Theologia Germanica*: 'Whosoever seeketh, loveth, and pursueth goodness, as goodness and for the sake of goodness, and maketh this his end – for nothing but the love of Goodness, not for love of the I, Me, Mine, Self, and the life – he will find the highest good, for he seek it aright, and they who seek it otherwise do err.' So al-Hallaj:

> Between You and me there *lingers*
> an 'It is I' that torments me.
> Ah, of your grace take away
> this 'I' from between us.

So Eckhart: 'God asks only one thing of you: that you dethrone the creaturely self and let him be God in you.' And Boehme: 'Love hates Self, or that which we call *I*, because it is a deadly thing, and the two of them, Love and Self, cannot well stand together.'

But in another sense the Self, the true Self, is to be found in God. As the *Chandogya Upanishad* puts it: 'The Self is below, the Self is above, the Self is to the west, to the east, to the south, to the north. Truly the Self is this whole universe. The man who sees and thinks and understands in this way has pleasure in the Self, plays with the Self, copulates with the Self, and has his joy with the Self: he becomes an independent sovereign. In every state of being freedom of movement is his.' (7, 25). The mystics are seeking this true Self. Thus Abu Yazid told the caller who was looking for Bayazid: 'I've been looking for him for thirty years without finding him,' and Schopenhauer answered the park-keeper's 'Who do you think you are?' with 'If only I knew!' Rumi has a magnificent poem on the finding of the Self in God.

> One went to the Beloved's door and
> knocked.
> A voice asked 'Who is there?'
> He answered 'I am.'
> The voice said 'There is no room for you
> and me.'
> The door was shut.
> After a year of lonely deprivation he
> returned and knocked.
> A voice from within asked 'Who is there?'
> The man said 'You are.'
> The door was opened for him.

So one of the RANTERS, Jacob Bauthumley, wrote in *The Light and Dark Sides of God*: 'If I say I see Thee, it is nothing but Thy seeing of Thyself; for there is nothing capable of seeing Thee but Thyself.'

Self-Realization Fellowship

Organization founded by Paramhansa Yogananda in 1920, with headquarters in Los Angeles and a hundred branches in three continents. Its object is the harmonizing of man's physical, mental and spiritual natures through yoga.

Seng-chao
(384–414)

Chinese Buddhist who drew together Buddhism with the TAO-TE-CHING and CHUANG-TZU. A mystic, he subordinated all else to the One, and held an advanced doctrine of meditation and contemplation. He was a master of paradox, who held that transcendental wisdom lay in the illuminating power of not-knowledge, and that the wise man in consequence is like an empty hollow, inactive in a world of apparent activity, living in a world which transcends speech amid all the noises around him. Seng-chao in many ways anticipates the doctrine of ZEN.

Seraphim of Sarov
(1759–1833)

Russian Christian mystic who spent fifteen years in a monastic community, withdrew for thirty years as an eremite, and returned in 1825 to human society, making his spiritual sensitivity and practical service available to all in need. His life is a classical pattern of withdrawal and return. Seraphim was an ascetic, but through his asceticism the note of joy rings loud and clear. He used the JESUS-PRAYER to help his contemplative life, and enjoyed the mystical vision of the divine uncreated Light. More, he received the Light into his own person, so that he became transfigured. One of his disciples, Nicholas Motovilov, was asking him how a man could be sure of being in the Spirit of God. Seraphim told him that they were both at that moment in the Spirit of God. The disciple found the light from Seraphim blinding. Seraphim testified that the disciple too was shining with splendour. Motovilov perceived the other's voice coming as from the sun, and the light spreading through the trees of the forest and the falling snow, and himself felt an immeasurable well-being, peace of soul and infinite joy in all his heart. Motovilov's account is one of the most impressive direct testimonies to spiritual experience.

Sex

Often the mysteries of the universe are expressed in sexual terms. This is natural, since sex is the obvious analogue of creative energy. So in China we have the YIN-YANG dualism, which may be paralleled in Indian thought by the dualism between *praktri* (nature, female) and *purusa* (spirit, male). In the TAOIST book *The Secret of the Golden Flower* the One, the Tao, produces *yin* and *yang*; from *yin* comes life, and the receptive female principle; from *yang* comes essence, and the creative male principle. A similar dichotomy can be found in numerous early cosmogonies from all over the world in which the cosmos is formed from the intercourse between the male power of the sky and the female power of the earth. In much Eastern thought cosmic sexuality and human sexuality are closely interrelated. The human act of love re-enacts the sacred marriage of heaven and earth, and Taoist sexology identifies thirty 'heaven-and-earth' postures. The artistic portrayal of the act of sexual union in Taoist or TANTRIC art is often accompanied by symbols giving it at the same time cosmic significance.

Many mystery-religions are based on a triple analogue. The image of sex reveals first the process of the initial formation of a cosmos, second, the present operation of the world we know (the fertilization of the land through river or rain) and third, from the past origin of life and the present continuation of life, the future promise of life beyond death. This is obviously strong in the Mediterranean mystery-religions, of ISIS AND OSIRIS, or DIONYSUS or ELEUSIS. We know that at Eleusis there was a call to the sky to rain and the earth to conceive, and that this was part of the revealed certainty of life beyond the grave, and that in the Dionysus mysteries there was a culminating revelation of a phallus.

Mystical writers often use sex as an image to express their mystical experience. The soul is identified with the woman. The experience is private and personal, joyful, receptive and ecstatic. So Macarius: 'Sometimes they are filled with a divine and intimate delight, like that of the bride when she rejoices in the presence of the bridegroom.' So too Bernard of Clairvaux spoke of Christ as his soul's bridegroom. *The Song of Songs* has much affected the imagery of Christian mysticism. The words often used of mystical experience, ravishing and rapture, are from the same root as 'rape'. François de Sales draws the parallel, though he calls the one good and exalting and the other base and degrading. There is a supreme example in sculpture in Bernini's portrayal of Teresa in ecstasy. Islamic mystics also use sexual imagery both in relation to the Prophet and even to Allah himself.

A Chinese cup of the Ch'ing dynasty showing a couple making love in the Taoist 'Autumn Days' position

See SPIRITUAL MARRIAGE, LOVE, MAITHUNA.

Shaftesbury, Anthony Ashley Cooper, 3rd Earl
(1671–1713)

British man of letters, forced to withdraw from politics through ill-health: Platonist philosopher; and author in 1707 of *A Letter concerning Enthusiasm* in which he declared that 'inspiration is a real feeling of the Divine Presence and enthusiasm a false one'.

Shakers

The United Society of Believers in Christ's Second Coming had its origins in a Quaker revival in England in 1747. Its founders were James and Jane Wardley. Jane Wardley preached the imminent Advent of Christ in the form of a woman. This preaching was heard with enthusiasm by a Manchester girl, Ann Lee, who joined in the proclamation. Their preaching was accompanied with spiritual exaltation, ecstasy and speaking with tongues. They were imprisoned for disturbing the peace: in prison Ann Lee had a visionary experience persuading her that she was the Bride of the Lamb, the female principle in Christ (Jesus being the male), the incorporation of the Second Coming. She became 'Mother Ann'. In 1774 she with a handful of others emigrated to America and settled at Watervliet near Albany. From there the numbers grew. The communities were communistic, pacifist, hardworking, temperate, and largely celibate. There was no salaried minister; there were many manifestations of ecstatic possession in worship which led to the name of Shakers. By the middle of this century only five communities and less than 100 members were left.

Shaiva Siddhanta

South Indian Hindu sect, honouring SHIVA as God. The souls of men are held in fetters, from which they are released by love of Shiva, who is the object of hymns of great personal devotion.

When You created me, You knew all about me.
I knew nothing of You. Only when Light
from You brought understanding of Your ways,
came knowledge. Now, wherever I sit,
or walk or stand, You are always close.
Can I forget you? You are mine, and I
am Yours and Yours alone. With my eyes I see,
with my heart realize that You are come
to me as lightning from a stormswept sky.

The path of salvation starts from self-discipline and meditation; at higher stages it depends on the guidance of a teacher; in the end enlightenment is by Grace of God. The soul is released from successive reincarnations, but is not wholly absorbed in God and retains its individuality.

Shakti

In Hindu thought, the power of creative energy, the female principle, spiritual power, personified as the divine female consort, often of SHIVA, and in some schools of Shaktism or Tantrism honoured through the act of sexual intercourse as a means of God-realization.

Shamanism

Strictly a religious phenomenon of Siberia and Central Asia, though the word has been widely used of similar practices in other parts of the world. The religious life of the community centres on the shaman, who is a master of ecstasy. But shamanism has a number of peculiar features. During his trance the shaman's soul is believed to leave his body and ascend to the sky or descend to the underworld; the shaman possesses and controls his spirits rather than being possessed by them; he holds special powers including magical flight and mastery over fire.

The profession of shaman is hereditary, but new shamans also appear through mystical vocation. Whether hereditary or not, the calling is ratified by a hysterical crisis and ecstasy, dreams and visions, and a sickness which seems to represent a death and resurrection. One shaman said that a prospective shaman must fall ill and have his body cut in pieces and his blood drunk by the spirit of dead shamans; and mystic dismemberment is a normal feature of initiation. Among the Eskimo the climax is QAUMANEQ or enlightenment, a mysterious light which the shaman suddenly feels inside himself enabling him to see in the dark. Sometimes there is an experience of spiritual marriage with a spirit of the opposite sex. The initiatory period often includes a rite of ascent, perhaps of a tree, which is linked with the power of flight. The first ecstasy is followed by a long period of training which is often also a means of communication with animals.

The shaman wears a complex costume, which is a whole symbolic system in itself. These vary in different parts, but they often include animal skins, and symbolic representations of different birds and animals (a wealthy Altaic shaman should have 1,070 'snakes' in his costume),

A Lapp shaman beating a painted drum to induce ecstasy (left) and being possessed by spirits (right)

apotropaic iron discs, mirrors to enhance the power of sight, symbols of the heavenly bodies, symbolic physical organs (a male shaman may appear with discs representing a woman's breasts) and above all a cap of power. Among his equipment are likely to be drums and bells, staves with horse-heads and weapons against the demons.

The shaman is a healer; he takes sacrifices to the sky or the underworld; he escorts the soul of the dead; he guards the spiritual health of society.

Shamanism has been the subject of an outstanding study by Mircea Eliade.

Shekhinah

In Jewish mysticism, the glory of God. In classical Jewish thought, the *Shekhinah* is never thought of as a feminine element in God; but the Kabbalists personify her as a woman, and indeed as the symbol of eternal womanhood, and she plays the part that Sophia plays in Gnostic thought. She is queen, daughter and bride of God, mother of every individual in Israel and, in the sufferings of Israel, Rachel weeping for her children.

Shelley, Percy Bysshe
(1792–1822)

English lyrical poet, who passed from atheism to a form of pantheism compounded of his own imagination playing over the natural world. Shelley speaks of a divine force in nature which

> Sweeps through the dull dense world,
> compelling there
> All new successions to the forms they wear.

Shelley, however, is not a NATURE-MYSTIC of the same colour as WORDSWORTH. He does not go to nature for charm and beauty, nor on the whole does he look outside nature to the transcendent. His reaction is emotional, not intellectual; there is no consistency in his doctrine. It is significant that he headed *Alastor* with words from Augustine: 'I was not yet loving; I was loving the state of loving, and in my love of the state of loving I was looking for something to love.' In *Adonais* he has a magnificent expression of Platonic mysticism:

> The One remains, the many change and pass;
> Heaven's light forever shines, Earth's
> shadows fly;
> Life, like a dome of many-coloured glass,
> Stains the white radiance of Eternity,
> Until Death tramples it to fragments. – Die,
> If thou wouldst be with that which thou dost
> seek.

Shelley was the subject of a percipient essay by the Catholic mystical poet Francis THOMPSON.

Shiflut

In Jewish mysticism, the humility which is essential to sainthood, without which there is no true love, and no experiences of mystical union.

Shiva

One of the three major gods of Hinduism, at once a destroyer and a saviour. He is regarded as a fertility power, with the lingam or phallus as his symbol. He is also characterized as the ascetic who keeps the world in existence by his meditation. He is the great God of the SHAIVA SIDDHANTA.

Shoichi Kokushi
(1202–80)

Japanese ZEN Master, educated in the more speculative anti-Zen Tendai school of Buddhism, and also in Confucianism. He was in China in 1235–41 studying Zen, and received the seal of the Mind. He was associated chiefly with the Tofokuji temple, south of Kyoto, where he introduced the pattern of Zen meditation.

Shugendo

Esoteric Japanese Buddhist sect, associated with mountains, and honouring the YAMABUSHI. Among the Shugendo the mountain is sacred, a meeting-place where the two worlds touch. Initiation is through the climbing of a mountain; the whole process is symbolical of passage through the Ten states of Existence. These are the Six Realms of the lower world, the world of transmigration (Hell, the Hungry Ghosts, The Animals, The Titans, human beings, the Gods); and above, the Four Holy States, of which the highest is complete enlightenment. In addition to the ceremonial climb there are many rites and practices associated with purification and escape from the lower realms. For Hell the appropriate act is 'weighing one's *karma* or active life', accompanied by confession; this was sometimes literally symbolized, the neophyte being swung out over a precipice with his hands tied on the scale pan of a gigantic balance. Fasting is the means of escape from the Realm of the Hungry Ghosts, abstinence from water was appropriate to the world of animals, wrestling to the Realm of Titans, repentance to the human world, and the dance of long life to the world of the Gods.

Siddhartha

See GAUTAMA.

Sikhism

World religion which sprang up in the Punjab in the early sixteenth century AD. It appears in measure as a reformist movement in Hinduism, and there remain important common features; but the development is distinct. Sikhism is compacted of three elements: the vision of its founder, Guru NANAK, the traditions of Punjab society and historical developments of nine other Gurus. The mystical elements are discussed under Guru NANAK.

Silence

'God is a silence rather than speech.' 'The most beautiful thing which one can say of God is silence in knowledge of God's inner riches. Do not be always talking about God.' 'Glory be to the Silence that spoke by the voice of the Logos.' 'The dog barks; the caravan passes.' 'He who knows does not speak; he who speaks does not know.' 'The Father uttered one Word; that Word is the Son, and He utters Him forever in everlasting silence; and in silence the soul has to hear it.' So the testimony comes from Spain and Arabia and India and China. There is something deeper still. Holiness distinguishes three degrees of silence – silence of the mouth, silence of the mind, and silence of the will. He who would hear the voice of God must practise all three.

Sixteen Revelations of Divine Love

An account of mystical experiences including a vision of Christ's wounds by an anchoress of Norwich, published in 1670.

Skovoroda, Grigori Savvitch

(1722–94)

Russian Christian visionary and mystical philosopher. His thought was influenced by Plato and the Church Fathers; perhaps also by Western Europe, where he travelled widely. A mystical ecstasy led to his conversion; he had a sense of complete union with God, as an undivided being on fire with God's love, circling round in space. The central principle of his philosophy is that the path to knowledge of God is knowledge of self; at the same time he is something of a pantheist, and at one point explicitly identifies nature and God.

Smith, John

(1618–57)

See CAMBRIDGE PLATONISTS.

Society of Friends

Body of Christians founded by George FOX; popularly known as Quakers. Friends are characterized by the doctrine of the INNER LIGHT, which leads to the rejection of many of the external observances associated with other Christians, such as a formal ministry, a formal liturgy, special sacraments, hymns, creeds and the like. Meetings are held in silence, waiting upon the Lord, except as members feel called to speak out loud. The sense of direct dependence on God's Spirit within is vital to Friends. It leads them in

An 18th-century American painting of a scene in a Quaker meeting house, with one of the Friends giving testimony

encounters with others to look towards that of God in every man. As with many other mystics, the experience of union with God leads to practical good works, and Friends have been noted for the integrity of their commercial dealings, for their philanthropy, for their pacifism, and for their active concern in such causes as prison-reform, world peace and the abolition of slavery. The Society of Friends is perhaps the most remarkable demonstration in history of the availability of mystical experience to groups of open but otherwise ordinary people.

Socrates
(469–399 BC)

Socrates was an Athenian, son of a stonemason, whose profession he followed physically, and of a midwife, whose profession he followed spiritually, claiming to help others to give birth to the thoughts that were in them. Socrates was associated with the New Enlightenment. At one time he was interested in scientific developments, but increasingly asked Why? rather than How? When the Delphic Oracle called him the wisest man in Greece he started quizzing others with a reputation for wisdom and exposing their pretensions. He was wise because he knew his own ignorance. So he did not teach, and his associates moved intellectually in vastly different directions. PLATO took off from Socrates, but the philosophy he put into Socrates's mouth was his own answer to Socrates's questions. Socrates was a supreme rationalist, with the courage to trust reason to the end. But he was also a mystic, who experienced a divine sign or *daimonion*, which was a voice within warning him against particular courses of action. He was condemned to death, nominally for religious innovation and corrupting the youth, but actually for his criticisms of the democracy; and his divine sign would not let him escape from prison.

A Greek portrait sculpture of Socrates

Solomon Ben Gabirol
(*c.* 1021–58)

Spanish poet and Jew, mystical theologian, also known as Avicebron. He was the intermediary between Judaism and Platonic philosophy for his day, as Philo had been a thousand years before. His book *The Source of Life* was immensely influential. All created things are constituted of form and matter. The Godhead, which is the primal Being alone, is not so compounded. The Godhead has no attributes, but matter or substance emanates from God as Being, and form from God as Will: Being and Will are aspects, not attributes, of God. God reveals Himself, but in His own Being is unknowable.

Soloviev, Vladimir
(1853–1900)

Russian Christian mystical philosopher, who tried to draw together the Christian doctrine of the Incarnation with the pantheistic ideas of German philosophy, and found in WISDOM, identified with Plato's world-soul, the principle of unity between God and the world. The cosmos was for him thus a living organism. Equally important was his 'theanthropy'; he revived the doctrine that salvation consists in the spiritual transformation of human to 'divine-human'.

Soma

Plant used in ancient India and Iran as the source of an invigorating drug, ritually drunk by the worshipper, 'the drink of immortality', found also in India as the name of a deity.

Song of Songs, The

Book of love poems, dating from Hellenistic Judaism, but attributed to Solomon, and appearing in the Canon of the Old Testament. Rabbi

The marriage of Christ and the Church in an illuminated initial (O) from Bede's Commentary on the Song of Songs

Akiba protested against its literal interpretation, and it has been a major quarry for mystics seeking to use the language of love to interpret the relations of God and the soul, from DIONYSIUS the Areopagite onwards. The high-water mark of such interpretations is to be found in BERNARD OF CLAIRVAUX's eighty-six homilies on the theme.

Sophia

Greek term for WISDOM; in Hellenistic Judaism an intermediary between God and man, and an important character in GNOSTIC mythology.

Soto

See FIVE HOUSES

Soul-loss

Term used by anthropologists for the view among many peoples that trance is caused by the withdrawal of the subject's soul.

Speaking with tongues

The utterance, in prayer and worship, of sounds expressing profound emotion. It is found in early Christianity on the Day of Pentecost (Acts 2) and in the church at Corinth, where Paul ranks it low among the spiritual gifts, and discourages it unless the speech can be interpreted to others (1 Cor. 12; 14). In the twentieth century it is particularly associated with PENTECOSTAL churches. Speaking with tongues is said to include sometimes speech in a language never consciously learned by the speaker; it also gives room for prayer in a 'non-rational, meditative language'.

Spinoza, Baruch
(1632–77)

Born in Amsterdam of Portuguese parents, Spinoza grew up in the Jewish faith, but was expelled for unorthodoxy. He is the leading philosopher of PANTHEISM in the West. God is infinite substance, and His attributes are infinite, though human beings can recognize only thought and extension. All individual objects are modes of these two. The human mind is a part of the workings of the divine Mind. There is no personal God, no immortal soul, no free will. The highest satisfaction of the human mind is *amor Dei intellectualis*, the intellectual love of God. 'And this intellectual love of the mind towards God is the very love of God with which God loves himself, not in so far as he is infinite, but in so far as he can be expressed by the essence of the human mind, considered under the form of eternity; that is, the intellectual love of the mind toward God is a part of the infinite love with which God loves himself.' God is the alpha and omega of his philosophy; Novalis described him as 'God-intoxicated'.

Baruch Spinoza

Spirit-possession

See POSSESSION.

Spiritual exercises

Spiritual exercises play in personal devotion the part which liturgy plays in public worship. They are part of the training of the soul for mystical experiences. One example of spiritual exercise is the MANTRA in various forms: in the Christian tradition John Cassian recommends a verse of a psalm, and *The Cloud of Unknowing* the alternation of the words *sin* and *God*; in Islam it is the DHIKR. Another is concentration on a symbolic object; lotus or crucifix; or meditation on God's attributes or some scene in the life of a saint or avatar (in Christianity often Christ's passion). A third is Brother LAWRENCE'S PRACTICE OF THE PRESENCE OF GOD. Love to the neighbour may itself be a spiritual exercise. Fasting, asceticism and deprivation have been so used. YOGA offers a whole range of spiritual exercises. In Buddhism two vital exercises are called the Way of Tranquillity, tranquillizing the mind by checking discursive thinking; and the Way of Wisdom, the constant application of insights received. Spiritual exercises are means to an end, but they do not inevitably secure that end, and if they lead to spiritual pride they will not do so.

Spiritual marriage

In TERESA DE JESUS's analysis, the highest stage of mystic union. It is marked by a sense of permanence. Teresa herself says, 'Unless the soul first deserts God, I believe He will never fail to make her sensible of His presence'. So Mary of the

Incarnation (1600–72) called the spiritual marriage her 'vested and permanent state'. It is marked also by a sense of transformation. Juan de la Cruz says that the soul 'becomes immediately enlightened by and transformed in God', and again that the spiritual marriage is 'beyond all comparison a far higher state than that of espousals, because it is a complete transformation into the Beloved'. Ruysbroeck, though his analysis of his experience is cooler, wrote of *The Spiritual Espousals* and of *The Adornment of the Spiritual Marriage*. Spiritual marriage is thus participation in the divine Life.

In Christian thought the idea of Spiritual Marriage goes back to Origen's allegorical interpretation of *The Song of Songs*. It passed to the Latin-speaking world through Jerome and Rufinus. It is found in Augustine and Gregory, but scarcely becomes common before BERNARD OF CLAIRVAUX. Bernard's mysticism of love naturally gave it wide currency. In the seventh chapter of *The Grades of Humility* he presents an account of the marriage between the soul-bride and her divine lover. The divine action, through humility and charity, has made the soul spotless. Reason is no longer preoccupied with itself, the will and reason no longer in conflict, and the Father joins Himself without more ado to His bride. More often the Word is the soul's Bridegroom. Sometimes Bernard uses the language of rape, the violent destruction of the soul's false selfishness.

There seems no doubt that mystics in the height of mystical union experience a sensation of being embraced with a kind of spiritual sexuality. Thus Gerson says, 'The object of mystic theology is an experimental knowledge of God in the embrace of unitive love.' Generally God is seen as the Bridegroom, the soul as the bride. So Sandaeus: 'The mystic union is an experimental and direct perception of God by a secret embrace; a mutual kiss between God, who is the Bridegroom, and the soul-bride', or Denys the Carthusian: 'When the soul has purified herself, when she burns with the fire of charity, when she shines by reason of her virtues, God takes His pleasure greatly in her. He holds her familiarly like a lovely bride clasping her, caressing her, embracing her, and communicating His blessings to her abundantly', or Thomas Aquinas: 'The soul, in the preceding stages, loves and is loved in return; she seeks and is sought; she calls and is called. But in this, in an admirable and ineffable way, she lifts and is lifted up; she holds and is herself held; she clasps and she is closely embraced, and by the bond of love she unites herself to God, one with one, alone with Him.'

Sometimes however the mystics edge away from the overt sexuality of the image. So Angela of Foligno: 'Never can father or mother embrace their child, nor any person embrace another with so much love as God Almighty embraces the rational soul.' There is a fascinating passage from TERESA DE JESUS's *Conceptions of the Love of God* (4) in which she oscillates between God as husband, wife and mother: 'When this most opulent Spouse is pleased to enrich and more eminently to caress souls, He so converts them into Himself that, as a person swooning through excessive delight and pleasure, the soul seems to herself to be suspended in those divine arms and to rest on that divine side and those divine breasts; and does nothing but enjoy, being sustained with divine milk with which her Spouse goes feeding her. . . . She sees herself . . . caressed by Him who knows how and is able to do it; she does not know what to compare it to, except the caress of a mother who loving her baby tenderly, nurses and fondles him in this way.'

Indian temple sculpture of a couple in sexual intercourse symbolizing the use of physical ecstasy to attain the spiritual

In some mysticisms and mystery-religions the spiritual union is expressed through physical union. A good example of this is the Tantric MAITHUNA, where the mystical nature of the union is shown in the fact that there must be no ejaculation of semen. The concept of the Sacred Marriage (*hieros gamos*) was important in ancient Greek religion; it was the union of sky and earth. Human union might be used as a means to promoting cosmic fertility. Ritual prostitution is found in one form or another widely in the eastern Mediterranean in classical times, on Cyprus and along the coast of Palestine, for example. In Armenia the daughters of the aristocracy regularly served a period as temple prostitutes of Anaitis before their marriage. At Tralles in Lydia one Aurelia Aemilia records proudly on an inscription her service and that of her mother and other ancestors. The experience itself was of a kind of mystical identity with the goddess. At Corinth there was a large company of sacred prostitutes attached to the temple of Aphrodite. In 464 BC a wealthy citizen named Xenophon dedicated in thanksgiving twenty-five girls to her service. Pindar wrote a hymn for the occasion: he says that the goddess has received a hundred new limbs:

> Hospitable girls, attendants
> on Beguilement in rich Corinth
> you who sacrifice the amber tears of fresh
> frankincense, often soaring in your souls to
> Aphrodite,
> heavenly Mother of loves.

But the great area for temple prostitution has been India; in the service of Shiva or Vishnu the priestesses are honoured as 'brides of God', and the dancing-girls attached to many temples were engaged in a religious service of ecstasy and fertility. No doubt in some mystery-religions the drama of the sacred marriage was re-enacted before the initiates.

The concept of the spiritual marriage is used all over the world to express the relationship between a spirit and the inspired human. Thus in Ethiopia the *zar*-initiate is called a bride and given two 'best men' to help in difficulties with her spiritual husband. In voodoo in Haiti men and women contract spiritual marriages with one of the *loa*; there are ceremonial marriages with marriage certificates, and a bed may even be made up for the spiritual partner. Among the Saora of Orissa dedication of the inspired priest is celebrated by marriage with a female spirit; the marriage may produce spiritual offspring; on death the priest leaves his earthly partner for his heavenly one. Among the Akawaio of Guyana the inspired human has the swallow-tailed kite as his spiritual partner. Among the Chukchee of the Arctic the male shaman often has a spirit-wife; but the women shamans have more difficulty, since their spirit-partners dislike child-birth, and leave them during the process. Similar beliefs are widespread in Asia and Africa.

See also LOVE, SEX.

Spiritual senses

Mystical symbolism (*see* SYMBOL) naturally expresses mystical experience through the analogy of sensory experience, and though some interpreters prefer to speak of a sixth sense, through which there is the direct apprehension of things divine, and though one or two of the mystics, like Bonaventura, use vision as the single expression of spiritual experience, in general the mystics speak of five spiritual senses corresponding with the five physical senses. A famous passage from Augustine's *Confessions* (10, 6) illustrates this well: 'When I love You, what am I loving? Not the beauty of a physical body, not the attractiveness of the season, not the brilliance of a light which our eyes love so well, not the charming melodies of songs of all kinds, not the sweet fragrance of flowers or scents or spices, not manna or honey, not limbs asking for physical embrace: when I love my God, it is not these that I love. Yet I do love a kind of light, a kind of sound, a kind of scent, a kind of food, a kind of embrace, in loving my God, the light, sound, scent, food and embrace of my inner man, where a light shines in my soul which space cannot contain, a melody rings which time cannot snatch away, a scent breathes which no wind can scatter, there is a savour which eating does not diminish, and an embrace which is not broken by satiety. When I love my God, it is this that I am loving.'

Of these the language of sight predominates. The ultimate experience is called the BEATIFIC VISION. Dante speaks of this vision as of a tri-coloured circle, but soon withdraws into the inadequacy of any language, and in the end cannot say more than that he has seen. Angela of Foligno says 'I beheld God . . . I beheld a beauty so great that I can say nothing concerning it, save that I saw the Supreme Beauty which contains within itself all goodness.' The language of light predominates (*see* LIGHT): it is enough here to note Walter Hilton's 'God is light, that is, God is truth and verity itself, for verity is spiritual light'. This language is common to mystics in all ages and of all creeds.

The language of hearing is also frequent. Sometimes it has to do with the voice of God. Here TERESA DE JESUS puts forward an important sign for distinguishing the voice of God from other voices: the words of God effect what they signify. Whereas vision often expresses awareness of the presence and being of God, hearing more often expresses ethical and moral commandments – 'Thus saith the Lord'. It is, says Farges, the most 'instructive' of the spiritual senses (though not always). Thus Hilton: 'The privy voice of Jesus, is full true, and it maketh a soul true . . . When it soundeth in a soul, it is of so great power sometimes, that the soul suddenly layeth aside all that was in hand . . . and listeneth thereto fully, hearing and perceiving in rest and in love the sweet sound of this spiritual voice, as it were, ravished from the mind of all earthly things, and then in this quiet, Jesus sometimes shareth Himself as an awful Master, and sometimes as a reverend Father, and sometimes as a lovely Spouse' (3, 14). Sometimes however the object heard is not a voice but a melody or harmony of sounds, in the Pythagorean-Platonic tradition the music of the spheres. Here is a passage from Sikh traditions about the heart where God dwells: 'The five forms of music resound in that happy house; in that happy house into which God has infused His might, the strains resound.'

The language of smell is less frequently used than the others. But the language of *The Song of Songs* led Christian mystics along this path: 'I will hie me to the mountains of myrrh and the hill of frankincense' (4, 6), 'Blow upon my gardens, let its fragrance be wafted abroad' (4, 16), 'His cheeks are the beds of spices, yielding fragrance, his lips are lilies, distilling liquid myrrh' (5, 13). So Teresa says of the prayer of quiet that it is 'as if some very sweet ointment were injected into the most intimate part of the soul, after the manner of an exquisite perfume'. So Cassian: 'It frequently happens, in the divine visits, that we are filled with perfumes, of a sweetness unknown to human skill; so that the soul, overwhelmed with delight, is lifted into a rapture and forgets that she is living in the flesh.'

So also with the language of taste. Here too there is a key text for Jewish and Christian mystics: 'O taste and see how gracious the Lord is' (Ps. 34, 8). Hugh of St Victor, for example says, 'To attain to God is to seek him incessantly by desire, to find him by knowledge, and to touch him by taste.' Often the language of taste is there indirectly in the thought of God as the food and drink of the faithful. The mystics are continually speaking of the sweetness of mystical union after the bitterness of sin, or the refreshment of the presence of God after the arid draught of being without Him.

Touch is sometimes described as the coarsest of the corporeal senses and the most delicate of the spiritual senses. In prayer, in the approach, to God, the soul is said to touch a spiritual substance and be touched by it again. So Juan de la Cruz speaks of ecstasy as a sublime touching of the holy and divine substance, and Ruysbroeck, describing the experience of union, says, 'We feel that we touch and are touched, that we love and are loved.' There are two forms which the sensation of spiritual touch commonly takes. One is the sense of being immersed. So Tauler: 'The spirit is submerged and absorbed in the depths of the divine ocean, so that we can exclaim: God is in me, God is outside of me, God is everywhere round about me.' The other is grounded in the analogy of sexual union, and is expressed in the language of the embrace or kiss.

See also SEX, SPIRITUAL MARRIAGE.

ŠT3

Ancient Egyptian word designating mystery. It has a secular meaning indicating anything hidden, difficult or unusual. Religiously it is used of the shaped earth-mould symbolizing the rising of the dead Osiris, and used frequently in funeral-texts of the secrets of the after-life, and the deeper wisdom a man attains through death.

Steger, Jane

See MONTAGUE, MARGARET PRESCOTT.

Steiner, Rudolph

(1861–1925)

Founder of ANTHROPOSOPHY, he blended together science and literature in his education, and combined a wide-ranging and scholarly intellect with a fantastic imagination. In 1902 he became a leading Theosophist, but moved away from them partly because he seems to have had no belief in a god; and in 1913 formed the Anthroposophical Society. He was a lecturer of considerable persuasive power; his aim was to liberate the spiritual potential of ordinary people.

St Francis receiving the stigmata, as painted by Giotto

Stigmata

When Jesus was crucified his body bore five wounds, two in the hands, two in the feet, and one in the side. Paul had written of himself: 'I bear the marks (*stigmata*) of the Lord Jesus in my body' (Gal. 6, 17). Mediaeval devotion brought these two passages together, and sought to be identified with them.

The most famous example of stigmatization is FRANCIS OF ASSISI. There are however two or three examples from earlier in the thirteenth century. Where the records are traceable the wounds seem to have been deliberately caused, either as a means to closer identification with Jesus, or for deliberate deception.

The evidence relating to Francis is impressive. Brother Elias wrote immediately after Francis's death, 'I announce to you great joy, even a new miracle. From the beginning of ages there has not been heard so great a wonder, save only in the Son of God, who is Christ our God. For, a long while before his death' – the reading here is a little uncertain – 'our Father and Brother appeared crucified, bearing in his body the five wounds which are in truth the Stigmata of Christ, for his hands and feet had as it were piercings made by nails fixed in from above and below, which laid open the scars and had the black appearance of nails; while his side appeared to have been lanced, and blood often trickled from it.' Our evidence is that Francis received the stigmata in an ecstatic vision, and that he was exceedingly reluctant to display them. We thus have good evidence that the physical marks were there (evidence from others besides Brother Elias), that it is unlikely that they were physically inflicted, and that they appeared during a mystical experience.

During the Second World War a man had been brutally treated by the Nazis, cruelly bound hand and foot, and left for dead. He was rescued by the Americans, nursed back to physical health, but was still a nervous wreck. He was put under hypnosis and asked to project himself back into his prison camp experiences. The deep weals of the ropes appeared on his wrists and ankles. Probably along these lines we may apprehend the physical results of mystical experience. The intense mystical identification with Jesus led to the physical appearance of the actual wounds.

There have been other stigmatics since Francis, mostly in conscious or unconscious emulation of him. Sometimes the wounds were physically caused. Even here mystical experience may be involved. Lukardis of Oberweimar (*c.* 1276–1309) in ecstasy would strike her palms with her finger and her feet with her toe, and in her ecstatic state her members took on the rigidity and piercing quality of a nail, as one onlooker found who tried to put his own hand in the way. Some of the later experiences are associated with the marks of the crown of thorns as well as the nails and spear. A number of examples bear the marks of, and some have been exposed as, deliberate imposture. But some, notably Domenica Lazzari of the Tyrol (1815–48), cannot be so explained, and are supported by excellent medical testimony. Here again there seems to have been some kind of religious ecstasy leading to a self-identification with Jesus which came out in physical form, to the great pain of the person concerned. Altogether there have been over 300 recorded instances of stigmatization.

One important feature of stigmatization is that it obviously takes place only within an awareness of the Christian story. Mystical experiences can be paralleled from one religion to another, but their exact form is influenced by the pattern of religious belief already held by the mystic.

Stoicism

Ancient Greek philosophy, initiated by Zeno (335–263 BC), developed in a religious and ethical direction by Cleanthes (331–232 BC) and monumentally synthesized by Chrysippus (*c.* 280–207 BC). Stoicism is one of the main European examples of PANTHEISM. Ironically one of the clearest expositions of Stoicism was penned by the Christian poet Alexander Pope in *An Essay on Man*:

> All are but part of one stupendous whole,
> Whose body, Nature is, and God the soul;

Zeno. Roman copy of a Greek original sculpture

> That chang'd thro' all, and yet in all the same,
> Great in the earth, as in th' aethereal frame,
> Warms in the sun, refreshes in the breeze,
> Glows in the stars, and blossoms in the trees,
> Lives thro' all life, extends thro' all extent,
> Spreads undivided, operates unspent,
> Breathes in our soul, informs our mortal part,
> As full, as perfect, in a hair as heart;
> As full, as perfect, in vile Man that mourns,
> As the rapt Seraph that adores and burns;
> To him no high, no low, no great, no small;
> He fills, he bounds, connects, and equals all.

God, who is all in all, may be called by many names. Often he is called Zeus or Jupiter. But the Roman Stoic Seneca writes: 'Every name is his. Would you call him Fate? You will not err. He it is on whom all things depend, the cause of causes. Would you call him Providence? You will be right. He it is whose thought provides for the universe that it may move on its course unhurt and do its part. Would you call him Nature? You will not speak amiss. He it is of whom all things are born, by whose breath we live. Would you call him Universe? You will not be deceived. He himself is this whole that you see, fills his own parts, sustains himself and what is his.' Sometimes he is called Reason or LOGOS. The Stoics took up a hint from HERACLITUS, adapted it, and in so doing passed on an idea of great significance for Jewish, Christian and Gnostic mysticism. Among the Stoics one important aspect of this is the concept of generative Reason, the Ultimate considered as creative power. A further identity of the Ultimate is with primal fire, from which all comes and to which all returns.

The omnipresence of God means that God is in man and it is there that we should seek for Him. So Seneca says 'God comes to man – no, nearer still, he comes into man. No mind is good without God. Divine seeds are sown in human bodies,' and again: 'God is near you, with you, within you. I say it, Lucilius, a holy spirit has his seat within us, spectator of our good and evil, and our guardian.' So Epictetus: 'You bear him in yourself and fail to see that you are defiling him with your impure thoughts and filthy acts. In the presence even of an image of God you would not have dared to do any of the things you do. But in the presence of God himself within you, who sees and hears all things you are not ashamed of your desires and acts.' So the wistful half-agnostic Stoic emperor, Marcus Aurelius, speaks of the true self as an emanation from God, a fragment of Zeus, an efflux of the Logos that orders the whole, the god within.

The life to which man is called is thus a life of acceptance. All is in the hands of God, for all is God. All we have to do is to live in accordance with nature, that is in accordance with the Logos, with Reason. There is a concept here closely parallel to that of the TAO. We may be cast for the role of emperor like Marcus Aurelius, or slave like Epictetus. Both are in the providence of God – and we can do nothing about either. Cleanthes put it in a famous hymn:

> Lead me, O Zeus, and thou, O Destiny,
> Lead thou me on,
> To whatsoever task thou sendest me,
> Lead thou me on.
> I follow fearless, or, if in mistrust
> I lag and will not, follow still I must.
>
> *(tr. C. F. Angus)*

All else is a matter of indifference, save only virtue. The Stoics reinforced this teaching with a series of paradoxes. You are either a spiritual king or a spiritual slave. He who offends in one point is guilty of the whole law. If you are not a sage (as they called their saints), you are a fool.

Stoicism thus tended to breed a kind of spiritual complacency. But the doctrine of living according to Nature had an important effect in humanizing the legal system. And there is something moving in Epictetus, 'a lame old man' (as he describes himself) seeing his only purpose as to make his life a hymn of praise to God.

Sudden illumination

ZEN doctrine. The object of Zen is to focus the mind on that which is real. The correction of false vision may require long and careful preparation, but as long as we are out of focus, however fractionally, our vision is blurred. At the moment when true focus is attained, Reality dawns on us, whole and complete. HUI HAI has a treatise on sudden illumination; he defines it as a 'sudden means of ridding yourself of deluded thoughts instantaneously'.

Sufism

Mystical movement in Islam, with affinities with the Christian monastic movement. The Sufis wore clothes of wool (*suf*) in token of penitence. Sufism is thus mysticism on the basis of monotheism.

In the *Risala*, written in 1046, al-Qushairi wrote a defence of Sufism. He claimed that it did not depart at all from the orthodoxy of Islam. He defended this by a series of sketches of Sufi saints, starting from IBRAHIM BEN ADHAM. He then proceeded to explain some of the language used by the Sufis, drawing out the distinction between *maqam*, a station or stage of spiritual attainment, and *hal*, a spiritual state granted by God. The first is of merit, the second of grace. But al-Qushairi does not mark the distinction rigidly.

The stations are conversion; earnest striving after the mystical life (a spiritualization of the *jihad* or holy war); withdrawal; awe of God; abstinence; renunciation; silence (the Greek 'speak words of good omen' was an injunction to silence); fear; hope; sorrow (for sin); hunger (discipline of appetite); humility; rejection of the 'flesh', especially envy and slander; contentment; trust in God; gratitude; faith; patience; the practice of the presence of God; satisfaction. This concludes the stations proper, but the list is somewhat extended: servanthood; desire (i.e. right desire); uprightness (some certainly would regard this as a state); sincerity (almost single-mindedness in devotion to God); truthfulness; shame; a free spirit; remembrance (of God); brotherhood to fellow-Moslems; insight (another state, it would seem); moral probity; generosity; jealousy (in the Biblical sense); sainthood (another state, literally being under God's care); prayer; poverty; purity; good manners. Here the states and stations seem to blur and blend. But we are clearly not yet done with the stations, for the next four are: travel; companionship; true belief in the One God; noble dying. Finally we have the three gifts and graces which are clearly states: knowledge (the Christian and sub-Christian *gnosis*); love (which is kindled by God's love); yearning (for God).

This is a complex analysis, but it is needful to see how complex it can be. For mysticism is not to be lightly undertaken. And the distinction between stations and states is basic to Sufism. A simpler analysis was given by al-Sarraj, who identified seven stations (conversion, abstinence, renunciation, poverty, patience, trust in God, satisfaction) and ten states (meditation, nearness to God, love, fear, hope, longing, intimacy, tranquillity, contemplation, certainty).

The Sufis had four great orders or Ways. The first, the Qadiriyya, became especially influential in the Indian subcontinent; it was noted for a stringent orthodoxy, combined with devotional exercises directed to religious experience. The second, the Suhrawardiyya, was also influential in India; here the orthodoxy was less stringent, and there was a tendency to pantheism. The third, the Shadhiliyya, spread in Egypt and North Africa; its members were noted for their devotional practices, and especially for their sense of utter dependence on God ('O God, seek me out of Thy Mercy that I may come to Thee; and draw me on with Thy Grace that I may turn to Thee'). The fourth, and in many ways the most interesting, was the Mevlevi order founded by the poet Rumi, with their famous whirling dance. There have been many others, but these stand supreme. The orders did much to bring isolated mystics into community with one another, and to preserve their experience and traditions.

Sufism is characterized by asceticism ('Sufism means an empty hand and a good heart'; 'Sufism has three basic traits: to embrace poverty, to show disinterested generosity and to abandon the will to interfere'; 'The Sufi possesses nothing and is possessed by nothing'), non-attachment ('Sufism is to be freed from the contemplation of the world of becoming'; compare the last quotation), purity ('Sufism is the purity of nearness to God supervening on the corruption of alienation'; 'The Sufi is defiled by nothing; rather does he purify everything'), closeness to God ('The Sufis prefer God to all else, as God prefers them to all else'; 'Sufism is to sit in God's presence without external cares'; 'Sufism means that God should cause you to die to yourself and to live to him').

Sufi teaching involves meaning at multiple levels. This can well be exemplified by Hujwiri's chapter on patched clothes. Immediately it is a reference to simple, austere, appropriately ascetic wear. But the Arabic root can provide an allusion to folly (the Sufi's behaviour is folly to worldly wisdom), carelessness (the Sufi is indifferent to worldly concerns), inebriation (a common metaphor for mystical ecstasy), the highest Heaven, a chessboard (some meeting-houses had a chequered floor: the interplay of light and darkness), hitting a target, producing epigrammatic wisdom, and repairing a well (the well of truth). The NASRUDIN stories offer similar examples of multiple-level meaning.

A famous and characteristic story tells how a Sufi was asked, 'Where do you come from?' 'From the Beloved.' 'Where are you going?' 'Near the Beloved.' 'What do you want?' 'To meet the Beloved.' 'What is your food?' 'The recollection of the Beloved.' 'What is your drink?' 'Longing for the Beloved.' 'What do you wear?' 'The veil of the Beloved.' 'Why is your face so pale?' 'Because of separation from the Beloved.' 'How long are you going to go on saying "The Beloved – the Beloved"?' 'Until I see the Face of the Beloved.'

A Persian dictionary contains the entry 'What is a Sufi?' 'A Sufi is a Sufi.' This is itself a mystical expression. 'He is a day that needs no sun, and a night that needs no moon or star, and a not-being that needs no being.'

For individual Sufis *see* ANSAR, ATTAR, DHU ʿL-NUN, AL-GHAZALI, AL-HALLAJ, IBN ʿARABI, IBN AL-FARID, IBRAHIM, JAMI, AL-JILI, AL-JUNAID, AL-MUHASIBI, ʿOMAR, RABIA, RUMI, SAʿDI. *See also* NASRUDIN, TASAWWUF.

Sulpician method

Method of meditation developed in the Society of Saint-Sulpice in Paris, based on the approach of J.-J. OLIER, particularly as developed in the last part of the seventeenth century by the third Superior General, L. Tronson. It is simpler and less intellectual than the other well-known method associated with IGNATIUS, FRANÇOIS DE SALES and PETER OF ALCANTARA. The Sulpicians have no special guidance about preparation, which will follow the normal practices of mortification, and recollection of God's presence. The meditation itself, which is specifically Christian, consists of three seemingly simple acts of Adoration (Jesus before the eyes), Communion (Jesus in the heart) and Co-operation (Jesus in the hands). The soul draws near to Jesus, opens itself to him, submits its active will to his.

Sundar Singh, Sadhu
(*c.* 1889–1930)

Sundar Singh was brought up a Sikh, but himself said 'I was not a Sikh, but a seeker – after Truth.' He was seeking Peace, in the sacred books of the Sikhs, the Hindus, the Moslems. He turned to the Bible, and it repelled him. Then at 4·30 am on 18 December 1904, he was praying, and suddenly the room was filled with a blaze of light, and he saw a vision of Jesus Christ in glory and love, saying to him in Hindustani, 'How long will you persecute me? I have come to save you; you were praying to know the right way. Why do you not take it?' With that he became a Christian, and renounced all possessions. He took Francis of Assisi as his model, but felt no impulse to form an order. His life was passed in prayer and preaching. He had a continuous sense of the presence of God, as well as a succession of vivid Christ-centred visions: 'Wherever I go there it is the same. Christ is always in the centre, a figure ineffable and indescribable. His face shining like the sun, but in no way dazzling, and so sweet that without any difficulty I can gaze at it – always smiling a loving glorious smile.' Christ, he said, 'is not the supreme mystic. He is the Master of mystics, the Saviour of mystics.' He never sought ecstasy; when it came it overwhelmed him. In it he experienced three heavens, Heaven on earth, the intermediate state of Paradise, and the true

Heaven. He described ecstasy: 'There are pearls in the sea, but to get them you have to dive to the bottom. Ecstasy is a dive to the bottom of spiritual things. It is not a trance; but it is like a dive, because, as a diver has to stop breathing, so in Ecstasy the outward senses must be stopped.' Sundar Singh insisted that every man has the capacity for religion, and prayer and meditation are for all; it is for God to grant ecstasy. He also insisted that visionary experience must lead to active service.

Sundar Singh is of particular importance, partly as a twentieth-century mystic, who was able to discuss his experiences with a high measure of objectivity, partly because of the way in which he bridges Hindu and Christian mystical experience, partly because he seems never to have experienced the Dark Night of the Soul.

In 1929 he disappeared into the Himalayas.

Sunyata

Buddhist term for the Void, that which is beyond cause, thought or conception, the object of mystical knowledge.

Superessential life

Term used by RUYSBROECK for MYSTIC UNION.

Supernatural state

See MYSTICAL STATE.

Surin, Jean Joseph
(1600–65)

French mystic, who joined the Jesuit order in 1616. In 1636 he was involved in the exorcism of the 'devils of Loudun', and for the next twenty years was subject to great spiritual tribulation from which he emerged into mystical exaltation. His spiritual teaching was directed to the necessity of a suffering self-sacrifice, the practice of the presence of God, and contemplative prayer leading to the overpowering of the soul by the love of God.

Suso, Henry
(*c.* 1295–1366)

More familiar form of the name of Heinrich Seuse, who entered the Dominican order at the age of thirteen, and lived most of his life by Lake Constance. At the age of eighteen he began to call himself the Servant of the Eternal Wisdom; his mystical experiences date from this point. He records the first of these. He went alone into the church on the Feast of St Agnes in the middle of the day, in considerable distress of spirit. Suddenly his soul was rapt in his body, or out of his body. What he saw and heard was inexpressible; he describes it as a Shining Brightness, a manifestation of the sweetness of Eternal Life in the sensations of silence and of rest; 'If this is not heaven, I do not know what heaven is.' It was an experience of joy and fulfilment, and it lasted between half an hour and an hour. When he came to himself he was in physical agony, but inside he was, in his own words, walking on air.

There followed a period of hair-raising asceticism. At some point in the 1320s he worked with Meister ECKHART, whom he always defended as the saintly or beloved Master. His first work, *The Little Book of Truth*, is an exposition of Eckhart's teaching in dialogue form. He returned to Constance, and somewhere about 1335 gave up the mortification of the flesh: he had now reached the stage of 'perfect resignation'. He was now an itinerant preacher, pastor of souls, leader of the FRIENDS OF GOD. He had to face hardship, opposition, scandal, but ended his life in peace.

Suso has a fine description of the ultimate entry into the joy of the Lord. It is an experience like intoxication. Consciousness of selfhood vanishes, human desires fall away. The divine Will is all. Those who experience this are changed to another form, the divine Nature and the divine Being, to another glory, the radiance of the inaccessible Light, to another power, achieved through union with the divine Personality.

Suso had a remarkable visual imagination: he could *see* the scenery of Heaven and its occupants. In one of his visions Jesus's mother allowed him to hold the Holy Child: 'He contemplated its beautiful little eyes, he kissed its tender little mouth, and gazed again and again at the infant member of the heavenly treasure. Then, lifting up his eyes, he uttered a cry of amazement that He who bears up the heavens is so small, so beautiful in heaven, and so childlike on earth.' One of his most magnificent visions brings together all creation in praise of God: 'I set before the eyes of my soul myself, all that I am, with body, soul, and all my powers, and set around me all creatures which God ever created in heaven, in earth, and in all the elements, each with its name, were it birds of the air, beasts of the forest, fish of the waters, leaf and grass of the earth, and all the unnumbered sand of the sea, and therewith all the little motes which shine in the sunbeam, and all the little drops of water, of dew, and snow, and rain, which ever fell or have fallen, and wished that each of them had a sweet instrument of music made ready out of my heart's innermost chords, and thus forth-sounding from first to last, should bring to the beloved tender God new and glorious praise.'

One of his most interesting passages describes how in early days he shut himself up in a spiritual entrenchment. He marked out three circles in his imagination. The first was his own cell, the second the monastery buildings, the third the circle of the outer gate. If his concentration remained in his own cell he was secure; if he allowed it to range beyond the gate of the monastery, he was like a hunted animal.

The object of Suso's mystical love is the Eternal Wisdom; he is a Christian, and for him the Eternal Wisdom is identified with Christ. He calls himself the Servant of the Eternal Wisdom, and his love for the Eternal Wisdom is the thread on which the beads of his work are strung.

Suso is perhaps the most poetic of all Western mystics. He has been called 'the last of the Minnesinger', and *The Little Book of Eternal Wisdom* remains perhaps the most attractive of all mystical treatises.

Suzuki, Daisetz Teitaro
(1870–1966)

Japanese ZEN scholar, who played a major part through his writings in introducing Zen to the Western world. He was born to a family of doctors, was a member of the Rinzai sect, was sympathetic but not converted to Christianity. He has left a vivid account of his difficulties with the KOAN 'the sound of one hand clapping' and with the syllable *Mu*. His final enlightenment came in the vivid realization of 'the elbow does not bend outwards' – restriction is freedom.

Swedenborg, Emanuel
(1688–1772)

Swedish visionary, he began as a scientist but turned increasingly to study the relationship of soul to body. At fifty-five he began to see visions, develop clairvoyant faculties and claim the power of communication with 'discarnate souls'. He asserted that his symbolic interpretation of scripture, *The Word Explained*, was dictated to him in automatic writing. He developed a vast pantheistic theosophy which he expounded in the eight volumes of *Arcana Coelestia* (1756) and other works, including *Heaven and Hell* (1758), *Divine Love and Wisdom* (1763) and *The True Christian Religion* (1771). According to Swedenborg the scriptures must be understood in a spiritual or mystical sense, according to a law of correspondences, by which natural things are in a full and real way united to spiritual things. The real world comprises three regions: the Heavens, the Hells and the World of Spirits. It is in this last, our world, that judgment takes place. Swedenborg's morality was in advance of his day: all acts were judged by intention. Similarly, marriage is an inner, not an external, tie: 'It is the life of our love which we live, and that life is of such quality as the love.' God is one in person and essence; there is a trinity of attributes – Love (the Father), Wisdom (the Son), Energy (the Spirit). This Trinity is found in Jesus Christ only, and he for Swedenborg is God; and much of Swedenborg's mysticism centres on him. Swedenborg influenced other mystics, notably BLAKE, who was however critical also. Among his followers in the New Church his revelations are sacrosanct. Swedenborgian ideas find remarkable expression in Balzac's novel *Séraphita*.

Emanuel Swedenborg

Symbol

There has been some controversy over the relation between mysticism and symbolism. Thus Récéjac actually defines mysticism as 'the tendency to approach the Absolute, morally, by means of symbols'. So too R. L. Nettleship: 'The True Mysticism is the belief that everything, in being what it is, is symbolic of something more.'

In mystical symbolism the symbol retains its own form, content, being and nature, but at the same time becomes the window through which spiritual truth is discerned. Thus the lily may symbolize purity; for the Christian the cross symbolizes the love of God revealed in Jesus. In mystical symbolism the divine dimension breaks into the human 'like a beam of light', and the perception of the divine takes place in the timeless *now*.

The basis of symbolism is analogy. In trying to express something which is beyond words, the mystics seek an analogy within their common experience which may convey or express an element of their mystical vision. The analogy is not intellectually contrived; it is accepted as an immediately perceived actuality. God *is* to mankind what the sun is to the earth. God *is* to the soul what water is to the swimmer. God *is* to sin what the farmer is to weeds. Platonic philosophy offers a support to this approach, since in Platonism the objects of the material world are in fact related, as dim shadows, to their exemplars in the spiritual world.

We can usefully divide the area of mystical symbolism into four parts. They reflect the immediate mystical experience, the process of growth in mystical understanding, the awareness of the Ultimate and the experience of complete union; they thus cover respectively experience, growth or process, being and relationship, and the sources of analogy naturally lie in sense-experience, physical activity, physical beings and powers and relationships. For the first of these *see* SPIRITUAL SENSES.

The second group of symbols includes most obviously the pilgrimage or journey. This has sometimes become a faded metaphor, as in the Pythagorean symbol Y (representing the parting of the ways), the Buddhist Eightfold Path, or the *via contemplativa* and all the other forms of the Way (indeed the Way was an early name for Christianity). We must remember that this was once a vivid symbol. We see it more clearly in Hilton's allegory of the pilgrimage to Jerusalem, Bunyan's *The Pilgrim's Progress*, or the symbolic use of the Quest for the Grail. In Farid al-Din Attar's *The Parliament of the Birds* the questers must pass through the valleys of Search, Love, Knowledge, Detachment, Unity, Wonder and Self-Annihilation. The thirty birds who win through see the Great *Simurgh* (which means Thirty Birds), and find they are seeing themselves; they look at themselves and see Him. In the Upanishads the journey is in a carriage driven by Reason. Catherine of Siena depicts a journey across a raging torrent by means of a bridge, which is Christ. The door at the end of the bridge leads not to land but to the Pacific Ocean of God. Sometimes, as in *The Cell of Self-Knowledge*, the journey is a voyage. Sometimes it is the ascent of a mountain, or stairway. Walter Hilton's title suggests the latter though he does not develop it. In the subtler symbol used by TERESA DE JESUS, it is the exploration of the inner rooms of a castle.

The journey is only one of many symbols for the progress of the soul. Another frequently used is warfare, whose finest example is the warfare of Arjuna in *The Mahabharata*. So too in Zoroastrianism the world is a battleground between the forces of light and the forces of darkness. The *militia Christi* is the Christian equivalent of this. Sometimes the soul is seen as a city under siege. Bunyan's second-best-known book has as its title *The Holy War made by Shaddai upon Diabolus, for the regaining of the metropolis of the world, or, the losing and taking again of the town of Mansoul*.

Again there are the symbols which Evelyn Underhill has called 'transmutational'. These are closely associated with ALCHEMY; the Philosopher's Stone and the Elixir Vitae are identified with the creative power behind the universe, or the saviour-mediator, according to the particular religious framework employed. Thus Fludd writes: 'That is the true alchemy . . . which can multiply in me that rectangular stone, which is the corner stone of my life and soul.' So the *Sophia* Hydrolith says that theology without alchemy is like a noble lady without her right hand, which is another way of saying that a dynamic religion involves the transmutation of the believer.

Another obvious and frequent symbol of progress is the thought of rebirth into new life, Dante's *vita nuova*. Sometimes the soul in its approach to God is compared with a new-born baby. In the Orphic-Dionysiac mysteries we encounter the formula, 'A kid I have fallen among milk', and the picture of the kid being suckled by a Panisca. Clement of Alexandria uses the term 'milk-drinkers' of Christians; they are as reborn babes. An example from a later mystic will be found in Teresa de Jesus. She says that in the prayer of quiet 'the soul is like a child that sucks still, who lying at his mother's breast, she to please him, without his moving his lips, spurts her milk into his mouth'. Such language is not uncommon: William James wrote: 'Christian devotional literature quite floats in milk, thought of from the point of view, not of the mother, but of the greedy babe.'

The Bride. *A modern Dutch artist's symbolic rendering of marriage*

Human growth is paralleled by natural growth. So in Hindu mysticism the soul is a tender creeper, which must be watered, protected from the trampling of wild animals, helped by having other overgrowth cut away, and encouraged to grow upwards. Among the Sikhs, it is said that woman (that is the soul) on meeting her beloved God extends the vine. So Guru NANAK: 'Make your mind the ploughman, good acts the cultivation, modesty the irrigating water, your body the field, the Name the seed, contentment the marrow, the garb of humility the fence; with the work of love the seed will germinate.' The vine is a basic symbol in the mysteries of Dionysus, as well as in Judaeo-Christian mysticism. Catherine of Siena says that each soul contains a vine which God expects her to prune and tend; Teresa similarly uses the image of watering a garden.

One other symbol must be cited under this second head. That is courtship, which leads to the SPIRITUAL MARRIAGE. This is strong in Hindu mysticism. It is found among the Sikhs: here for example is Guru Nanak: 'I am dying with the pang of separation; the flash of lightning terrifies me. I am alone on my bed and in much distress. O mother, my pain is as bad as death. Say, how can sleep and appetite come to me without God?' It is strong also in the Christian tradition, where it takes its start from *The Song of Songs*.

We turn next to the third group of symbols, which point to the very being and nature of God or the Ultimate. Here we shall have to be highly selective. Probably the commonest of all such symbols is LIGHT. Closely associated with that is the sun, which Plato took as symbol of the Form of the Good. Of other natural forces the sea or ocean is frequently found: we have noted its appearances in Catherine of Siena. Sometimes more subtly we find the wind. In many religions the phallus is the symbol of the ultimate life-giving power of the universe; in the Dionysiac Villa of the Mysteries at Pompeii there is a great phallus waiting to be unveiled at the moment of revelation. In the Eleusinian Mysteries an ear of corn performed the same symbolic function.

A number of such symbols are taken from human relationships of various kinds. Some are relations of kinship. So the Sikh Guru Arjan: 'You are my Father, my Mother, my Kinsman, my Brother'; or Julian of Norwich: 'Thus I saw that God rejoices that he is our Father, and God rejoices that he is our Mother, and God rejoices that he is our very husband and our soul is his loved wife. And Christ rejoices that he is our Brother, and Jesus rejoices that he is our Saviour.' Elsewhere she says, 'Our Saviour is our Very Mother in whom we be endlessly born, and never shall come out of him.' In relation to religion generally the language of fatherhood is commonest, but to express mystical union, the language of SPIRITUAL MARRIAGE is more frequent though the image of God as father or mother tends to supervene upon it.

Many other human images are used of the Ultimate as personally conceived. Such are king, lord or master (often slave-owner), commander-in-chief, captain or judge. Shepherd is a common image in Christianity and is found elsewhere; so are guide, doctor and schoolmaster. Some images are less functional and more personal, such as friend, comrade, ally and guest.

It is important to realize that many of the symbols which refer to the Ultimate and appear in the highest visions of the mystics are in fact conditioned by the religion on which they have grown up: the cross in Christianity is a good example. Important too to recognize that the idea of the symbol may be misused. Emerson once said: 'Mysticism (in a bad sense) consists in the mistake of an accidental and individual symbol for an universal one.'

Finally there are the symbols which express the actual experience of union. We may begin from the idea of God as a FIRE, consuming or transforming the soul. It is an experience of pain as impurities are burned away, but also of warmth and of union. Thus Rabia prays, 'Consume with fire, O God, a heart which presumes to love you', and Catherine of Genoa describes her experience: 'The holy soul, yet in the flesh, found herself placed in the purgatory of God's burning love, which consumed and purified her from whatever she had to purify.' Zeb un Nissa describes himself as melting like wax within love's flame, but with a hard core of stone in his heart, which will not be melted. But Rumi depicts the soul as iron heated in the fire till it takes on the colour of the fire and can say, 'I am the fire'. Attar has a magnificent allegory in which a society of butterflies are curious about a candle-flame. One flies over and reports on what he has seen, but is silenced, because he has no real knowledge. A second singes his wings, and comes back and describes his sensations, but this too is not enough. A third envoy is sent: 'He was intoxicated with love for the flame, and flung himself wholly into it: he lost himself, and identified himself with it. It embraced him completely, and his body became fiery-red as the flame itself. When the presiding butterfly saw from afar that the flame had absorbed the devoted butterfly and communicated its own qualities to it, "That butterfly", he exclaimed, "has learnt what he wished to know, but he alone understands it".' We remember the poignant entry in Pascal's notebooks, 'From half past ten to half past twelve, Fire.'

Another similar symbol of the absorbing power of God is the ocean or river. In eastern mysticism the soul is often seen as a drop of water in the ocean of deity: 'The Dewdrop slips into the shining Sea.' So Tauler: 'The spirit is submerged and absorbed in the depths of the divine ocean.' Rumi uses a slightly different image, by which the soul is a fish swimming in the ocean of deity. A similar notion is found in Catherine of Siena, who calls God the Pacific Ocean.

A particular symbol from nature, which we have already noted, and which also expresses the relationship of God and the soul, is the tree. In Hindu mysticism Radha is the beloved of Krishna, and each believer is a leaf on the vine that is Radha. Guru Arjan says of God, 'You are the tree; your branch has blossomed.' The image is familiar from Jesus (Jn 15, 5–6) 'I am the vine, you are the branches.'

The union between God and the soul may be seen in terms of the nourishment of food and drink. We have noticed examples of this when the mystical experience is conceived as a rebirth into new life. Even without this there are plenty of grounds for the image. Thus among Christian mystics, the centrality of the sacrament of the EUCHARIST, and such words of Jesus as 'Whosoever drinks of the water that I shall give him shall never thirst', or 'I am the Bread of life', predisposed them to this symbolism. So Ignatius of Antioch: 'I desire God's bread, which is the flesh of Christ . . . and for drink I desire the blood of him who is incorruptible love,' (Rom. 7) or Ruysbroeck: 'The first token of love is that Jesus has given us his flesh to eat and his blood to drink: Thus is the miracle of miracles before which we wonder and adore.' But both Ignatius and Ruysbroeck also reverse the image, and see God as hungry to consume them. Ignatius describes himself as 'God's grain'. Ruysbroeck goes on: 'The property of love is to be always giving and always receiving; and the love of Jesus is hungry and generous . . . His insatiable hunger would possess us utterly. . . . The more lovingly we give to his hunger the more fully do we possess him.'

But of course the commonest symbol of mystical union is the *hieros gamos*, the SPIRITUAL MARRIAGE. Says the Sikh Guru Amar Des: 'The women' (i.e. souls) 'on whom God looks with favour are happy wives; they recognize their Husband, and offer Him their bodies and their souls. When they drive away their pride, they find their husband in their own homes.' Or as *The Cell of Self-Knowledge* has it: 'The true spouse of the soul is God.'

It is the function of symbols to point beyond themselves, relating the immediate to the Ultimate. Because of this mystical symbols are capable of being interpreted on a variety of different levels; they reveal aspects of the World which are not immediately discernible, and express patterns of ultimate reality which cannot be conveyed in any other way. At the same time they relate the Ultimate to the immediate; that is to say, they are existential; they throw light on present life.

Symeon of Studion
(949–1022)

Symeon began training for the Imperial Service at Constantinople, but early turned to the life of a monk. After a period at the Studion he was for a quarter of a century abbot of St Mamas in Constantinople, and won such a reputation that he was known as the New Theologian or the Younger Theologian, second only to Gregory Nazianzen, who was the Theologian. Symeon was perhaps the greatest of the mediaeval Orthodox mystics. The centre of his mystical faith was that deification, the sharing of the divine Essence through grace, was the highest point of the spiritual life. He uses continually the symbolism of Light and Fire and calls the divine Light, as he himself experienced it, 'fire uncreated and invisible, without beginning and immaterial'.

Synteresis

A supposed faculty of the soul which is divinely implanted and can never consent to sin.

Syzygy

A pair, literally 'yoked together', a technical term of GNOSTICISM for a pair of cosmological opposites, male and female.

T

Tagore, Rabindranath
(1861–1941)

Indian thinker and poet, endowed with a singularly impressive and harmonious personality. His best-known work is probably the volume of poems called *Gitanjali* (Song of Offerings). He is waiting for God:

> I am only waiting for love to give myself up at last unto his hands. (17)

But sometimes he is waiting in darkness – and sometimes God comes while he is asleep. He is a prisoner who has forged his own fetters. But he sends up the cry, 'I want thee, only thee.' And sometimes he feels himself at one, with the joy of all creation, with the mirth which spreads from leaf to leaf, with the earth flowing over in the riotous excess of the grass. He sees God as light:

> Light, my light, the world-filling light, the eye-kissing light, heart-sweetening light! (57)

So he calls his readers to the vision of the all-undying whole in the parable of the stars which panicked and thought one of them was missing:

> Only in the deepest silence of night the stars smile and whisper among themselves – 'Vain is this seeking! Unbroken perfection is overall!' (78)

Tagore's philosophy is centred on the progressive realization of the divine in men:

> Let only that little be left of me whereby I may name thee my all.
> Let only that little be left of my will whereby I may feel thee on every side, and come to thee in everything, and offer to thee my love every moment.
> Let only that little be left of me whereby I may never hide thee. (34)

Taizé

French village where Roger Schutz, a Franco-Swiss brought up in the Reformed Tradition, bought a deserted manor-house. In 1949 seven brothers took their *engagements* there, and formally established a community, dedicated to struggle and contemplation (*Lutte et Contemplation*). The struggle is for reconciliation between the nations, for Church unity, and for an end to the exploitation of some men by others. Common worship holds together those dedicated to the cause, brings unbelievers to God, gives them all strength; thousands of under-twenty-fives from all over the world have found new life in the worship of Taizé. But personal prayer is also essential; it is understood as the renewal of personal intimacy with Jesus. Its deepest form is contemplative prayer, which is essential for purification. In the supplementary directions to the Taizé Rule is written: 'What do we understand by contemplation? Nothing else than that disposition by which our whole being in its totality is seized by the reality of the love of God. When we understand a truth only on its natural level by our intelligence, we are seized by it, but often only partially. On the other hand we can be seized entirely, including our affections, by supernatural truth, by God's own love. One can say that love here is a touchstone. Contemplation strengthens our love for God. By an intimate union with the love of God contemplation makes us loving also towards our neighbour. If it is authentic, this love of our whole being for Christ cannot but show itself in love towards our neighbour. The love which we bear to others remains the mark of the authenticity of our contemplation' *(tr. Mark Gibbard)*.

Tantrism

Movement appearing in India about AD 400 and operating within both Hinduism and Buddhism. The word *tantra* means a work. It may simply mean a book. But it also has an implication of the right way to do something, to perform ritual, for example. And there seems to be allusion to weaving and spinning, the skilled work of women: the world too is woven like a tissue. The *Tantras* are texts intended for a close circle of devotees:

> Not to all and any should this hymn be revealed,
> For be it made known to one who is unworthy,
> Then ill falls upon him,
> Therefore should it be carefully concealed.

Their principal theme is ritual and worship; they are involved with what one critic calls 'baroque forms of yoga'; women, goddesses, and fertility and sexual energy generally are important for religious understanding; wine and meat are also important. Tantric ritual has in fact been summed up as 'the five *ms*': *madya* (intoxicating drinks), *mamsa* (meat), *matsya* (fish), *mudra* (ritual gestures), *maithuna* (ritual sexual union). Thus whereas Hinduism tends to deny this world, Tantrism in general affirms it. In Hinduism this world is to be escaped from, in Tantrism to be enjoyed. In Tantrism joy, vision and ecstasy are the fundamentals of religious experience, and in sexual union, properly conceived as a total

The lingam (male principle) set in the yoni (female principle). A tantric depiction of the reconciliation of opposites

uniting of two personalities dwelling on one another eye to eye, there is a glimpse of union with the Ultimate.

In Hindu Tantra everything is the active play of a female creative principle: 'Whatever power anything possesses, that is the Goddess.' She is often called Sakti: 'The truth which is the conclusion of all those people imbued with the Veda and its highest philosophy is that which the yogis see as the One, all-pervasive, subtle, beyond qualities, motionless and static; it is the ultimate state of the Great Goddess. What yogis see as the eternal, unwasting, solitary, pure, supreme Brahman, that is the ultimate state of the Great Goddess. That all-embracing existence, higher than the highest, universal, benevolent and faultless, which is in the genitals of Prakriti, that is the ultimate state of the Great Goddess. That which is white, spotless, pure, without qualities and distinctions, that which is realized only in the self, that is the ultimate state of the Great Goddess.'

Though there is strong emphasis on the female, visually and imaginatively, the ultimate creative power is bisexual, and often portrayed as a single bisexual being, or as a divine couple, or symbolized by the two sex-organs, the *lingam* (male) set in the *yoni* (female).

The *Devatas* or divine principles are portrayed in human shape. Many temples show divine beings making love. This is all part of the sense that energy and joy and creativity throughout the universe is one and the same.

Tantrism is a mystery-religion. The aim is that the energy and creative impulses of the individual shall be one with the energy and creative impulses of the cosmos. This is achieved through an exact pattern of repeated rituals, and of meditation directed to the realization that even the smallest object or movement, the rising of a bubble, the twitch of a gnat's foot, emanates from the creative joy of the Goddess and is an essential part of the bliss of the cosmos. Sexual union with an initiate of the opposite sex, who is thus an instrument of the divine energy, is a part of the mystery. Complex symbolism of YANTRAS and MANTRAS help to concentrate the mind and develop the understanding. The individual initiate will catch occasional glimpses of the cosmic bliss; he ultimately seeks union with the Divine.

Tao

Chinese concept meaning 'the Way', the ultimate reality in the universe, the way the universe works. Man's aim thus is to live in harmony with the Tao. To do this he has to discard his civilization and artifice and put on simplicity:

> Banish wisdom, discard knowledge,
> and the people will be benefitted a
> hundredfold.
> Banish human kindness, discard morality,
> and the people will be dutiful and
> compassionate.
> Banish skill, discard profit,
> and thieves and robbers will disappear.
> If when these three things are done, they
> find life too plain and unadorned,
> then let them have accessories.
> Give them Simplicity to look at, the
> Uncarved Block to hold,
> give them selflessness and fewness of desires.
>
> *Tao-Te-Ching* (19)

But the Absolute is ineffable. So in TAO-TE-CHING (1):

> The way that can be told is not the
> immutable Way;
> The name that can be named is not the
> immutable name.
> It was from the Nameless that Heaven and
> Earth sprang;
> The named is but the mother that rears the
> ten thousand creatures, each after its kind.

So the Tao may be called the Void, or Quietude, a deep pool which never runs dry; ultimate Emptiness. But all things come from it, and it gives them their characters.

The Tao is the central concept of the Taoists. But the term is also used by Confucians, Mohists and Buddhists. As a Ming inscription puts it (the Golden Man is the Buddha):

> Vast indeed is the Ultimate Tao,
> Spontaneously itself, apparently without
> aching,
> End of all ages and beginning of all ages,

Existing before earth and existing before
Heaven,
Silently embracing the whole of time,
Continuing uninterrupted through all eons,
In the East it taught Father Confucius,
In the West it converted the Golden Man,
Taken as pattern by a hundred kings,
Transmitted by generations of sages,
It is the ancestor of all doctrines,
The mystery beyond all mysteries.

Chinese Christians have equated the Tao with the LOGOS.

Tao-hsin
(580–651)

Fourth of the ZEN patriarchs, an ascetic scholar with a magnetic personality, who developed self-supporting community life among his followers, 'working, dwelling, sitting, resting'. Tao-hsin was a great exponent of ZAZEN. 'Sit earnestly in meditation. Sitting in meditation is basic to everything else. By the time you have done this for three to five years, you will be able to keep off starvation with a handful of meal. Close the door and sit! Do not read the sutras. Do not speak to anyone. If you will practise this and apply yourself to it for a long period, the fruit will be as sweet as the kernel the monkey extracts from the nutshell. But such people are very rare.'

Taoism

Ancient religion of China. As a philosophy it goes back to the legendary LAO-TZU, and its great classic is TAO-TE-CHING. As anything like a mass religious movement it can be traced to the second century AD when there was a Taoist-inspired and Taoist-led insurrection (which hardly seem to accord with the principle of quietude) sustained by apocalyptic promises of the millennium and the hope of establishing a Taoist state. Taoist traditions go back to one Chang Liang who in the early second century BC was 'in search of immortality'. Seven generations later a descendant of his began a mass movement in west China.

Taoism became a religion of salvation with an organized Church and hierarchy. For its ordinary adherents it offered confession and atonement through gifts ('the five pecks of rice doctrine') and pious observances, and was replete with divination and magic, designed to knowing and controlling the Way. For others it offered the way of abstinence, almsgiving and service. All these might attain bliss beyond death. The true initiate sought to escape death, purging his mortal element by fasting and dietary regimens, breathing exercises, sexual discipline and the like. The three principal techniques were known as 'nourishing the life principle', 'nourishing the spirits', and 'keeping the One intact'. In the higher stages these led to contemplation, rapture, visionary experiences and so to immortality. But the highest aim of all was to renounce even immortality for the state of identification with and absorption by the Tao.

See also TAOISM IN ART.

Taoism in art

Taoism as a religious philosophy depends on recognition of the Way. The typical Western artwork stops the flow of reality as does a cinema still. But the Tao 'is a seamless web of unbroken movement and change, filled with undulations, waves, patterns of ripples and temporary "standing waves" like a river'. The Great Whole, the uncarved block, does not itself change; it consists of a mighty web of change. And within that web nothing ever repeats itself. Within this change the YIN-YANG dialectic is always at work. *Yin* is the female principle, dark and deep, blue or green or black exemplified by scudding cloud and moving water, by winter and the north, by valley and receptacle, by fish and flower and

Seeking the Tao in the Mountains, *a 10th-century Chinese painting*

The heavenly dragon of Taoism. Detail of a vase decoration of the 18th century

fruit and fungus, and associated with earth. *Yang* is the male principle, brilliant and lofty, red or gold, exemplified by jade, by summer and the south, by mountain and projecting objects, by male animals; and associated with Heaven.

Taoism is expressed in art particularly in three ways. First, through the expression of flow, of the unending mobility of change. Secondly, in the symbolic representation of the harmony of *yin* and *yang*, as on an eighteenth-century porcelain plate where we see a male Feng-bird flying down to two women seated in a garden of flowers, or in a magnificent soapstone carving of a dragon among swirling clouds. Thirdly, through various formal symbols, such as the circle representing Heaven and the square representing earth, or a whole series of trigrams, each with its own set of meanings, or calligraphic script itself with its special brushwork or the special mystic scripts of the Taoists with their own symbolical meanings. So in Taoist art the objects represented, their shapes and colours, and the brush-strokes with which they were portrayed, may all be charged with hidden meaning: a love scene may speak of the harmony of earth and Heaven, a landscape be the setting for a spiritual journey, a moving line be an expression of the Cosmic Vital Energy.

Tao-Sheng
(*c*. 360–434)

A Chinese monk who brought together Taoist and Buddhist thought, and identified the Buddha with the Tao. Tao-Sheng's originality lay in his doctrine of sudden enlightenment. The Absolute *is* absolute; you cannot enter it gradually or by stages. The way is never the goal: 'When the mountain is climbed, the landscape of the goal appears all at once.' For this reason Tao-Sheng has been called 'the actual founder of Zen'.

Tao-Te-Ching

One of the great works of mystical religion, traditionally ascribed to the shadowy LAO-TZU, but undoubtedly an anthology of quite short discrete passages from different sources, some of which may go back to the legendary sage, some of which is undoubtedly later. The individual *pericopae* belong in form to oral tradition, and in fact rather more than half the work is rhymed. Editorial work has been careless. Passages are repeated in different contexts (e.g. 40, 53; 12+118, 129; 66, 154). The connection between consecutive passages is often tenuous, and the editor has sometimes been misled by superficial resemblances (e.g. 14, 15) into juxtaposing two sayings. On general grounds we may place the compilation to the late fourth or early third century BC.

The book is about the TAO, the Way, the Ultimate Truth of the Universe. It is nameless (1, 72, 92). It was the beginning of all things (2), the source of the One, and so of plurality (93). But sometimes the Tao is called the One:

> Heaven in virtue of the One is limpid;
> Earth in virtue of the One is settled;
> Gods in virtue of the One have their
> potencies;
> The valley in virtue of the One is full;
> The myriad creatures in virtue of the One
> are alive;
> Lords and princes in virtue of the One
> become leaders in the empire (85).

It can be called great, but that is a makeshift name (56). It is shadowy and indistinct (49), silence and emptiness (56), the Nothing from which Something emerges (89).

How can we know the Way. The dilemma of mysticism has never been more clearly put:

> Rid yourself of desires in order to observe
> its secrets;
> But always allow yourself to have desires in
> order to observe its manifestations.
> These two are the same
> But diverge in name as they issue forth.
> Being the same they are called mysteries,
> Mystery upon mystery.
> The gateway of the manifold secrets.

One thing we can know. The Way leaves nothing undone by doing nothing. It just is. Paradoxically we may say

> Turning back is how the Way moves;
> Weakness is the means the Way employs (88).

There is a lesson here for men. The meek may not inherit the earth, but they inherit the universe. This may be a simple lesson for a turbulent age; 'he that is down needs fear no fall'.

There is no crime greater than having too many desires;
There is no disaster greater than not being content;
There is no misfortune greater than being covetous.

But there is more to it than that. There is a whole philosophy of life. 'To hold fast to the submissive is called strength' (119). Hence the profound pacifism of the book: 'When two armies confront one another it is the man of sorrows who is victorious' (169). Hence also the *laissez-faire* politics. The Tao gives life but claims no possession, and grants benefit but exacts no gratitude (116). So 'The best of all rulers is but a shadowy presence to his subjects' (39). It is through learning the same lesson that we find life. Grass and bushes are supple and fragile while living, dried and shrivelled in death. Life is in suppleness and weakness (182). This too is the secret of mystical intuition.

Without stirring abroad
One can know the whole world;
Without looking out of the window
One can see the way of heaven.
The further one goes
The less one knows (106).

Tariki

Japanese for another's strength, contrasting with *jiriki*, one's own strength; though in mystical terms the two ultimately coincide.

Tasawwuf

The practice of SUFISM. In an article in the *Journal of the Royal Asiatic Society* for 1906, R. A. Nicholson collected a number of definitions as:

'*Tasawwuf* is to grasp the verities and to renounce that which is in the hands of men.'

'*Tasawwuf* is this: that actions should be passing over the Sufi which are known to God, and that he should always be with God in a way that is known to God only.'

'*Tasawwuf* is a name including three ideas. The Sufi is he whose light of divine knowledge does not extinguish the light of his piety; he does not utter esoteric doctrine which is contradicted by the exterior sense of *The Qur'an* and the Sunna; and the miracles vouchsafed to him do not cause him to violate the holy ordinances of God.'

'*Tasawwuf* is wholly discipline.'

'*Tasawwuf* is: to eat little, and to take rest with God, and to flee from men.'

'*Tasawwuf* is this: that you should possess nothing, and that nothing should possess you.'

'*Tasawwuf* is not a system composed of rules or sciences, but it is morals.'

'*Tasawwuf* is freedom, and generosity, and absence of self-constraint, and liberality.'

'*Tasawwuf* is to renounce all selfish gains in order to gain the Truth.'

'*Tasawwuf* is hatred of the world and love of the Lord.'

'*Tasawwuf* is thus: that the Truth should make you die from yourself and live in Him.'

'*Tasawwuf* is to be non-attached and to be with God.'

'*Tasawwuf* is praise of God with concentration, ecstatic with hearing, practice with conformity.'

'*Tasawwuf* is to be chosen for purity.'

'*Tasawwuf* is to purify the heart from the recurrence of unborn weakness, and to take leave of one's natural characteristics, and to extinguish the attributes of humanity, and to hold aloof from sensual temptation, and to dwell with the spiritual attributes, and to mount aloft by means of the Divine sciences, and to practise that which is eternally the best, and to bestow sincere counsel on the whole people, and faithfully to observe the truth, and to follow the Prophet in respect of the law.'

'*Tasawwuf* is purity of heart, and to do what is pleasing to God Almighty, and to have no personal volition although you mix with men.'

'*Tasawwuf* is to make a show of wealth, and to prefer being unknown, and to abstain from everything useless.'

'*Tasawwuf* is the self-abandonment of the soul with God according to His will.'

'*Tasawwuf* is based on three qualities: a tenacious attachment to poverty and indigence; a profound sense of sacrifice and renunciation; and absence of self-obtrusion and self-will.'

'*Tasawwuf* is to become quit of all persons except Him, and to make oneself clear of all others except Him.'

'*Tasawwuf* is to enter into every lofty disposition and to leave every low disposition.'

'*Tasawwuf* is to be open to God in all circumstances and to be constant in self-discipline.'

'*Tasawwuf* is to behold the imperfection of the phenomenal world – or rather to close the eye to everything imperfect in contemplation of Him who is free from all imperfection.'

'*Tasawwuf* is a good disposition.'

'*Tasawwuf* is purity and spiritual vision.'

'*Tasawwuf* is to alight and wait at the Beloved's door, even though you are driven away from it.'

'*Tasawwuf* is the purity of nearness after the defilement of farness.'

'*Tasawwuf* is to let oneself be led to the Truth.'

'*Tasawwuf* is patience under the events of destiny, and acceptance from the hand of Almighty God, and travelling over desert and highland.'

'*Tasawwuf* is to sit with God without care.'

'*Tasawwuf* is a burning flash of lightning.'

'*Tasawwuf* is this: that the Sufi should be just as he was before he came into existence.'

'*Tasawwuf* is discipline of the faculties, and breath-control.'

'The whole of *Tasawwuf* consists in abandonment of superfluities.'

'*Tasawwuf* is deficiency of hope and incessant devotion to work.'

'*Tasawwuf* is to throw oneself into servility

and to come out from humanity and look wholly to God.'

'*Tasawwuf* is to be patient under commandment and prohibition.'

'*Tasawwuf* is this: that the Sufi does not take rest or comfort in anything in the world except God, and that he commits his affairs to Him who is the Lord and who Himself oversees that which He has predestined.'

'*Tasawwuf* is to have a heart pure from the defilement of oppositions.'

'*Tasawwuf* is severance of ties, rejection of created things and union with reality.'

'*Tasawwuf* is to keep one's state hidden and to bestow honour on one's brethren.'

'*Tasawwuf* is to lay aside what you have in your head, to give away what you have in your hand, and not to recoil from whatever happens to you.'

Tat Tvam Asi

'That art Thou': the mystic copula of Hinduism bringing together individual and universal self. 'That is the Real. That is the Self. That art thou' (Chandogya Upanishad, 6, 8–16).

In most mysticism that is not seen as complete identification between God and man. For in the first place it is an overcoming of the duality which divides Creator from creature; it is something which must happen. The Gospel According to John speaks of 'those to whom he gave power *to become* children of God'; and a phrase frequently found of Jesus in early Greek Christianity is 'He became a man in order that we might *become* God'. So Angelus of Silesia: 'He who seeks God must *become* God.' And secondly the mystical immanence does not abolish transcendence, union does not abolish distinction, identification does not mean identity. As Eckhart puts it: 'The more God is in all things, the more he is outside them. The more he is within, the more he is without.' Only God can plumb the depths of the soul. Not even the soul can plumb the depths of God.

Tauler, Johann
(*c.* 1300–61)

Not much is certain about Tauler's life, except that he was born in Strasbourg, that his family were wealthy, that he became a Dominican, that his life was mainly associated with Strasbourg, that his thinking owed a debt to Eckhart, and that he was a great preacher who 'set the world ablaze with his fiery tongue'.

His certainly authentic works consist of sermons and one letter, all in German. Tauler is a practical mystic; in view of Eckhart's condemnation he avoids any wild flights of speculation. He insists on a religion of experience: 'The man who truly experiences the pure presence of God in his own soul knows well that there can be no doubt about it.' There is 'an entrance into union

Johann Tauler

of the created spirit with the uncreated Spirit of God', so that the human is swallowed up in the divine and becomes one spirit with God; and this truth is to be learned not from the schools of theology, but from the experience of 'entering in and dwelling in the Inner Kingdom of God, where pure truth and the sweetness of God are found'. Within man there is the image of God, but hidden. Tauler, in a magnificent simile, speaks of God finding it as the sculptor finds his statue in the unhewn block. Tauler does not use Eckhart's language of the spark of the soul, though he speaks of the ground of the soul, the apex of the soul, 'the kingdom of God in the innermost recesses of the spirit' and 'the unseen depths of the spirit, where lies the image of God'. He is careful to avoid pantheistic language: 'God is the Being of all beings, but He is none of all these things'; He is 'the Unity in which all multiplicity is transcended'. Tauler insists that God must be born in the soul, but that Creator and creature are distinct, and the union requires the operation of divine grace. He often speaks of God shining in the soul. 'God illumines his true Friends, and shines within them with power, purity and truth, so that such men become divine and supernatural persons.' This inner Light gives man all Truth; it produces an enlightened understanding; peace and joy; it makes the soul of the recipient luminous so that the Light shines through to others.

Tauler sometimes talks of the hidden God, the divine Darkness, 'the calm waste of the Godhead'. The way to such a God is by dying to self. The first stage in this remains self-centred; self-denial springs from fear rather than from love. In the second the soul is subjected to humility, barrenness and spiritual destitution and leads to the stage where it ceases to be preoccupied with itself. The third is the perfect denial of all self-love and union of the human will with the divine Will. Tauler is an introspective mystic. All external things, even works of love, may be distractions: 'We shall never find God anywhere so perfectly, so fruitfully, and so truly as in retirement and in the wilderness.' At most the external world offers a first step only: 'God draws us in three ways: first, by His creatures; secondly, by His voice in the soul, when an eternal truth mysteriously suggests itself, as happens not infrequently in morning sleep; thirdly, without resistance or means, when the will is quite subdued.' In the glorious thirty-sixth *Sermon* he speaks of man as the temple of the Holy Spirit, a house of prayer; he must drive out the 'traders', fancies and imaginations, self-gratification and concentration on the temporal.

That Tauler experienced the things he writes about, it is impossible to doubt: 'What this is and how it comes to pass is easier to experience than to describe. All that I have said of it is as poor and unlike it as a point of a needle is to the heavens above us!'

One attractive feature of Tauler's mysticism is his practicality. Like Plato's philosopher he returns from the cave; he descends from the mount of Transfiguration. 'Spiritual enjoyments are the food of the soul, but they are to be taken only for nourishment and support to help us in our active work.' 'Works of love are more acceptable than contemplation.' 'No virtue is to be trusted until it has been put into practice.' There is no more remarkable passage in any of the mystics than this: 'One man can spin, another can make shoes, and all these are gifts of the Holy Ghost. I tell you, if I were not a priest, I should esteem it a great gift that I was able to make shoes, and I would try to make them so well as to be a pattern to all.'

Taurobolium

Ritual associated with the cult of CYBELE under the Roman Empire. We hear of it first in the early second century AD and have a full description from Prudentius in the fourth. The name suggests the lassoing of a bull, but the fact was a baptism in bull's blood. It was a rebirth, efficacious perhaps for twenty years, though some describe themselves as 'reborn for eternity'. The rite was also used as a public sacrifice for the safety of the emperor or of the Empire. There was a similar ritual involving a ram, called CRIOBOLIUM.

Taylor, Jeremy
(1613–67)

Anglican devotional writer, who became Bishop of Down and Connor and Vice-Chancellor of Dublin University. His lasting fame depends on *The Rules and Exercises of Holy Living* (1650) and *The Rule and Exercises of Holy Dying* (1651), which, in Heber's words, 'may be said to offer a complete summary of the duties, and specimen of the devotions, of a Christian'. Taylor insists that 'God is wholly in every place', though none contains him, 'filling heaven and earth with His present power, and with His never absent nature'. 'We can no more be removed from the presence of God than from our own being.' How is God present everywhere? First because His infinite Essence cannot be contained within any limits of place. Second by His power in creation. Third by special manifestations of Himself. Fourth through the Holy Spirit in the hearts of His servants. Realization of this can give a new meaning to life. 'In the face of the sun you may see God's beauty; in the fire you may feel His heart warming; in the water His gentleness to refresh you.' So 'every act of rejoicing or of mourning is a going to God' and even in the busiest day we can retire into the chapel of our heart and converse with God.

Te

In Confucian philosophy, virtue or morality; in Taoist mysticism, the revelation or power of the *tao* in anything.

Tears

In Christian and Moslem mysticism the gift of tears is sometimes accounted a special grace, and the title 'Weeper' is an indication of sainthood. Thus it was said of Ephraem of Syria: 'As with all men to breathe is a natural function unceasing in exercise, so with Ephraem was it natural to weep. There was no day, no night, no now, no moment, however brief, in which his eyes were not wakeful and filled with tears, while he bewailed the faiths and follies now of his own life, now of mankind.' Isaac of Nineveh too stresses the value of weeping: 'What is the meditation of the solitary in his cell but weeping?' Constant tears keep down sensual desires, and lead the seeker beyond the visible world to the complete love of God. So Shawana, a Moslem woman mystic, was continually weeping and would say, 'I wish that I could weep blood.' Abd al-Wahid ben Zayd cries, 'O brethren, will you not weep in desire for God? Shall the man who weeps in longing for his Lord be denied the Vision of Him?' So too Abu Suleiman al-Darani depicts God as looking down with compassion upon the tears of His people, and because of their tears unveiling His face to them. 'When the heart weeps for what is lost, the spirit laughs for what is found.' There are thus three different aspects of the gift of tears. The first is penitence, the second compassion, the third yearning.

Teilhard de Chardin, Marie-Joseph-Pierre
(1881–1955)

Jesuit palaeontologist, who had a vision of a Christianity renewed through the spiritual understanding of evolution, and of the Church as widening till it becomes the true all-comprehensive body of the cosmic Christ. His views may be formulated scientifically, somewhat as follows: matter contains the potentiality of life and thought. The movement of evolution is towards greater complexity and higher consciousness. There is a logically necessary end-term, which he calls Point Omega. Man has the power of understanding and transforming the evolutionary process. The movement of history is towards greater cohesion, culturally and psychically. There is a threefold convergent evolution, chemical, organic, psychosocial, in what Teilhard calls the hydrosphere, the biosphere and the noosphere. Mankind is converging into a kind of super-organism. But Teilhard's is more of a mystical vision than a scientific hypothesis, and his real thought is theological, in terms of evolution controlled through continuous creation by God and His Word, who by entering the evolutionary process controls history as well as cosmology and directs Man to his ultimate goal of Love: Teilhard's thought is much influenced by John and Paul. He once declared that 'neither in its impetus nor its achievements can science go to its limits without becoming tinged with mysticism and charged with faith'.

At the end of his life Teilhard made a distinction between what he called the pantheism of identification and the pantheism of unification. The first is unity at the base; it starts from the universe, and works by diffusion or dissolution; its cry is 'God is the All.' The second is unity at the top; it starts from God and Love, and works by ultra-differentiation; its cry is 'God is All in all things.' Yet these antipodal poles become terribly alike, and sometimes he writes as if God can be reached only through the world of matter.

Teilhard's first mystical experience was at Hastings in 1911 when he suddenly became aware of the universe not as an abstract notion but as a presence. Then in 1916, while serving as a stretcher-bearer, he was in a church near the front and had a vision associated with a picture of Christ; the outlines melted, 'it seemed as though the surface that separated Christ from the world about him was changing into a film of vibration in which all limits were confounded', and he had a sense of phosphorescent trails of light reaching the outermost spheres of matter and of the whole universe vibrating.

In 1933 he wrote out his creed in words which began 'We cannot be fundamentally happy but in a personal unification with something Personal (with the Personality of the Whole) in the whole. This is the ultimate call of what is termed "love".' We have a passionate human heart, but also 'The Ocean collecting all the spiritual streams of the Universe is, not only something, but *somebody*. He has, Itself, a face and a heart.' So all life (including death) becomes a discovery of the divine Presence, which enlightens the secret Zones of everything and everybody around us. 'We can reach it in the *achievement* (not in the mere enjoyment) of everything and everybody.'

Teiresias

Legendary Greek seer who had experienced what it was to be both man and woman. His blindness was coupled with inward sight.

Tennyson, Alfred
(1809–92)

English poet. In a letter to B. P. Blood he gave an account of his own mystical experience: 'I have never had any revelations through anaesthetics, but a kind of waking trance – this for lack of a better word – I have frequently had quite up from boyhood, when I have been all alone. This has come upon me through repeating my own name to myself silently, till all at once, as it were out of the intensity of the consciousness of individuality, individuality itself seemed to dissolve and fade away into boundless being, and this not a confused state but the clearest, the surest of the surest, utterly beyond words – where death was an almost laughable impossibility – the loss of personality (if so it were) seeming no extinction, but the only true life. I am ashamed of my feeble description. Have I not said that state is beyond words?' On another occasion he said of the experience: 'By God Almighty! there is no delusion in the matter! It is not nebulous ecstasy but a state of transcendental wonder, associated with absolute clearness of mind.'

Tennyson had an unusually sensitive appreciation of mystical experience. In an early poem which he suppressed he describes 'The Mystic': 'Angels have talked with him, and showed him thrones.'

> Always there stood before him, night and day,
> Of wayward vary coloured circumstance,
> The imperishable presences serene,
> Colossal, without form, or sense, or sound . . .

In another early poem, 'The Two Voices', he describes the state where

> Heaven opens inward, chasms yawn,
> Vast images in glimmering dawn,
> Half shewn, are broken and withdrawn.

'The Higher Pantheism' shows another aspect of mysticism:

> The sun, the moon, the stars, the seas, the
> hills and the plains –
> Are not there, O Soul, the Vision of Him
> who reigns? . . .
>
> Dark is the world to thee: thyself art the
> reason why;
> For is He not all but that which has power
> to feel 'I am I'?

This is marvellously put in some untitled lines:

Flower in the crannied wall,
I pluck you out of the crannies,
I hold you here, root and all, in my hand,
Little flower – but *if* I could understand
What you are, root and all, and all in all,
I should know what God and man is.

Teoqualo

Mystical god-eating communion recorded among the Aztecs in the sixteenth century AD. It was a celebration of the god Huitzilopochtli, and of the ceremony they said, 'The god is eaten', and participants in the communion were said to 'guard the god'.

Teresa de Jesus

(1515–82)

Popularly known as Teresa of Avila. Spaniard of noble birth who in 1533 became a Carmelite nun, and after a long period of indifferent spirituality, despite a spiritual vision of Christ in 1539 'in an attitude of great sternness', found a new purpose in 1555. Soon afterwards she began 'to see certain visions and experience revelations', and in 1557 she was seized by her first ecstasy. Of this she says, 'It always carried me out of myself' and records how she heard the words 'I will have thee converse now, not with me but with angels.' For two years she remained uncertain, without visions, in a state of utter exhaustion. Then she heard the words 'Do not be afraid, daughter, for it is I, and I will not forsake you: do not fear.' From this point the mystical experiences came more frequently. She had a consciousness of Christ at her side; she saw him, with the eye of the soul, in his resurrection-body 'in very great beauty and majesty', revealed through 'a soft whiteness and infused radiance'; she saw him on the cross; he marked her rosary with precious stones which only she could see; she experienced the transverberation of her heart by an angel with a red-hot spear. Sometimes her visions were of devils and Hell; she learned to dispose of Satan by a considered disrespect: she called him 'Goose!' All these experiences, she insists, were spiritual, not corporeal. She did not seek them: indeed she resisted them and was embarrassed by them.

In 1562 despite opposition she founded a convent at Avila with more stringent rules, and from 1567 was concerned with the extension of this work. This was the period of her association with JUAN DE LA CRUZ; it was also the period of the consummation of her mystical life in her experience of spiritual marriage. This balance of spiritual experience and practical service is a noteworthy feature of her life, the inward and the outward, the contemplative and the active, hand in hand. The soul which becomes one with the God who gives Himself in love cannot but give itself in love to others.

Teresa de Jesus as portrayed by the contemporary painter Fray Juan de la miseria

Teresa, in her *Life*, and in her treatises *The Way of Perfection*, *The Interior Castle* and others, has left one of the fullest and most important of all accounts of mystical experience. For her teaching on prayer see PRAYER, STAGES OF. In one of her finest images she compares the four stages with methods of watering a garden. Recollection is like drawing water from a well; the prayer of quiet is the same with the use of windlass and bucket, 'less laborious and giving more water'. 'Tumescence' is irrigation by a river. Here God 'may almost be said to be the gardener Himself, for it is he who does everything'. The highest stage is 'by heavy rain, when the Lord waters it with no labour of ours'.

In *The Interior Castle* she depicts the soul as a castle in which there are many rooms or mansions. It was a vivid picture which suddenly came to her of 'a most beautiful crystal globe, made in the shape of a castle, and containing seven mansions, in the seventh and uppermost of which was the King of Glory, in the greatest splendour, illumining and beautifying them all'. She tells of the journey from the outer gate to the centre. In the courtyard it is dark and cold, and the toads and reptiles of distracting thoughts diverted her. She first entered the Rooms of Humility, then the Rooms of the Practice of Prayer, then the Rooms of Meditation. Then came the Rooms of Quiet, where she gradually realized her dependence on God. Here is the antechamber of the Prayer of Recollection leading to the Prayer of Quiet. Next were the Rooms of Illumination, corresponding to the third stage of prayer and to the Spiritual Betrothal. At this point Teresa introduces the image of the silkworm, feeding on mulberry-leaves till it is full-grown and then spinning the cocoon in which it is to die itself, and from which it will rise again as a butterfly. Now came the Rooms of the Dark Night. The 'little butterfly' cannot go back and it cannot rest here. The account of the sixth Mansion is almost as long as all that has gone before. Finally we are led to the Rooms of Union. This is the account of her own journey. But she wrote it to help others, and to help others at all stages. Not all will reach the Rooms of Union, but all should be encouraged to come in out of the chill slime of the courtyard.

Her experience of union is caught in Bernini's famous statue. She herself wrote: 'The soul neither sees, hears nor understands while she is united to God – God establishes himself in the interior of this soul in such a way that, when she comes to herself, it is impossible for her to doubt that she has been in God and God in her. So does that Beauty and Majesty remain stamped on the soul that nothing can drive it from her memory. The soul is no longer the same, always enraptured.'

Teresa was a warm, human person, a little tubby, bright-eyed, vivacious, and fun to be with. She would play the tambourine and dance with her 'daughters'; they would greet her with song. She would laugh at dignitaries standing on their dignity. She had a strong sense of humour, and a sturdy, earthy commonsense. She knew long periods of spiritual drought. She knew also the dangers of interpreting every experience as transcendental, even more of wallowing in an emotional bath. One of her prayers runs 'From foolish devotions may God deliver us!' She might be formidably trying; her own confessor said, 'Good Lord, good Lord! I would rather argue with all the theologians in creation than with that woman.' She could be round even with her Lord. One famous story tells how on one of her last journeys when she was desperately ill, she complained to him. 'But that is how I treat my friends.' 'Yes – and that's why you have so few of them.'

After her death these words – sometimes called St Teresa's Bookmark – were found in her breviary:

> Let nothing disturb you;
> Let nothing dismay you;
> All things pass:
> God never changes.
> Patience attains
> All that it strives for.
> He who has God
> Finds he lacks nothing:
> God alone suffices.
>
> *(tr. E. A. Peers; altered)*

Tersteegen, Gerhard
(1697–1769)

German Protestant mystic, who retired from the world in his early twenties to live ascetically, earning his livelihood by weaving ribbons; then ten years later turned to the idea of religious community. He was influenced by the Catholic mystics, though rejecting their 'sensual religion', and by French QUIETISM. In his notebook he records humbly and carefully his own mystical experience: 'I occasionally seem to experience something of a divine communication, which is exceedingly precious, but which lasts only a few moments.' This is through no action of his own; we are not to act; God acts if we resign ourselves to him. Tersteegen has a fine account in Christian terms of inward or spiritual prayer, which is an approach of the soul to God, in the name of Jesus, and an abiding in His presence. The God who is love draws us to Him as a magnet draws iron. Our sole task is to remove any obstacles and to commit ourselves entirely to Him. Then we are led to Him by love 'even as a stream flows towards the ocean, and as a stone, pendant in the air, sinks down to the earth which is its centre of attraction. . . . Our spirits then become the temples, in which the glory of God, as in the Holiest of Holies, is near to us.' Tersteegen's warm devotional spirit lives on in his hymns.

Tetragrammaton

Literally the fourfold lettering. In the *Kabbalah* the Hebrew name for God Y-H-V-H without the vowel points.

Theologia Germanica

Anonymous mystical treatise, well edited by Martin Luther in 1516 and 1518. It has had a chequered history: Calvin declared it 'poison supplied by the Devil', and Pope Paul V placed it on the Index of Banned Books, where it still very oddly remains.

According to this great mystic the true Christian life calls for humility and self-denial, for the annihilation of selfishness and self-centredness to such an extent that religion is not accepted for fear of Hell or desire for Heaven but out of acceptance of God's will even though that were to mean eternal damnation. Religion is a quest for deification, for the elimination of creatureliness, for a union with God in which man's will is destroyed and God's takes its place. There is no room for spiritual pride, certainly no room for the sort of libertarianism which claims to be above ethical rules. But man has within him an eye which can look into eternity (7, 17, 18–20), and this vision leads him to strive actively towards union – even though his appropriate action may be to wait patiently.

Theology of Aristotle, The

Neo-Platonic mystical treatise, which gave currency to Neo-Platonic ideas under the authority of Aristotle, and was influential in shaping

Islamic philosophical mysticism. It is possible that it incorporates material from Aristotle's early Platonic works. In it Aristotle is made to say: 'Often I was alone with my soul. I entered as pure substance into my real self, turning away from all that is external to what is within. I became pure knowing, at once the knower and the known. How astonished I was to behold beauty and splendour in my own self and to recognize that I am a part of the sublime Divine World, endowed even with creative life! In this discovery of self, I was lifted up above the world of the senses, even above the world of spirits, up to the Divine, where I beheld a Light so beautiful that no tongue could express it or ear understand it.'

Theory of Forms (or Ideas)

See PLATO.

Theosis

Greek term for DEIFICATION.

Theosophy

'Divine Wisdom', literally, the term is applied to a number of esoteric systems, particularly those which profess a detailed and complex knowledge of the nature of the Divine and its relation to the cosmos, such as those of GNOSTICISM, BOEHME (known as 'the Teutonic Theosopher') and SWEDENBORG.

It is more precisely applied to a movement which began in the Western world in about 1875. Knowledge of Indian religion began to permeate through to Britain and America. From this emerged a new synthesis or syncretism, drawing together aspects of Hindu, Buddhist and Christian wisdom, together with other strands. The Theosophical Society was founded by Madame Helena Petrovna Blavatsky, a Russian aristocrat, and Col. H. S. Olcott, in 1875 in New York. The adherence of the well-known secularist and orator Annie Besant gave the movement a considerable fillip.

Man is essentially a spiritual being, and his spirit is an emanation from the Universal Spirit God. To know himself is to know God. Out of this experience come the two central tenets of theosophy, the immanence and transcendence of God, and the unity in God of all living beings. These can be expanded into four: the unity of God, who is the One without a second, the superlife and superconsciousness in whom all lives and consciousnesses inhere; the manifestation of God in the Trinity of Will, Wisdom and Mind; the hierarchy of beings, including a vast army of superhuman intelligences and another of subhuman intelligences; and universal brotherhood. The spirit is eternal; the individual climbs the ladder of being through a series of reincarnations, until he reaches the stature of the perfect man, 'beyond birth and death, "fitted for immortality", ready for work in the larger life'.

The individual exists on three planes: he acts through his physical body, desires or receives sensation with his astral body, thinks with his mental body. In death the consciousness passes from the physical plane to the astral plane or intermediate world, and so to the mental plane or 'heaven' till ready for a new incarnation. People who are called 'psychic', visionaries, endowed with second sight, are living on the astral plane.

A spirit which has through noble and virtuous living and through the guidance of a higher power reached the goal of human perfection, becomes a Master or *Mahatma*. Such a one may pass into other worlds, or remain as guardian of this world offering spiritual support to others on their way; or, in exceptional circumstances, put himself into a human body and become one of the founders of the world religions.

Membership of the Theosophical Society requires adherence to three objects: 'To form a nucleus of the Universal Brotherhood of Humanity, without distinction of race, creed, sex, caste or colour.

'To encourage the study of comparative religion, philosophy, and science.

'To investigate the unexplained laws of Nature and the powers latent in man.'

Thérèse de l'Enfant-Jésus
(1873–97)

Thérèse Martin was born in Alençon to a devout family who destined their five girls for the convent. Thérèse's development was conditioned, but none of her sisters had her experiences. She was certain of her vocation, and, though she did not dare to say so at the time, certain of the direct hand of God on her life, without intermediacy. She had a sense of special destiny and special relationship to God. The language in which she speaks of this sometimes seems arch; she describes herself as Jesus's 'doll' or 'little flower' or 'girl-friend'; but it would be a mistake to dismiss the experience she is trying to express. Her determination on her vocation led her to persuade the authorities to accept her as a Carmelite long before the normal age, and the last nine years of her brief life were spent in a convent at Lisieux. They were not years of easy self-delusion. On the contrary, she passed through desiccating periods of spiritual aridity, which she faced with simple heroism. Through this she found her vocation – love – and poured out affection and practical help for birds and animals, her fellow nuns and the world outside. It is a simple story of a simple girl; but her simple profundity made a tremendous impact on the outside world, and Thérèse the dove of Lisieux has been an inspiration in the same way as Teresa the eagle of Avila.

Theurgy

The direct action of God through a human subject. Strictly, theosophy has its culmination in wisdom and understanding, theurgy in supernatural powers of action; strictly too theurgy applies to the action of God, though the word is loosely used of other spiritual powers. R. A. Vaughan wrote: 'I would use the term theurgic to characterize the mysticism which claims supernatural powers generally, – works marvels, not like the black art, by help from beneath, but as white magic, by the virtue of talisman or cross, demi-god, angel, or saint.' Theurgy was prominent among some of the GNOSTICS, who claimed that divine power was made open to the initiate. It was markedly prominent among the later NEO-PLATONISTS, especially IAMBLICHUS and PROCLUS, who believed in 'Intelligences' or divine powers which would come into the soul of the mystic and endow him with superhuman power. There was a considerable revival of theurgy at the Renaissance in the Neo-Platonists such as PICO, and theosophists such as AGRIPPA, PARACELSUS and BOEHME. One of the best accounts of theurgy comes from the pen of one J.F., who translated Agrippa's *Occult Philosophy* in 1651. In his preface he wrote: 'This is true and sublime Occult Philosophy. To understand the mysterious influence of the intellectual world upon the celestial, and of both upon the terrestrial; and to know how to dispose and fit ourselves so as to be capable of receiving the superior operations of these worlds, whereby we may be enabled to operate wonderful things by a natural power – to discover the secret counsels of men, to increase riches, to overcome enemies, to procure the favour of men, to expel diseases, to preserve health, to prolong life, to renew youth, to foretell future events, to see and know things done many miles off, and such like as these. These things may seem incredible, yet read but the ensuing treatise and thou shalt see the possibility confirmed both by reason and example.' SHAMANISM is one of the best examples of theurgy.

Thierry of Chartres
(12th century)

Mediaeval theologian and Platonist, who identified the Holy Spirit with Plato's World-Soul, proclaimed the divine Form as the Platonic Form of the universe, and identified this with the Son. If the divine Form is the *forma essendi* of all things, then we find our true being only therein.

Thomas à Jesu
(1564–1627)

Diaz Sanchez de Avila entered the Carmelite order in 1587, taking the name of Thomas à Jesu. He became known for his learning and austerity. His thinking and approach to the contemplative life were much influenced by TERESA DE JESUS, and it was his achievement to give her genius scholastic form in his mystical treatises *De Contemplatione Divina* and *Divinae Orationis Methodus*.

Thomas à Kempis
(*c.* 1379–1471)

Born in a village not far from Cologne, Thomas went to Holland to be educated by the BRETHREN OF THE COMMON LIFE, and entered their community at the Agnietenberg, living and writing, preaching and offering spiritual guidance there for more than seventy years. His great work was the compilation of THE IMITATION OF CHRIST.

Thomas Aquinas
(*c.* 1225–74)

Dominican philosopher and theologian, the great systematizer of mediaeval Christian thought. Thomas was not a mystic in his general approach (though it has been calculated that in the *Summa*, his *magnum opus*, he quotes Dionysius 1,760 times). But about two years before his death he had a profound mystical experience while celebrating mass. He put his pen on one side and left his great *Summa* unfinished. For, he said, 'I have seen that which makes all I have written and thought look small to me.'

Thomas Aquinas. Detail of a fresco portrait by Francesco Traini

Thompson, Francis
(1859–1907)

English Roman Catholic poet, who was rescued from destitution and opium by Wilfrid Meynell. He is an uneven poet with a flamboyant vocabulary, but a startling vision. For him nothing in this corporal earth of man can lack correlated greatness. The filigree petal of the snowflake speaks of God the craftsman, with His hammer of wind and His graver of frost. The cloud contains a parable that we should face the Is and with To-Be trust Heaven. The field-flower is musical of the mouth of God and mystical with the mouth of God. In 'Any Saint' he describes man as a

> . . . swinging-wicket, set
> Between
> The Unseen and the Seen.

In his best-known poem the tremendous Lover follows the human soul with 'deliberate speed, majestic instancy' as it twists and turns, till its eventual surrender to the Hound of Heaven. There is here no cloying sweetness but a numinous authority. His last lyric 'The Kingdom of God' tells that the Kingdom is to be seen even in the streets of London:

> But when so sad thou canst not sadder,
> Cry; – and upon thy so sore loss
> Shall shine the traffic of Jacob's ladder
> Pitched betwixt Heaven and Charing Cross.

So he views the invisible world.

Thoreau, Henry David
(1817–62)

American poet and essayist, who scandalized polite society by advocating civil disobedience and retiring to commune with nature on the shores of Walden Pond. He described himself as 'a mystic, a transcendentalist and a natural philosopher to boot'. In his posthumously published *Journals* he gave some record of his mystical experiences alone among trees and flowers, insects and birds and animals, clouds and water and winds, sun, moon and stars. There he has experienced ecstasy: 'There comes into my mind such an indescribable, infinite, all-absorbing, divine, heavenly pleasure, a sense of elevation and expansion, and have had nought to do with it [*sic*]. I perceive that I am dealt with by superior powers.' 'I am like a feather floating in the atmosphere, on every side is depth unfathomable.' It concerns him that his ecstatic states seem to yield so little fruit, but he decides that they provide him with the 'gold-leaf' to help him to better report to others the truth he has discerned. The art of life is to prepare ourselves, and to help others to prepare, to receive our portion of the Infinite.

Throne

See MERKABAH. The 'throne' verse in the QUR'AN is also beloved by SUFI mystics.

Tibetan Book of the Dead, The

Manual of instructions for dead souls for the period of forty-nine days between death and rebirth; used by Tibetan Buddhists as a manual of mystical teaching, 'a book for the living as well as for the dying'. It gives an account of three stages of mystical experience, the first of self-loss, the sight of the Clear Light of Reality, transcendent ecstasy; the second of visions and images, some peaceful, some wrathful; the third the process of rebirth into the physical world.

Within this is a complex system involving the formation of the world from five elements emerging in turn, Fire, Air, Water, Earth and finally, Aether, 'the green light-path of the Wisdom of Perfected Actions'; a doctrine of three bodies, the Divine Body of Truth (the Qualityless Void), the Divine Body of Perfect Endowment, and the Divine Body of Incarnation, which explains the descent of the great Teachers from the Higher to the Lower and their passage again to *nirvana*. Associated with the elements are five Wisdoms. Water produces the life-stream, the passion of Anger, the aggregate of Consciousness and the Mirror-like Wisdom; Earth produces the physical body, the passion of Egoism, the aggregate of Touch, and the Wisdom of Equality; Fire produces Vital Heat, the passion of Lust, the aggregate of Feelings and the Wisdom of Discrimination; Air produces breath of life, the passion of Envy, the aggregate of Will and the All-Performing Wisdom; Aether produces the mind, and the fully enlightened consciousness, a state beyond our ordinary humanity.

Tikhon of Zadonsk
(1724–83)

One of the greatest Russian Christian mystics, he learned alike from Orthodox, Catholic and Protestant. Much of his personal experience was rooted in his constant meditation on the passion of Jesus and his profound sense of prayer; his enlightenment came only through the DARK NIGHT OF THE SOUL. Tikhon was an eloquent preacher, an attractive writer and a beloved friend of the outcast. He was the model for Zossima in DOSTOYEVSKY's *The Brothers Karamazov*.

Time

See ETERNITY.

Tolstoy, Count Lev Nikolayevich
(1828–1910)

Russian author of aristocratic family, deeply divided between an enjoyment of life as it is and a search for ultimate meaning. His magnificent masterpiece *War and Peace* (1867–9) projects his own search on to two of the characters, Andrey and Pierre, against the back-cloth of the Napoleonic Wars. In *Anna Karenina* Levin, who combines exterior happiness with inner restlessness, learns the secret – of universal love and brotherhood – from a simple peasant. So Tolstoy was himself converted to a radical Christianity. He tells the story in *Confession*; his philosophy is henceforth expressed in the title of one of his pamphlets, *The Kingdom of God is within You*.

Traherne, Thomas
(*c.* 1636–74)

Traherne was a minor but worthy country cleric, who wrote poems which remained unpublished for more than two centuries after his death till their rediscovery and publication in 1903, followed in 1908 by prose reflections entitled *Centuries of Meditation*. Traherne is something of a nature-mystic, and seeks to recapture the 'divine intuitions' of childhood: 'The corn was orient and immortal wheat which never should be reaped nor was ever sown. I thought it had stood from everlasting to everlasting. The dust and stones of the street were as precious as gold: the gates were at first the end of the world. The green trees when I saw them first through one of the gates transported and ravished me; their sweetness and unusual beauty made my heart to leap, and almost mad with ecstasy, they were such strange and wonderful things. . . . Eternity was manifest in the Light of Day, and something infinite behind everything appeared, which talked with my expectation and moved my desire.' The same thought of childhood comes in his poems 'Wonder', 'Eden' and 'Innocence'.

But in his poems there is not merely aspiration, there is also mystical fulfilment. He writes in 'The Vision':

From one, to one, in one to see all things,
To see the King of kings,
But once in two; to see His endless treasures
Made all mine own, myself the end
Of all his labours! 'Tis the life of pleasures!
To see myself His friend!
Who all things finds conjoined in Him alone,
Sees and enjoys the Holy One.

Again in 'A Hymn upon St Bartholomew's Day' he writes:

An inward Omnipresence here,
Mysteriously like His within me stands,
Whose knowledge is a sacred sphere
That in itself at once includes all lands.
There is some angel that within me can
Both talk and move,
And walk and fly and see and love
A Man on earth, a man
Above.

And the ecstasy of the mystic is powerfully conveyed in 'Love':

O nectar! O delicious stream!
O ravishing and only pleasure! Where
Shall such another theme
Inspire my tongue with joys, or please mine
ear?
Abridgement of delights
And queen of sights!
O mine of rarities! O kingdom wide!
O more! O cause of all! O glorious Bride!
O God! O Bride of God! O King!
O soul and Crown of everything!

Trance

A condition of dissociation, characterized by the lack of voluntary movement, and frequently by automatisms of act and thought. It can be scientifically induced by hypnosis. As a worldwide religious phenomenon it is usually explained either by spirit-possession or by soul-loss.

Transcendence

That which relates to the Absolute and is 'beyond' the world of sense-perception; applied for example to Plato's Forms or to God in His eternal nature; opposed to IMMANENCE. Mystics who stress the transcendence of the Ultimate are naturally concerned to detach the individual soul from the material world, and tend to stress asceticism as a means to that end, and interior meditation.

Transcendental meditation

Term coined by Maharishi Mahesh Yogi for his technique in drawing on the innate ability of the nervous system to rid itself effortlessly of stress and fatigue. Each practitioner of transcendental meditation is given a *mantra*, a sound without meaning, the vehicle for the natural tendency of the mind to find its relaxation. It made some impact in Europe and America in the 1960s because of the adherence of 'The Beatles'.

Transmigration of souls

See REINCARNATION.

Trappists

Notre Dame de la Trappe is an abbey in Normandy, founded by the Benedictines in 1122 and adopting the Cistercian reform in 1148. In 1636 de Rancé at the age of ten became commendatory abbot. For many years he lived a life of worldliness, but in the late 1650s experienced conversion and in 1664 was consecrated abbot at La Trappe, recalling the monks to their earlier rule, combined with new austerities. The Trappists (as they are familiarly called) are a contemplative order, with a strong emphasis on liturgical worship, simplicity of living (including vegetarianism) and silence.

Tree of Life

Religious symbol of which the Norse YGGDRASIL is an immediately obvious example; it was in hanging from the tree that Wotan achieved mystical knowledge. The BUDDHA found illumination under the Bo-tree; it appears in the myth at the beginning of Genesis, both as a Tree of Life and as a Tree of Knowledge. The maypole of spring festivals is a good example of the Tree of Life. Trees play a powerful part in the myths associated with the mysteries of ISIS AND OSIRIS, and CYBELE and Attis. The SHAMANS climb a tree to the Heaven, where they find knowledge. The cross of Jesus is often called and thought of as a tree. The inverted tree by which the single God manifests Himself from above is an important image in Hinduism ('The threefold Brahman has its root above' – *Maitreya Upanishad*), and in THE KABBALAH ('The Tree of Life extends from above downwards, and is the sun which illuminates all' – The ZOHAR). The Tree appears frequently in all forms of religious art.

Trevelyan, Katharine
(b. 1909)

Niece of the historian G. M. Trevelyan, she published in 1962 *Fool in Love*, the 'autobiography of a natural mystic'. In it she describes how, realizing her own weakness and folly, she offered them to God, and how she 'saw face to face at last': 'Light streamed down from the sky such as I have never beheld. The sun shone with a new light, as though translucent gold were at its heart. I saw not only the physical sun but the spiritual sun also, which poured down on me as I walked in the garden at Coombe.' She speaks of a sense of unimaginable wonder. She was primal man, Adam with no need of Eve, for both combined within her; she experienced complete human fulfilment. Everything around spoke to her of Paradise. But more wonderful than the Light within the light was the presence of God, 'radiant, burningly pure, holy beyond holy'. 'When I breathed, I breathed Him; when I asked a question He both asked and answered it. . . . Never again the need to meditate for He was here, to be STOOD in, SAT in, as a child might play on the edges of a great sunny river.' She felt herself a child, playing in Him, laughing with Him. 'When I stood with Him, He gave and was everything.' It was an experience of wonder and joy.

Trigger

A term used by Marghanita Laski conveniently to describe factors which can be identified as inducing ecstatic experience. They include natural scenery, sexual love, childbirth, physical exercise, works of art or literature, creative activity, mathematics, various factors associated with religion, beauty and the exercise of memory.

Trinitarian Mysticism

Mystical union is usually experienced as union with the absolute simple, modeless God. But the mystical experience of Christians combined with the doctrine of God as a Holy Trinity, sometimes takes an explicitly Trinitarian form; this is known as Trinitarian Mysticism.

Troubadour

Mediaeval singers of romantic love. It has been argued that the derivation of their name and song comes from SUFI mystical love poetry. The Arabic roots *t-r-b* and *r-b* offer a series of wordplays of a type beloved by the Sufis, including the words for God, mistress, minstrel and education.

Truth

There are three important uses of the word 'truth' in relation to mystical religion. The first is applied to statements about the Ultimate. Here the mystics themselves are as clear as twentieth-century linguistic philosophers that statements about the Ultimate cannot be true, since the language and categories of thought which we use of our ordinary experiences are inescapably inappropriate when used of the Ultimate, which is thus incomprehensible and ineffable. 'Why prate about God?' asked Eckhart. 'Whatever you say of Him is untrue.' The second use of the word is to express an attitude of approach to God through direct apprehension; it is excellently exemplified in the most mystical of the Christian Gospels, According to John, when Jesus says, 'The hour is coming and is already here when the true worshippers shall worship the Father in spirit and in truth' (4, 23).

The third use is as a synonym for ultimate reality. Thus to Plato true reality is in the unchanging Forms, not the changing world; and the more intellectual forms of mysticism (such as that of the Cambridge Platonists) tend to concentrate attention on God as Truth. In the Christian tradition this is one aspect of the revelation of God in Christ, who said, 'I am the Way, the Truth, and the Life.' But there is a strong sense that the ultimate Truth is not to be caught within an intellectual net, and is not communicable by normal human means. So in the Buddhist *sutras* we read 'What is known as the teaching of the Buddha is not the teaching of the Buddha' and 'The truth indeed has never been preached by the Buddha, seeing that one has to realize it within oneself.' This is admirably put by Hui-Neng:

> There is nothing true anywhere,
> The True is nowhere to be found.
> If you say you see the True,
> This seeing is not the true one.
> When the True is left to itself,
> There is nothing false in it for it is Mind
>   itself.

When Mind in itself is not liberated from
the false,
There is nothing true; nowhere is the True
to be found.

Hence all the paradoxes of Zen Buddhism. Elsewhere Hui-Neng says, 'The Truth is not to be spoken but lived.' Here all three meanings of 'truth' are coming together.

Ts'ao-tung

See FIVE HOUSES

Two Ways, The

1 In mysticism the Two Ways usually refer to the inward and outward search for God, the one approaching God through the self, the other through the unity in or behind the sensible universe. Both are well illustrated in Plotinus. The former appears in the sixth *Ennead*: 'Often when I awake from the slumber of the body and come to myself, and step out of the outward world in order to turn in upon myself, I behold a wonderful beauty. Then I believe unshakably that I belong to a better world; most glorious life works strongly in me and I am become one with the Godhead. Transferred into this I have reached that vital energy and have raised myself above all intellectual things. When I then climb down from this rest in the lap of the Godhead to intellectual understanding I ask myself how there can possibly be a sinking back out of that condition.' Here God is found in the depths of our being; the knowledge of God is in some sense self-knowledge. We might call this Introspective Mysticism, or Introverted Mysticism. The *Mandukya Upanishad* says of this that it is 'beyond the senses, beyond the understanding, beyond all expression. . . . It is the pure unitary consciousness, wherein awareness of the world and of multiplicity is completely obliterated. It is ineffable peace. It is the Supreme Good. It is One without a second. It is the Self.' Similarly Ruysbroeck says of the 'God-seeing man' that 'his spirit is undifferentiated and without distinction, and therefore it feels nothing but the unity'.

On the other hand mystics have approached God through the sensible universe and the Unifying Vision (as we may call it). Here again is Plotinus, this time in the fifth *Ennead*: 'They see all not in process of becoming, but in Being, and they see themselves in the other. Each Being contains within itself the whole intelligible world. Therefore all is everywhere. Each is there all and all is each. Man as he now is has ceased to be the All. But when he ceases to be an individual he raises himself again and penetrates the whole world. Then, become one with the All, he creates the All' (5, 8). The Unifying Vision begins from the annihilation of the division between sensible things, so that there is an awareness, not of Many, but of All, and so of One. So Eckhart: 'In the eternal goodness of the divine nature (as in a miraculous mirror) the essence of all creatures is seen as one.' So to the perceiving soul 'all is one and one is in all'. The sensible world carries division and contradiction in itself; in essential Being these cannot remain. As long as a man sees one thing separated from another he remains in a state of mere intellectual understanding. When he sees all in all, then a man stands beyond mere understanding. But this alone is not enough. There is a process of discernment. First Many is seen as one. Then Many is seen as the One. Then the One is seen in the Many. Finally the One is seen in Itself.

Some thinkers have brought the Two Ways together. Rudolf Steiner says, 'The outer world, with all its phenomena, is filled with divine splendour, but we must have experienced the divine within ourselves, before we can hope to discover it in our environment.'

2 Another dichotomy to which the idea of the Two Ways is sometimes applied is the VIA AFFIRMATIVA and the VIA NEGATIVA, the positive and negative approaches to God, the appeal (as William James puts it) to the yes-function and to the no-function in us. On the one hand the approach to God through his love or his goodness, the vision of him as superlucent, supersplendent, superessential, supersublime, on the other the assertions of DIONYSIUS that the Absolute is not reason, or intelligence, or number or order, or magnitude or smallness, or equality or inequality, or time or eternity, not even truth or wisdom or unity or divinity or goodness, but, to go further with ERIGENA or BOEHME, it is NOTHING and (so the Upanishads) not to be described except by 'No! No!' Of course there is a sense in which these roads come together. The mystics start from the goodness they know only to leave it behind; so the positive leads to the negative. Or else in denying that God is essence they point to Him as superessential; so the negative leads to the positive.

3 There is also an important concept of the Two Ways relating to moral choice. Here however there are not two alternative routes to the same destination; they lead to different destinations. The PYTHAGOREANS used the letter Y to symbolize that choice, representing a fork in the road. They listed opposites in two columns: on one side, the right, good, light, rest, straight, the definite; on the other, the left, bad, darkness, motion or change, curved, the indefinite. Prodicus, one of the 'sophists' of the fifth century BC, used to tell a fable about Heracles, sometimes called 'Heracles at the Crossroads'. The hero was confronted by two women, one seductively made up, the other sober, steadfast and demure. The first, Vice, offered him a short and easy road, the other, Virtue, a long toilsome one. This teaching of the Two Ways was familiar throughout the Greek-speaking world. It made its way early into CHRISTIANITY and is found in *The Teaching of the Twelve Apostles* which begins 'There are two Ways, one of life and one of

death, and there is a great difference between the two Ways.' There is a sense in which all mystery-religions proclaim the same doctrine. There is a good saying of the Chinese sage Mencius: 'The ways are two: love and lack of love – that is all.'

Typology of Mysticism

One typology, based on W. T. Stace, suggests the following analysis:

1 Unity (a) External: a sense of cosmic oneness.
(b) Internal: fading of ego into a state a pure awareness.

2 Transcendence of time and space.

3 Positive sensations: joy, bliss, love, peace.

4 Sense of the numinous.

5 Sense of certitude: the reality of the mystical experience.

6 Paradox. So in the *Isa Upanishad* (5)
It moves. It does not move.
It is far. It is near.
It is within this whole universe.
It is outside it.

7 Ineffability.

8 Transience: the experience does not last.

7 Resultant change of attitude and behaviour.

Another, produced by C. Jinarajadasa, has been presented in tabular form as follows:

TYPE	THEME	METHOD	OBSTACLE	IDEAL
Grace	Gulf between man and God	Prayer	Self-reliance	Righteous man
Love	God's love to man	Adoration	Worry over unworthiness	*Bhakta* or Saint
Pantheistic	God and man are one	Affirmation	Matter (i.e. Illusion)	Yogi
Nature	God revealed in nature	Contemplation	Ignorance, superstition	Philosophic
Sacramental	'Real Presence'	Symbolism in ritual	Invalid ritual	Priest
Theosophical	Plan of the Logos	Discipleship		Master of Wisdom

U

Unamuno y Jugo, Miguel de
(1864–1937)

Spanish philosopher and poet, whose intellectual and artistic life was a search for immortality. Part of this search was the breaking down of hypocrisy and cosy dogmatism: 'My painful duty is to irritate people. We must sow in men the seeds of doubt, of distrust, of disquiet, even of despair.' Part was the comic vision: he loved Don Quixote, and even looked on Jesus as a divine fool. Part was the tragic vision, which emerges from the tension between faith and reason, opposed but needing one another. In his poem *The Christ of Velázquez* he saw Christ as having achieved the conquest of death for himself and others:

It's a sleep,
Christ, life, and death is a watch.
While the earth sleeps in loneliness
there on watch is the white moon; there
on watch is the Man,
Watching from the cross, while men lie
asleep;
there on watch is the Man, drained of blood,
the Man white
as the moon in the blackness of night.
(tr. Eleanor L. Turnbull)

Unamuno held that dreaming, not systematic thought, is the essence of life; he held to the wholeness of primal man; he held to faith as the source of truth. He regarded himself as descendant of saints and mystics.

Unifying vision

See TWO WAYS.

Unio Mystica

See MYSTICAL UNION.

Unitive Way

In Christian mysticism the third and culminating stage of the spiritual life in which the soul after purgation and illumination attains to union with God.

Universalism

There is a strong stream of mysticism which holds that all human beings are one in and with God. In Indian Vedantism there is a single Self common to all; in neo-Platonism all souls are one; in the Christian mystics 'all creatures that have flowed out from God must become united into One Man' (Eckhart) or 'all the children of God are but one in Christ, which one is Christ in all' (Boehme); in the philosophy of Spinoza, Hegel and Schopenhauer there is the unity of all consciousness.

Upanishads

Spiritual treatises composed in Sanskrit, the oldest and greatest of them between 800 and 400 BC in prose and verse. The title means something like 'Sitting at the Master's Feet'. The Upanishads contain the core of Hindu philosophy. They are about the relationships of our being to the being of the universe. The *Isa Upanishad* begins 'Behold the universe is the glory of God' and goes on to speak of the divine Spirit as both immanent and transcendent, both far and near, within all and outside all. The *Mandukya Upanishad* speaks of the pure unitary consciousness, which is 'beyond the senses, beyond the understanding, beyond all expression', in which 'awareness of the world and of multiplicity is completely obliterated. It is ineffable peace. It is the supreme good. It is One without a second. It is the Self.' The Upanishads centre on Brahman, God as Spirit, transcendent and immanent, and one with the Self in man. As the *Svetasvatara Upanishad* puts it, 'Like butter or cream is the Self in everything. Knowledge of the Self is gained through meditation. This is Brahman.' An important message of the Upanishads is *tat tvam asi* ('Thou art that'), the identity of the Self in man and the Divine in the universe. The *Chandogya Upanishad* says, 'These rivers flow, the eastern towards the West and the western towards the East; from ocean to ocean they flow. They actually become the ocean. And as they do not know which one they are, so all these creatures here, though they have come forth from Being, do not know that they have come forth from Being. Whatever they are, whether tiger, lion, wolf, boar, worm, fly, gnat, or mosquito, they all become That. That which is the subtlest of the subtle, the whole world has it as its self. That is reality. That is the Self, and That art thou.' The mystical paradox is well expressed in some lines from the *Kena Upanishad*:

It is conceived by him whom It is not
conceived of;
He by whom It is conceived of does not
know It.
It is not understood by those who
understand It;
It is understood by those who do not
understand It.

V

Vaishnavism

Devotional movement in Hinduism centred on Vishnu, especially in his manifestation as Krishna and Rama. The movement is foreshadowed in the BHAGAVAD GITA, and from the seventh to the twelfth century produced saints from both sexes and all castes, as well as ecstatic devotional poetry. It remained for centuries a movement of personal devotion; then in the eleventh century AD received theological formulation from RAMANUJA. Ramanuja challenged the impersonal philosophy of SANKARA, who had refused to have any truck with dualism. The personal devotion which was the basis of the Vaishnava movement implied that God was not identical with the soul, but was outside the soul waiting to be loved. Ramanuja therefore proclaimed a qualified Monism. A major controversy within the sect had to do with grace and individual response in salvation. Is man like a baby monkey clinging to its mother, or like a kitten being carried with no effort of its own?

Valentinus
(2nd century AD)

GNOSTIC leader, founder of the Valentinian sect, he offered a theosophy of extraordinary complexity. The *pleroma*, or fullness of the godhead, consists of thirty æons or spiritual beings, arranged in pairs or syzygies. First came four pairs: Abyss and Silence, Mind and Truth, Word (Logos) and Life, Man and Church. From Word and Life come five more pairs, and from Man and Church six more pairs, completing the *pleroma*. The thirtieth and weakest æon is called Achamoth, Sophia or Wisdom. She has an incestuous desire to know the Father of all; in her passion she produces formless Matter. Now Abyss and Mind produce the first Redeemer, Horus (the name of the reborn Osiris in Egyptian religion, and a Greek word meaning 'limit'), who fences off Wisdom from heaven, though she does not lose her heavenly origin. She now produces Iadabaoth, Child of Chaos, the creator-god of the Old Testament Yahweh, Plato's divine craftsman. He tries to imitate the perfection of the *pleroma* in the realm of matter and the eternity of the *pleroma* in the world of time. The world and the living things in it are thus ultimately of heavenly derivation, but in need of redemption. Mind counters by bringing out two more æons, the perfect offspring of the *pleroma*, Jesus and the Holy Spirit. The divine Saviour comes down to redeem and wed Wisdom and bring her back to the *pleroma*, and to redeem the souls of the Gnostics, who are the true children of their mother, from the realm of matter. Mankind is divided into three groups – the *carnal*, who are beyond redemption; the *psychic*, who live by faith and good works but not by light and knowledge, and who are redeemed from this world without attaining the *pleroma*; and the *pneumatic*, the illuminated, the true Gnostics, who have perfect knowledge and a brighter destiny, and whose feminine souls will be united in the *pleroma* with male angels.

Valentinus thus offered an esoteric gospel of salvation, expounded more simply in The GOSPEL OF TRUTH. He is highly original in the way he links religion and sexuality; we can today see in Sophia the repression of incestuous desire, and in Horus the censor or superego.

Vallabha
(1473–1531)

Hindu philosopher, whose system was one of pure non-dualism (ADVAITA). The highest reality is the Lord Krishna, who appears as Brahman in the *Upanishads*, and by other names elsewhere. He is One; he is existence, intelligence and bliss;

Vallabha

he is eternal, unchanging, omnipotent, omniscient. He is the origin of all nature and all intelligence, and in him the differences apparent in nature and in human experience disappear, so that the world and souls are all in essence one with Brahman. Those who have known Brahman can see the objects of the world as Brahman. Liberation for man comes through action, knowledge and devotion. There are nine progressive stages in devotion: hearing, reciting, remembering, obeisance, worship, salutation, service, friendship and self-dedication. The end is the love of the Lord merging into union with him.

Vallombrosan Order

Monastic order of contemplatives founded at Vallombrosa near Florence in the 1030s by John Gualbert, who was at the time attached to the CAMALDOLESE. The principles are broadly Benedictine with a greater emphasis on asceticism and silence. Galileo was for a period a novice in the order.

Varèse, Edgard
(1885–1965)

French composer who emigrated to the US in 1915. He has held that industrial society calls for a harsh, alienated music. His mastery of acoustics has given strength to his 'organized sound' and control to his inventiveness, which has been encouraged by electronic music, and by his combination of western and eastern expression. He claims that his message reaches the listener unadulterated by interpretation. His *Arcana* (1927) was inspired by PARACELSUS, and was an attempt to explore the arcane essence of the arts.

Vaudois

See WALDENSES

Vaughan, Henry
(1622–95)

Welsh doctor and poet, nicknamed the Silurist. For his first and principal collection of poems *Silex scintillans* (*The Flashing Flint*) he was indebted to George Herbert.

One of Vaughan's great themes is the restlessness of man:

> Lord! what a busie restless thing
> Hast thou made man!
>
> Man is the shuttle, to whose winding quest
> And passage through these looms
> God order'd motion, but ordain'd no rest.

This is because man has moved away from his true self, and in 'The Retreate' Vaughan uses a Platonic conceit, to express this:

> When yet I had not walkt above
> A mile or two from my first Love,
> And looking back, at that short space,
> Could see a glimpse of his bright face;
> When on some gilded Cloud or Flowre
> My gazing soul would swell an houre,
> And in these weaker glories spy
> Some shadows of eternity.

Something of the same experience of 'recollection' is still open to us as we look for God in the world of nature. Vaughan's attitude to nature is close to that of the Spanish mystic LUIS DE GRANADA:

> Grant I may so
> Thy steps track here below,
> That in these masques and shadows I may see
> Thy sacred way;
> And by those hid ascents climb to that Day
> Which breaks from Thee,
> Who art in all things, though invisibly.

This is nature-mysticism. So Vaughan hears God through a bird's song and sees Him through the rainbow.

But Vaughan knows the experience of spiritual drought, finely expressed in 'The Ecclipse':

> Whither, O whither did'st thou fly
> When I did grieve thine holy Eye?
> When thou did'st mourn to see me lost,
> And all thy Care and Councels crost.
> O do not grieve, where e'er thou art!
> Thy grief is an undoing smart,
> Which doth not only pain, but break
> My heart, and makes me blush to speak.
> Thy anger I could kiss, and will:
> But O! thy grief, thy grief doth kill!

But this is more than compensated by his positive vision:

> I saw Eternity the other night,
> Like a great ring of pure and endless light,
> All calm as it was bright;
> And round beneath it, Time, in hours, days, years,
> Driven by the spheres,
> Like a vast shadow moved; in which the world
> And all her train were hurl'd.

Plato (as Vaughan knew) had called Time 'the moving image of eternity'). Most profound of all his expressions of mystical experience is 'The Night':

> There is in God, some say,
> A deep but dazzling darkness; as men here
> Say it is late and dusky, because they
> See not all clear.
> O for that night! where I in him
> Might live invisible and dim!

Vedanta Hinduism

Indian mystical philosophy. Within Vedantism a variety of approaches may be found. Underlying the philosophy is a belief in reincarnation, but at the same time a pessimistic rejection of the material world. The object then is to attain to a mystical identification with Brahman which will lead to liberation. The first step towards this is the development of a mystical consciousness through which the multiplicity of the material world is annihilated and the Many swallowed up in the One; the individual self must be emptied of all that pertains to the world of multiplicity, sensations, images, thoughts, desires and the like. What is left is then the true Self. And this individual Self, purified of all externals, is one with the Universal Self, the Absolute, Brahman. This identity of the microcosm with the macrocosm, of man's true inmost nature with the Divine is the secret of blessedness. In realizing through mystical consciousness its oneness with Brahman, the soul finds release.

Vernazza, Battistina
(1497–1587)

Tommasina Vernazza was born at Genoa. At the age of thirteen she entered the monastery of S. Maria delle Grazie, with the name of Battistina, rising to be prioress. She wrote a number of meditations, spiritual songs and mystical treatises, particularly *The Union of the Soul with God*, *On the Knowledge of God*, *On Prayer* and *On heavenly joys and the means of attaining them*, revealing through them something of her own experience of illumination.

Via affirmativa

The way of affirmation is an approach to God through positive assertion about His attributes. He is good, just, wise, loving and so on. From that point we have to expand our concept from goodness as we know it to infinite goodness. Many theologians claim that the *via affirmativa* is inadequate without the *via negativa*, because it can speak only of the attributes of God, never of His eternal nature.

Via illuminativa

See ILLUMINATIVE WAY.

Via negativa

Converse of the VIA AFFIRMATIVA. The way of God through negation, a commonplace of all mysticism, whether Eastern or Western. No predicates attach to God; no words may legitimately be used to describe him. He is 'not this, not this'. But in stripping from our mind its delusions about God we prepare it for the truth, and in eliminating all that is not God, we begin to penetrate to the heart of the mystery. A magnificent expression of the *via negativa* will be found under DIONYSIUS THE AREOPAGITE.

Via purgativa

See PURGATIVE WAY.

Via Unitiva

See UNITIVE WAY.

Victoria, Tomas Luis de
(*c.* 1540–1611)

Spanish musical composer, who worked for a period in Rome, and was a friend of Palestrina. Both were deeply concerned with appropriate settings of the liturgy, and Victoria's most celebrated work is his *Office of Holy Week* (1585), polyphonic settings of all the Proper chant-texts from Palm Sunday to Easter. But whereas Palestrina was a serene composer, Victoria is charged with a passionate mysticism which has often led him to be compared with JUAN DE LA CRUZ: to express this he uses rich chromatic harmonies, and the device of repeated notes often charges his words with ineluctable emphasis.

Vijnana-vada

See YOGACARINS

Villa of the Mysteries

Ancient Roman villa on the outskirts of Pompeii, belonging to the *gens* Istacidia. One room was plainly set aside for the celebration of mysteries associated with DIONYSUS, and the walls are painted with a sequence of events. First we see the lady of the house presiding hieratically over the events. A neophyte with hand on hip and scarf on head is listening to the divine liturgy read by a boy under the guidance of a seated matron. A maidservant is carrying ritual offerings from the neophyte to a priestess seated at a table with two attendants, one of whom is pouring a libation. This is the prooemium. Now come the mysteries. A gross Silenus is playing the lyre; so is wanton excess turned to music and beauty in the god's service. A young Pan is playing the flute, and a charming boyish Panisca is offering her breast to a kid: we recall the phrase which the ORPHICS took up, 'A kid, I have fallen into milk.' But now in the corner is a woman starting back in terror, perhaps playing a part in some divine drama, perhaps horrified at some scene on the next wall. The initiate who has followed so far is reminded that the path to heaven is not all joy. Next, on the wall at right angles is a scene of ecstatic divination, or perhaps of the search for a new identity. A satyr is peering into a bowl held by a Silenus with head averted; behind him another Silenus is holding up a grotesque mask, which presumably the satyr sees reflected where he expects to see his own face. Next, sadly damaged, are the figures of Dionysus and his consort Ariadne; they would

Frieze from the Villa of the Mysteries

face the worshipper on his first entering the room. A kneeling woman is unveiling a phallus, that great symbol of potency. Beyond her a great winged figure, perhaps Telete, the very spirit of mystery-initiation, stands wielding a long rod; and far to the left our initiate kneels with her back bared to the blows of the rod, which brings a symbolic death, and yet whose touch means fertility. Her head is in the lap of a woman who comforts her; another stands anxiously by. Now the ordeal is over. The neophyte rises again and engages in a triumphant swirling dance, to the clashing of cymbals, and goes to prepare for the mystical marriage in which she will be one with Ariadne and receive the power of the god within her.

Vincent de Paul
(*c.* 1581–1660)

Son of a French peasant, he was ordained priest in 1600. While in his twenties he was captured by pirates and sold as a slave, but converted his owner's Turkish wife and, through her, his owner. Returning to France he came under the spiritual influence of Pierre de BÉRULLE, who found him the office of tutor to the family of the General of the Galleys, an office which he used to alleviate the sufferings of the galley-slaves. In 1625 he established the Congregation of the Mission (popularly known as Vincentians or Lazarists), and in 1633 the Daughters of Charity. He was active alike in overseas missionary work and in care for the needy everywhere. The good works of 'Monsieur Vincent' sprang from his practice of the interior life; it was well said of him that he was charitable because he was a saint, not a saint because he was charitable.

Virasaivism

Religious movement in mediaeval India, fostering personal devotion (*bhakti*) and conversion through illumination. Virasaivism produced some notable poetry, known as *vacana* ('what is said'), often using simple, homely illustrations, but sometimes using high symbolism to express mystical experience. Here are three examples from Allama Prabhu:

They don't know the day
is the dark's face,
and dark the day's.
    A necklace of nine jewels
    lies buried, intact, in the face of the night;
    in the face of the day a tree
    with leaves of nine designs.
When you feed the necklace
    to the tree
    the Breath enjoys it
in the Lord of the Caves.

The jewel of wisdom is found in the experience of the ignorant; but joy comes only when it enters the awareness of the discriminating.

Looking for your light,
I went out:
    it was like the sudden dawn
    of a million million suns,
        a ganglion of lightnings
        for my wonder.
    O Lord of Caves,
    if you are light,
    there can be no metaphor.

Here the traditional image of mystical illumination is used and then seen in its limitation.

For all their search
    they cannot see
    the image in the mirror.
It blazes in the circles
    between the eyebrows.
    Who knows this
    has the Lord.

(*all tr. A. K. Ramanujan*)

The Virasaiva is perhaps the best-known sect of devotees of Shiva, a supreme Deity and a god of healing, who is often symbolized in his potency by the *lingam* or phallus.

Vision

See SPIRITUAL SENSES.

Vision of Arda Viraf, The

Zoroastrian mystical work of uncertain date, some time about the middle of the first millennium AD. The visionary Arda Viraf, accompanied by Good Thought, Good Word and Good Act, reaches the bridge to the other world. There he sees an encounter between a soul and its *fravashi*, its personified pious acts, its Escort. He himself is escorted by two angelic spirits, Divine Obedience and Flaming Fire of Thought. He sees the 'purgatory' of those in whose lives right and wrong were nicely balanced and who remain immobile till the resurrection, the Star Tract where Good Thoughts are rewarded, the Moon Tract where Good Words are rewarded, the Sun Tract where Good Actions are rewarded, and the Place of Bliss, where he is in the presence of the radiance and voice of Ahura Mazda, the great god of Light. He then sees an encounter between a wicked soul and its deformed, misshapen *fravashi*, and places of punishment, physical and brutal, corresponding to those of reward. There are pages of physical torment described in evocative detail. After this Arda Viraf is taken back to the presence of Ahura Mazda, and commissioned to carry to mankind the lesson of what he has seen.

Visitandine Order

Order of contemplative women founded by FRANÇOIS DE SALES and JEANNE FRANÇOISE DE CHANTAL, directed to the contemplative life together with the service of the ill and needy, and practical work in education, without the extremes of asceticism. The most notable product of the order was MARGARET MARY ALACOQUE.

Vivekananda, Swami
(1862–1902)

Follower of RAMAKRISHNA; at Chicago in 1893 he effectively introduced Vedanta Hinduism to the Western world. He too was an ascetic. But where Ramakrishna was simple, Vivekananda was sophisticated: his aim was a society compounded of Western science and socialism and Indian spirituality.

Voices

See SPIRITUAL SENSES.

Voodoo

Religion of Haiti, followed by over 90 per cent of the population, and regarded with suspicion by Catholic orthodoxy. The word Voodoo is derived from a West African word, *Vodu*, for a god. Voodoo has been much influenced by Catholic belief and practice; in Lent the sanctuaries are closed, and Christmas is a time of celebration; Christian saints including Mary are found among the voodoo spirits. These spirits are called *loa*; they are protectors who help their protégés. Cult of the *loa* includes mystical marriage, dancing and spirit possession.

W

Waldenses

Christian sect (also called Vaudois) founded by Peter Waldo (d. 1217), a rich merchant of Lyons, who essayed a return to primitive Christianity, which led them to suffer persecution. They were especially strong in the Alps, but under duress spread to Bohemia, Spain and elsewhere. Their simple faith has been understandably idealized by later radicals.

Wang Pi

(226–49)

Commentator on TAO-TE-CHING and I CHING, who found ultimate reality in non-being. 'If we want to say it is Non-being, yet things from it gain completeness. If we want to say it is Being, yet we do not see its form.'

Weber, Max

(1864–1920)

Religious sociologist, who in his difficult work *The Sociology of Religion* argued that the change from traditional, magical religion to rational, ethical religion is the work of religious specialists whom he called prophets, endowed with charisma, and with a belief in their own transcendent mission, and enthusiastic proclaimers of a 'religious truth of salvation through personal revelation'.

Weil, Simone

(1909–1943)

French philosopher and mystic. In a letter to Father Perrin she outlined her 'spiritual autobiography'. In youth she held Christian concepts, especially neighbourly love, unconsciously. At the age of fourteen she went through a period of despair, emerging after some months to the faith that every human being can penetrate to the kingdom of truth, beauty, goodness, if he longs for it and concentrates all his attentions on it. But she avoided churches, and was agnostic about God. She avoided reading mystical works too. But she was attracted by George Herbert's poem 'Love bade me welcome' and learned it by heart; and one day, while she was repeating it to herself, 'Christ himself came down and took possession of me'. She did not reason about Jesus as the incarnation of God; she could not think of him without thinking of him as God. But she found the same sort of mystical experience in Plato and indeed in the Mysteries of Osiris or Dionysus. After this initial experience, the sense of Christ's presence returned to her with increasing clarity, and his passion entered into her being. But she remained on the threshold of the Church, 'waiting in patience'. Dogged by agonizing headaches and ill-health all her life, she died young. The last words she wrote were 'The most important part of education – to teach the meaning of *to know* (in the scientific sense).' Her spiritual legacy is a small volume of letters and papers under the title *Waiting on God.*

Wei-yang

See FIVE HOUSES

Wesley, John

(1703–91)

Founder of Methodism. His father was a High Church Anglican, whose dying words were 'The inward witness, son, the inward witness, that is the proof, the strongest proof of Christianity.' At Oxford John was the central figure in the 'Holy Club'. At this time he was attracted to mystical and contemplative thought, particularly in the writings of Henry More and William Law (whom he went to see). He went for a period as a missionary to Georgia. On his return in 1737, contact with the MORAVIANS led him to feel that his religious life was inadequate; and on 24 May 1738 he had a conversion experience. From that point his expressed aim was 'to promote as far as I am able vital practical religion and by the grace of God to beget, preserve, and increase the life of God in the souls of men'. This was just what he did. In the next fifty-two years he made the world his parish. He rode 225,000 miles and preached more than 40,000 sermons, calling the people to salvation, perfection and love. His preaching moved great crowds of people to an almost ecstatic response. Critics, like Sydney Smith, derided this power of ENTHUSIASM. But Wesley's own instructions to preachers show that he discerned a difference between an enthusiasm imposed by a preacher, and an enthusiasm which arises from the opening of the inner self to – as he would say – Christ, 'the giving God all our heart'. He was himself a loyal member of the Church of England, but the Methodists were driven to operate outside the framework of the established Church.

Whichcote, Benjamin

(1609–83)

See CAMBRIDGE PLATONISTS.

Walt Whitman

Whitman, Walt
(1819–92)

One of America's greatest poets, poet of the body and of the soul; he described himself as a cosmos, and said he could experience the whole world widening within him. He declared himself 'standing at ease in Nature'. A live-oak in Louisiana speaks to him of a joy even beyond his own; he demands, of the prairie-grass dividing, the spiritual corresponding. He ebbs with the ocean of life. One of his poems begins

Spontaneous me, Nature.
The loving day, the mounting sun, the
  friend I am happy with,
The arm of my friend hanging idly over
  my shoulder,
The hillside whiten'd with blossoms of the
  mountain ash . . .

In the famous 'Song of Myself', in celebrating himself he takes the exact dimensions of the gods of old. He ends one of his later poems, 'Chanting the Square Deific':

Santa Spirita, breather, life,
Beyond the light, lighter than light,
Beyond the flames of hell, joyous, leaping
  easily above hell,
Beyond Paradise, perfumed solely with mine
  own perfume,
Including all life on earth, touching, including
  God, including Saviour and Satan,
Ethereal, pervading all (for without me what
  were all? what were God?)
Essence of forms, life of the real identities,
  permanent, positive, (namely the unseen)
Life of the great round world, the sun and
  stars, and of man, I, the general soul,
Hence the square finishing the solid, I the
  most solid,
Breathe my breath also through these songs.

It is not surprising that this vast cosmic vision could not be expressed through a formal verse-structure; yet Whitman's use of anaphora and parallelism also expresses something of the unity of his vision. For he sings of the universal and is preoccupied with perfection, and in perhaps his finest poem, 'Out of the Cradle Endlessly Rocking', reality is in the unfolding Word.

In 1882 he published *Specimen Days*, a volume of prose, which contains some notable passages of nature-mysticism.

William of St Thierry
(*c.* 1085–1148)

Of noble birth, he entered the religious life, being associated particularly with the Cistercian abbey of Signy, where he divided his time between prayer and study. Theologically he was an opponent of Abelard. He was a close friend of BERNARD OF CLAIRVAUX, and himself a contemplative and mystic: we may note especially his work *De Deo Contemplando*, which owes some debt to Augustine, and his commentary on *The Song of Songs*.

Williams, Charles Walter Stansby
(1886–1945)

English scholar and author. He was professionally employed by Oxford University Press, but his public reputation depended on his writing and lecturing; he was also an exacting teacher and stimulating conversationist. He wrote poetry and drama, criticism, biography, theology. Perhaps his most interesting achievement lay in seven novels, which he called 'psychological thrillers', and whose themes are supernatural and mystical. For example, in *The Place of the Lion* (1931) the Platonic Forms seek to take over the world.

Windesheim

Village in Holland where in 1387 Florentius Radewyns – who had succeeded Geert de GROOTE as head of the community at Deventer, and was a leading member of the BRETHREN OF THE COMMON LIFE – together with six others from one of RUYSBROECK's foundations, formed a community of Augustinian Canons. The house flourished through the fifteenth and sixteenth centuries, and had priors of notable ability and saintliness, especially John Vos, Ian Busch (the historian of the community) and John of

Brussels, and nurtured THOMAS À KEMPIS and the philosopher Gabriel Biel. The community were the outstanding representatives of the DEVOTIO MODERNA; there was dedicated meditation on Christ's passion, frequent Communion interpreted in a strongly mystical way and a passionate pursuit of spiritual perfection. The house itself was destroyed in 1581, but the community continued in exemplary fashion till 1802.

Wine

Image used by mystical writers to describe the object of mystical experience, the experience itself being a kind of intoxication. So Macarius: 'Sometimes the communication of the divine mysteries induces in them a holy inebriation.'

Among the Sufis where several levels of meaning operate simultaneously, drinking songs, while literally meant, also speak of spiritual ecstasy: we can see this in Omar Khayyam or Hafiz.

In the Christian EUCHARIST wine is one of the two consecrated elements.

Winstanley, Gerrard
(*c.* 1609–55)

Winstanley's place in history arises from his leadership of the Christian communist group known as the Diggers. But Winstanley was also a mystic with an intense belief in the divine Light within: 'Man looks abroad for a God and doth imagine or fancy a God in some particular place of glory beyond the skies. But the Kingdom of Heaven is within you, dwelling and ruling in your flesh.' He looked for a God outside himself, but came to see God as the Spirit and Power of Light shining within the individual. Winstanley is a believer in waiting upon God in silence. Truth must be manifested within: 'You shall no longer feed upon the oil that was in other men's lamps, for now it is required that every one have oil in his own lamp, even the pure testimony of truth within himself.' But experience must come out in action; 'for action is the life of all, and if thou dost not act thou dost nothing'. Winstanley in all this shows himself a firm Christian; it is Christ who validates the inner experience: 'this is to believe in Christ, when the actings and breathings of your soul are within the centre of the same spirit in which the man Jesus Christ lived, acted, and breathed'.

Wisdom

In the Hellenistic age, the Jews became concerned about the gulf between God and man. Wisdom is one of the powers which bridge that gap. In Ecclesiasticus (1, 4) she is described as 'first of all created things'. In Proverbs (3, 19) and Job (28, 27) God employs Wisdom in creation. In *The Wisdom of Solomon* we read (7, 25–8, 1) 'Like a fine mist she rises from the power of God, a pure effluence from the glory of the Almighty. . . . She is the reflection of everlasting light, the flawless mirror of the active power of God and the image of his goodness. She is but one, yet can do everything; herself unchanging, she makes all things new; age after age she enters into holy souls, and makes them God's friends and prophets. She is more radiant than the sun, and surpasses every constellation; compared with the light of day, she is found to excel; for day gives place to night, but against wisdom no evil can prevail. She spans the world in power from end to end, and orders all things benignly.' This language is close to that which many mystics use of God or the Ultimate.

In Christian thought there is some tendency to identify Wisdom with the LOGOS; this may be seen in the dedication of the great cathedral church at Constantinople to Holy Wisdom (Santa Sophia). In GNOSTIC mysticism Wisdom is a divine EMANATION, sometimes appearing as the bride of the Logos, with a part to play in the creation and redemption of the world. In the late nineteenth century the Russian Orthodox mystical philosophers BULGAKOV and SOLOVIEV found a place for Wisdom in their systems. They distinguished between created and uncreated Wisdom, but found in Wisdom the unity between God and the world.

Woolman, John
(1720–72)

American Quaker, whose journal is one of the great testaments of spiritual devotion. He tells how while only six years old he had an urge to search for the pure River of Water of Life, how he came to see God in all His creatures, how he was lifted from worldliness by the power of Truth. One of his notable visionary experiences came towards the end of his life during a desperate illness. He had a vision of a mass of dull colour to the south-east, and learned that this was human beings in misery and he among them. Then he heard a melodious voice saying 'John Woolman is dead.' Then he was carried in the Spirit to mines where pagans were oppressed by Christians. He lay seeking to understand, and into his mouth were put the words 'I am crucified with Christ, nevertheless I live, yet not I, but Christ liveth in me.' The death was the death of his own will.

Wordsworth, William
(1770–1850)

Born in Cumberland; a sympathizer with the French Revolution; friend of Coleridge, with whom he collaborated in the *Lyrical Ballads*; one of those who led others to share in the beauty and majesty of the English Lake District; poet laureate from 1843; both one of the best and worst of English poets; and a secular or natural mystic. In early days he was something of a pantheist; later he came to a more orthodox

William Wordsworth painted by Richard Carruthers in 1817

Christianity. But even in early days he spoke of God as the object of mystical experiences. So in *The Prelude* he writes of

> one interior life
> In which all beings live with God, themselves
> Are God, existing in the mighty whole.

Wordsworth's mysticism has a strongly impersonal element. He writes in *Tintern Abbey* of

> A motion and a spirit, that impels
> All thinking things, all objects of all thought,
> And rolls through all things. Therefore am
> I still
> A lover of the meadows and the woods.

Human beings seem to enter this as depersonalized elements

> Rolled round in earth's diurnal course,
> With rocks, and stones, and trees

as he puts it in the little epitaph. 'A slumber did my spirit seal'.

Whether Wordsworth had himself the experience properly called mystical seems doubtful. But he could enter into it in such a way as to write about it with empathy.

In one passage he seems to suggest that mystical experience comes from within us:

> Not Chaos, not
> The darkest pit of lowest Erebus . . .
> – can breed such fear and awe
> As fall upon us often when we look
> Into our Minds, into the Mind of Man –

a remark which profoundly shocked a mystic of a different temper, William Blake.

Wu

Chinese term for illumination, equivalent to the Japanese SATORI.

Wu-wei

Non-activity, an important doctrine of TAOISM.

Y

Yamabushi

Japanese holy men who seek ecstatic inspiration in the heights of the mountains. They blend ancient mountain-worship with Buddhism; and the Buddhists equate the climbing of the mountain with the eightfold path which leads to enlightenment. The charisma of the Yamabushi is passed on within the family.

Yantra

Sanskrit word for a mystical diagram. TANTRA is something done, MANTRA is something spoken, YANTRA is something seen, a visible form in which cosmic energies are concentrated, which offers a starting-point and direction for meditation, and evokes mental imagery of the higher sort. The MANDALA is a form of *yantra*. The typical pattern of *yantra* is an enclosure, to contain the meditating self, with multiple triangles to the outside representing the grosser forms of energy, and concentric circuits within the whole helping to focus the mind on the centre. *Mantras* or anthropomorphic deities may be shown at key points. The ultimate aim is for the mind to move from the outer perimeter to the central point where a dot represents the invisible source of Being. There are many *yantras* of different kinds: for example a temple in its design may be a *yantra*, and the human body is sometimes called 'the best of *yantras*'.

Yggdrasil

The World Tree in ancient Scandinavian mythology. Its branches spread over the whole world. Under its roots are wells of wisdom, from which the Norns draw water, and by which the gods deliver their dooms. Thomas Carlyle said that the tree 'has its roots deep down in the Death-kingdoms, among the oldest dead dust of men, and with its boughs reaches always beyond the stars, and in all times and places is one and the same Life-tree.'

Yin, Yang

In Chinese philosophy the principles of dark and light. Everything in the universe is classified under these categories. *Yin* is the negative, female, principle, and includes earth, moon, water, winter; *yang* is the positive, male principle, and includes heaven, sin, fire, summer. But these are not, like the Pythagorean opposites, dualistic principles of evil and good. Both are complementary parts of a single cosmic harmony, and merge and change and interact with one another.

Yoga

The root meaning is 'yoke' or 'bind'. Yoga is thus a method of discipline and linking oneself to the spirit world. The BHAGAVAD GITA is the great scripture of yoga. In it due honour is paid to *karma-yoga* (the approach to the Divine through good works) and *jñana-yoga* (the approach to the Divine through knowledge); each is valid for different people. But there is a higher form of yoga, *bhakti-yoga* (the approach to the Divine through personal devotion).

Many treatises teach different practices and postures to help the attainment of unity with the spirit world, of which breath-control and meditation are perhaps the most important.

The beginning of yoga meditation is concentration on a single point. This may be something physical, a point of light on the wall, or the tip of your own nose, or it may be a single thought, or it may be the very Being of God. All scattered thoughts and diffused attention thus become integrated and focused. The effect is to control, almost to censor, all distractions, whether arising from the senses or the inward consciousness. The true *yogin* can practise this concentration on a single point at any moment, and so eliminate distractions.

To achieve this requires discipline and practice. These practices and spiritual exercises are analysed by Patanjali under eight heads. First 'restraints' (*yama*). These are five moral restrictions on action tolerated by the rest of society: *ahimsa* (not to kill or do violence), *satya* (not to lie or deceive), *asteya* (not to steal), *brahmacarya*

*A shepherdess (*yin*) surrounded by three sheep (*yang*) on a Ch'ing dynasty porcelain dish*

Two sections of an 18th-century Indian manuscript illustrating various yoga postures

(to abstain from sex), *aparigraha* (to avoid avarice). Second, 'disciplines' (*nijama*). These include cleanliness of body, tranquillity of mind, asceticism, religious study and the dedication of all actions to God. Third, 'postures' (*asana*). The body must be in a stable and comfortable position. There must be relaxation and the avoidance of physical effort and fatigue: 'Posture becomes perfect when the effort to attain it disappears.' Patanjali does not try to describe suitable postures, except in general terms; they shall be learned by imitating a master. One of the most familiar, the *padmasama* is one of thirty-two described in the *Gheranda Saniluta*: 'Place the right foot on the left thigh and similarly the left foot on the right thigh; cross the hands behind the back and firmly catch the big toes of your crossed feet (the big toe of the right foot with the right hand, of the left foot with the left hand). Place the chin on the chest and fix the gaze on the tip of the nose.' Fourth, 'respiration' (*pranayama*). Breathing should be disciplined, first by prolonging inhalation and exhalation; the irregular breathing of the average man produces a dangerous psychic fluidity. Fifth, withdrawal of sensory activity from external objects (*pratyahara*). Sixth, 'concentration' (*dharana*), fixing the attention on a single point of thought. Seventh, 'meditation' (*dhyana*), 'a current of unified thought, a kind of extension of the concentration on a single point of thought'. Finally, 'union' (*samadhi*).

The *yogin* who attains to the state of union is said to be in touch with Brahman. He perceives himself in all things and all things in himself, for he is in union with God, and perceives God in all things and all things in God. So he is at one and the same time in communion with God, and in a loving relationship with the world. He is free from his lesser self, and finds his greater self in God. He is beyond the range of *meum* and *tuum*: the *Gita* calls yoga a state of equality. And the experience is one of ecstatic joy.

Yogacarins

Buddhist Mahayana school, founded perhaps by Maitreyunatha, and developed in the fourth century AD by Asanga and Vasubandhu in N.W. India and attaining considerable influence about AD 500, notable for their emphasis on withdrawal into trance, in contrast to the ABHIDHARMA approach. Their complex system is based on 'Thought-only' or 'Mind-alone': the Absolute is Thought. Where the *Abhidharma* sought analytical awareness, the Yogacarins tried to reach the transcendental infinite by withdrawal. Being is of three kinds: the *apparent* existence of an object apart from others; the aspect of *interdependence* with other objects; and the real undifferentiated being in which the thing no longer appears as an object at all. One of the odder Yogacara doctrines is of *store-consciousness*, a supra-personal consciousness in which the impressions of all past experience are stored, and which is the foundation of all acts of thought. Yogacara is also called Vijnana-vada because of its teaching that external objects have no reality and consciousness (*vijnana*) alone is real.

Yün-men

(d. 949)

Chinese ZEN Master, founder of the Yün-men sect, one of the FIVE HOUSES. He specialized in single-word answers. 'What is the meaning of the Patriarch's coming from the West?' 'Master!'

Z

Zarathustra
(*c.* 618–541 BC)

See ZOROASTRIANISM

Zazen

A posture for meditation, associated with Zen, with legs crossed and body upright, and fostered particularly by Dogen. It has been called a process of 'non-thinking'. Here is Dogen's own account of it:

'If you wish to attain enlightenment, begin at once to practice *zazen*. For this meditation a quiet chamber is necessary, while food and drink must be taken in moderation. Free yourself from all attachments, and bring to rest the ten thousand things. Think of neither good nor evil and judge not right or wrong. Maintain the flow of mind, of will, and of consciousness; bring to an end all desires, all concepts and judgements. Do not think about how to become a Buddha.

'In terms of procedure, first put down a thick pillow and on top of this a second (round) one. One may choose either a full or half cross-legged position. In the full position one places the right foot on the left thigh and the left foot on the right thigh. In the half position only the left foot is placed upon the right thigh. Robe and belt should be worn loosely, but in order. The right hand rests on the left foot, while the back of the left hand rests in the palm of the right. The two thumbs are placed in juxtaposition.

'The body must be maintained upright, without inclining to the left or to the right, forward or backward. Ears and shoulders, nose and navel must be kept in alignment respectively. The tongue is to be kept against the palate, lips and teeth are kept firmly closed, while the eyes are to be kept always open.

'Now that the bodily position is in order, regulate your breathing. If a wish arises, take note of it and then dismiss it. In practising thus persistently you will forget all attachments and concentration will come of itself. That is the art of *zazen*. *Zazen* is the Dharma gate of great rest and joy.'

(tr. R. Masunaga)

Zen

Zen (Chinese *ch'an*) is the School of Meditation in Mahayana Buddhism introduced into China by BODHIDHARMA *c.* AD 520, though traceable in its essence to TAO-SHENG in the previous century. Almost inevitably there were sooner or later sects or divisions, especially the Five Houses. These were the Wei-yang sect, whose special contribution was the use of circular figures to symbolize the enlightened consciousness and help the process of enlightenment; the Yün-men sect, with their laconic, single-word answers to spiritual questions; the Fa-yen sect, which held the interpretation of the six attributes of being, totality and distinction, identity and difference, coming-to-be and passing away; the Ts'ao-tung sect, which analysed reality, or our awareness of reality under five 'ranks', the Absolute within the relative, the relative within the Absolute, the Absolute alone, the relative alone, the Absolute and the relative at one, of which the last is the highest; and the Lin-chi sect, with its emphasis on the liberating nature of enlightenment, and the surprising use of shouting and beating to help disciples towards enlightenment. After Zen developed in Japan through the work of Eisai in the late twelfth century it was these last two, known in Japan as Soto and Rinzai, which flourished.

Zen depends upon the techniques of ZAZEN (an upright cross-legged posture) and KOAN (paradoxical questions and answers leading the mind away from the contradictions of sense-perception and the material world into the Truth). The experience of enlightenment comes in an intuitive grasp of the units of being. Zen has had a significant impact on the arts, and inspired the painter Sesshu and the poet Bashō. Through the work of D. T. Suzuki and others it has become popular with Westerners seeking enlightenment.

The essence of Zen is summarized in four statements:

> A special transmission outside the Scriptures.
> No dependence upon words and letters.
> Direct pointing to the soul of man.
> Seeing into one's nature and the attainment of Buddhahood.

Zen used startling verbal methods almost to shock the listener into fresh thought. Paradox for instance. As Fudaishi puts it:

> Empty-handed I go and yet the spade is in my hands.
> I walk on foot, yet am riding on an ox's back
> When I pass over the bridge,
> look, the water is not flowing, the bridge is flowing.

This is one way of directing attention to the unity of all being. One famous Zen sermon is reminiscent of some words of Jesus: 'If you have a staff I will give you one; if you have not, I will take it away from you.' This is in a sense a denial

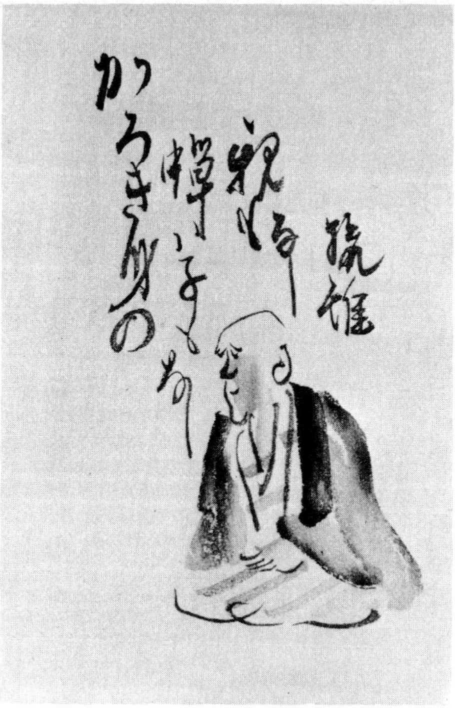

A 19th-century Japanese portrait of a haiku *poet*

of the law of contradiction. A thing *can* be both A and not A, and the Zen masters are liable to answer Yes or No impartially to the same question. But Zen is in the end a religion of affirmation. One form of affirmation is repetition. 'What is the Buddha?' 'The Buddha.' 'What is the Tao?' 'The Tao.' 'What is the Dharma?' 'The Dharma.' Another is to meet a question with an exclamation or with silence: both are forms of affirmation. Another form of affirmation is a simple act, the raising of a stick, a movement of the finger; for Zen is life.

One of the fascinations of Zen is that it can start anywhere. A German philosopher, Eugen Herrigel, wanted to penetrate the mystery of Zen. He did not try to analyse Zen philosophically. He took up, under a Master, one of the arts which exemplify Zen. As he was a good rifle-shot, he chose archery. The lessons lasted six years, practising every day, and it was four years before he was allowed to face a target. The Japanese hold the bow above the head and then pull the hands apart until the left hand comes down to eye-level and the right hand above the right shoulder. Then after a pause the arrow is shot. Herrigel found that this very exercise was a strain which left him weak and trembling. He nearly gave up; he said it was impossible for him. The Master explained that it was because he was not breathing properly. So Herrigel started breathing exercises, and gradually it became effortless, second nature, for the bow to come into position. Now he concentrated on the shooting, but try as he would he either jerked or let the arrow go indifferently. The Master explained that he must practise to work not by effort but by instinct, like a child: then the string would loose itself at the right moment, like snow sliding from a leaf. He practised and after one shot the Master suddenly said, 'Just then *it* shot. Not you, but *it*.' Then came the target. To his surprise the Master forbade him to aim. In that case he challenged the Master to hit the target in the dark. After a period of meditation the Master shot two arrows by the light of a single taper. The first hit the bullseye, the second splintered the first. '*It* shot the second arrow, and *it* brought it to the centre of the target.' Herrigel understood. He let the bow and arrow take over, and gradually came to achieve perfect shots. In so doing he had become a Zen Master himself. Zen must be lived, not analysed.

Similarly a Zen Master offered to train a pupil in sword-play. For weeks the young man was given menial tasks to perform. From time to time the Master would suddenly, without provocation, cudgel him. He learned to be on the alert against such blows, but never evaded them all. He kept asking for training in swordsmanship, but never received it. One day he saw the Master crouching over a cooking-pot with his back to him. He thought he would have his revenge; he aimed to thwack at the Master, only to find that the Master without turning round had parried the blow with the saucepan lid. The essence of swordsmanship lay in the effortless perception and avoidance of danger, in the complete unity of thought and action, in the fusing of mind and body, perception and reaction, into an instantaneous whole.

The Buddha's most famous sermon consisted in holding up a flower. A Chinese Master, when asked 'What is a Buddha?', held up his index finger. A monk asked a Master 'Has a dog a Buddha-nature too?' and the Master answered 'Wa!' This implies (a) No, (b) the Chinese word for 'Enlightenment', (c) the noise a dog makes when it barks.) In those three stories is the nucleus of Zen.

Zen has affected social life and the arts in a variety of ways. For example the Sumiye school of painters, who sketch in black and white on thin paper, swiftly, without deliberation or correction. The Sumiye artist does not attempt to copy objective reality, but to realize it. The line he draws does not represent the mountain; it *is* the mountain. In one sense his work is impressionist; he catches the moment; this is the essence of Zen. The Japanese *haiku* or seventeen-syllable poem, does the same thing with words. Here is Bashō (1643–94)

> A branch shorn of leaves
> A raven perching on it –
> This autumn evening.

Swordsmanship is another part of life deeply affected by Zen, as was the whole way of life of the Samurai. Even such a simple act as taking tea may reveal the Ultimate.

One of the wisest statements of the nature of Zen was made by Ch'ing-yuan Wei-hsin: 'Before a man studies Zen, to him mountains are mountains and waters are waters; after he gets an insight into the truth of Zen through the instruction of a good master, mountains to him are not mountains and waters are not waters; but after this when he really attains to the abode of rest, mountains are once more mountains and waters are waters.'

See also BODHIDHARMA; BUDDHISM; DOGEN; HAKUIN; HUI-NENG; KOAN; NIRVANA; SATORI; TAO-SHENG; ZAZEN.

Zinzendorf, Nikolaus Ludwig, Graf von

(1700–60)

Born in Dresden, and a member of the Central European aristocracy, Zinzendorf became actively involved in a colony of MORAVIAN refugees at Herrnhut on one of his estates. He gave up government service in 1727 to concentrate on the religious life, was consecrated to a bishopric in 1737, and did more than any other individual to bring about the revival in the Moravian Church. Zinzendorf stood for 'a religion of the heart' based on personal devotion to and fellowship with Christ as creator, sustainer and redeemer of the world.

Zohar, The

Strictly *Sefer Ha-Zohar, The Book of Splendour*, but usually called *The Zohar*. Written in Castile towards the end of the thirteenth century, in an artificial Arabic, it is thought to be the work of Moses de Leon. The leading document of Jewish Kabbalism, it consists in its main bulk of eighteen parts: (a) a lengthy commentary on the *Torah*; (b) *The Book of Concealment*, a brief and difficult commentary on the opening chapters of Genesis; (c) *The Greater Assembly*, a dramatic, literary composition, comprising a series of speeches about mystical truth, culminating in death by ecstasy; (d) *The Lesser Assembly*, a similarly dramatic account developing *The Greater Assembly*; (e) *Assembly for a Lecture on the Tabernacle*, a dramatized exposition of mystical prayer; (f) *The Halls*, an account of the seven Halls of God's chariot-throne or *Merkabah*; (g) *The Old Man*, an address on the mysteries of the soul set in a dramatized context; (h) *The Child*, an address on the mysteries of the *Torah* attributed to a young child; (i) *The Head of the Academy*, a visionary journey through Paradise including a celestial address; (j) *The Secrets of the Torah*, allegorical interpretation; (k) a highly literary attempt to reproduce an archaic style of commentary on the *Torah*; (l) a Kabbalistic commentary on the opening verses of *The Song of Songs*; (m) *The Mystical Standard of Measure*, a mystical commentary on Deuteronomy 6, 4; (n) *Secrets of the Letters*, a Kabbalistic interpretation of the letters in the name of God; (o) a commentary on Ezekiel's vision of the *Merkabah*; (p) *Mystical Midrash*, further dramatized commentaries on the *Torah*; (q) interpretations of *The Book of Ruth*. To these are appended three further volumes of commentary which patently do not come from the same hand.

The Zohar is closely linked to the text of the Jewish scriptures in general and the *Torah* in particular. Four methods of interpretation are used: the literal, the homiletic, the allegorical and the mystical, and in the end the last alone counts. It is an attempt to use mystical interpretation in defence of a basically simple faith. Behind the world we know is the Infinite, *En-Sof*. The ultimate world of God is knowable to none but Him, but there is a secondary world, the world of attributes, through which He may be known. These attributes, applied by scripture to God, are not mere analogies. The arm of God is not a groping attempt to describe God in human terms; it is the name of that which gives any sort of existence to human arms: 'all names and attributes are metaphoric with us but not with him', said Isaac ibn Latif. This means that there cannot be an absolute discontinuity between God and the world. *The Zohar* is in fact ambivalent to the material world; it describes it as 'the world of separation' where things are isolated from God and from one another; yet at the same time 'if one uses mystical meditation to contemplate material objects, everything is revealed as one'. Primarily, however, *The Zohar* is a revelation, based on a mystical interpretation of the *Torah*, of the hidden life of God.

Zoroastrianism

Zarathustra or Zoroaster (*c*. 618–541 BC) appeared in Persia as a prophet probably in the early sixth century BC. He saw himself as the messenger of Ahura Mazda, Lord of Light, the one Wise Lord, and only God, creator and sustainer of all that is good. Life, to Zarathustra, was a battleground between light and darkness, good and evil, the beneficent Spirit (Spenta Mainyu) and the maleficent spirit (Angra Mainyu). Zarathustra looked forward to the appearance of a Saviour, the victory of the forces of good over the forces of evil, and the establishment of a golden age for the righteous. There will be judgement: 'Powerful in immortality shall be the soul of the follower of Truth, but lasting torment shall there be for the man who cleaves to the Lie.' Zoroastrianism thus offers an ESCHATOLOGY, which had a profound influence on Judaic and Christian eschatology. It has little in it which can be called mystical, but Zarathustra's successors (or he himself later in life) introduced a communion in haoma juice (the Hindu SOMA), which was regarded as a foretaste of eternal life. Zoroastrian religion survives among the Parsis.

ABELSON, J. *The Immanence of God in Rabbinical Literature*, London, 1912.

—— *Jewish Mysticism*, London, 1913.

ABERLE, D. *The Peyote Religion among the Navaho*, Chicago, 1965.

ADDISON, C. M. *The Theory and Practice of Mysticism*, New York, 1918.

AEGERTER, E. *Madame Guyon, une aventurière mystique*, Paris, 1941.

—— *Le Mysticisme*, Paris, 1952.

ALLEN, H. E. *Writings ascribed to Richard Rolle, hermit of Hampole, and materials for his biography*, New York and London, 1927.

ALSTON, W. 'Ineffability', *Philosophical Review*, 65 (1956), 506–22.

ALTMANN, A. *Studies in Religious Philosophy and Mysticism*, London, 1969.

ANCELET-HUSTACHE, JEANNE *Mechtilde de Magdebourg (1207–82): Etude de psychologie religieuse*, Paris, 1926.

—— *Le bienheureux Henri Suso*, Paris, 1943.

—— *Master Eckhart and the Rhineland Mystics*, Eng. tr., London, 1957.

ANDREWS, C. F. *Sadhu Sundar Singh: a personal memoir*, London, 1934.

ANGUS, S. *The Mystery Religions and Christianity*, New York, 1925.

ANRICH, G. *Das antike Mysterienwesen in seinem Einfluss auf das Christentum*, Göttingen, 1894.

ARBERRY, A. J. *Sufism: An Account of the Mystics of Islam*, London, 1950; New York, 1970.

ARINTERO, J. G. *Cuestiones misticas*, Salamanca, 1916.

—— *Evolucion mistica*, Salamanca, 1921.

ARMSTRONG, A. H. *The Architecture of the Intelligible Universe in Plotinus*, Cambridge, 1967.

AUCLAIR, M. *Saint Teresa of Avila*, Eng. tr., London, 1953.

AUGER, A. *Etude sur les Mystiques des Pays Bas au Moyen Age* (Acad. Roy. de Belge 46), Brussels, 1892.

AVALON, A. *Shakti and Shakta*, Madras, ³1939.

—— *Principles of Tantra*, Madras, ²1952.

BACH, J. *Meister Eckhart, der Vater der deutschen Speculation*, Vienna, 1860.

BAETA, C. G. *Prophetism in Ghana*, London, 1962.

BALLARD, P. H. *Psychedelic Religion?*, Cardiff, n.d. (*c.* 1970).

BARTLETT, F. C. *Religion as Experience, Belief, Action*, London, 1950.

BASTIDE, J. *The Mystical Life*, Eng. tr., London, 1934.

BAUDISSON, W. W. *Adonis und Esmun*, Leipzig, 1911.

BAXTER, I. F. G. 'Justice and Mysticism', *Revue Internationale de Philosophie*, 17 (1963), 353–80.

BENNETT, C. A. *A Philosophical Study of Mysticism*, New Haven, 1931.

BENSON, R. H. *Mysticism*, London, 1907.

BERDYAEV, N. *Freedom and the Spirit*, Eng. tr., London, 1935; Plainview, NY, 1972.

—— *Spirit and Reality*, Eng. tr., London, 1939.

BERGER, P. *William Blake: Poet and Mystic*, Eng. tr., London, 1914; New York, 1969.

BERGMAN, J. *Ich bin Isis*, Uppsala, 1968.

BERGSON, H. *Les deux sources de la morale et de la religion*, Paris, 1932.

BERLIÈRE, U. *L'ascèse bénédictine des origines à la fin du xiie siècle*, Paris, 1927.

BERTHOLET, A., *Das Geschlecht der Gottheit*, Tübingen, 1934.

BERTOCCI, P. A. *The Empirical Argument for God in Late British Philosophy*, Cambridge, Mass., 1938.

BESANT, W. *The Eulogy of Richard Jefferies*, London, 1888; Philadelphia, 1889.

BETT, H. *Nicholas of Cusa*, London, 1932.

BLEEKER, C. J. (ed.) *Initiation*, Leiden, 1965.

BLOFIELD, J. *The Tantric Mysticism of Tibet*, New York, 1970.

BOLLE, K. W. *The Persistence of Religion*, Leiden, 1965.

BOLLEA, B. L. C. *Il mysticismo di S. Bonaventura studiato nelle sue antecedenza e nelle sue esplicazione*, Turin, 1901.

BOLZA, O. *Meister Eckhart als Mystiker. Eine religiongeschichtliche Studie*, Munich, 1938.

BONETTI, I. *Le Stimate della Passione: Dottrina e Storia della Devozione alle Cinque Piaghe*, Rovigo, 1952.

BORNKAMM, H. 'Μυστήριον', in G. Kittel (ed.) *Theologisches Wörterbuch zum Neuen Testament* IV, Stuttgart, 1942, 809–34.

BOURQUE, L. B., and BACK, K. W. 'Values and Transcendental Experiences', *Social Forces*, 47 (1968), 34–8.

BRADEN, W. *The Private Sea: An Enquiry into the Religious Implications of L.S.D.*, London, 1967.

BRAITHWAITE, W. C. *The Beginnings of Quakerism*, London, 1912.

BRANDON, S. G. F. (ed.) *The Saviour God*, Manchester, 1963.

BRÉHIER, E. *La Philosophie de Plotin*, Paris, 1928.

—— *Les Idées philosophiques et religieuses de Philon d'Alexandrie*, Paris, ²1925.

BREMOND, H. *Apologie pour Fénelon*, Paris, 1910.

—— *Histoire Littéraire du Sentiment religieux en France*, 8 vols, Paris, 1916–28.

BRENAN, G. *St John of the Cross*, Cambridge and New York, 1973.

BRIANCHANINOV, BISHOP IGNATIUS *On the Prayer of Jesus*, Eng. tr., London, 1952.

BRINTON, H. H. *The Mystic Will*, New York, 1930.

BROAD, C. D. *Religion, Philosophy and Psychical Research*, London, 1953; New York, 1969.

BROERS, B. C. *Mysticism in the neo-Romanticists*, Amsterdam, 1923.

Brown, J. P. *The Dervishes*, London, 1927; Portland, Ore., 1968.
Brunner, E. *Die Mystik und das Wort*, Tübingen, 1928.
Buber, M. *Ekstatische Konfessionen*, Jena, 1909.
—— *Die chassidischen Bücher*, Hellerau, 1928.
—— *Jewish Mysticism and the Legend of the Baal Shem*, London, 1931.
—— *Hasidism*, New York, 1948.
Bucke, R. M. *Cosmic Consciousness: A Study in the Evolution of the Human Mind*, Philadelphia, 1905.
Buhlmann, J. *Christuslehre und Christusmystik des Heinrich Seuse*, Lucerne, 1942.
Bullett, G. *The English Mystics*, London, 1950; Folcroft, Pa., 1973.
Bultmann, R. 'Geschichte der Lichtsymbolik in Altertum', *Philologus*, 97 (1946), 1–36.
Buonaiuti, E. *Il Misticismo Medioevale*, Pinerolo, 1928.
Burel, J. *Isis et Isiaques sous l'Empire roman*, Paris, 1911.
Burkert, W. *Lore and Science in Ancient Pythagoreanism*, Oxford, 1971; Cambridge, Mass., 1972.
Burkitt, F. C. *Jewish and Christian Apocalypses*, London, 1914.
Burnaby, J. *Amor Dei: A Study of the Religion of St Augustine*, London, 1938.
Butler, C. *Western Mysticism*, New York, 1924; London, [2]1926.
Caird, E. *The Evolution of Theology in the Greek Philosophers*, 2 vols, Glasgow, 1904; Millwood, NY, 1968.
Campagnac, E. T. *The Cambridge Platonists*, Oxford, 1901.
Campbell, J. (ed.) *The Mysteries*, London and Princeton, NJ, 1955.
Camus, J. P. *The Spirit of St François de Sales*, London, n.d.
Capitan, W. H., and Merrill, D. D. *Art, Mind and Religion*, Pittsburgh, 1967, 133–58; N. Smart, 'Mystical Experience'; N. Pike, Comments; P. F. Schmidt, 'Comments'; and N. Smart, 'Rejoinders'.
Carcopino, J. *Aspects mystiques de la Rome paienne*, Paris, [5]1941.
Cassirer, E. *The Platonic Renaissance in England*, London, 1953; New York, 1970.
Chadwck, Nora *Poetry and Prophecy*, Cambridge, 1942.
Chadwick, O. *John Cassian*, New York, 1968; Cambridge, 1970.
Chandler, A. *Ara Coeli: Studies in Mystical Religion*, London, 1908.
Chapman, Dom John *Spiritual Letters*, London, 1935.
Chevallier, P., *et al. Dionysiaca*, Paris, 1937.
Clark, J. M. 'Marquard von Lindau and his "Dekalogerklärung"', *MLR* 34 (1939), 72–8.
—— *The Great German Mystics: Eckhart, Tauler and Suso*, Oxford, 1949; New York, 1970.
—— *Meister Eckhart*, London, 1957.
Clark, W. H. 'A Religious Approach to the Concept of the Self,' *Annals of the New York Academy of Science* 96 (1962), 831–42.
—— *Chemical Ecstasy*, New York, 1969.
Clarke, J. J. 'Mysticism and the Paradox of Survival', *International Philosophical Quarterly* 6 (1971), 165–79.
Clemen, C. *Der Einfluss der Mysterienreligionen auf das älteste Christentum*, Giessen, 1913.
Cohn, N. *The Pursuit of the Millennium*, London, 1957; New York, 1970.
Coleman, T. W. *English Mystics of the Fourteenth Century*, London, 1938.
Colledge, E. *The Mediaeval Mystics of England*, London, 1962; New York, 1972.
Connolly, J. L. *John Gerson, Reformer and Mystic*, St Louis, 1928.
Conze, E. *Buddhism, its Essence and Development*, Oxford, 1951; New York, 1959.
—— *Buddhist Meditation*, London, 1956.
—— *Buddhist Thought in India*, London, 1962; Ann Arbor, Mich. 1967.
Cook, R. *The Tree of Life*, London and New York, 1974.
Coomaraswamy, A. K. *Buddha and the Gospel of Buddhism*, New York, 1916.
—— *The Transformation of Nature in Art*, Cambridge, Mass., 1935.
Corless, R. J. 'The Function of Recollection in Theravadin and Ignatian Ascesis', *Monastic Studies* 8 (1972), 159–69.
Coulton, G. G. *Five Centuries of Religion*, 4 vols, Cambridge, 1923–50; New York, 1974.
Courcelle, P. 'Tradition néoplatonicienne et traditions chrétiennes de la "region de dissemblance"', *Archives d'histoire doctrinale et littéraire du Moyen Age* 24 (1957), 5–33.
Creed, J. M. 'The Hermetic Writings,' *Journal of Theological Studies* 15 (1914), 513–38.
Crookall, R. *The Interpretation of Cosmic and Mystical Experiences*, London and Greenwood, SC, 1969.
Cumont, F. *The Mysteries of Mithra*, Chicago, 1910.
—— *Oriental Religions in Roman Paganism*, Chicago, 1911.
Curtis, A. M. *The Way of Silence*, Burton Bradstock, 1937.
Dahlmann, J. *Nirvana*, Berlin, 1896.
Darbishire, Helen *The Poet Wordsworth*, Oxford and New York, 1950.
D'Arcy, M. C. *The Meeting of Love and Knowledge*, London, 1958.
—— *The Mind and Heart of Love*, London, [2]1860.
D'Asbeck, M. *La mystique de Ruysbroeck l'Admirable*, Paris, 1930.
Dasgupta, S. *Hindu Mysticism*, Chicago, 1927.
—— *A History of Indian Philosophy*, 5 vols, Cambridge, 1922–55.
Dasgupta, S. B. *An Introduction to Tantric Buddhism*, Calcutta, 1958.
David-Neel, A. *With Mystics and Magicians in Tibet*, London, 1931.
—— *Initiation and Initiates in Tibet*, London, 1958.
—— *Magic and Mystery in Tibet*, London 1967; Baltimore, 1971.

DAVIES, W. D. *Paul and Rabbinic Judaism*, London, 1955.

D'AYGALLIERS, A. W. *Ruysbroeck the Admirable*, Eng. tr., London, 1925; Port Washington, NY, 1969.

DEIKMAN, A. J. 'Experimental Meditation', *Journal of Nervous and Mental Disease* 136 (1963), 329–43.

—— 'Implications of Experimentally Induced Contemplative Meditation', *Journal of Nervous and Mental Disease* 142 (1966), 101–16.

—— 'De-automatization and the Mystic Experience', *Psychiatry* 29 (1966), 324–38.

DEISSMAN, A. *St Paul*, London and New York, 1912.

DE JONG, K. H. E. *Das antike Mysterienwesen*, Leiden, [2]1919.

DELACROIX, H. *Essai sur le mysticism speculatif en Allemagne au quatorzième siècle*, Paris, 1900.

—— *Etudes d'Histoire et de Psychologie du Mysticisme*, Paris, 1908.

DEMPF, H. *Meister Eckhart: Eine Einführung in sein Werk*, Leipzig, 1934.

DENIFLE, H. S. *Das geistliche Leben: Blumenlese aus den deutschen Mystikern des 14 Jahrhunderts*, Graz, 1895.

DEREN, M. *Divine Horsemen: The Voodoo Gods of Haiti*, London, and New York, 1953.

DEUSSEN, P. *The Philosophy of the Upanishads*, London, 1906; New York, 1966.

DEVANDRADAN, P. D. *The Concept of Maya*, London, 1950.

DICKEN, E. W. TRUEMAN *The Crucible of Love*, London, 1963.

DOBBINS, D. *Franciscan Mysticism*, New York, 1927.

DODD, C. H. *The Meaning of Paul for Today*, New York, 1920; London, 1935.

—— *The Interpretation of the Fourth Gospel*, Cambridge, 1953.

DODDS, E. R. *Pagan and Christian in an Age of Anxiety*, Cambridge, 1968, 69–101; New York, 1970.

DORESSE, J. *The Secret Books of the Egyptian Gnostics*, Eng. tr., London, 1960; New York, 1972.

DORRIES, H. *Zur Geschichte der Mystik: Erigena und der Neoplatonismus*, Tübingen, 1925.

DOUGLAS-SMITH, B. 'An Empirical Study of Religious Mysticism', *British Journal of Psychiatry* 118 (1971), 549–54.

DROWER, E. S. *The Secret Adam: A Study of Nasorean Gnosis*, Oxford, 1960.

DUMOULIN, H. 'Methods and Aims of Buddhist Meditation – Satipatthana and Zen', *Psychologia* 5 (1962), 175–80.

—— *A History of Zen Buddhism*, Eng. tr., London, 1963; Boston, 1969.

DUPONT-SOMMER, A. *The Jewish Sect of Qumran and the Essenes*, Eng. tr., London, 1954.

DURANTEL, J. *Saint Thomas et le Pseudo-Denis*, Paris, 1919.

DURRER, R. *Bruder Klaus*, 2 vols, Sarnen, 1917–21.

DYSON, W. H. *Studies in Christian Mysticism*, London, 1913.

EDMAN, I. 'The Logic of Mysticism in Plotinus', *Studies in the History of Ideas* 2 (1924), 51–81.

EDSMAN, C. M. *Le Baptême de feu*, Uppsala–Leipzig, 1940.

EDSMAN, C. M. (ed.) *Studies in Shamanism*, Stockholm, 1967.

ELIADE, M. *Birth and Rebirth*, Eng. tr., New York, 1958.

—— *Yoga, Immortality and Freedom*, Eng. tr., London, 1958; Princeton, NJ, 1970.

—— *Myths, Dreams and Mysteries*, Eng. tr., London, 1960; New York, 1961.

—— *Shamanism: Archaic Techniques of Ecstasy*, Eng. tr., New York, [2]1964.

—— *The Two and the One*, London, 1965, 19–77; New York, 1969.

ELLINGER, G. *Angelus Silesius: Ein Lebensbild*, Breslau, 1927.

ENNIS, H. E. 'Ecstasy and Everyday Life', *Journal for the Scientific Study of Religion* 6 (1967), 40–48.

ELWIN, H. V. 'Light Mysticism', *Modern Churchman* 17 (1927), 69–86.

EVANS-WENTZ, W. Y. *The Tibetan Book of the Dead*, London, 1927; New York, 1960.

—— *Tibet's Great Yogi, Milarepa*, London, 1928; New York, 1951.

—— *Tibetan Yoga and Secret Doctrines*, London, 1935; New York, 1967.

EWER, M. A. *A Survey of Mystical Symbolism*, London, 1933.

FAKHRY, M. 'Three Varieties of Mysticism in Islam', *International Journal for Philosophy of Religion* 2 (1971), 193–297.

FARGES, A. *Mystical Phenomena compared with their Human and Diabolical Counterfeits: a treatise . . .*, Eng. tr., London, [2]1926.

FARRER, A. *A Rebirth of Images*, London and Westminster, Md, 1949.

FAYE, E. DE *Gnostiques et Gnosticisme*, Paris, [2]1925.

FERGUSON, J. *The Religions of the Roman Empire*, London and Ithaca, NY, 1970.

FERNBERGER, S. W. 'Observations on taking peyote', *Am. J. Psych.* 34 (1923), 267–70.

FESTUGIÈRE, A. J. 'Les mystères de Dionysos', *Rev. Bibl.* 44 (1935), 192–211, 366–96.

—— *L'Hermétisme*, Lund, 1948.

—— *Personal Religion among the Greeks*, Berkeley, 1954.

FIELD, C. *Mystics and Saints of Islam*, London, 1910.

FILTHAUT, E. (ed.) *Johannes Tauler: Ein Deutscher Mystiker*, Essen, 1961.

FINDLAY, J. N. 'The Logic of Mysticism', *Religious Studies* 2 (1967), 145–62.

FINGARETTE, H. 'The Ego and Mystic Selflessness', *Psychoanalysis and the Psychoanalytic Review* 45 (1958), 5–40.

FLEMING, W. K. *Mysticism in Christianity*, London, 1913.

FLITCH, J. E. C. *Angelus Silesius*, London, 1932.

FONCK, A. 'Mystique (Théologie)', *Dictionnaire de Théologie Catholique* 10, cols 2599–2674.

FOUCART, P. *Les Mystères d'Eleusis*, Paris, 1914.
FRAZER, J. G. *Adonis, Attis, Osiris*, London, ^{3}1914.
FREMANTLE, ANNE *The Protestant Mystics*, London, 1964.
FROST, BEDE *Saint John of the Cross*, London, 1937.
—— *The Art of Mental Prayer*, London, 1940.
FRYE, NORTHROP *Fearful Symmetry: A Study of William Blake*, Princeton, NJ, 1947.
FUNG YU-LAN *A History of Chinese Philosophy*, 2 vols, Princeton, NJ, 1952–3.
GALE, R. 'Mysticism and Philosophy', Journal of Philosophy 57 (1960), 471–81.
GANDILLAC, M. DE *La philosophie de Nicolas de Cues*, Paris, ^{2}1941.
GARDNER, ALICE *Studies in John the Scot*, New York, 1900.
GARDNER, E. G. *St Catherine of Siena*, London, 1907.
—— *Dante and the Mystics*, London, 1913.
GARDNER, HELEN 'Walter Hilton and the Mystical Tradition in England', *Essays and Studies* 22 (1936), 103–27.
GARRIGOU-LAGRANGE, R. *Perfection Chrétienne et Contemplation selon S. Thomas d'Aquin et S. Jean de la Croix*, 2 vols, Paris, 1939.
—— *Traité de Théologie ascetique et mystique*, 2 vols, Paris, 1939.
GEBHART, E. *Mystics and Heretics in Italy*, Eng. tr., London and New York, 1922.
GEM, S. H. *William Law on Christian Practice and Mysticism*, Oxford, 1905.
GERLICH, F. *Die Stigmatisierte Therese Neumann von Konnersreuth*, Munich, 1929.
GIBBARD, M. *Twentieth-Century Men of Prayer*, London, 1974.
GILBERT, J. 'Mystical Experience and Public Testability', *Sophia* 9 (1970), 13–20.
GILSON, E. *La Philosophie de S. Bonaventure*, Paris, 1924.
—— *La théologie mystique de St Bernard*, Paris, 1934.
—— '"Regio Dissimilitudinis" de Platon à St Bernard de Clairvaux', *Med. St.* 9 (1947), 108–30.
—— *A History of Christian Philosophy in the Middle Ages*, London and New York, 1955.
GINSBURG, C. D. *The Kabbalah*, London, 1865.
GLASGOW, W. D. 'Knowledge of God', *Philosophy* 32 (1957), 229–40.
GOERRES, J. *Die Christliche Mystik*, 4 vols, Regensburg and Landshut, 1836–42.
GOLDSCHMIDT, V. *La Religion de Platon*, Paris, 1949.
GOMBRICH, E. H. 'Botticelli's Mythologies', *J. Warburg and Courtauld Institutes* 8 (1945), 7–60.
GOODENOUGH, E. R. *By Light, Light: The Mystic Gospel of Hellenistic Judaism*, New Haven, 1935.
—— *An Introduction to Philo Judaeus*, New Haven, 1940.
GORDON, R. 'Mithraism and Roman Society', *Religion* 2 (1972), 92–101.
GOVINDA, LAMA A. *Foundations of Tibetan Mysticism*, London, 1959; Berkeley, 1971.
GRABMANN, M. *Wesen und Grundlagen der katholischen Mystik* (Der Katholische Gedanke 2), 1922.
GRAEF, HILDA *Mystics of Our Time*, London, 1961; New York, 1963.
GRANT, R. M. *Gnosticism: An Anthology*, London, 1961.
—— *Gnosticism and Early Christianity*, New York, ^{2}1966.
GRÖBER, C. *Der Mystiker Heinrich Seuse*, Freiburg, 1941.
GUARNIERI, R. 'Il movimento del libero spirito', *Arch. ital. per la storia della pieta* 4 (1965), 501–635.
GUÉNON, R. *Man and His Becoming according to the Vedanta*, Eng. tr., London, n.d. (1928).
—— *East and West*, Eng. tr., London, 1941.
—— *Introduction to the Study of the Hindu Doctrines*, Eng. tr., London, 1945.
GUIGNEBERT, C. *The Jewish World in the Time of Jesus*, Eng. tr., London, 1939; New York, 1959.
GUILLAUME, A. *Prophecy and Divination among the Hebrews and Other Semites*, London, 1938.
GUTHRIE, W. K. C. *Orpheus and Greek Religion*, London, ^{2}1952.
GUY, H. A. *New Testament Prophecy*, London, 1949.
HAHN, G. 'Les phénomènes hystériques et les révélations de Sainte Thérèse', *Rev. quest. sci.* 13–14 (1883).
HALL, W. W. *Recorded Illuminates*, London, 1937.
HAMILTON, C. H. *A psychological interpretation of Mysticism*, Chicago, 1916.
HANKAMER, P. *Jakob Böhme: Gestalt und Gestaltung*, Hildesheim, ^{2}1960.
HANSON, R. P. C. *Allegory and Event*, London, 1959.
HAPPOLD, F. C. *Mysticism: A Study and an Anthology*, Harmondsworth and Baltimore, ^{3}1970.
HARDMAN, O. *The Ideals of Asceticism: An Essay in the Comparative Study of Religion*, London, 1929.
HART, B. *Psychopathology*, Cambridge, 1927.
HEIGL, B. *Antike Mysterienreligionen und Urchristentum*, Münster, 1932.
HEILER, F. *Prayer*, Eng. tr., London, ^{2}1937.
HEMBERG, BENGT *Die Kabiren*, Uppsala, 1950.
HERMANN, E. *The Meaning and Value of Mysticism*, New York, ^{3}1922.
HERMANNS, M. *Mythen und Mysterien, Magie und Religion der Tibeter*, Cologne, 1956.
HERTZ, J. H. 'Mystic Currents in Ancient Israel' in *The Jews at the Close of the Bible Age*, London, 1926, 127–56.
HESCHEL, A. J. 'The Mystical Element in Judaism' in L. Finkelstein, *The Jews*, New York, 1949, II xiii.
HEUSCH, L. DE 'Cultes de possession et religions initiatiques de salut en Afrique', *Annales du Centre d'Etudes des Religions*, Brussels, 1962.
HINNELLS, J. R. (ed.) *Mithraic Studies*, 2 vols, Manchester 1973; Totowa, NJ, 1974.

HOBHOUSE, S. *William Law and Eighteenth-Century Quakerism*, London and New York, 1927.
—— *Selected Mystical Writings of William Law*, London, 1938.
HOCKING, W. E. *The Meaning of God in Human Experience*, New Haven, 1912.
—— 'The meaning of mysticism as seen through its psychology', *Mind* 21 (1912), 38–61.
HODGKIN, T. *George Fox*, London, 1896.
HODGSON, PHYLLIS *The Cloud of Unknowing*, London, 1958.
HOFFMANN, E. *Das Universum des Nicolaus von Cues*, Heidelberg, 1930.
HOLLENWEGER, W. J. *The Pentecostals*, London and Minneapolis, 1972.
HOLMYARD, E. J. *Alchemy*, Harmondsworth, 1957.
HOPKINS, A. J. *Alchemy, Child of Greek Philosophy*, New York, 1934.
HORNSTEIN, X. DE *Les grands mystiques allemands du xive siècle: Eckhart, Tauler, Suso*, Fribourg, 1922.
HORSBURGH, H. J. N. 'The Claims of Religious experience', *Australasian Journal of Philosophy* 35 (1957), 186–200.
HORSTMAN, C. (ed.) *Richard Rolle of Hampole and his Followers*, 2 vols, London and Philadelphia, 1895–6.
HOWLEY, J. *Psychology and Mystical Experience*, London, 1920.
HUCK, J. C. *Joachim von Floris und die joachitische Literatur*, Freiburg im Breisgau, 1938.
HÜGEL, F. VON *The Mystical Element of Religion as Studied in Saint Catherine of Genoa and her friends*, 2 vols, London, 1908–23; New York 1961.
HUGHES, T. H. *The Philosophic Basis of Mysticism*, Edinburgh, 1937.
HUXLEY, A. *The Perennial Philosophy*, Plainview, NY, 1945; London, 1946.
—— *The Doors of Perception*, London, 1954.
HYMA, A. *The Christian Renaissance*, New York, 1925.
—— *The Brethren of the Common Life*, Grand Rapids, 1950.
IKBUL, ALI SHAH *Islamic Sufism*, London, 1933.
IMBERT-GOUBEYRE, A. *La Stigmatisation, l'extase divine et les miracles de Lourdes*, 2 vols, Clermont-Ferrand, 1894.
INGE, W. R. *Studies of English Mystics*, London and Plainview, NY, 1906
—— *The Philosophy of Plotinus*, 2 vols, London, 1918; Westport, Conn., 1929.
—— *Christian Mysticism*, London, [6]1925.
—— *Mysticism in Religion*, London, n.d. (1947).
IQBUL, M. *The Development of Metaphysics in Persia*, London, 1908.
JEAGHER, P. DE *An Anthology of Mysticism*, Westminster, Md, 1950.
JAMES, J. *The Way of Mysticism*, London, 1950.
JAMES, W. *The Varieties of Religious Experience*, London, 1910; New York, 1958.
JEANMAIRE, H. *Dionysos*, Paris, 1951.
JENNINGS, J. G. *The Vedantic Buddhism of the Buddha*, London, 1948.
JINARAJADASA, C. *The Nature of Mysticism*, Madras, 1917.
JOHNSON, A. R. *The One and the Many in the Israelite Conception of God*, Cardiff, [2]1961.
JOHNSON, F. E. (ed.) *Religious Symbolism*, New York, 1955.
JOHNSON, R. C. *The Imprisoned Splendour*, London, 1953.
—— *Watcher on the Hills*, London, 1959.
JOHNSTON, W. 'Zen and Christian Mysticism: A Comparison in Psychological Structure', *International Philosophical Quarterly* 7 (1967), 441–69.
JOLY, H. *Psychologie des Saints*, Paris, 1897.
JONAS, H. *Gnosis und spätantiker Geist*, Göttingen, 1934.
—— *The Gnostic Religion*, Boston, [2]1963.
JONES, RUFUS. *Studies in Mystical Religion*, London, 1909; New York, 1970.
—— *New Studies in Mystical Religion*, London and New York, 1927.
—— *Spiritual Reformers in the 16th and 17th Centuries*, London, 1928; Gloucester, Mass., 1959.
—— *Some Experiments of Mystical Religion*, New York, 1930.
—— *George Fox, Seeker and Friend*, London, 1930.
—— *The Flowering of Mysticism*, New York, 1939.
JONES, RUFUS, *et al.* 'Mysticism', *Encyclopedia of Religion and Ethics* 9, 83–117.
JORET, PÈRE *La contemplation Mystique d'après S. Thomas d'Aquin*, Paris, 1923.
JORGENSEN, J. *Saint Catherine of Siena*, Eng. tr., London, 1938.
JUNDT, A. *Essai sur le Mysticisme speculatif de Maître Eckhart*, Strasbourg, 1871.
—— *Histoire du panthéisme populaire au moyen âge*, Paris, 1878.
—— *Les Amis de Dieu au XIV siècle*, Paris, 1879.
—— *Rulman Merswin et l'Ami de Dieu de l'Oberland*, Paris, 1890.
JUNG, C. G. *Psychology and Religion*, New York, 1938.
—— *Psychology and Alchemy*, London, 1953; Princeton, NJ, 1968.
KARPPE, S. *Etude sur les origines et la nature du Zohar*, Paris, 1901.
KARRER, O. *Meister Eckhart, das System seiner religiösen Lehre*, Munich, 1926.
KASAMATSU, A., and HIRAI, T. 'An Electro-encephalographic Study on the Zen Meditation (Zazen)', *Psychologia* 12 (1969), 205–25.
KEAY, F. E. *Kabir and his Followers*, London, 1931.
KEITH, A. B. *Buddhist Philosophy in India and Ceylon*, Oxford, 1923.
—— *The Religion and Philosophy of the Veda and Upanishads*, Cambridge, Mass., 1925.
KENNEDY, H. A. A. *St Paul and the Mystery Religions*, London, 1913.
—— *Philo's Contribution to Religion*, London, 1919.

KERENYI, K. *Eleusis: Archetypal Image of Mother and Daughter*, Eng. tr., London, 1967.
KERN, O. *Die griechischen Mysterien der classischen Zeit*, Berlin, 1927.
KING, RACHEL H. *George Fox and the Light Within 1650–1660*, Philadelphia, 1940.
KING, W. L. 'A Comparison of the Theravada and Zen Buddhist Meditational Methods and Goals', *History of Religions*, 9 (1970), 304–15.
KINGSLAND, V. *Rational Mysticism*, London, 1924.
KINGSLAND, W. *An Anthology of Mysticism and Mystical Philosophy*, London, 1927.
KLOSSOWSKI DA ROLA, S. *Alchemy: the Secret Art*, London, 1973.
KNIGHT, H. *The Hebrew Prophetic Consciousness*, London, 1947.
KNOWLES, D. *The English Mystics*, London, 1927.
—— 'The Excellence of the *Cloud*', *Downside Review* 52 (1934), 76–92.
KOCH, J. *Humanismus, Mystik und Kunst in der Welt des Mittelalters*, Cologne, 1953.
KÖRTE, A. 'Zu den eleusinischen Mysterien', *Archiv für Religionswiss.* 18 (1915).
KOYRÉ, A. *La Philosophie de Jacob Boehme*, Paris, 1929.
—— *Mystiques, Spirituels, Alchimistes*, Paris, 1955.
KROLL, W. '*Hermes Trismegistos*' in Paully-Wissowa, *Real-Encyclopädie der classischen Altertumswissenschaft* 8, 791–823.
KROVOSHEINE, ARCHBISHOP BASIL *The Ascetic and Theological Teaching of Gregory Palamas*, London, 1954.
LABARRE, W. *The Peyote Cult*, New Haven, 1938.
LACOMBE, O. *L'Absolu selon le Védanta*, Paris, 1937.
LAGRANGE, M. J. *Les Mystères: L'Orphisme*, Paris, 1937.
LAMBALLE, E. *Mystical Contemplation*, Eng. tr., London, 1914.
LANGER, Suzanne K. *Philosophy of Reason, Rite and Art*, Cambridge, Mass., 1942.
LASKI, M. *Ecstasy*, London, 1961; Westport, Conn., 1968.
LEARY, T., ALPERT, R., and METZNER, R. *The Psychedelic Experience*, New York, 1964.
LECLÈRE, A. *Le Mysticisme catholique et l'âme de Dante*, Paris, 1906.
LECLERQ, J. *Pierre le Vénérable*, Saint-Wandrille, 1946.
—— *La Spiritualité de Pierre de Celle*, Paris, 1946.
—— *St Bernard Mystique*, Paris, 1948.
LECLERQ, J., and BONNES, J. P. *Un maître de la vie spirituelle au xie siècle, Jean de Fécamp*, Paris, 1946.
LECLÈVE, L. *Sainte Angèle de Foligno: Sa vie – ses oeuvres*, Paris, 1936.
LEGGE, F. *Forerunners and Rivals of Christianity*, 2 vols., Cambridge, 1915; New York, 1950.
LEHMANN, E. *Mysticism in Heathendom and Christendom*, Eng. tr., London, 1910.
LEHMANN, W. *Meister Eckhart, der gotische Mystiker*, Lübeck, 1933.
LEISEGANG, H. *Die Gnosis*, Stuttgart, 1955.
LEJEUNE, P. *An Introduction to the Mystical Life*, Eng. tr., London, 1915.
LENORMANT, CH. 'Mémoire sur les representation qui avaient lieu dans les mystères d'Eleusis', *Mem de l'Acad. d'inscr. et de belles lettres* 24 (1861), 343–445.
LEONARD, A. 'Studies on the Phenomena of Mystical Experience', *Mystery and Mysticism*, London, 1956.
LERNER, A. B., CASE, J. D., and HEINZELMAN, R. V. 'The Structure of Melatonin', *Journal of the American Chemical Society* 81 (1959), 6084.
LERNER, R. E. 'The Image of Mixed Liquids in Late Mediaeval Mystical Thought', *Church History* 40 (1971), 397–411.
LESSER, A. 'Cultural Significance of the Ghost Dance', *American Anthropologist* 35 (1933), 108–15.
LEUBA, J. H. 'Les tendances fondamentales des mystiques chrétiens', *Rev. Phil.* 54 (1902), 1–36.
—— 'Les tendances religieuses chez les mystiques chrétiens', *Rev. Phil.* 54 (1902), 441–87.
—— *The Psychology of Religious Mysticism*, Eng. tr., New York, [2]1929.
LÉVY, P. *Buddhism: a 'Mystery Religion'?*, London, 1957; New York, 1968.
LEWIS, C. S. *The Four Loves*, London, 1960.
LEWIS, I. M. *Ecstatic Religion*, New York, 1960; Harmondsworth, 1971.
LINFORTH, I. M. *The Arts of Orpheus*, Berkeley, 1941.
LING, T. 'Buddhist Mysticism', *Religious Studies* 1 (1966), 163–75.
LINHARDT, R. *Die Mystik des hl. Bernard von Clairvaux*, Munich, 1926.
LIPPMANN, E. O. VON *Entstehung und Ausbreitung der Alchemie*, Berlin, 1919–31.
LITTLE, K. D. *Francis de Fénelon: Study of a Personality*, New York, 1951.
LOISY, A. F. *Les mystères paiens et le mystère Chrétien*, Paris, [2]1930.
LOOKER, S. J., and PORTEOUS, L. C. *Richard Jefferies: Man of the Fields*, Mystic, Conn., 1964; London, 1965.
LOSSKY, V. *The Mystical Theology of the Eastern Church*, Eng. tr., London, 1957; Greenwood, SC, 1968.
—— *Théologie négative et connaissance de Dieu chez Maître Eckhart*, Pari, 1960.
LOUNSBERRY, G. C. *Buddhist Meditation in the Southern School*, London, 1935.
LUBAC, H. DE *The Faith of Teilhard de Chardin*, London, 1965.
—— *The Religion of Teilhard de Chardin*, London, 1967.
LUDDY, J. A. *St Gertrude the Great*, Dublin, 1930.
MCCANN, J. *The Cloud of Unknowing and other Treatises*, London, [6]1957.
MACDONALD, D. B. *The Religious Life and Attitude in Islam*, Chicago, 1909.
MACNICOL, N. *Indian Theism from the Vedic to the Muhammadan Period*, London, 1915; Mystic, Conn., 1968.
MAETERLINCK, M. *Ruysbroeck and the Mystics*,

Eng. tr., London, 1908.
MAITRA, S. K. *An Introduction to the Philosophy of Sri Aurobindo*, Benares, 1945.
MARÉCHAL, J. *Etudes sur la psychologie des mystiques*, 2 vols, Paris, 1938.
MARQUETTE, J. DE *Introduction to Comparative Mysticism*, New York, 1949.
MARTENSEN, H. L. *Jacob Behmen: His Life and Teaching*, Eng. tr., London, 1885.
MARTIN, C. B. *Religious Belief*, New York, 1959, 64–94.
MARY CATHERINE, SISTER *Henry Suso, Saint and Poet*, Oxford, 1947.
MASLOW, A. H. *Religions, Values and Peak Experiences*, Columbus, 1964.
MASPERO, H. *Le Taoisme*, Paris, 1950.
MASSIGNON, L. *La Passion de Al-Hallaj*, Paris, 1921.
MASTERS, R. E. L., and HOUSTON, JEAN. *The Varieties of Psychedelic Experience*, London and New York, 1966.
MASUNAGA, R. *The Soto Approach to Zen*, Tokyo, 1958.
MATTER, M. *Le Mysticisme en France au Temps de Fénelon*, Paris, 1865.
MAW, M. B. *Buddhist Mysticism: A Study based upon a Comparison with the Mysticism of St Teresa and Juliana of Norwich*, Bordeaux, 1924.
MEAD, G. R. S. *Quests Old and New*, London, 1913.
—— *Fragments of a Faith Forgotten*, London, ^{3}1931; New York, 1960.
MEECH, S. B., and ALLEN, H.E. *The Book of Margery Kempe*, London and New York, 1940.
MEHTA, P. D. *Early Indian Religious Thought*, London and Totowa, NJ, 1956.
MERKELBACH, R. *Roman und Mysterium in der Antike*, Munich and Berlin, 1967.
MERTON, T. *Mystics and Zen Masters*, New York, 1967.
MÉTRAUX, A. *Voodoo in Haiti*, Eng. tr., London, 1959; New York, 1972.
MEYENDORFF, J. *S. Grégoire Palamas et la mystique orthodoxe*, Paris, 1959.
—— *A Study of Gregory Palamas*, London and Tuckahoe, NY, 1964.
MILBURN, R. G. *The Religious Mysticism of the Upanishads*, London, 1924.
MILOSH, J. E. *The Scale of Perfection and the English Mystical Tradition*, Madison, 1960.
MISCIATELLI, P. *Mistici Senesi*, Siena, 1911.
MOLINARI, P. *Julian of Norwich: the Teaching of a Fourteenth-Century Mystic*, London, 1957; Norwood, Pa., 1974.
MONTMORENCY, J. E. G. DE *Thomas à Kempis: His Age and Book*, London, 1906; Port Washington, NY, 1970.
MOONEY, J. 'The Ghost-Dance Religion and the Sioux Outbreak of 1890', *14th Annual Report of the Bureau of American Ethnology 1893–4*, Part 2, Washington, 1896.
MUKERJEE, R. *Theory and Art of Mysticism*, London, 1937.
MÜLLER, E. *History of Jewish Mysticism*, London, 1956.
MÜLLER, H. F. *Dionysius, Proclus, Plotinus*, Münster, 1918.
MURAT, E. 'Mistica', *Enciclopedia Cattolica*, vol. 8, cols 1135–43.
MYLONAS, G. E. *Eleusis and the Eleusinian Mysteries*, Princeton, NJ, 1961.
NANDIMATH, S. C. *A Handbook of Vira Saivism*, Dharwar, 1942.
NARANJO, C., and ORNSTEIN, R. E. *On the Psychology of Meditation*, New York, 1971; London, 1972.
NEEDHAM, R. 'Percussion and Transition', *Man* 2 (1967), 606–14.
NEENAN, MARY P. *Some Evidences of Mysticism in English Poetry of the Nineteenth Century*, Washington, 1916.
NICHOLSON, D. H. S. *The Mysticism of St Francis of Assisi*, London, 1923.
NICHOLSON, R. A. 'A Historical Enquiry concerning the Origin and Development of Sufism', *JRAS* (1906), 303–48.
—— *The Mystics of Islam*, London, 1914; Boston, 1970.
—— *Studies in Islamic Mysticism*, Cambridge, 1921.
—— *The Idea of Personality in Sufism*, Cambridge, 1923; New York, 1970.
—— *Rumi, Poet and Mystic*, London, 1950.
NILSSON, M. P. *The Dionysiac Mysteries of the Hellenistic and Roman Age*, Lund, 1927.
NOACK, F. *Eleusis, die baugeschichtliche Entwicklung des Heiligtumes*, Berlin and Leipzig, 1927.
NOCK, A. D. *Essays on Religion and the Ancient World*, 2 vols, Oxford and Cambridge, Mass., 1972.
NYGREN, A. *Agape and Eros*, Eng. tr., New York, ^{2}1953.
O'BRIEN, E. *Varieties of Mystic Experience*, London, 1965.
ODEBERG, H. *The Fourth Gospel*, Uppsala, 1929.
OESTERREICH, T. K. *Possession, Demoniacal and Other, among Primitive Races, in Antiquity, the Middle Ages and Modern Times*, Eng. tr., London, 1930; Secaucus, NJ, 1974.
OHASAMA, S., and FAUST, A. *Zen, der lebendige Buddhismus in Japan*, Gotha, 1925.
OLIVER, M. *St Gertrude the Great*, Dublin, 1930.
OLSCHAK, B. C., and WANGYAL, G. T. *Mystical Art of Ancient Tibet*, London, 1973; New York, 1974.
ORGAN, T. 'The Language of Mysticism', *Monist* 47 (1963), 417–43.
OSMOND, P. H. *The Mystical Poets of the English Church*, London and New York, 1919.
OTTAVIANO, C. *L'ars compendiosa de R. Lull*, Paris, 1930.
OTTO, R. *The Idea of the Holy*, Eng. tr., London, 1923; New York, 1958.
—— *Aufsätze das Numinose betreffend*, Gotha, 1923.
—— *Mysticism, East and West: A Comparative Analysis of the Nature of Mysticism*, Eng. tr., New York, 1932.
OVERTON, J. H. *Law: Nonjuror and Mystic*, London, 1881.

Owen, H. P. 'Christian Mysticism: A Study in Walter Hilton's *The Ladder of Perfection*', *Religious Studies* 7 (1971), 31–42.

Pacheu, J. *Introduction à la psychologie des mystiques*, Paris, 1901.

—— *Psychologie des Mystiques Chrétiens*, Paris, 1909.

—— *L'expérience mystique et l'activité subconsciente*, Paris, 1911.

Pahnke, W. N. 'Drugs and Mysticism', *International Journal of Parapsychology* 8 (1966), 295–314.

Paquier, J. *L'orthodoxie de la Théologie Germanique*, Paris, 1922.

Payne, R. *The Holy Fire*, London, 1958.

Peacock, J. L. 'Mystics and Merchants in Fourteenth Century Germany', *Journal for the Scientific Study of Religion* 8 (1969), 47–59.

Peers, E. A. *Studies of the Spanish Mystics*, London, 1927.

—— *Spirit of Flame: A Study of St John of the Cross*, London, 1943.

—— *Mother of Carmel: A Portrait of St Teresa of Jesus*, London, 1945.

—— *Fool of Love: The Life of Ramon Lull*, London, 1946; Philadelphia, 1973.

—— *The Mystics of Spain*, London and New York, 1951.

—— *Handbook to the Life and Times of St Teresa and St John of the Cross*, London, 1954.

Percheron, M. *Buddha and Buddhism*, Eng. tr., London, 1957.

Petrocchi, M. *Il quietismo italiano del seicento* (*Storia e letteratura* 20), Rome, 1948.

Petrullo, V. *The Diabolic Root: A Study of Peyotism, the New Indian Religion among the Delawares*, Philadelphia, 1934.

Petry, R. C. 'Social Responsibility and the Late Medieval Mystics', *Church History* 2 (1952), 3–19.

Petry, R. C. (ed.) *Late Medieval Mysticism*, London and Philadelphia, 1957.

Pettazoni, R. *I Misteri: Saggo de una teoria storico-religiosa*, Bologna, 1924.

Pick, B. *The Cabala, its Influence on Judaism and Christianity*, Chicago, 1913.

Plard, H. *La Mystique de Angelus Silesius*, Paris, 1943.

Pletcher, G. K. 'Agreement among Mystics', *Sophia* 11 (1972), 5–15.

Plöger, O. *Theokratie und Eschatologie*, Neukirchen, 1959.

Pott, P. H. *Yoga and Tantra*, The Hague, 1966.

Poulain, R. P. A. *The Graces of Interior Prayer*, Eng. tr., London, 1916.

Pourrat, P. *Christian Spirituality*, Eng. tr., 3 vols, London, 1922–6.

Poussin, L. de la Vallée *The Quest for Nirvana*, Eng. tr., London, 1917.

Powicke, F. J. *The Cambridge Platonists*, London, 1926; Hamden, Conn., 1971.

Prabhavananda, Swami *The Spiritual Heritage of India*, London, 1962; Garden City, New York, 1963.

Pratt, J. B. *The Religious Consciousness, a Psychological Study*, New York, 1920.

—— *The Pilgrimage of Buddhism*, New York, 1928.

Preger, W. *Geschichte der deutschen Mystik im Mittelalter*, 3 vols, Leipzig, 1874–93.

Prem, Sri Krishna *The Yoga of the Bhagavad Gita*, London, 1938.

Prince, M. *The Unconscious*, New York, 1914.

Probst, J. H. 'La mystique de Ramon Lull et l'art de contemplacio', *Beiträge*, 13 parts, 2–3 (1914), 1–126.

Puech, H. C. *Le Manichéisme, Son Fondateur, Sa Doctrine*, Paris, 1949.

Radhakrishnan, S. *The Philosophy of Rabindranath Tagore*, Baroda, ²1961.

—— *The Philosophy of the Upanishads*, London, 1924.

—— *The Vedanta according to Samkara and Ramanuja*, London, 1928.

Radhakrishnan, S. (ed.) *History of Philosophy Eastern and Western*, 2 vols, London, 1952–5; New York, 1967.

Radin, P. *Primitive Man as Philosopher*, New York and London, 1927.

Raine, Kathleen *Blake and Tradition*, 2 vols, Princeton, NJ, 1968; London, 1969.

Ramanujan, A. K. *Speaking of Siva*, Harmondsworth and Baltimore, 1973.

Rangachari, K. *The Sri Vaishava Brahmans*, Madras, 1931.

Rawson, P. *The Art of Tantra*, London and Boston, 1973.

Rawson, P., and Legeza, L. *Tao: The Eastern Philosophy of Time and Change*, London and New York, 1973.

Récéjac, E. *Essay on the Bases of the Mystic Knowledge*, Eng. tr., London, 1899.

Reichelt, K. L. *Religion in Chinese Garment*, London, 1952.

—— *Meditation and Piety in the Far East*, London, 1953.

Reitzenstein, R. *Poimandres: Studien zur griechischen-ägyptischen und frühchristlichen Literatur*, Leipzig, 1904.

—— *Die Hellenistischen Mysterienreligionen*, Leipzig and Berlin, ³1927.

Renda, A. *Il Pensiero Mistico*, Milan and Palermo, 1902.

Rhine, J. B., *et al. Extra-Sensory Perception after Sixty Years*, New York, 1940.

Rhys Davids, C. A. F. *Buddhist Psychology*, London, 1914.

Ribet, J. *La Mystique Divine*, 3 vols, Paris, 1879.

Rieder, C. *Der Gottesfreund von Oberland*, Innsbrück, 1905.

Riesenfeld, H. *Jésus transfiguré*, Lund, 1941.

Rist, J. M. *Plotinus, the Road to Reality*, Cambridge, 1967.

Ritschl, A. *Geschichte des Pietismus*, 3 vols, Bonn, 1880–86.

Robb, A. A. *Neo-Platonism of the Italian Renaissance*, London, 1969.

Robinson, H. W. *Inspiration and Revelation in the Old Testament*, Oxford, 1946.

Robinson, T. H. *Prophecy and the Prophets in*

Ancient Israel, London, 1923.
ROCHÉ, P. *Etudes manichéennes et Cathares*, Paris, 1952.
ROHDE, E. *Psyche*, 2 vols, Eng. tr., London, 1925.
ROLT, C. E. *Dionysius the Areopagite*, London, 1920.
ROSTOVTZEFF, M. I. *Mystic Italy*, New York, 1928.
ROWLEY, H. H. *The Relevance of Apocalyptic*, London, ³1963.
RUBENSOHN, O. *Die Mysterienheiligtümer in Eleusis und Samothrake*, Berlin, 1892.
SABATIER, P. *Vie de S. François*, Paris, 1893.
SABBALUCCI, D. *Saggio sul misticismo greco*, Rome, 1965.
SACKVILLE-WEST, V. *The Eagle and the Dove*, London, 1943.
SAGNARD, F. M. M. *Le gnose Valentinienne et le témoignage de S. Irénée*, Paris, 1947.
SALTER, W. H. *Zoar*, London, 1961.
SAUDREAU, A. *Les degrès de la vie spirituelle*, 2 vols, Paris, 1896.
—— *L'Etat mystique, sa nature, ses phases*, Paris, 1903.
—— *Les faits extraordinaires de la vie spirituelle*, Paris, 1908.
—— *La vie d'union à Dieu et les moyens d'y arriver d'après les grands maîtres de la spiritualité*, Paris, ³1921.
SAUPPE, H. *Die Mysterieninschrift von Andanu*, Göttingen, 1860.
SAUVÉ, C. *L'Homme intime*, Paris, 1901.
SCHECHTER, S. *Studies in Judaism*, 2 vols, London, 1896–1908; New York, 1970.
SCHERBATSKY, T. *The Conception of Buddhist Nirvana*, Leningrad, 1927.
SCHLESINGER, M. *Geschichte des Symbols*, Berlin, 1912.
SCHNEIDERMAN, L. 'Psychological Notes on the Nature of Mystical Experience', *Journal for the Scientific Study of Religion* 6 (1967), 91–100.
SCHOLEM, G. G. *Major Trends in Jewish Mysticism*, London, 1955; New York, 1961.
—— *Jewish Gnosticism, Merkabah Mysticism and Talmudic Tradition*, New York, 1960.
—— *On the Kabbalah and Its Symbolism*, London and New York, 1965.
—— 'Mysticism and Society', *Diogenes* 58 (1967), 1–24.
SCHOLZ, H. *Eros und Caritas: Die platonische Liebe und die Liebe im Sinne des Christentums*, 1929.
SCHROEDER, L. VON *Mysterium und Mimus in Rig-Veda*, Leipzig, 1908.
SCHUBERT, K. *The Dead Sea Community*, London, 1959; Westport, Conn., 1974.
SCHUON, F. *The Transcendent Unity of Religions*, Eng. tr., London, 1953.
SCHWANN, L. *Nikolaus von Cues*, Düsseldorf, 1953.
SCHWEITZER, A. *The Mysticism of Paul the Apostle*, Eng. tr., London, ²1953; New York, 1968.
SEDGWICK, H. D. *Ignatius Loyola*, London, 1923.
SEESHOLTZ, ANNA GROH *The Friends of God: Practical Mystics of the Fourteenth Century*, New York, 1934.
SEISDEDOS SANZ, J. *Principios fundamentales de la mistica*, 5 vols, Madrid, 1913–17.
SENCOURT, R. *Carmelite and Poet: St John of the Cross*, London, 1943; Folcroft, Pa., 1973.
SENZAKI, N. *Zen Meditation*, Kyoto, 1936.
SENZAKI, N., and MCCANDLESS, R. *Buddhism and Zen*, New York, 1953.
SETON, W. (ed.) *St Francis of Assisi: 1126–1926. Essays in Commemoration*, London, 1926.
SHAH, IDRIES *The Sufis*, New York, 1964.
—— *The Way of the Sufi*, London, 1968; New York, 1970.
SHARPE, A. B. *Mysticism, Its True Nature and Value*, London, 1910.
SHIVAPADASUNDARAM, S. *The Shaiva School of Hinduism*, London, 1934.
SIEDEL, G. *Die Mystik Taulers*, Leipzig, 1911.
SILBERER, H. *Problems of Mysticism and its Symbolism*, Eng. tr., New York, 1917.
SLATER, R. L. *Paradox and Nirvana*, Chicago, 1951.
SLOTKIN, J. S. *The Peyote Religion: A Study in Indian-White Relations*, Glencoe, Ill., 1956.
SMART, N. 'Mystical Experience', *Sophia* 1 (1962), 19–25.
—— 'Interpretation and Mystical Experience', *Religious Studies* 1 (1965), 75–87.
—— *The Religious Experience of Mankind*, New York, 1969.
SMITH, D. 'Lysergic Acid Diethylamide', *J. Psychedelic Drugs* (1967).
SMITH, H. 'Do Drugs Have Religious Import?', *Journal of Philosophy* 61 (1964), 517–30.
SMITH, MARGARET *Rabia the Mystic and her Fellow-Saints in Islam*, Cambridge, 1928.
—— *An Introduction to the History of Mysticism*, London and New York, 1930.
—— *Studies in Early Mysticism in the Near and Middle East*, London, 1931.
—— *An Early Mystic of Baghdad*, London, 1935.
—— *Al-Ghazali the mystic*, London, 1944.
SOLMSEN, F. *Plato's Theology*, New York, 1942.
SPALDING, K. J. 'From Empiricism to Mysticism' in Inge, W. R., *et al.*, *Radhakrishnan*, London, 1951, 118–38.
SPAMER, A. *Texte aus der Mystik des 14. und 15. Jahrhunderts*, Jena, 1912.
SPENCER, S. *Mysticism in World Religion*, Harmondsworth, 1963.
SPINKS, G. S. *Psychology and Religion: An Intro to Contemporary Views*, London, 1963.
SPURGEON, C. F. E. *Mysticism in English Literature*, New York, 1913.
SRINIVASACHERI, P. N. *Mystics and Mysticism*, Madras, 1951.
STACE, W. T. *Mysticism and Philosophy*, Philadelphia and New York, 1960; London, 1961.
—— *The Teachings of the Mystics*, New York, 1960.
STEIN, R. A. *Recherches sur l'épopée et le barde au Tibet*, Paris, 1959.
STELZENBERGER, J. *Die Mystik des Johannes Gerson*, Breslau, 1928.

STEPHEN, C. E. *Light Arising – Thoughts on the Central Radiance*, Cambridge, 1908.
STIERNOTTE, A. P. (ed.) *Mysticism and the Modern Mind*, New York, 1959.
STÖCKERL, D. *Bruder David von Augsburg. Ein deutscher Mystiker aus dem Franziskanerorden*, Munich, 1914.
STOUDT, J. J. *Sunrise to Eternity*, Philadelphia, 1957.
STREETER, B. H., and APPASAMY, A. J. *The Sadhu: A Study in Mysticism and Practical Religion*, London, 1921.
SUNDKLER, B. G. M. *Bantu Prophets in South Africa*, London, 1948; New York, 1961.
SUZUKI, B. L. *Mahayana Buddhism*, London, ³1959; New York, 1969.
SUZUKI, D. T. *An Introduction to Zen Buddhism*, London, 1949; New York, 1973.
—— *The Zen doctrine of No-mind*, London, 1949.
—— *Manual of Zen Buddhism*, London, 1950; New York, 1974.
—— *Living by Zen*, London, 1950.
—— *Essays in Zen Buddhism*, 3 vols, London, 1949–53; Montgomery, Ala., 1971.
—— *Studies in Zen*, London, 1955.
TAYLOR, F. SHERWOOD *The Alchemists*, New York, 1949.
THAMERY, E. *Le mysticisme de S François De Sales*, Arras, 1906.
THÉRY, G. *Etudes Dionysiennes*, 2 vols, Paris, 1932–7.
THOMAS, E. J. *History of Buddhist Thought*, London, ²1933.
THOMPSON, A. H. 'The Mystical Element in English Poetry', *Essay and Studies* 8 (1922), 90–108.
THORNDIKE, LYNN *A History of Magic and Experimental Science from the Twelfth to the Sixteenth Century*, London and New York, 1923–41.
THOROLD, A. *An Essay in Aid of the better appreciation of Catholic Mysticism illustrated from the writings of Blessed Angela of Foligno*, London, 1900.
THOULESS, R. H. *An Introduction to the Psychology of Religion*, Cambridge, ²1924; New York, 1972.
—— *The Lady Julian: A Psychological Study*, London, 1924.
THURSTON, H. *The Physical Phenomena of Mysticism*, London, 1951.
—— *Surprising Mystics*, London, 1955.
TILLYARD, A. *Spiritual Exercises*, London, 1927.
TILNEY, F., and WARREN, L. F. 'The Morphology and Evolutionary Significance of the Pineal Body', *American Anatomical Memoirs* 9 (1919), 257 ff.
TIMMONS, B., and KAMIYA, J. 'The Psychology and Physiology of Meditation and Related Phenomena: A Bibliography', *Journal of Transpersonal Psychology* 2 (1970), 41–59.
TOUTAIN, J. F. *Les Cultes paiens dans L'Empire Roman*, Paris, 1907.
TRINE, R. W. *In Tune with the Infinite*, London, 1905; Indianapolis, 1970.
TUCCI, G. *The Theory and Practice of the Mandala*, London, 1961.
TYRRELL, G. N. M. *The Personality of Man*, Harmondsworth, 1947.
UNDERHILL, E. *Ruysbroeck*, London, 1919.
—— *Practical Mysticism*, London and New York, 1914.
—— *Jacopone da Todi*, London and Plainview, NY, 1919.
—— *The Essentials of Mysticism*, London and New York, 1920.
—— *The Mystics of the Church*, London, 1925; New York, 1964.
—— *Mysticism: A Study in the Nature and Development of Man's Spiritual Consciousness*, London, ¹²1930.
UNTERLEIDER, J. T. *The Problems and Prospects of L.S.D.*, Springfield, 1968.
URBAN, W. M. *Language and Reality, the Philosophy of Language and the Principles of Symbolism*, London and Plainview, NY, 1939.
URWICK, E. J. *The Message of Plato*, London, 1920.
UTTENDÖRFER, O. *Zinzendorfs religiöse Grundgedanken*, Herrnhut, 1935.
VAN DUSEN, H. P. *Dag Hammarskjöld: A Biographical Interpretation*, London, 1967.
VAN DYKE, P. *Ignatius Loyola, the Founder of the Jesuits*, London and Port Washington, NY, 1926.
VANNESTE, J. 'Is the Mysticism of Pseudo-Dionysius Genuine?', *International Philosophical Quarterly* 3 (1963), 286–306.
VAUDEVILLE, CH. *Kabir Granthavali*, Pondicherry, 1957.
VERMASEREN, M. J. *Mithras, The Secret God*, Eng. tr., London, 1963.
VERNET, F. *La Spiritualité Médiévale*, Paris, 1929.
VETTER, F. *Ein Mystikerpaar des vierzehnten Jahrhunderts, Schwester Elsbeth Stager in Toss und Vater Amandus in Konstanz*, Basle, 1882.
VEZZANI, V. *Le Mysticisme dans le monde*, Fr. tr., Paris, 1955.
VIDMAN, L. *Isis und Sarapis bei den Griechen und Römern*, Berlin, 1970.
VILLER, M., *et al. Dictionnaire de Spiritualité*, Paris, 1937.
VREESE, W. L. DE 'Jean de Ruysbroeck' in *Biographie Nationale de Belgique* 20, Brussels (1907).
WACH, J. *Types of Religious Experience*, London and Chicago, 1951.
WAINWRIGHT, W. J. 'Stace and Mysticism', *Journal of Religion* 50 (1970), 139–54.
WAITE, A. E. *The Doctrine and Literature of the Kabalah*, London, 1902.
—— *The Hidden Church of the Holy Grail: its Legends and Symbolism*, London, 1909.
—— *The Way of Divine Union*, London, 1915.
—— *The Holy Kabbalah: A Study of the Secret Tradition in Israel*, London, 1929; New York, 1960.
WALEY, A. *Zen Buddhism and its Relation to Art*, London, 1822.
—— *Three Ways of Thought in Ancient China*,

London, 1939; New York, 1956.
WALLACE, A. F. C. 'Revitalization Movements', *American Anthropologist* 58 (1956), 264–81.
—— *The Death and Rebirth of the Seneca*, New York, 1970.
WALLACE, R. K. 'Physiological Effects of Transcendental Meditation', *Science* 167 (1970), 1751–54.
WALTON, C. *Notes and materials for an adequate biography of William Law*, London, 1859.
WATKIN, E. I. *The Philosophy of Mysticism*, New York, 1920.
—— *Poets and Mystics*, London and Plainview, NY, 1953.
WATSON, H. A. *The Mysticism of St John's Gospel*, London, 1916.
WATTS, A. W. *The Supreme Identity*, London, 1950.
—— *The Way of Zen*, London, 1959.
WENSINCK, A. J. *La Pensée de Ghazzali*, Paris, 1940.
WERBLOWSKY, R. J. ZWI 'Mystical and Magical Contemplation', *History of Religions* 1 (1961), 9–36.
—— 'On the Mystical Rejection of Mystical Illuminations', *Religious Studies* 1 (1966), 177–84.
WESTON, J. L. *The Quest of the Holy Grail*, London, 1913; New York, 1973.
—— *From Ritual to Romance*, Cambridge, 1920; New York, 1957.
WHELAN, J. P. *The Spirituality of Friedrich von Hügel*, London, 1971; New York, 1972.
WHITE, HELEN *The Mysticism of William Blake*, Madison, 1927.
WHITEHEAD, A. N. *Symbolism, its Meaning and Effect*, New York, 1927.
WHITEMAN, J. H. M. *The Mystical Life*, London, 1961.
WHYTE, A. *Character and Characteristics of W. Law*, Edinburgh, 1893.
—— *Jacob Böhme: An Appreciation*, Edinburgh, 1894.
—— *Santa Teresa: An Appreciation*, Edinburgh, 1897.
WIDENGREN, G. *Mani and Manicheism*, Eng. tr., London, 1965.
WILHELM, R. *Lao-Tse und der Taoismus*, Stuttgart, 1925.
—— *The Secret of the Golden Flower: A Chinese Book of Life*, Eng. tr., London, 1931; New York, 1974.
WILLIAMS, W. *Studies in St Bernard of Clairvaux*, London, 1927.
—— *The Mysticism of St Bernard of Clairvaux*, London, 1931.
—— *St Bernard of Clairvaux*, Manchester, 1938.
WILLINCK, A. D. R. *The Prophetic Consciousness*, London, 1824.
WILLMART, A. *Auteurs spirituels et textes dévots du moyen âge latin*, Paris, 1932.
WILLOUGHBY, H. R. *Pagan Regeneration*, Chicago, 1929.
WILSON, R. McL. *The Gnostic Problem*, Oxford, 1958.
WISDOM, W. A. 'A Phenomenological Review of Mysticism and Childhood Experience', *Philosophy and Phenomenological Research* 21 (1961), 397–401.
WITT, R. E. *Isis in the Graeco-Roman World*, London, 1970; Ithaca, NY, 1971.
WOLFSON, H. A. *Philo: Foundations of Religious Philosophy in Judaism, Christianity and Islam*, 2 vols, Cambridge, 1947; Cambridge, Mass., 1962.
WOOD, E. *Yoga*, Harmondsworth, 1959; Baltimore, 1961.
WOODROFFE, SIR JOHN *Shakti and Shakta*, Madras, [4]1951.
WORSLEY, P. *The Trumpet Shall Sound*, London, 1957; New York, 1968.
WOSIEN, MARIA-GABRIELE *Sacred Dance*, London and New York, 1974.
YABLONSKY, L. *The Hippie Trip*, New York, 1968.
YASUTANI-ROSHI 'Commentary on the Koan Mu', in P. Kapleau (ed.), *Three Pillars of Zen: Teaching, Practice, Enlightenment*, New York, 1966.
YOUNG, K. *The Drama of the Mediaeval Church*, 2 vols, Oxford and New York, 1933.
ZAEHNER, R. C. *Mysticism, Sacred and Profane*, Oxford, 1957; New York, 1961.
—— *Hindu and Muslim Mysticism*, London, 1960; New York, 1969.
—— *Concordant Discord*, Oxford, 1970.
—— *Drugs, Mysticism and Make Believe*, London, 1970.
ZAHN, J. *Einführung in die christliche Mystik*, Paderborn, 1908.
ZUNTZ, G. *Persephone*, Harvard, 1972.

The following periodicals have articles too numerous to mention individually: *Etudes Carmelitaines; La Vie Spirituelle; Revue d'Ascétique et de Mystique; Zeitschrift fur Aszese und Mystik*, continued since 1947 as *Geist und Leben*. Standard encyclopaedias such as *Catholic Encyclopaedia, Encyclopaedia Judaica, Encyclopaedia of Religion and Ethics, International Encyclopaedia of the Social Sciences, Jewish Encyclopaedia, New Catholic Encyclopaedia, Oxford Dictionary of the Christian Church*, have proved useful for consultation.

ACKNOWLEDGMENTS

The author is grateful to the undermentioned for permission to quote copyright material:

George Allen & Unwin Ltd, *Sufism: An Account of the Mystics*; A. J. Arberry, copies distributed by Humanities Press in the U.S.A.; *Cherubinic Wanderer*, Angelus Silesius, translated by J. E. C. Flitch; *Rumi, Poet and Mystic*, Rumi, translated by R. A. Nicholson. George Allen & Unwin Ltd and Macmillan Publishing Co., U.S.A., *A Moslem Saint of the Twentieth Century*, Martin Lings. Cambridge University Press, *St John of the Cross*, G. Brenan; *Studies in Islamic Mysticism*, R. A. Nicholson. Johns Hopkins University Press, *The Poems of Unamuno*, translated by Eleanor Turnbull. The Trustees of the Tagore Estate, Macmillan London and Basingstoke and Macmillan Publishing Co., U.S.A., *One Hundred Poems of Kabir*, translated by Rabindranath Tagore; *Collected Poems*, Rabindranath Tagore. The Executors of the Estate of C. M. Bowra and Macmillan London and Basingstoke, *The Heritage of Symbolism*, C. M. Bowra. Penguin Books Ltd, three poems by Allama Prabhu from *Speaking of Siva*, edited and translated by A. K. Ramanujan, Penguin Classics, 1973, pp. 153, 168, 167, Copyright © A. K. Ramanujan, 1973, reprinted by permission of Penguin Books Ltd. Vision Press Limited, *Poems from the Book of Hours*, Rainer Maria Rilke, translated by Babette Deutsch.

Photographic acknowledgments
(numerals refer to folios)

Antiquario Comunale, Rome: 121
Art Institute of Chicago, Albert H. Wolf Memorial Collection: 113
Biblioteca Estense, Modena: 20
Bibliothèque Nationale, Paris: 24
Trustess of the British Museum, London: 11, 15, 29 (*lower*), 48, 124, 153, 215
Castello Sforzesco, Milan: 43
Cathedral Library, Winchester: 150
Chiesa di Badia, Florence: 27
Chiesa di S. Maria Novella, Rome: 60
City Art Gallery, Manchester: 44 (*lower*)
Convento de Carmelitas Descalzas de Sta Teresa, Seville: 193
Etnografiska Museet, Stockholm: 169
The Frick Collection, New York: 62
Goethe Museum, Düsseldorf: 75
Gulbenkian Museum of Oriental Art, Durham: 168, 212
Herzog-August Bibliothek, Wolfenbüttel: 173
Hessische Landesbibliothek, Wiesbaden: 77
India Office Library, London: 18
Kings College, Cambridge, Ms. 19, f. 21v: 172 (*lower*)
Kröller-Müller Museum, Otterlo: 182
Kunsthistorisches Museum, Vienna: 84
Library of Congress, Washington: 209
Louvre, Paris: 120, 158, 176
Collection Ajit Mookerjee, New Delhi: 32 (*lower*), 90, 105, 117, 186, 213
Museo Nazionale, Naples: 172 (*upper*), 177
Museo Provincial, Valladolid: 94
Museum of Fine Arts, Boston: 65, 171
National Gallery, London: 132
National Gallery of Ireland, Dublin: 21
National Library of Medicine, Bethesda, Maryland: 74
National Museum, Athens: 53
Nationalmuseum, Stockholm: 181
National Palace Museum, Taipei: 102, 187
National Portrait Gallery, London: 79
New Statesman: 160
Österreichische Nationalbibliothek, Vienna: 122
Private Collection: 114, 140, 188, 211
Royal Ontario Museum, Toronto: 68
Sta Caterina, Pisa: 196
S. Tomé, Toledo: 70
Staatliche Graphische Sammlung, Munich: 30
Staatliche Museen, Berlin: 44 (*upper*), 52
Unterlinden Museum, Colmar: 92
Victoria and Albert Museum, London: 38, 154
Nicolaes Witsen, *Noord en Oost Tartarye*, 1705: 17 (*upper*)
Zenrin-ji, Kyoto: 35
Zentralbibliothek, Zurich, Cod. rhenovacensis 172: 13

Sources of illustrations
(numerals refer to folios)

Archives Photographiques, Paris: 176
Bassano & Vandyk Studios: 82
Giraudon: 120, 158
Hirmer: 43, 48
Mansell-Alinari: 27, 60
Mansell-Anderson: 19, 51, 172 (*upper*), 177, 186, 196
The Mansell Collection: 53
Foto Marburg: 71, 92
Mas, Barcelona: 70, 94, 111, 193
Courtesy of Piccadilly Gallery, London: 140
Josephine Powell: 46
Radio Times Hulton Picture Library: 98
Soprintendenza alle Antichità, Rome: 87
Jeff Teasdale: 32 (*lower*), 90, 105, 114, 117, 135, 174, 188, 213